China in the Local and Global Economy

The history of China dates back thousands of years, with periods of decline followed by periods of growth and innovation. This book puts the last 50 years – China's most recent period of growth – into perspective. It explores the changing national and international connections within China and between China and other parts of the world, and their importance for understanding the past, current and future developments of the Chinese economy.

The book brings together leading international contributors from China, Japan and Europe to consider the historical developments of these connections, the importance of natural and man-made connections for the Chinese economy, the role of institutions and policies for understanding the connections and their sustainability.

This book will be of interest to scholars and researchers focusing on China, economics, geography or international trade.

Steven Brakman is Professor of International Economics at the University of Groningen, the Netherlands.

Charles van Marrewijk is Professor of Economics at Utrecht University, the Netherlands.

Peter J. Morgan is Senior Consultant for Research at the Asian Development Bank Institute, Japan.

Nimesh Salike is Associate Professor of Economics at Xi'an Jiaotong-Liverpool University, China.

Regional Studies Association
THE GLOBAL FORUM FOR CITY AND REGIONAL RESEARCH, DEVELOPMENT AND POLICY

Routledge
Taylor & Francis Group

Regions and Cities

In today's globalised, knowledge-driven and networked world, regions and cities have assumed heightened significance as the interconnected nodes of economic, social and cultural production, and as sites of new modes of economic and territorial governance and policy experimentation. This book series brings together incisive and critically engaged international and interdisciplinary research on this resurgence of regions and cities, and should be of interest to geographers, economists, sociologists, political scientists and cultural scholars, as well as to policy-makers involved in regional and urban development.

For more information on the Regional Studies Association visit www.regionalstudies.org

There is a **30% discount** available to RSA members on books in the *Regions and Cities* series, and other subject related Taylor and Francis books and e-books including Routledge titles. To order just e-mail Joanna Swieczkowska, Joanna.Swieczkowska@tandf.co.uk, or phone on +44 (0)20 3377 3369 and declare your RSA membership. You can also visit the series page at www.routledge.com/Regions-and-Cities/book-series/RSA and use the discount code: **RSA0901**

129. Fragile Governance and Local Economic Development
Theory and Evidence from Peripheral Regions in Latin America
Edited by Sergio Montero and Karen Chapple

130. The Production of Alternative Urban Spaces
An International Dialogue
Edited by Jens Kaae Fisker, Letizia Chiappini, Lee Pugalis and Antonella Bruzzese

131. Creating Smart Cities
Edited by Claudio Coletta, Leighton Evans, Liam Heaphy and Rob Kitchin

132. China in the Local and Global Economy
History, Geography, Politics and Sustainability
Edited by Steven Brakman, Charles van Marrewijk, Peter J. Morgan and Nimesh Salike

For more information about this series, please visit: www.routledge.com/Regions-and-Cities/book-series/RSA

China in the Local and Global Economy

History, Geography, Politics and Sustainability

Edited by Steven Brakman, Charles van Marrewijk, Peter J. Morgan and Nimesh Salike

Routledge
Taylor & Francis Group
LONDON AND NEW YORK

First published 2019
by Routledge
2 Park Square, Milton Park, Abingdon, Oxon OX14 4RN

and by Routledge
52 Vanderbilt Avenue, New York, NY 10017

First issued in paperback 2020

Routledge is an imprint of the Taylor & Francis Group, an informa business

British Library Cataloguing-in-Publication Data
A catalogue record for this book is available from the British Library

Library of Congress Cataloging-in-Publication Data
A catalog record for this book has been requested

ISBN 13: 978-0-367-66439-8 (pbk)
ISBN 13: 978-1-138-30798-8 (hbk)

Typeset in Times New Roman
by Apex CoVantage, LLC

Contents

Figures

Tables

Contributors

Steven Brakman is Professor of International Economics at the University of Groningen, the Netherlands.

Yang Chen is Lecturer at Xi'an Jiaotong Jiaotong-Liverpool, Suzhou, China.

Ming He is Lecturer at Xi'an Jiaotong Jiaotong-Liverpool, Suzhou, China.

Shiwei Hu is Assistant Professor of Economics at Beijing Foreign Studies University, Beijing, China.

Yanghua Huang is Associate Professor at the Institute of Industrial Economics, Chinese Academy of Social Sciences, Beijing, China.

Bas van Leeuwen is Researcher at the IISH and Utrecht University, the Netherlands.

Charles van Marrewijk is Professor of Economics at Utrecht University, the Netherlands.

Peter J. Morgan is Senior Consultant for Research at the Asian Development Bank Institute, Japan.

Paulo José Regis is Associate Professor of Economics at Xi'an Jiaotong-Liverpool University, Suzhou, China.

Simon Rudkin is Lecturer at the University of Manchester, United Kingdom.

Nimesh Salike is Associate Professor of Economics at Xi'an Jiaotong-Liverpool University, Suzhou, China.

Julia Swart is Assistant Professor at Utrecht University, the Netherlands.

Willem Thorbecke is Senior Fellow at the Research Institute of Economy, Trade, and Industry (REITI), Tokyo, Japan and an affiliate at the Center for International Development at Harvard University, USA.

Jan Luiten van Zanden is Professor of Global Economic History at Utrecht University, the Netherlands.

Preface

The history of China dates back thousands of years. With a history this long one can easily distinguish upswings and downswings in Chinese development. In this respect, China is not different from other old cultures; periods of decline are followed by periods of growth and innovation. Presently China is undergoing a period of growth. Arguably, the seeds of this most recent period started in the 1960s. The disastrous economic policies by Mao Zedong – the Great Leap Forward, and the subsequent Cultural Revolution – were an enormous setback to the Chinese economy. A reaction was inevitable. After Mao Zedong's death in September 1976, a scramble of successions took place, ending in the appointment of the more liberal Deng Xiaoping in 1977. Most crucially, in 1978 the new Chinese leadership adopted economic reforms that allowed more entrepreneurial autonomy, reduction in capital controls and reduction in central planning in general.

The consequences of these policies were enormous. More inward foreign direct investment (FDI), more focus on industrialization, increased access to world markets through international trade, membership of the World Trade Organization (WTO) in 2001 and more concentrated investments in large cities, resulted in unprecedented growth rates for decades in the past and likely in the future.

This was not always a smooth process. For some, especially liberal-oriented students, policies to relax the Chinese society were too slow, and by the end of the 1980s the students were demanding more freedom and a swifter move towards a liberalized society and economy. In contrast, old party members feared that the reform policies were leading to social instability and were demanding more party control on the Chinese society and economy. Although there were temporary setbacks during this period, the reforms had brought in economic development in the country, and the reform process continues to this date.

This book is the result of a collaboration between institutes in China, Japan and Europe. More specifically, Xi'an Jiaotong-Liverpool University in Suzhou, China, the Asian Development Bank Institute in Tokyo, Japan, and the Universities of Groningen and Utrecht, both in the Netherlands. For some chapters, individual researchers from Beijing Foreign Studies University (China), the Chinese Academy of Social Sciences (China), the University of Manchester (UK) and the Research Institute of Economy, Trade, and Industry (Japan) also contributed.

In our work we put this most recent period in Chinese history – the last 50 years – into perspective. In Part I we look into the historical development of China. Bas van Leeuwen and Jan Luiten van Zanden highlight important periods in Chinese history starting in 221 BC, and show that periods of decline are associated with a top-down governance structure, and periods of growth with more liberal government structures, but also social instability. In Chapter 2, Paulo José Regis focusses on the most recent period that started in 1978. He highlights that opening up to international trade in combination with capital liberalization was pivotal for growth. In Chapter 3, Shiwei Hu completes this historical overview by zooming in on the importance of FDI for the Chinese growth process.

In Part II we concentrate on the geographical dimension of China. In Chapter 4, Steven Brakman analyses, from an urban perspective, how more liberal policies could affect the Chinese landscape. One of the conclusions is that more liberal economic policies, especially the relaxation of the Hukou migration system, could result in more economic concentration in the already large cities. Migration is important for this conclusion. This is the focus in Chapter 5, where Charles van Marrewijk highlights the importance and size of migration within China. He argues that the peak of Chinese industrialization was in 2006, and that China is now rapidly developing into a modern, service-oriented economy. Nimesh Salike and Willem Thorbecke, in Chapter 6, finish this analysis by analysing the link between trade and FDI. They point out that globalisation in China also implies a strong role in global supply chains.

In Part III policy is the main topic. Yanghua Huang, in Chapter 7, highlights the specific institutional changes that have been made in China and also points out what is still needed. If China is going to make further economic progress additional improvements in the property rights system, market-based allocation of factors of production, and improving the system for managing different types of state assets is still needed. In Chapter 8, Yang Chen, Ming He and Simon Rudkin add to this analysis by arguing that macro-economic policies need to be improved. They focus on monetary policy, fiscal policy and trade policy. In a large country like China, the infrastructure is important. This is the topic of Chapter 9, where Ming He and Yang Chen highlight the contribution of the Chinese infrastructure to Chinese growth. However, it has also increased the huge public debt problem, which is one of the key risk factors in modern China.

Part IV looks at the future of China. In Chapter 10, Charles van Marrewijk looks at demographic pressures in modern China. He describes the nexus of an aging population and increasing economic inequality. Despite impressive economic growth in China over the last three decades, demographic pressures are among the key risk factors of China. Another major risk is pointed out by Julia Swart. She points out that economic growth in China is accompanied by environmental degradation. Only recently has China introduced policies to deal with environmental issues that should make the Chinese economy somewhat greener.

Finally, in Chapter 12 Peter J. Morgan looks ahead and stresses that the enormous growth in China is also reflected in an increased international political responsibility for China; its role in the international financial architecture is rapidly increasing, and so is its responsibility.

The chapters in this book discuss the rapid development of the Chinese economy in the last 50 years also from a longer-run perspective. The benefits are many; a reduction in poverty, a more open society, migration possibilities and so on. The authors of the chapters also express that given the size of the Chinese economy, responsibilities for China have grown as well; the Hukou system is still restrictive, environmental issues are being addressed but are far from being solved, rapid growth of financial debt is a risk to international finance and many more risk factors are being analyzed in this book. Furthermore, China still needs to find a stable place in international politics that matches its economic size. There is no end to history for China yet.

Part I

Historical connections

1 China as a nation

Bas van Leeuwen and Jan Luiten van Zanden[1]

1.1 Introduction

Worldwide, China is one of the oldest unified states that has persisted to the present day. At the end of the Warring States period (ca. 475–221 BC), during which all regions competed for control, the Qin Dynasty (221–206 BC) rose to power through a series of victories over competing states. This resulted in China's unification in 221 BC. One reason for the success of the Qin was its location in the heartland of Shaanxi Province, which was effectively shielded from invasions and simultaneously enabled access to the large fields in the north of China (Peralta 2014). Moreover, the Qin managed to exploit the resources of the country – basically men and land – more intensively than did its competitors, creating a solid basis for its ultimate victory.

The unification of China by the Qin was already viewed as important at the time. For example, in the following dynasty (Han, 206 BC–AD 220), the history of the Han (Hanshu) acknowledged that 'the Qin unified the world' (Swann 1950). Moreover, three interrelated sets of ideas and policies introduced by the Qin laid the basis for the state that has persisted to this day. The first of these was the introduction of legalism as a replacement for Confucianism as the basic philosophy of the state. Whereas Confucianism essentially preached the good of the people and the importance of family and education, legalism developed during the Warring States period, ca. 476–221 BC, (which was characterized by intense warfare) and started from the belief that it was the task of the state to direct all persons for the good of the state. Consequently, people derived their value from their usefulness to the state. Related to this is a second aspect, namely a distrust of education. Because education could drive people to independent thinking and criticism of the state, it was discouraged; books were burned, and scholars were executed. Although this policy was reversed during the following Han Dynasty, the prominence of the state remained an important feature of the education system. Third, the Qin started to build physical infrastructure such as the Great Wall and the Grand Canal. Combined, these three policies would unite China.

This process of unification has lasted essentially to the present day. Although China has known major dynastic cycles and even extended periods during which different political entities competed for control over the entire empire, the gradually expanding territory of the empire remained the basic framework for these cycles and this competition. Likewise, the three policies described previously were continued, to some extent. After the fall of the Qin, the policy of legalism was reversed and replaced by Confucianism mixed with a soft form of legalism. Likewise, schooling was resurrected to a certain extent, but only for the purpose of creating a class of loyal government officials to feed the bureaucracy (the famous civil examination system). The trade links established by the Grand Canal and by other infrastructural projects made it possible for new rulers to extract tribute from the various regions of China as soon as they took power. Hence, new dynasties were able to make full use of the existing system.

Of course, China as a state did not remain unchanged after the Qin. In terms of population, an indicator of political and economic change, the centre of gravity of the empire relocated many times over the course of its long existence. The ancient heartland of the empire was in the North, in the Yellow River valley, with capital cities such as Xi'an (home of the first emperor) and Kaifeng (capital during the 960–1127 Northern Sung Dynasty). Part of the population migrated to the South, to the Yangtze valley (and even further south to the Pearl River valley), driving out the non-Han population. From the Southern Sung onwards, the Yangtze valley became the economic centre and remains so to the present day. During the Qing, there was a further expansion to the North, the East, and the Southeast – incorporating new regions such as Tibet, Xinjiang, Manchuria, and Taiwan.

Other changes occured in trade. Until about 1500, when the geography of world trade changed dramatically, China was the eastern hub of the Great Silk Road, which, in practice, was a set of interrelated caravan routes that connected the empire with India, Persia, and the Middle East. The world economy was dominated by an urban belt stretching from Egypt and the Ottoman Empire to the great metropoles of China, together forming the core area of world trade and industry. During the Han Dynasty (206 BC–AD 220), intense commercial exchange along this network connected China with the Roman Empire; similarly, the Sung Dynasty (960–1279) coincided with the flowering of the Arab world. In particular, when strong states dominated both ends of the Silk Route, facilitating commercial exchange via 'law and order'; and/or when the regions in between the two nodes where unified into one polity, as occurred during the Great Mongol Empire of the 13th and 14th centuries, trade via these routes expanded rapidly and connected the great cities of the East and West into one dynamic urban system (Abu-Lughod 1989). Europe, especially Western Europe, was at the margin of this commercial system until the rise of the Italian city-states (Venice, Genova). However, from the late Middle Ages onwards, Western Europe became increasingly dynamic, developing new commercial routes in the 15th and 16th centuries – basically via the circumnavigation of Africa – that would fundamentally change the geography of international trade from the 17th to the 19th centuries. Initially, European commercial enterprises such as the Dutch East India Company were relatively weak compared with the vast powers of the Chinese Empire. For example, the Dutch attempted to establish a strong base on the island of Taiwan but were unable to control it. The terms of international trade were set by the empire, which allowed trade to take place only in Quandong (Kanton/Guangzhou) during much of the 17th and 18th centuries. However, this changed dramatically in the early 19th century, as demonstrated forcefully by the First Opium War (1839–1842). The Chinese state continued to decline in power and was humiliated by foreign powers – first the British, followed soon after by all of the major Western countries. This set in motion (or rather accelerated) a process of fragmentation of state power that ended in the long war with Japan (1937–1945) and the subsequent civil war.

In Section 1.2, first we take a closer look at China's dynastic cycles, finding that the end of a dynasty, which was often accompanied by massive warfare, was characterized by population declines. The dynastic cycle theory is further confirmed by looking at population indicators such as urban primacy (the capital city's share of the total population), which is often considered a proxy for the extractive capacity of the state, and which declined at the end of dynasties. This pattern weakened during the Qing Dynasty. Although the dynastic cycles persisted, urban primacy had been weak from the beginning of the Qing period and decreased even further over the course of the dynasty and the subsequent Republican period. To understand why the pattern of strong and weak state capacity existed and why the pattern declined (though it did not disappear) during and after the Qing, in Sections 1.3 and 1.4 we deal with the two aspects of a strong bureaucracy (centralization and the civil examination system), which is a proxy for state success. This provides a measure of state success, but not a link to economic development. Hence, in Section 1.5, we turn to the importance of state success with regard to economic development, with reference to the so-called 'Needham puzzle' (i.e. why Chinese development was at or above the level of development in Europe in the 15th century but then fell behind later).

1.2 Population development and state capacity

As pointed out earlier, the various dynasties since the Qin moved away from a patriarchal system in which the ruler shared power with his subjects to one of autocratic rule, resulting in the massive building of infrastructure, a theory of obedience to the state, and, eventually, an education system for training reliable civil servants. Both Elvin (1973) and Von Glahn (2016) claim that the rise of metalworking was one of the reasons for this shift, as it increased the value of a standing army under one ruler.

However, as was also pointed out earlier, state power was not the same either during or between dynasties. For example, during the course of the Eastern Han Dynasty (AD 25–220) there was a shift away from the autocratic mode into a more market-oriented system, causing a rise in land inequality that lasted well into the subsequent warring period of the Three Kingdoms (AD 220–280) (Von Glahn 2016). Stability, along with autocracy, returned at the end of this period and further strengthened during the following Jin Dynasty (AD 265–420) that once again united China. Just as during the late Han, during the Tang Dynasty (AD 618–907), we see a move away from a state-regulated economy towards the end of the reign (Von Glahn 2016, 206), which was further extended in the period of turmoil during the subsequent Five Dynasties and Ten Kingdoms periods (AD 907–960).

Opinions vary regarding the subsequent Song (960–1279), Ming (1368–1644), and Qing (1636–1912) dynasties – Von Glahn (2016) argues that there was essentially a gradual development of market forces over time, whereas Elvin (1973) favours a rapid development during the Song, followed by a stable system, with the exception of the highly disruptive Yuan Dynasty (1271–1368). Although we agree with Von Glahn to some extent, we stress that this move towards market-related forces, combined with declining state capacity, was still very limited. As we point out in subsequent sections of this chapter, although less severe than the those of previous dynasties, the first Ming emperors were strong rulers who aimed to impose restrictions of various kinds on society; e.g., by introducing an integrated monetary system. In that respect, the Song did not prove to be a watershed. However, this was different during the Qing: As a non-Han (i.e., Manchu) dynasty, the pressure the Qing was able to exert on society – through taxation or otherwise – was much more limited. However, even during the Qing, we witness an increasing rise of market forces over time that continued during the Republic of China period (1911–1948), which was characterized once more by warfare. It can be argued that this continuous pattern of a strong and then weakening state, followed by the rise of market forces, persists to the present day, with the initial phase of New China (1948–present) being characterized by a much stronger role of the state followed by the increasing dominance of market forces since the 1980s.

One way to look at this pattern is by assessing population development and state capacity. Focusing on population development, we argue that the phases of growth were often accompanied by losses in terms of population and state capacity. Indeed, China is unique in at least one respect: It has been by far the largest state in the world in terms of population size, making up at least around 20–25% of the world's population, both before and after the Qing. During the Qing, China's relative size was even larger, comprising no less than 35% of the global population (Maddison 2007). However, population growth in China has been rather unbalanced, characterized by extreme swings. In Europe, sudden drops in population levels because of wars or epidemics in one region were more or less compensated for by growth in other regions, resulting in a rather smooth European population growth (with the exception of the pan-European Black Death epidemic of 1348, during which about one-third of the European population died) (see e.g. Ko et al. 2017). Chinese population shifts were much more extreme, however, and dramatic declines were often related to the wars and civil unrest that accompanied the transition from one dynasty to the next. The conquest of the empire by the Mongols (establishing the short-lived Yuan Dynasty), the collapse of the Yuan Dynasty and establishment of the Ming, and the transition from the Ming to the Qing all had dramatic consequences for population numbers, as is clear from Figure 1.1. Population losses during these transitions were much more extreme than anything we find in European history (see also Chi 1934). Even the effects on Germany of the Thirty Years War seem rather moderate in comparison.

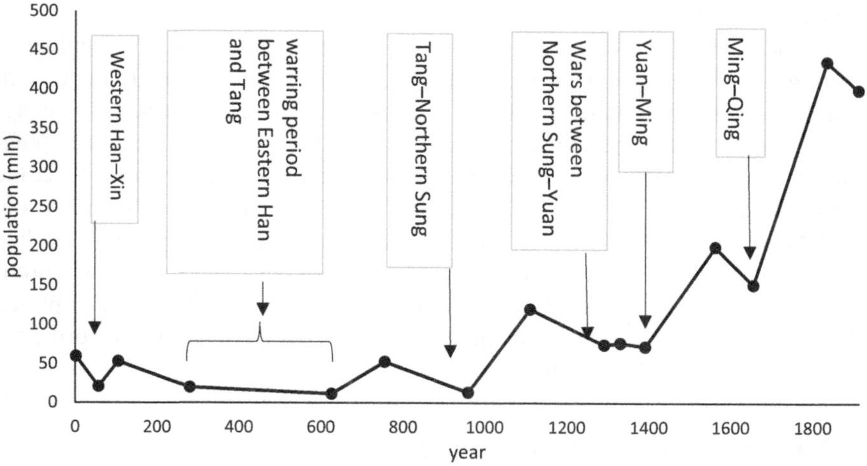

Figure 1.1 Population development in China, AD 1–1911, by period of dynastic change
Source: Deng (2004)

Table 1.1 Urban primacy in China and Western Europe (capital city/total population, %)

	China	*Western Europe*
1100	1.0	0.2
1200	0.8	0.2
1300	1.5	0.2
1391/1400*	1.4	0.2
1500		0.4
1600/30	0.7	0.4
1644/1700**	0.4	0.6
1800	0.3	0.7
1850	0.3	1.1
1900	0.2	2.3
1918	0.4	

* 1391 China, 1400 Western Europe
** 1644 China, 1700 Western Europe

Source: Xu *et al.* (2018)

That these periods of turmoil and population loss coincided with declining state capacity can be seen by assessing urban primacy (the capital city's share of the total population), which is often considered a prime indicator of state capacity and the ability of the state to extract revenue from other regions (Ades and Glaeser 1995, 224; Bosker et al. 2013). Indeed, looking at Table 1.1, we may arrive at two conclusions. First, up to ca. 1700, urban primacy was lower in Western Europe than in China, which is arguably related to the fragmented nature of the European state system. Yet this clearly changed over time with Europe overtaking China around the 17th century.

Second, whereas urban primacy in China declined during the Ming and again during the Qing, as we have argued previously, it increased strongly in Western Europe together with state formation. The size of the largest Chinese city, Guangzhou, was relatively unchanged between 1100 and 1900, whereas the total population of China had increased dramatically over this time. These trends reflect the divergence in terms of state capacity and are confirmed by similar disparities in fiscal capacity. In the 19th century, the state's share of gross domestic product (GDP) was ~10% in Western Europe, vs 2% in China (Ma 2011), which was probably connected to China's weakening as an international trade hub, as exemplified by the change from a strong position in the Silk Road to eventual defeat during the Opium Wars in the 19th century.

1.3 Centralization and bureaucracy

To this point, we have considered the phoenix-like character of the Chinese state with regard to its ability to repeatedly re-emerge after the toppling of each dynasty, facilitated by the state-centred ideology combined with an education system geared towards supplying the bureaucracy with new members and an infrastructure able to extract revenue from all parts of the empire.

This pattern is also known as the dynastic cycle, an 'old-fashioned' idea (especially unappreciated by Western scholarship) that might, however, have some value for understanding Chinese economic history. During the chaos of the final years of a dynasty, a strong clan leader arises and uses great force to establish a new regime and to extract resources using the existing infrastructure – forced labour, for example, is very common in this part of the cycle. In this way, a new alignment of incentives is achieved: Bureaucrats are disciplined, obeying the law and their Confucian conscience. The first Qin and Ming emperors were true authoritarian rulers who managed to build a new, centrally guided economy that did what they wanted almost completely; this was also thanks to an efficient, disciplined bureaucracy that saw it as their duty to obey the ruler. Later dynastic rulers, however, tended to be less successful in controlling the bureaucracy, leading to the eventual collapse of the dynasty, which was often accompanied by wars and population losses, as discussed in Section 1.2.

Indeed, a key problem of the Chinese state was its size and that communication between the centre and the rest of the empire was time-consuming and costly. There were clearly limits to the degree to which the emperor could monitor his 'agents' – the civil servants of the professional bureaucracy – at the provincial and district levels. It may have been in their long-term interest to be impartial officials with integrity, much like Confucian ideology told them to be; however, in the absence of countervailing powers at both the local and the national level, there was always the temptation to profit from the huge powers bestowed upon them. Recent game-theoretical research has shown that people are motivated by a mix of economic and social incentives. They usually want to be good citizens, or, in this case, good officials in the best Confucian tradition, but they often also cannot resist the lure of the market (Bowles 2016). Strong material incentives can undermine people's social preferences, but a state can appeal to and work with the citizenship of its inhabitants – and, again, in this case, particularly the bureaucrats who rule the country. In other words, only when either a proper infrastructure is managed by a strong bureaucracy or when government is supported by a strong civil society can a dynasty remain in effective control of the vast empire.

Force is often inefficient, and markets are an attractive alternative for organizing public goods (ranging from palaces for the imperial family to irrigation works for agriculture). After some time, force is replaced by market incentives. As pointed out in Section 1.2, there are various examples of this, such as during the 8th century AD at the end of the Tang Dynasty. This period witnessed a strong decline of the old elite and the rise of powerful non-office-holding economic elites such as businessmen (Tackett 2008). A similar situation occurred during the 'commercial revolution' of the 16th century (during the Ming Dynasty) and at the end of the Qing (19th century). A clear example showing the role of the rise of market forces in the weakening of the state is the sale of offices, which began in the Ming Dynasty in the early 15th century in certain regions and became a national phenomenon during the late 15th century when the dynasty weakened (Tang 1991). The Qing Dynasty, however, was exceptional (as we will return to in the following sections) in that the sale of offices was already witnessed at the start of this dynasty (e.g. Xu 1950). Hence, the move from force to market was quite universal in imperial China, and also, we can perhaps add, after the death of Mao in 1976.

As argued earlier, this turn to market incentives tends to undermine the social incentives of bureaucrats and other members of the elite. It would probably be beneficial for all if social preferences – bureaucrats' honour as members of the mandarin class – continued to dominate their behaviour. However, the temptation of corruption is always present after the market becomes predominant in the rest of the economy, and social preferences may slowly be eroded by material incentives. Growing corruption then tends to undermine the effectiveness of the state. In practice, it is almost impossible to monitor officials in the vast empire, resulting in the fragmentation of state power. Once one official defects, others tend to do the same, and the intricate balance of power relations within the state may disintegrate. This cumulative process of disintegration continues until the state falls apart, and a powerful leader has to stand up to start the whole process all over again.

These processes of state erosion by rising market forces are well recorded; the focus of late Tang local elites on economic benefits over social prestige led to the disintegration of the empire (Tackett 2008). Indeed, as pointed out by Hartwell (1982, 395), the end of the Tang was characterized by a reduction in influence of the central government and mid-level administration (the prefecture), combined with the increasing importance of the lowest administrative levels (counties). Similar turns towards economic regionalism have been recorded for the end of the Ming and Qing dynasties. For example, the number of judicial matters dealt with at the prefecture level and the amount of direct contact (via memorials) of the prefecture with the throne were reduced.

This pattern of increased regionalism at the end of a dynasty held true until the Qing. Although it worsened at the end of this dynasty as well, economic and social regionalism were strong already from the very start of the Qing. In fact, one of the first Qing emperors, Kangxi (1654–1722), ordered counties to submit memorials directly to the emperor rather than via higher administrative levels. One might even consider that this also applies to the New China reform period after Mao's death in 1976. Indeed, it has been argued that, in the case of taxes for example, China had been unified until 1976 in the sense that regions had very little bargaining power. After the reforms of 1978,[2] regions obtained much more freedom to bargain with the central government, and this led to differences in regional development (Shu-ki and Yuk-sing 1994). This point is also made by Xu (2011), who argues that the post-Maoist period was characterized by a central government that tried to control personnel, with regional governments controlling the main parts of the economy; this gave regional governments considerable leverage to negotiate with the central government.

1.4 Education and bureaucracy

Education played a key role in keeping the empire together but was both a strength and a weakness of the central state. Almost all education from the Qin onwards was focused on training for government positions. The first examination system started in the Han Dynasty after the anti-education campaign of the Qin had ended. In principle, the examination system was open to all. However, in practice, until the Ming, education remained characterized by some form of co-optation, and the new literati came from elite groups that were already established. This system changed formally in the Ming but changes were already discernible in the late Tang (Tackett 2008, 112), when 'men of virtue' could also pass the examination system, even though social background continued to play an important role (Elman 2000, 5–7). The regulations on entering the civil examination were further relaxed at the start of the Qing Dynasty (1644) when the new emperor (actually his regent, because the emperor himself was only 5 years old) reinvigorated the civil examination system. More people than ever before were then allowed to take the exams. Interestingly, the exams contained various questions about how the Han and Manchu (the Qing Dynasty was of Manchu origin) populations could live harmoniously side-by-side, thus suggesting that the government remained interested in dynastic stability and that it realized being a 'non-Han' dynasty made it weak from its inception. Nonetheless, education remained largely focused on government positions.

Even after the modernization of the education system at the turn of the 19th/20th century, the focus remained on furthering government policy, and also on the importance of education for training reliable civil servants to some extent (Becker et al. 1932). Indeed, if only for a few years after the introduction of the modern system, the old title of *shengyuan*, which was obtainable via the civil examination system, continued to be given to persons passing a certain level in modern schooling. As late as the 1930s, a report of the League of Nations stated that higher education levels continued to lead mainly to government positions.

It is important to realize the relatively small scale of Chinese education. We have very little quantitative historical data on Chinese education, but some data give an impression of the participation in formal education in the late 19th century. The available data for two counties – the semi-urban county of Chengong and the rural region of Yugan – are the basis for the ratios of school enrolment by level of education ca. 1880–1930. The enrolment rate was 10% – 13%, which is quite low compared with 77% in the United Kingdom, 80% in the Netherlands, and 60% in Italy around 1880 (Lee and Lee 2016), and education in China also remained geared mostly towards government positions. Indeed, the education system had little effect – or even an impact opposite to that expected – on technology. For example, Bai (2013) found that, in the last years of the Qing, modern factories arose only in regions with the lowest numbers passing the civil examinations.

This appears as a paradox of educational development: Education in China was always highly regarded, and relatively large investments were made by private families for their children to obtain degrees. However, before recent times, the general level of education was not very high, and the effect of education on the economy (outside the government bureaucracy) was limited. The enormous growth of education in recent years is therefore deeply rooted in China's past and culture. Education was also an effective instrument for recruiting and 'reproducing' the ruling elite; however, it allowed only very limited social mobility, it reached few women (except for a small number of highly educated women from the elite), and had almost no transformational effect on the lives of the Chinese people prior to 1912, or even 1949. In this respect, the Cultural Revolution (1966–1976) was a radical departure from Chinese traditions because it was aimed mainly against the educated (urban) elite. The post-Mao reforms of the 1980s and 1990s, in combination with the one-child policy, brought the country back to its historical development path.

1.5 Needham's puzzle and growth

As discussed previously, a delicate balance has existed between market forces and state capacity over the long term, from the Qin Dynasty to the present day, although the balance shifted somewhat towards the market from the Qing Dynasty onwards. This long-run stability, combined with the large population, leads to the puzzle first formulated in 1969 by Joseph Needham, the great expert on the science and technology of China: 'Why did modern science, the mathematization of hypotheses about Nature, with all its implications for advanced technology, take its meteoric rise only in the West at the time of Galileo [but] had not developed in Chinese or Indian civilization?' This puzzle actually concerns two questions: First, why was China more technologically advanced than the West prior to the 15th century? Second, why did China fall behind in modern science after the 15th century (Jin 2016, 29)? Alternatively, applied to the realm of economic history, the following question becomes relevant: Why did the Industrial Revolution not arise in China, but instead in Northwestern Europe? If we chart the long-term evolution of per capita GDP (Figure 1.2), we indeed witness similar values for China and England up to the 15th century. After the 15th century, a modest – and later accelerating – divergence occurred. Only from the 1950s, with the forced industrialization policy, was there convergence, which then accelerated following the reforms that started in the late 1970s.

The question of why China developed so successfully until the 15th century is perhaps not difficult to answer. If economic development is based on new technologies resulting from new ideas, and new ideas are produced by people, it follows that population size and density (increasing the interaction of ideas) determine development (Kremer 1993; Galor 2005). From this perspective, it is natural that the largest and arguably the most stable state will produce the most ideas, and hence greater economic development compared with small states with tiny populations, which might even regress in their level of economic development because they lose technologies (the example of Tasmania is often cited in this respect). Moreover, in cultural terms, China was relatively homogeneous, facilitating interaction and integration; the Han Chinese people shared a single language and common values and customs (albeit with significant regional variation). Compared with India, for example, or the Middle East (before the conquest by the Arabs), China was a much more homogeneous empire, bringing together a sizeable part of the global population. The stability of institutions – in a state governed by

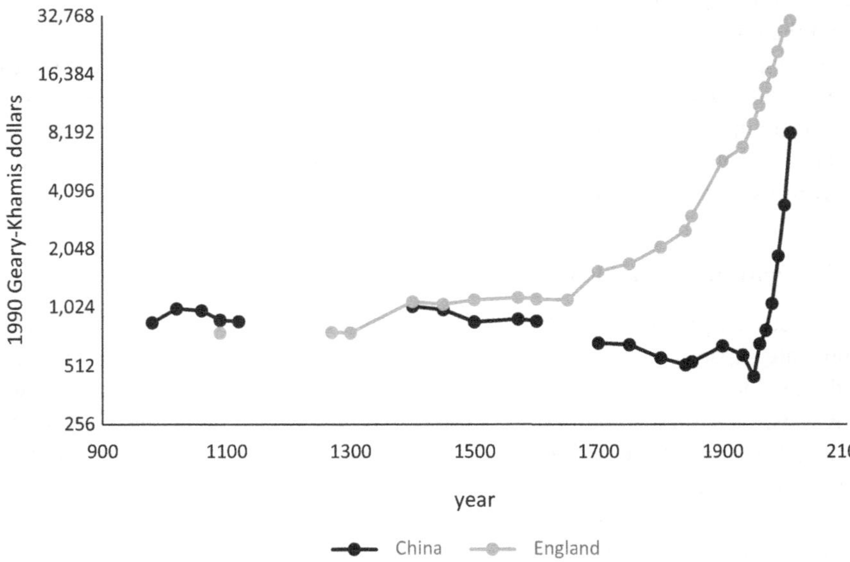

Figure 1.2 Per capita GDP, AD 980–2010 (log 2 scale, 1990 Geary–Khamis dollars)

Source: Broadberry et al. (2017, Table 6); The Maddison Project (2013); Xu et al. (2017)

an 'independent' bureaucracy – enhanced the effect of pure population size (e.g. Fairbank and Reischauer 1960). It is therefore more or less in line with economic theory that large states – such as the Roman and Chinese empires – that allow a certain degree of market exchange and offer some protection of property rights are the natural foci of economic development.

China was indeed the breeding ground for many inventions up to the Sung period, including the so-called 'four great inventions': the compass, gunpowder, papermaking, and printing. Therefore, the true Needham puzzle seems to be the question of why China did not continue to develop after the Sung period – or, if it did, why it did not develop in the direction of industrialization and 'modern' economic growth. Here, opinions are much more divided. Revisionists such as Bozhong Li have argued that China – or at least its most advanced 'core region', the Yangtze delta – did continue to develop and increased its agricultural productivity and structural transformation to new levels. This idea was the basis for the 'Great Divergence' thesis developed by the 'California School', which argues that, until about 1750, levels of economic development in China were comparable to those in Western Europe (Pomeranz 2001). However, there is increasing evidence that the development path of institutions in China was fundamentally different from that of those in Western Europe and that this had a large impact on relative prices and wages. In parts of Western Europe, real wages stabilized at a relatively high level after the Black Death, whereas interest rates fell to very low levels (~5–6%). This created the right incentives for labour-saving technologies to appear: The printing press was one of the first notable examples (the European version was much more capital-intensive than the comparable Chinese technology). This, in combination with low prices for energy (coal), set Western Europe on the road to industrialization, albeit initially very slowly.

China followed a different trajectory, characterized by low real wages, high interest rates, and increased labour-intensive industrialization and agricultural intensification, which is perhaps typical for rice-based irrigation agriculture; e.g., Chao (1986). This was arguably the 'usual' Boserupian and Smithian development path of a pre-modern economy. What was perhaps unusual is that during the Qing Dynasty, this trajectory resulted in a decline in the rate of urbanization (from about 12% to about 7%), partially because most demographic growth occurred in the periphery rather than in the core regions. Similarly, the current estimates of GDP per capita show a long-term decline that runs more or less parallel to the process of de-urbanization.

Additionally, after 1500, China also fell behind the West in terms of education – especially mass education. Although it was acknowledged in the late Tang period that outside of the capital, skills rather than birth dominated the civil examination system (Tackett 2008, Table 1.2), there was still no real mass education, let alone government-sponsored education (Lin 1995). This does not mean there was no demand for such education. Indeed, in a study on the quality – quantity tradeoff in terms of education for Chinese clans, Shiue (2017) found that from the Ming Dynasty onwards, more highly educated families had fewer sons. Hence, they preferred fewer, but better-educated, children.[3] The type technology had also

Table 1.2 Enrolment ratios in Chinese education in Chengong and Yugan counties, 1880–1930

Region	*Education level*	*1880*	*1900*	*1930*
Chengong county (Yunnan)	No school	89.4%	86.2%	84.5%
	Popular school	10.0%	13.3%	12.8%
	Mid-level school	0.6%	1.0%	2.5%
	Higher education	0.0%	0.1%	0.1%
Yugan county (Jiangxi)	No school		89.7%	89.0%
	Popular school		9.8%	7.9%
	Mid-level school		0.5%	3.1%
	Higher education		0.0%	0.0%

Source: Mengxia and Tian (2009, vol. 11); Yugan county household books (ca. 1947, unpublished)

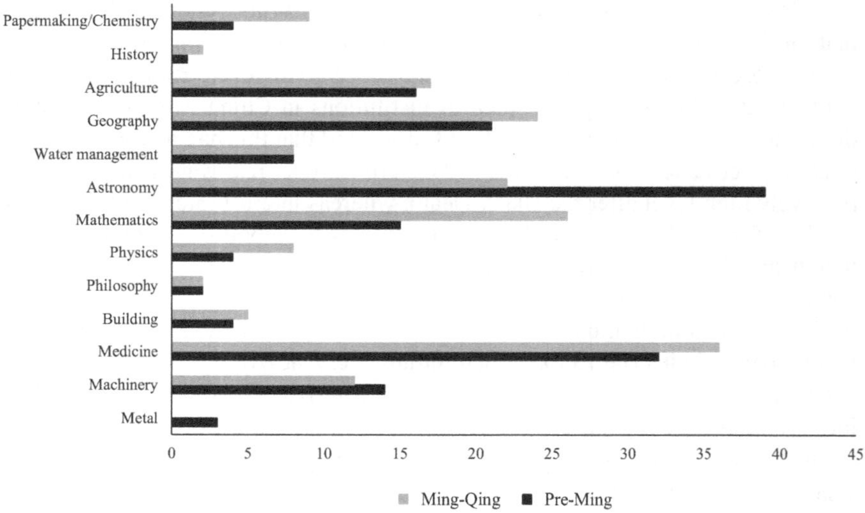

Figure 1.3 Number of scientists in China by field before and after 1368

Source: Du (1992)

changed (see Figure 1.3), with an increased focus on mathematics and practical industries such as papermaking compared with, for example, astronomy.

Hence, in terms of state capacity, the Qing Dynasty was different. As mentioned earlier, this was perhaps because they were a dynasty 'outside' the Han population.[4] The Manchus, who took over the Chinese state in the mid-17th century, more or less skipped the stage of 'forced development' based on coerced labour and massive repression; although they did occur in this period, they took place on a lesser scale.[5] The strategy of allowing the market economy of the late Ming period was essentially copied, and the market remained the dominant allocation mechanism during the entire Qing Dynasty. Moreover, as they were of a different ethnicity to the Han Chinese, the Manchus were probably unable to mobilize the same social preferences (such as loyalty) from officials and the population. Knowing this, they tried to impose a kind of social contract by implying that taxes would not be raised (in particular, land taxes were frozen, despite rapid growth of the population) and they tried to rule the empire in a more or less enlightened way. Indeed, as pointed out earlier, they attempted to combine the Manchu and Han populations, even stimulating intermarriage. This strategy was successful until the final decades of the 18th century, when corruption inevitably began to erode state capacity as well as the civic attitudes of officials and the population at large. For example, Figure 4.7 in Yeung (2007) showed that rebellions co-existed with decreases in the share of top bureaucrats who were of Han origin, most markedly during the 1850s. From then onward, state capacity declined rapidly, as evidenced by the reduction in GDP per capita; accelerating population growth also played a role.

Indeed, the humiliating defeat by the British during the First Opium War (1839–1842) followed by the Taiping rebellion (1850–1864) almost ended the dynasty. However, the state rebounded somewhat after the Taiping rebellion, although corruption remained a key concern. Accordingly, the idea of the dynastic cycle should not be taken too literally, as the declining part of the cycle may still have some periods of prosperity. Nevertheless, almost all attempts to reform the state and society failed. The official abolition of the empire and the beginning of the Republic in 1911 did not lead to political stability, but the period that followed was not at all bad in economic terms. The declining trend in GDP per capita ended, economic modernization accelerated, and the Yangtze again rose to prominence in the newly industrializing economy. The trend towards increased political fragmentation was not reversed, however. Japan contributed markedly to this decline with the First Sino-Japanese War (1894–1895), the invasion of Manchuria in 1931, and the Second Sino-Japanese War (1937–1945).

A new cycle began only with the victory of the Chinese Communist Party under the leadership of Mao in 1949. In a way, the new cycle followed classic patterns, beginning with flawed practices (the Great Leap Forward [1958–1962] was the most extreme experiment in this respect), followed after 1978 by radical market-oriented reforms that unleashed the underlying forces of economic growth to produce miraculous growth previously unheard of in history. The succession of central planning (modelled after the example of the Soviet Union) and market reforms fits nicely into the classical pattern of the dynastic cycle, in which the 'mandate from heaven' was replaced by a contract with Marxist ideology. It will obviously take some time before this situation is undermined by corruption and the erosion of social preferences, but China seems to be on the 'same' historical track in this respect.[6] The rest of this book speaks much more authoritatively about these recent developments.

1.6 Conclusion

China is arguably the oldest unified state. The unification that occurred during the Qin Dynasty (221–206 BC) has essentially remained in place to the present day. Although not without periods of unrest, invasions, or partitions, China has always reunited within roughly the same borders. In this chapter, we have attributed this to three main factors that occurred during the Qin reign: The introduction of legalism (an ideology that attaches value to a person only in her/her use for the state), an educational system that trains people for government positions (established during the subsequent Han Dynasty), and the building of a physical infrastructure that allowed easy extraction of tribute from all parts of China. Until about 1500, China was also the eastern terminus of the Great Silk Route, which connected it with the urban centres of the Middle East, India, and Persia. In many ways, this formed the core of the world economy until about 500 years ago, when new routes were developed that used cheaper transport via the high seas, which fundamentally changed the global economic system.

The persistent (although weak) stability of this system, along with a large population, enabled the development of new technologies, as has been explained in various growth theories. However, it has remained a puzzle that the acceleration in technological development from the 15th century onwards occurred in Europe, rather than in China. We consider that the same system that persisted throughout the dynasties led to weak stability and low levels of education, preventing major changes in technological progress and therefore restricting economic development.

The cyclic dynastic process, outlined by its foundation, the period of weakening towards its end, followed by increased growth, dynastic unrest, and the rise of a new dynasty, has continued in various ways to the present day. However, some changes that occurred in the Qing Dynasty were a departure from the norm. First, in contrast to the preceding dynasties, the Qing was a 'non-Han' dynasty. Its basis was therefore less strong than that of the other dynasties, and market forces had a prominent role from its inception. The longevity of the dynasty is remarkable under such circumstances, and can probably be attributed to the quality of its civil servants. Second, beginning in the late 19th century, we witness educational modernization, even though these changes were initially small. Third, early in the New China era, a period of forced industrialization occurred on a new scale, although this was not a real break with the past, considering the government-led industrialization seen during the Ming Dynasty.

This analysis shows that Chinese development was partly hindered by its persistent governance structure and legalism-induced education system. Weakening of these systems enabled growth, but also caused instability and dynastic change. From the Qing Dynasty onwards, this cycle weakened but did not disappear.

Notes

1 Bas van Leeuwen, International Institute of Social History/UU, Cruquiusweg 31, 1019AT, Amsterdam, The Netherlands. Telephone: *31 20 668 5866. Email: bas.van.leeuwen@iisg.nl.

Jan Luiten van Zanden, Utrecht University Economic and Social History, Drift 6, 3512 BS, Utrecht, The Netherlands. Telephone: *31 30 253 1739. Email: j.l.vanzanden@uu.nl.

The research leading to these results received funding from the European Research Council under the European Union's Horizon 2020 Programme/ERC-StG 637695 –

HinDI, as part of the project 'The historical dynamics of industrialization in Northwestern Europe and China ca. 1800–2010: a regional interpretation'.

2 At least until the next tax reform of 1994.

3 Beginning in the late Qing period, this negative relation between number of children and investment in education disappeared, mostly because the population increased while the number of government positions declined.

4 Besides this reason, it is not entirely clear why the Qing cycle of economic and socio-political change was different from the preceding ones (the Sung and the Ming – the Yuan is yet another story).

5 The first emperor of the Qing period was 5 years old when he ascended the throne. In fact, many of the conquests were carried out by his regent Dorgon. Although Dorgon is known for policies reconciling the Manchu and Han populations, he is also known for his policy of forced labour of the Han population during labour shortages, as well as forced prescriptions for hairstyles and clothing.

6 Setting it apart from previous cycles were the resulting massive changes to the structure and productivity of the economy. Forced industrialization under strict communist rule set the initial stage, and guided industrialization, in which the Communist Party still tries to keep control of the complex processes, has followed.

References

Abu-Lughod, J. L. (1989), *Before European Hegemony: The World System A.D. 1250–1350*, New York and Oxford: Oxford University Press.

Ades, A., and E. Glaeser (1995), "Trade and Circuses: Explaining Urban Giants," *Quarterly Journal of Economics* 110(1): 195–227.

Bai, Y. (2013), "The Incentive Effect of Abolishing China's Imperial Civil Examination on the Adoption of Western Technology: A regression Discontinuity Design," Paper from Hong Kong University of Science and Technology.

Becker, C. H., M. Falski, P. Langevin, and R. H. Tawney (1932), *The Reorganization of Education in China*, Report of the League of Nations' Mission of Educational Experts, League of Nations' Institute of Intellectuel Co-operation, Paris.

Bosker, M., E. Buringh, and J. L. van Zanden (2013), "From Baghdad to London, Unraveling Urban Development in Europe, North Africa and the Middle East, 800–1800," *Review of Economics and Statistics* 95(4): 1418–1437.

Bowles, S. (2016), *Moral Economy. Why Good Incentives are no Substitute for Good Citizens*, New Haven and London: Yale University Press.

Broadberry, S. N., H. Guan, and D. Li (2017), "China, Europe and the Great Divergence: A Study in Historical National Accounting, 950–1850," University of Oxford Discussion Papers in Economic and Social History, no. 155.

Chao, K. (1986), *Man and Land in Chinese History: An Economic Analysis*, Stanford: Stanford University Press.

Chi, C.-T. (1934), "The Economic Basis of Unity and Division in Chinese History," *Pacific Affairs* 7(4): 386–394.

Deng, K. (2004), "Unveiling China's True Population Statistics for the Pre-Modern Era with Official Census Data," *Population Review* 43(2): 1–38.

Du, S. (1992), *Biography of Chinese Ancient Scientists* (2 Volumes), Beijing: Science Press. (杜石然, 中国古代科学家传记 (上下), 科学出版社1992年10月).

Elman, B. A. (2000), *A Cultural History of Civil Examinations in Late Imperial China*, Berkeley: University of California Press.

Elvin, M. (1973), *Pattern of the Chinese Past: A Social and Economic Interpretation*, Stanford: Stanford University Press.

Fairbank, J. K., and E. O. Reischauer (1960), *East Asia: The Great Tradition*, Boston: Houghton Mifflin Company.

Galor, O. (2005), "From Stagnation to Growth: Unified Growth Theory," in: Ph. Aghion and S. N. Durlauf (eds.), *Handbook of Economic Growth, Volume 1A*, North Holland: Elsevier, pp. 171–293.

Hartwell, R. M. (1982), "Political, and Social Transformations of China, 750–1550," *Harvard Journal of Asiatic Studies* 42(2): 365–442.

Jin, D. (2016), *The Great Knowledge Transcedence: The Rise of Western Science and Technology Reframed*, Basingstoke: Palgrave Macmillan.

Ko, C., M. Koyama, and T.-H. Sng (2017), "Unified China and Divided Europe," *International Economic Review* 59(1): 285–327.

Kremer, M. (1993), "Population Growth and Technological Change: One Million B.C. to 1990," *Quarterly Journal of Economics* 108(3): 681–716.

Lee, J.-W., and H. Lee (2016), "Human Capital in the Long Run," *Journal of Development Economics* 122(C): 147–169.

Lin, Y. (1995), "The Needham Puzzle: Why the Industrial Revolution did not Originate in China," *Economic Development and Cultural Change* 43(2): 269–292.

Ma, D. (2011), "Rock, Scissors, Paper: The Problem of Incentives and Information in Traditional Chinese State and the Origin of Great Divergence," LSE Working Paper 152/11.

Maddison, A. (2007), *Contours of the World Economy, 1–2030 AD. Essays in Macro-Economic History*, Oxford: Oxford University Press.

Mengxia, Y., and Q. Tian (2009), *Population Collection in the Period of the Republic of China Volume 1*, Fuzhou City: National library Press. (殷梦霞, 田奇, 民国人口户籍料汇编 第11册, 国家图书馆出版社 北京市 2009年9月).

Needham, J. (1969), *The Grand Titration: Science and Society in East and West*, London: Allen & Unwin.

Peralta, G. (2014), "Qin Dynasty." *Ancient History Encyclopedia*. Last modified January 22, 2014. Available at: www.ancient.eu/Qin_Dynasty/.

Pomeranz, K. (2001), *The Great Divergence: China, Europe, and the Making of the Modern World Economy*, Princeton and Oxford: Princeton University Press.

Shiue, C. (2017), "Human Capital and Fertility in Chinese Clans before Modern Growth," *Journal of Economic Growth* 22(4): 351–396.

Shu-ki, T., and Ch. Yuk-sing (1994), "Tax Reforms of 1994: Breakthrough or Compromise?" *Asian Survey* 34(9): 769–788.

Swann, N. (1950). *Food & Money in Ancient China: The Earliest Economic History of China to AD 25. Han Shu 24 with Related Texts, Han Shu 91 and Shih-Chi 129*, Princeton: Princeton University Press.

Tackett, N. (2008), "Great Clansmen, Bureaucrats, and Local Magnates: The Structure and Circulation of the Elite in Late-Tang China," *Asia Major* 21(2): 101–152.

Tang, W. (1991), *The Taxes and Corvee System in the Ming Dynasty*, Beijing: China Social Sciences Publishing House. (唐文基，明代赋役制度史，中国社会科学出版社，1991)

The Maddison-Project, Available at: www.ggdc.net/maddison/maddison-project/home.htm, 2013 version.

Von Glahn, R. (2016), *The Economic History of China: From Antiquity to the Nineteenth Century*, Cambridge: Cambridge University Press.

Xu, C. (2011), "The Fundamental Institutions of China's Reforms and Development," *Journal of Economic Literature* 49(4): 1076–1151.

Xu, D. (1950), *The Institutions of the Sale of Officer Positions in the Qing Dynasty*, Harvard–Yenching Institute, Yanjing University. (许大龄，清代捐纳制度，哈佛燕京学社出版，1950)

Xu, Y., Z. Shi, B. van Leeuwen, Y. Ni, Z. Zhang, and Y. Ma (2017), "Chinese National Income, ca. 1661–1933," *Australian Economic History Review* 57(3): 368–393.

Xu, Y., B. van Leeuwen, and J. L. van Zanden (2018), "Urbanization in China, ca. 1100–1900," *Frontiers in Economics* 13(3): 322–368.

Yeung, K. t. (2007), *Surpressing Rebels, Managing Bureaucrats: State-building during the Taiping Rebellion, 1850–1864*, Dissertation submitted to the Graduate School-New Brunswick Rutgers, The State University of New Jersey.

Yugan county, Shangrao City, Jiangxi Province, fifth township, fourth district, *Household registration books*, ca. 1947 (江西上饶市余干县五都乡第四保户籍登记簿).

2 Changing structure of the Chinese economy

Paulo José Regis[1]

2.1 Introduction

The study of structural change implies a transformation of the economy from a reliance on certain sectors to others. A long-run perspective is required in order to distinguish significant changes in the use of the factors of production and productivity levels. However, data limitations apply to the study of the Chinese economy, and because of that the time span concentrated upon here will be when the economic reforms started in 1978.

The establishment of the People's Republic of China introduced important changes to the degree of control of the central government. The country became a centrally planned economy under the Soviet model. The new form of governance and the expropriation of private property affected all sectors: local governments, agriculture, industry and the household. The second most important characteristic of the new economic system was its isolation from the world economy. In comparison to the former foreign dominance over Chinese matters, the rise of Chinese nationalism under the Communist Party represented another important differentiator with regards to the previous regime. These two tendencies were reversed with the economic reforms that started in 1978.

Even before the reforms, the Communist Party had been more successful than its predecessors in terms of economic performance, even taking into account the disastrous effects of the Great Leap Forward (1958–62) and the Cultural Revolution (1966–76). The reforms after 1978 brought about a great acceleration of economic growth, which has been sustained over the subsequent 40 years. The economic system has been changed from its roots, with an increasing decentralization of the country towards a market economy, and an opening up to international trade and foreign investment. In this period, China has grown faster than any other country, becoming the largest exporter in the world and the second-largest economy, behind the United States alone.

In the 1970s, after the Cultural Revolution, China had experienced difficult economic times. The economy was weak, and the Communist Party experienced political turmoil. There was a faction inside the party that sought market-oriented reforms to boost the economy, while the more conservative faction was reluctant to abandon the centrally planned institutions of the communist tradition. However, due to a vacuum of power caused by the death of Mao Zedong, an opportunity for political change emerged. Deng Xiaoping and his ideas for economic reform gained support, leading to a new phase, starting in 1978, of structural change and institutional reorganization, based on the market model from the west.

The most important reforms of the late 1970s and early 1980s involved the agricultural sector. With the introduction of the household responsibility system, peasants could sell any excess of production over the government quotas at unregulated prices. Significantly large increases in agricultural productivity allowed production to be expanded while workers were relocated to the industrial and service sectors, generating a structural transformation of the productive sectors. This was complemented by an opening up to international trade and foreign investment. The new labor market, with low salaries by international standards, provided manufacturers with the necessary competitive advantage to obtain a dominant position in the world markets.

However, the industrial sector still remained the monopoly of the public sector. The second wave of reforms in the late 1980s and 1990s led to the beginning of the privatization of state-owned industrial firms, generating large changes in the work force of urban cities, which accelerated after 1998. Prices were liberalized and entrepreneurship in the private sector was supported. Private firms would become the most dynamic sector of the economy, and the main engine of employment creation. After China joined the WTO in 2001, the private sector benefited from greater access to foreign markets, as well as SOEs. Taking full advantage of market liberalization, private firms have become the dominant agents in the industrial and service sectors.

However, some sectors remain under the domain of the public sector, the financial system being probably the most important. It is dominated by the big four state-owned banks, which concentrate most of the market. Although tight regulation may constrain competitiveness, policymakers have protected state-owned banks to facilitate financial stability. Likewise, the banking sector may lack sufficient incentives to expand its business, favoring state-owned and other large firms in credit allocation. Due to the lack of competitiveness of commercial banks, the remaining firms raise most of their capital through other means, such as loans from the informal financial sector, but mostly from internal finance, which is the method most successful firms use to fund their activities. Access to finance for medium and small-sized firms remains an area that may benefit from further economic reform.

2.2 Macro perspective: factors of production and technological change

The starting point for this chapter is the comparison of the macroeconomic performance of China in the post-reform period with that in the previous centrally planned period. The most common aggregate measure of performance of a country is the Gross Domestic Product (GDP). Factors of production, such as labor and capital services, play a predominant role in the generation of product. China has experienced important changes in the last 60 years regarding these two factors. Capital accumulation has been a top priority of the Chinese government, and was so particularly before the reforms. Likewise, the one-child policy has had very important implications for employment. An important difference between the pre- and post-reform periods has been the gains in GDP that have occurred due to technological changes.

2.2.1 Labor

Among the factors that explain the success of China's development strategy is the high availability of labor at low salaries. Prior to 1978, labor was allocated inefficiently by the centrally planned economy, with too much employment in rural activities. Rural China was very important to the ethos of the Communist Party and its agrarian socialist interpretation of the communist revolution. The household registration system (*hukou*) was strictly implemented, with very few opportunities for rural households to move to urban cities where they would have had access to better salaries and welfare services.

Although there are still many restrictions to internal migration, key to the success of the reforms has been the relaxation of the *hukou* system. In 1978, around 50% of the population was living in rural areas, while this number had fallen below 30% by 2015. With such a large rural population, the productivity of this sector was extremely low and the relocation of many of these workers to urban centers has generated important gains in productivity. A large surplus from the agricultural sector has been absorbed by the industrial and service sectors.

The level of education of the population has increased significantly. When the Communist Party came to power, it advocated the expansion of primary and secondary education, achieving an important expansion in coverage (although there is still room for improvement in rural areas). On the contrary, higher education did not follow suit, and for a long time remained stagnated. During the time of the Cultural Revolution, universities were shut down, teachers marginalized, and many relocated to rural areas. With the new economic reforms since 1978, higher education enrollment has risen steadily. The demand has risen faster than the domestic supply provided by Chinese universities, leading to a large surplus of international Chinese students pursuing their studies abroad. Initially, these students would remain abroad looking for new opportunities, but with the rise of the Chinese economy the new trend is for them to come back to look for job opportunities within China.

This new demand for higher education has been fueled by the aspirations of households that have observed a steady increase in their income and, at the same time, a reduction in the number of newborns. This is one of the consequences of the one-child policy implemented since 1979. With only one child per household, parents are willing to invest a large proportion of their rising income in education.

The one-child policy has also had important implications for the structure of employment, and the availability of a surplus work force at low wages. Not only has population growth been constrained but also the age composition of China has changed. The average age of the population has risen and is still rising steadily, which will lead to problems inherent to an aging society. Figure 2.1 shows the steady decrease in the total population growth rate since 1980. The population is projected to peak around 2030, before decreasing and returning to one billion inhabitants in 2100 or soon after.

The main impact has been seen in the young population (14-years-old and under), which has been in steady decline since 1978. It has taken decades but the one-child policy has affected the working-age population (15–64 years), which peaked in 2015. The elderly population (65 and over) continues to increase, with acceleration after 2015 and set to peak around 2060. The result has been a decrease in the dependency ratio (i.e. non-working to working-age population) up until 2015, which has been beneficial to the growth potential of the economy. However, we have reached a turning point, such that the new trend is heading towards a decrease in the working-age population and an increase in the elderly population and the dependency ratio. This is the basis of the structural change and demographic transition theory of Lewis (1954): the economy grows while labor from the rural sector with low productivity is absorbed by the high-productivity industrial sector. This is the demographic dividend. However, there is a turning point after which labor can no longer be relocated and growth stops. Cai (2012) presents the argument that the turning point has already been reached due to the aging population in China, and warns of the negative prospects for further growth. Chapter 10 presents further discussion on the demographic dividend hypothesis and its application to China.

The increase in the participation of women has helped raise employment over and above the growth rate of the population. The one-child policy pushed women

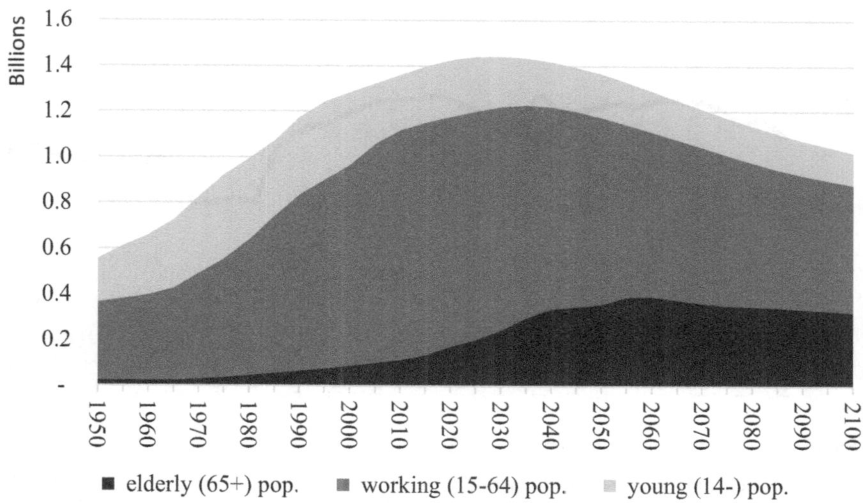

Figure 2.1 Total population by age group, 1950–2100

Source: United Nations, World Population Prospects 2017. Figures are in millions.

to participate in the labor force since most households had only one child. However, given the favoritism for boys over girls due to cultural preferences, the low fertility has been aggravated by an increase in the sex ratio (i.e. number of males for every 100 females). Therefore, some members of the male population will not be able to expand their household since they will not find a suitable partner.

2.2.1.1 Labor share of income

The distribution of national income has experienced some changes. The most important dimension of income inequality remains geographic: rural areas are much poorer and cannot catch up with urban areas.[2] In comparison, the labor share of income in Figure 2.2 is relatively stable, within the range 50–62%. Factor shares are derived from GDP figures using the income approach, which are only available at the provincial level, and only since 1978. The labor share is obtained as the share of labor remuneration within the sum of gross domestic income across provinces. Implicit is the assumption of distributing net taxes on production proportionally between labor and capital. Therefore, the capital share will be one minus the labor share.

The most recent empirical studies in China concerning labor share were motivated by the decline in the labor share from 1995 to 2007. For example, Cai (2005, 2006) first noticed the falling trend. The main explanations for the declining labor share in China, proposed by previous studies, include (a) the change from agriculture to industry and services (Bai and Qian 2010; Li et al. 2009), (b) privatization of SOEs and the change in the ownership structure of the economy (Bai and Qian 2010; Luo and Zhang 2009) and (c) FDI (Luo and Zhang 2009; Shao and Huang 2010). Most studies have proposed that the decline was driven

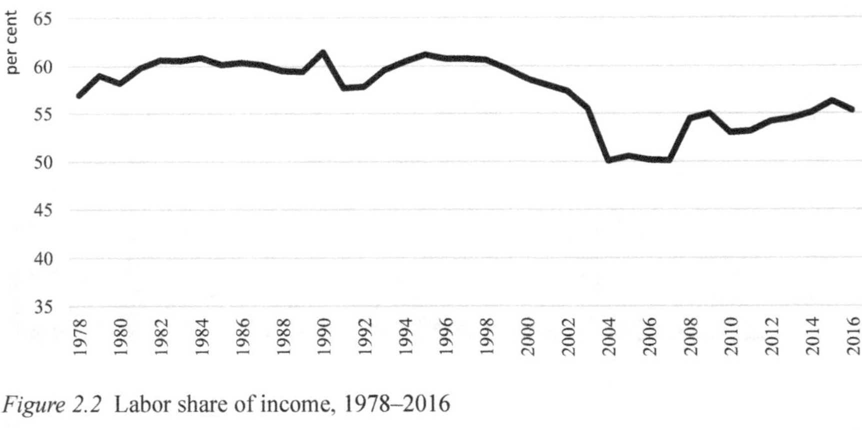

Figure 2.2 Labor share of income, 1978–2016

Sources: Hsueh and Li (1999) for the period 1978–1993. The series is then updated, applying the growth rate of the labor share from NBS (2007) for the period 1994–2004 and from CEIC for the period 2005–2016. The CEIC data are obtained from provincial yearbooks and other sources, with the values for 2009–2015 being the same as in the China Statistical Yearbook (www.stats.gov.cn/english/Statisticaldata/AnnualData/).

Note: The share of labor compensation in GDP net of indirect taxes.

by economic forces, while Bai and Qian (2010) argued that measurement changes could explain a large proportion of the drop, implying that the reported fall in the labor share was largely overstated. Moreover, since then, the labor share has shown a positive trend, bouncing back by half to the 55–60% range. As long as this positive trend continues, there is clear indication of a lasting change in the labor share.

2.2.2 Capital

Capital has been at the top of the priority list since the early days of the Communist Party being in charge of the central government. Capital accumulation was considered the key factor for boosting the secondary sector, with heavy industries being particular favored. Figure 2.3 shows two measures of the change in capital stock for the period 1952–2015. In the 1950s, the growth was extremely high, at greater than 20%, during the process of recovery from the war effort. After the expulsion of Japanese forces in World War II, and the end of the Chinese civil war, there was a large potential for growth based on catching up through capital accumulation. This is the period when the Soviet influence was the greatest. Capital accumulation was very high in communist countries in general. Investment deaccelerated in the early 1960s but recuperated soon after, especially after 1970. The positive trend remained after the reforms of 1978, with a 15% growth rate reached in 2010.

These large capital growth rates reflect another key characteristic of the Chinese economy: the high saving rate. During the time of the centralized economy,

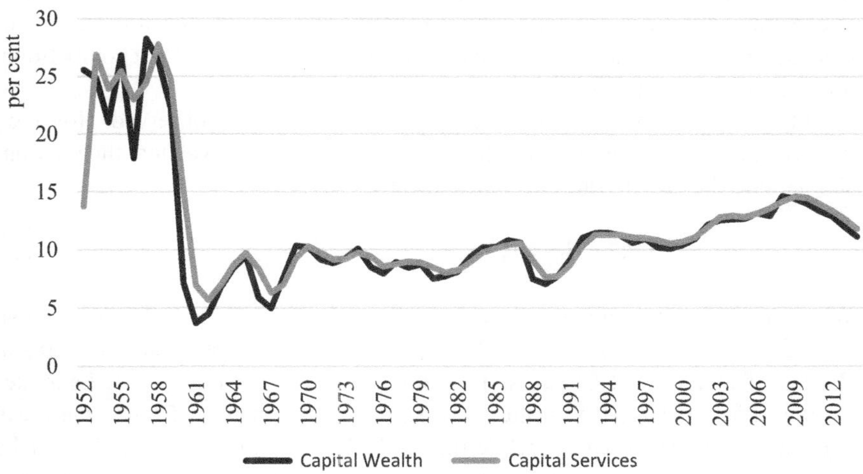

Figure 2.3 Capital stock growth

Source: Holz and Sun (2018). Capital wealth is the growth rate of the stock of capital, while capital services takes into account the use and level of productivity of capital of different ages. The selected series are based on hyperbolic age-efficiency.

investment came from the public sector, which pushed down consumption and kept wages low. Since the market-oriented reforms, high savings from the household, private sector retained earnings, and foreign investment have become very important sources of investment, although public investment still plays an important role, especially in major infrastructure related projects. Since 2010, we can observe a deceleration of investment, which coincides with the new focus on the domestic economy and the service sector. However, it is not yet clear whether this is the new norm or a temporary deviation.

The physical capital series used here are maintained by the China Center for Human Capital and Labor Market Research (CHLR) at the Central University of Finance and Economics (China). They provide wealth capital stock and capital services series using age-efficiency profiles. Wealth capital stock, also called net capital stock, is the value of the stock of capital at market prices, and its first difference is a measure of net investment. On the other hand, capital services is a flow measure (such as net investment), which represents the amount of capital used in the period for the production of new goods. It is the second of these measures that is relevant for measuring the economic activity of a particular period. However, Figure 2.3 shows there is little difference in using one or the other.

2.2.3 Total factor productivity

Total Factor Productivity (TFP) is a measure of technological change. It is usually obtained from a growth accounting exercise, based on aggregate measures of factors of production, such as the ones described in the last two sections. Growth accounting starts from a production function[3] of the form $GDP = A\,K^{1-\alpha}\,L^{\alpha}$, where GDP depends on the technology index (A), capital (K) and employment (L). The technology parameter α is the output elasticity of labor, while the capital elasticity is constrained to be $1 - \alpha$. Under the constraint whereby the technology parameters of labor and capital add up to one and the assumption of perfect competition, α is also the labor share of income in Figure 2.2.

TFP is the growth rate of technology A_t, which cannot be observed. However, it is feasible to estimate TFP from the production function, given that the relationship among the growth rates becomes linear[4]:

$$TFP = g^{GDP} - \alpha g^{L} - (1-\alpha)g^{K} \qquad 2.1.$$

Where g^{X} is the growth rate of a variable X and $g^{A} = TFP$. Table 2.1 derives two sets of estimates of TFP, using GDP and employment figures from the National Bureau of Statistics of China, and Capital Services from Figure 2.3. Estimates for the period 1952–2015 on the left assume a labor share of 57.4% (the mean over the period 1978–2015), while the 1978–2015 estimates on the right make use of the observed labor share from Figure 2.2. Overall, the figures show little difference, regardless of whether we assume the labor share to be constant or variable over the period 1980–2015. Unfortunately, we are not able to make this

Table 2.1 Growth accounting and total factor productivity

Period	g_t^{GDP}	$(1-\alpha)g_t^K$	αg_t^L	TFP_t	*Period*	g_t^{GDP}	$(1-\alpha)g_t^K$	αg_t^L	TFP_t
1952–1955	8.8	9.1	1.4	−2.0					
1955–1960	9.7	10.7	1.7	−2.7					
1960–1965	0.9	3.7	1.2	−4.1					
1965–1970	6.9	3.5	2.1	1.3					
1970–1975	5.9	4.1	1.2	0.6					
1975–1980	6.5	3.8	1.2	1.5	1978–1980	7.7	3.7	1.6	2.4
1980–1985	10.6	3.7	1.9	5.0	1980–1985	10.6	3.4	2.0	5.2
1985–1990	9.0	4.3	1.5	3.2	1985–1990	9.0	4.0	1.6	3.4
1990–1995	12.3	4.2	0.6	7.5	1990–1995	12.3	4.0	0.6	7.7
1995–2000	8.6	4.7	0.7	3.3	1995–2000	8.6	4.4	0.7	3.6
2000–2005	9.8	5.1	0.4	4.3	2000–2005	9.8	5.5	0.4	4.0
2005–2010	11.3	5.8	0.2	5.3	2005–2010	11.3	6.5	0.2	4.6
2010–2015	7.9	5.6	0.2	2.0	2010–2015	7.9	6.0	0.2	1.7
1952–2015	8.0%	5.0%	1.1%	2.0%	1978–2015	9.0%	4.4%	0.8%	3.9%

Notes: All growth rates expressed in per cent. On the left, the TFP computations assume the labor share is 57.4% (i.e. the mean of the period 1978–2015), while the TFP values on the right use the actual labor share as presented in Figure 2.2.

comparison for the full period, since there is no information about income distribution before 1978.

Table 2.1 shows the remarkable growth experience of China, with capital accumulation being the most important engine of growth. Before 1978, this was the only significant source of growth, with a minor but sustained contribution from employment of around 1.4% of GDP. On average, capital would provide a growth rate of almost 10% of GDP in the 1950s. Capital accumulation shrank by more than half after that but still provided a growth rate of 3.5% or more. TFP was not very important, and was even negative for the period 1952–1965, more than cancelling out the contribution from employment. After that, TFP became positive but was still not strong enough to provide significant growth.

After 1978, capital accumulation did not deteriorate but rather increased, reaching its maximum in 2005–2010. The main difference here, in comparison to the period before 1978, is the importance of the contribution of TFP as an engine of growth, rivaling that of capital accumulation. This suggests that the economic reforms have encouraged growth beyond capital accumulation, increasing overall productivity and innovation at the same time. The contribution of TFP has been sustained over time, except in the last period where it is down to 2% or less. The effect of the one-child policy is reflected after 1990, when the contribution of labor becomes consistently less than 1% of GDP growth, and only 0.2% in the last 10 years. Given the aging of the population, this is expected to become negative over time.

The growth rate of each period has been annualized. All subperiods include five years, except for 1952–1955 (three years) and 1978–1980 (two years), due to data constraints.

2.3 Patterns of structural change

This section first documents the main shifts in GDP and employment across the three main sectors of the economy: agriculture, industry and services. First, there is a clear decline in the participation of agriculture, while the industry first, and more recently services, have become the leading sectors in the development of the economy. Second, labor productivity is analyzed by means of a decomposition into intra-industry and industry-reallocation productivity gains across 10 sectors. Intra-industry gains are dominant; however, there are periods of important gains in productivity coming from the reallocation effect. Third, the structural change in urban employment towards privatization is presented to show the rise of private firms and self-employment in the economy. Private firms have replaced state-owned firms as the dominant organization of employment.

2.3.1 Sector shares of GDP and employment

Economic activity is usually divided into three main sectors: agriculture (primary), industry (secondary) and services (tertiary). The dominant view is that economic development requires the economy to move from the primary to the secondary sector first, and then to the tertiary sector. Therefore, poor economies are incentivized to develop their secondary sector (manufacturing in particular) since low salaries provide a potential source of growth in both employment and productivity. The relocation of labor from the primary to the secondary sector may also raise productivity in agriculture, since labor becomes scarcer in that sector.

Figures 2.4 and 2.5 provide GDP and employment shares from 1952 to 2016, split in terms of the three main sectors. Other than the effect of the Great Leap Forward (1958–1962), the pattern in the data is straightforward. The share of agriculture in both GDP and employment diminishes over time. Starting from over

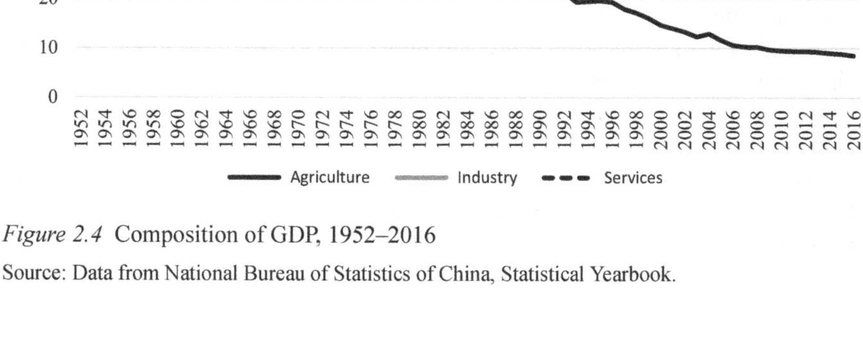

Figure 2.4 Composition of GDP, 1952–2016

Source: Data from National Bureau of Statistics of China, Statistical Yearbook.

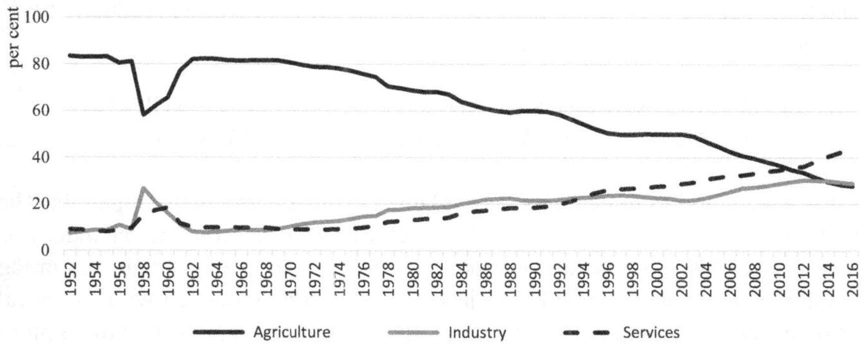

Figure 2.5 Employment participation of the three main sectors of the economy, 1952–2016

Source: Data from National Bureau of Statistics of China, Statistical Yearbook.

50% in 1952, the share of agriculture in GDP is less than 10% by 2016. Likewise, employment shrank from a share of 80% in 1952 to less than 30% in 2016. This is a remarkable transformation of the economy in the same direction as most developed countries. Although this transformation started before the reforms of the late 1970s, its pace has increased significantly since 1978. It is the change from a centrally planned to a market-oriented economy that has provided an energetic private sector that has in turn carried out most of the transformation, absorbing an increasing proportion of the labor force.

Initially, even before the pro-market reforms, the secondary sector generated most of the new employment, with significant gains in productivity, reaching almost 50% of GDP in 1978. Its employment participation has increased further over the whole period. The service sector has also increased its GDP participation, especially since the economic reforms. Before 1978, the government favored the secondary sector, relegating the tertiary sector to a small role in the economy. Following the reforms, the tertiary sector was in a better position to develop, reaching 50% of GDP in 2015, and 40% of total employment in 2016. Since the early 1990s, the employment share of the service sector has increased steadily, surpassing industry in 1994 and becoming the main generator of employment by 2011. Employment relocation to the service sector provides new opportunities for further growth of the economy, beyond manufacturing and the relocation of cheap labor. Figure 2.5 shows that 30% of total employment is still dedicated to agriculture. However, given the demographic constraints described in section 2, one of the most important challenges ahead is the shrinking of the labor force. Therefore, the service sector may be in a better position than industry to transform the economy further.

2.3.2 Structural change in labor productivity

Section 2.2.3 describes patterns in aggregate total output (GDP), while section 2.3.1 presents employment shares across sectors. This section looks at the evolution of aggregate labor productivity (i.e. *Y*, measured as GDP per employee) and its disaggregation across 10 sectors. The change in aggregate productivity (*Y*) can be decomposed into three terms:

$$\Delta Y = \text{INTRA INDUSTRY CHANGES} + \text{STATIC STRUCTURAL CHANGES} + \text{DYNAMIC STRUCTURAL CHANGES} \quad 2.2.$$

Equation 2.2 and its three terms are explained in more detail in the appendix. The first term represents the increase in productivity without structural change. It is measured as the weighted average productivity growth across sectors, assuming employment has not changed. The last two terms are associated with structural change, and represent the gains in productivity due to the reallocation of employment across sectors. The second term is the static structural change and is the gain in productivity due to shifts in employment from less productive to more productive industries, assuming there is no change in productivity within each industry. The third term is referred to as dynamic structural change and is the joint effect of changes in employment shares and changes in productivity across sectors.

The decomposition results for the period 1952–2010 are shown in Figure 2.6 and Table 2.2. Labor productivity is defined as the value added per employee.

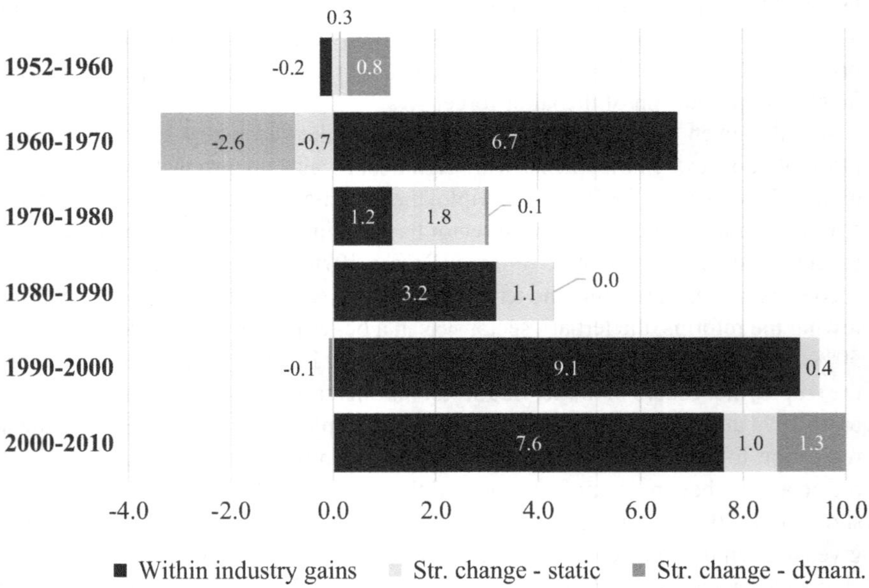

Figure 2.6 Labor productivity decomposition

Source: The data source is the GGDC Ten-Sector Database from Timmer et al. (2015).

Notes: Labor productivity gains by decade decomposed into three parts (within-industry gains, and static and dynamic structural-change gains). The changes in labor productivity are expressed as annualized growth rates.

Table 2.2 Labor productivity gains before and after 1978

	Intra industry	*Structural change*	*Total*
Centrally planned period: 1952–1978	*1.6*	*0.9*	*2.5*
Economic reform period: 1978–2010	*5.5*	*2.1*	*7.6*
1978–2010: sectoral analysis			
1. Agriculture	0.87	–0.70	0.17
2. Industry	2.83	1.24	4.07
Mining	0.48	–0.16	0.33
Manufacturing	2.01	0.91	2.92
Utilities	0.13	0.12	0.25
Construction	0.21	0.37	0.58
3. Services	1.80	1.54	3.34
Trade, restaurants & hotels	0.43	0.64	1.07
Transport, storage & communication	0.44	0.31	0.75
Finance, insurance, real estate & business services	0.39	0.28	0.67
Government services	0.51	0.17	0.68
Community, social & personal services	0.02	0.15	0.18

Source: GGDC Ten-Sector Database from Timmer et al. (2015).

Note: Within-sector and structural-change labor productivity gains are expressed as annualized growth rates (per cent).

The data come from the Groningen Growth and Development Centre (GGDC) database (Timmer et al. 2015) and considers ten sectors: agriculture, four industries (mining, manufacturing, utilities and construction) and five services (trade, restaurants & hotels; transport, storage & communication; finance, insurance, real estate & business services; government services; and community, social & personal services).

Figure 2.6 presents the decomposition of productivity gains according to Equation 2.2 by decade. Since the reforms started in 1978, the first three decades can be associated with the pre-reform centrally planned economy, while the last three are the result of the market-oriented economic transformation. Although there is little increase in productivity (only 0.9%) in the first decade, all of this gain is due to structural change, mostly dynamic gains from a relocation of employment to the most productive sectors, while the average productivity change is actually negative. However, this structural-change gain was more than reversed in the 1960s because of the negative effects of employment relocation during the Great Leap Forward and the Cultural Revolution. Overall, there was a gain of productivity (3.4%) in this period, but this could potentially have been larger if labor were not relocated to less productive sectors (agriculture). In the 1970s, the increase in productivity (3%) is mainly due to structural change, mostly though static gains (1.8%) from a relocation of employment from agriculture to other sectors, especially manufacturing, since the intra-sector gains in productivity were modest in all sectors.

In the last three decades, the economic reforms have provided opportunities for some very important gains in productivity, as shown by the figures: 4.3% (1980–1990), 9.4% (1990–2000) and 9.9% (2000–2010). Most of the gains in productivity have been within-sector, mostly in the industry and service sectors, but with some also coming from agriculture. In the 1990s, almost all of the productivity gain is within-industry. However, in the first and third subperiods after the reforms, structural transformation also provided important gains. In the period 1980–1990, there was a static structural change gain obtained from the relocating of employees from agriculture to industry. In the most recent period, there has been a combined gain from both types of structural change of 2.3% growth: 1% due to the relocation of workers from agriculture to other sectors (especially manufacturing) and 1.3% due to the increase in productivity of these more productive sectors to which labor was relocated during this 10-year period (i.e. dynamic gains).

Table 2.2 provides the decomposition of labor productivity for the pre- (1952–1978) and post- (1978–2010) reform periods, in which the static and dynamic structural change productivity gains have been grouped together. For the post-reform period, further details of the sectoral composition of these productivity gains are provided. Productivity grew by an annual growth rate of 2.5% in the period 1952–1978, with most of this change originating from within-industry productivity increases (1.6%), while structural change provided less than a 1% productivity gain. The economic reform period has seen a substantial increase in labor productivity (7.6%), most of which corresponds to gains in productivity within industries (5.5%). However, structural change has provided an additional 2.1% productivity growth, which is a significant contribution in this period.

Table 2.2 shows that the productivity gain of this period is generated by both the industry (4.07%) and service (3.34%) sectors. The contribution of the service sectors becomes increasingly important in the later years. Manufacturing is the most important sector, with more than two thirds of the productivity gains coming from the within-industry effect. Among services, the contributions are more evenly distributed, both among the different sectors and between within-industry and structural-change gains. The trade, restaurants & hotels sector is the most important, contributing 1.07% of overall productivity growth, more than half coming from structural-change gains. This is an encouraging sign since the service sector seems to provide a good alternative to the secondary. Further economic growth in China will require an increase in the contribution of the service sector, both in terms of employment and productivity.

2.3.3 The rise of the private sector in urban employment

Before 1978, industry and service economic activities were under direct control of the government. The main role was played by SOEs, which were the largest organizations in the economy, providing relatively large salaries and benefits.

Collective-owned firms were much fewer and smaller. Employment was guaranteed, while private organizations were not allowed and self-employment was quite rare. The reforms since 1978 have made fundamental changes to these limitations.

Figure 2.7 shows urban employment since 1978. Table 2.1 shows slow growth in the labor force since 1990, an important change with regards to pre-1990 data. However, urban employment displays steady growth in Figure 2.7 and, if anything, this growth may have accelerated in the 1990s. This rapid increase has been possible due to the continuous transfer of population from rural to urban employment.

Until 1978, the sector grew at the pace of public firms.[5] Eventually, the private sector emerged, while state enterprises peaked in 1992. After 1992, state enterprises deepened their reform, increasing their competitiveness and downsizing their operations. Self-employment became a significant source of employment. However, it is the private firm[6] which has dominated the expansion of the sector, as it is shown by the diagonal stripes area in Figure 2.7. Especially since 2000, it has become the most dynamic component of this sector. By 2016, state enterprises were generating only around a fourth of the employment of private enterprises.

Figure 2.7 also shows a "residual". This is employment which cannot be explained by the figures reported by legally registered firms. In other words, it captures employment generated either by the informal sector or by informal jobs within the formal sector. From 1997 to 2002, the residual was the most important source of the urban employment increase. These figures show the importance of informal employment at the time when the private sector was first starting to develop and the government was eliminating many of the protections afforded

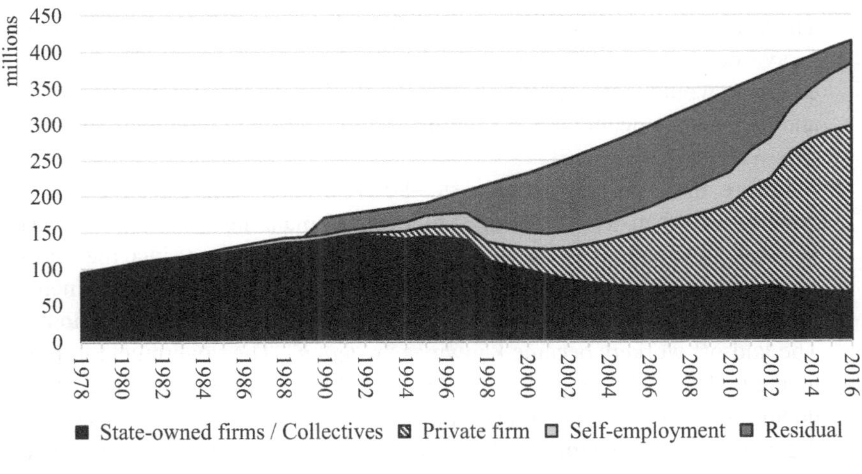

Figure 2.7 Changes in employment structure since the reform

Sources: National Bureau of Statistics. There is no statistic available about the "residual" before 1991, the starting year of the Sample Survey on Population Change.

to the employees of public firms. The informal sector provides opportunities although the positions it offers may be less stable and under poor conditions.

The informal sector has been an important source of employment for migrant workers moving from rural to urban regions. Many of these workers are working but not presented in the official numbers of firms (i.e. informal jobs within the formal sector). Other migrant workers are absorbed by the informal sector. Informal employment is, to the illegal migrant, an escape from low rural income and poverty, providing an improvement in his living standards. However, these informal workers face uncertainty since they lack access to the social security system, social protection networks and education for their children in their households.

In economies undertaking large structural changes, the informal sector may provide, in the short run, the flexibility required to ameliorate the negative effects of labor relocation. One example is rural-urban migration. Another example, which explains how the residual reached 40% of total urban employment in 2003, was the market privatization reforms of 1998 onwards. SOEs laid off a large number of staff, a large proportion of which ended up moving into informal jobs. Cai (2004) presents evidence of the importance of the informal sector in dealing with the restructuring and the laying off of workers from state-owned companies over the period 1998–2003. By 2015, however, the residual was less than 10% of total urban employment. Box 2.1 provides more details on the role the reforms played in the rise of the informal sector.

Box 2.1 Reforms and the restructuring of state-owned enterprises and banks

The structural transformations and economic reforms have meant to move away economic activity from the state to the private sector. The market economy would increase efficiency in production. The raise of private firms and banks also meant state-owned firms and banks had to change to compete with them.

Before the reforms, the iron-rice-bowl program guaranteed employment to all urban workers. Under this central planning system, there was no unemployment. With the reforms, unemployment raised since the state-owned firms had to reduce the number of employees and labor cost. Unemployment emerged as the result of the transition to the market economy. The laid-off workers became known as "*xiagang*". The government implemented a form of unemployment *xiagang* subsidies (three years) and other unemployment subsidies. Laid-off workers with unemployment subsidies did not count as unemployed in official statistics. They are part of the "residual" in Figure 2.7 and account for an important share of its increment since 1998. In recent years, the residual has steadily decreased since 2012.

In addition to adopt new management practices to increase competition, state-owned banks also laid off a large number of workers. During the centrally planned economy, loans were allocated to state-owned firms and local governments. With the marketization of the banking sector, restructuring also required loans to be allocated according to market principles. However, the links with the public sector remained strong for most of the 1990s. The result was an accumulation of bad loans by state-owned banks to state-owned firms and local governments. The large size of Non-Performing Loans (NPLs) was a serious threat to the stability of the financial sector.

The government implemented a bailout of state-owned banks in 1998 and established asset management companies to transfer a large share of their NPLs. With improvements in the practices of loan allocation of state-owned banks, it took many years to significantly decrease the size of NPLs. By 2008, the proportion of NPLs decreased considerably. However, in recent years, there is a new increase in NPLs signaling new concerns over systemic risk in the banking sector, although NPL to total loan ratios are still far from the levels of late 1990's. For further discussion on the evolution of NPL and NPL ratio, see Okazaki (2017).

2.4 Opening up

In addition to factors of production reallocation and private ownership, economic reforms introduced international competition. This has been a significant change with the past. Traditionally, exchange of goods with other countries has not been an important activity. China has been mostly self-sufficient through its long history. It has been the rest of the world that has been interested in integrating China and its rich economy to world trade. With the Communist Party's ascension to power, isolation became the norm once more. Likewise, Western countries did not recognize the new government and broke relationships to isolate the rising new communist power, with the US not normalizing the relationship as late as 1970's. In the 1950's, most imports came from the Soviet Union, especially in capital goods which were crucial for many investment projects. However, the relationship also became distant due to changes in leadership in the Soviet Union in 1960's. Figure 2.8 shows the export performance of China since 1960 as percentage of GDP. Before the 1978 reforms, exports were always less than 5% of GDP, reaching the lowest point in 1970 with 2.5% of GDP.

Diplomatic relationship with occident start normalizing in 1960s and, from 1978, economic reforms increasingly put emphasis on the exchange with outside world and performance of the export sector. By early 1980s, China enthusiastically initiated a process of opening up its economy in trade and foreign direct investment, modifying the law and introducing private property and market liberalization reforms. In industrial policy, the creation of special economic zones for the experimentation of new market friendly policies and the adoption of new technologies were very important (see Chapter 6 on international trade and special economic zone policies). Financial markets and FDI expanded in the 1990s, and

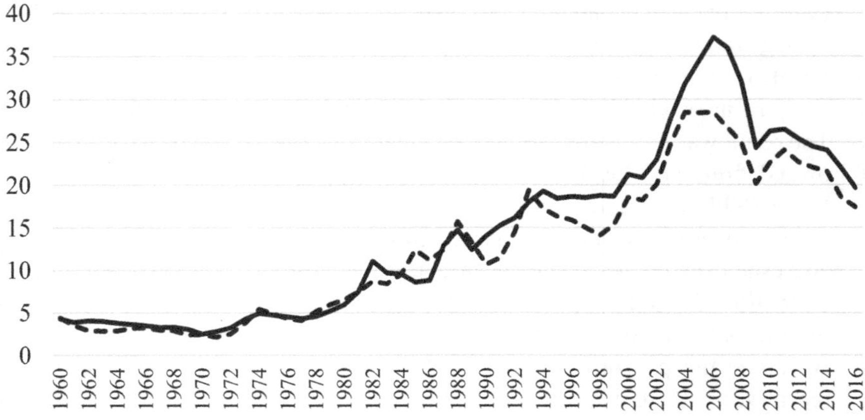

Figure 2.8 Exports and imports (% of GDP)

Source: World Development Indicators (World Bank). The solid and dashed lines are exports and imports as percentage of GDP, respectively.

especially after China's introduction as a new member of the World Trade Organization (WTO) in the year 2001.

The share of exports in GDP continues rising in the 1980s and 1990s, reaching over 20% of GDP in 2000. After the membership in the WTO, international trade boomed once more in China, reaching 37% of GDP in 2006. Since then, exports have grown slower than the rest of the economy but remaining still over 20% by 2016. However, taking into account total exports and imports accounted for more than 65% already in 2006, it is not surprising there is a drop in GDP participation. This has been a dramatic transformation in the Chinese economy and its integration with the rest of the world, becoming the largest trading country in the world by 2013.

Table 2.3 compares the destinations of exports and imports before the opening up (period 1974–1978) and after becoming integral part of the world economy (period 2010–2014). Before the opening up, China traded mostly with other Asian countries, both in terms of imports and exports. Especially the latter was concentrated in Asia. Europe was also important, as well as imports from North America (including some primary goods from Canada). Trade with other regions was rather small. Japan was by far the most important trade partner of China in this period. Germany is the largest trade partner of Europe, even more important than the US. Two small economies are at the top of the exports list as well: Hong Kong and Singapore. In the case of Hong Kong, it was the most important destination of Chinese exports. This is because of its importance as international port: most of those exports are routed to other destinations from Hong Kong. At the time, other ports in China lacked the infrastructure and know-how of international trade.

Table 2.3 Exports and imports – top destinations (%)

	2010–2014			*1974–1978*	
	Exports	*Imports*		*Exports*	*Imports*
By region:			By region:		
Africa	3.7	4.8	Africa	6.7	2.2
Asia	44.7	61.1	Asia	69.5	45.9
Europe	23.4	17.6	Europe	18.8	25.2
North America	20.9	9.5	North America	4.4	12.1
Latin America	7.3	6.9	Latin America	0.5	3.7
Top countries:			Top countries:		
USA	19	8	HKG	26.5	0.2
HKG	11	4	JPN	25.3	39.6
JPN	8	10	SGP	4.6	0.9
DEU	5	6	DEU	4.2	10.6
KOR	4	10	USA	3.4	8.2

Notes: Data for the period 2010–2014 is from the BACI database (Gaulier and Zignano 2009) while data for the period 1974–1978 is from Feenstra et al. (2005). Both sources rely on the COMTRADE database as primary source.

The second part of Table 2.3 shows the composition in 2010–2014. The most important change is now imports are mostly concentrated in Asian markets; however, exports are better distributed regarding Europe and North America. Latin America is still a small market but has increased in importance considerably. The US is by far the new top destination of Chinese exports. Japan is still an important trade partner but is much less important than before the reforms while Korea has gained importance, especially as source of imports to China. Hong Kong is still routing an important share of Chinese exports to other destinations but this is far less important than before. For a comparison of the export performance of China relative to a group of countries, see Chapter 3.

Table 2.4 and Table 2.5 show the analysis by product of Chinese exports in the same two periods. In the first period, Chinese products are small in size regarding world exports, no matter the product classification. In this period, China minimized international trade interaction to the level that could import some necessary capital goods (or paying its international loans). Some primary goods (food and live animals) were the most competitive of Chinese exports with the largest revealed comparative advantage index (2.38). This type of product is also the item with the largest share of export (26.7%). Manufactures also have a large participation of 24.2% which can be complimented with miscellaneous manufactured goods (12.8%). Both items show revealed comparative advantages larger than one. In this period, China also export some natural resources but only crude materials show a large revealed comparative advantage.

Table 2.5 reveals some important changes in the export sector in China since the start of the economic reforms. The participation in world exports has increased

Table 2.4 Exports 1974–1978 – product classification

	% of China	*% of world*	*RCA*
Food and live animals	26.7	1.6	2.38
Beverages and tobacco	0.9	0.6	0.84
Crude materials, inedible, except fuels	12.7	1.1	1.59
Mineral fuels, lubricants and related materials	13.5	0.5	0.72
Animal and vegetable oils, fats and waxes	0.4	0.4	0.62
Chemicals and related products, n.e.s.	5.4	0.5	0.70
Manufactured goods classified chiefly by material	24.2	0.9	1.33
Machinery and transport equipment	3.0	0.1	0.12
Miscellaneous manufactured articles	12.8	1.1	1.64
Commodities and transactions not elsewhere classified.	0.3	0.3	0.39

Source: Based on bilateral data from the NBER-United Nations Trade Data of Feenstra et al. (2005), which makes use of the SICT revision 2 product classification.

Notes: RCA is the revealed comparative advantage index and is equal to the proportion of exports of good X in China's total exports divided by the proportion of world exports of good X in the world total exports. An RCA = 1 implies the importance of good X in total exports of China is the same than the average country in the world.

Table 2.5 Exports 2010–2014 – product classification

	% of China	*% of world*	*RCA*
Animal & animal products	0.7%	4.3%	0.35
Vegetable products	0.9%	3.3%	0.26
Foodstuffs	1.1%	4.3%	0.35
Mineral products	1.3%	0.8%	0.07
Chemicals & allied industries	4.7%	6.3%	0.50
Plastics/rubbers	3.7%	10.2%	0.82
Raw hides, skins, leather, & furs	1.4%	30.6%	2.47
Wood & wood products	1.7%	8.7%	0.70
Textiles	11.2%	33.7%	2.71
Footwear/headgear	3.0%	47.3%	3.81
Stone/glass	2.7%	8.2%	0.65
Metals	7.2%	12.2%	0.98
Machinery/electrical	47.6%	24.6%	1.98
Transportation	3.4%	4.3%	0.35
Miscellaneous	9.6%	22.4%	1.80

Notes: Based on the 15 top categories of the bilateral trade BACI database of CEPII, which contains data using the Harmonized System product classification (see Gaulier and Zignano 2009). RCA is the revealed comparative advantage index and is equal to the proportion of exports of good X in China's total exports divided by the proportion of world exports of good X in the world total exports.

drastically. China is responsible for one third of textiles exports of the world as well as almost half of footwear and headgear and 30% of skins, leather and furs. These three items also display the highest revealed comparative advantage of China with values larger than 2.[7] The world clothing industry would not be the same without China.

Machinery and electrical products is the most important item regarding participation in total Chinese exports, with almost 48%. Likewise, the revealed comparative advantage index is almost 2. The last item, miscellaneous, also include many manufacturing goods (e.g. clocks & watches, toys & games, optical, medical and surgical goods). China shows an important participation in world trade as well as high revealed comparative advantage. On the contrary, unlike the 1974–1978 period, food-related products (top three items in Table 2.5) have a very low participation in Chinese exports and low RCA values. This is partially due to the specialization in new products as well as the increase of the population to 1.4 billion and the rise of living standards, which have increased considerably the domestic demand for food, and China's food production could barely cover its population needs.

China has used industrial policy actively in the last 25 years (Wang and Wei 2010). Rodrik (2006) attributes the rapid economic development of China since 1992 to the country's capacity at exporting goods associated with higher income levels than its own (e.g. namely consumer electronics). Besides the rapid expansion of trade volume, the level of sophistication of exports has also increased significantly. Wang and Wei (2010) attribute the increase in China's export variety and sophistication since 1996 to the establishment of economic and technological development zones which provide both tax breaks and opportunities for developing new products. Producing new goods with a relatively high value generates positive externalities in the country as it removes most uncertainties for potential followers in the new markets. Desmarchelier et al. (2018) show the conquering of the product space by China, expanding its coverage of the world network of products. However, their simulations also show that subsidy policies may generate important shocks when they are applied and when they are removed. In Chapter 6, Chinese trade policy and the role of China in the East Asian regional production network are discussed in more detail.

2.5 The financial sector

The financial intermediation in China is heavily dominated by banks. This is partly motivated by the Communist Party's desire to have a dominant role in the sector by regulating the rules of engagement among banks. Although the policy objective of financial regulation has been both to pursue credit expansion so as to promote steady economic growth of the real economy as well as to safeguard the stability of the financial sector, the priority is on the stability of the sector. Interest rates have been heavily regulated until very recently (2015), to provide control over financial resource allocation; however, this has constrained efficiency, since there has been no price competition among banks. Thus, this sector has been less dynamic than the private sector. Innovation and entrepreneurship has been heavily regulated in this sector. Despite a large amount of reform of financial intermediation, it is still largely dominated by few large state-owned banks.

As China has increasingly promoted market-oriented reforms and integration into the international markets, the development of the private sector has required the availability of credit. Therefore, the Chinese banking sector has experienced major reforms during the last three decades. A larger and more efficient financial sector is considered key to the flourishing of private firms. The Chinese government initiated banking reforms as part of the comprehensive post-1978 economic reform. These reforms were aimed at transforming the policy-driven and monopolistic banking system into one that adopted market-oriented practices and greater competition.

Under the Communist Party's rule of China, the financial sector was initially heavily concentrated into a single institution: the People's Bank of China. Three other banks[8] existed: the Agricultural Bank of China, the Bank of China and the China Construction Bank; however, they acted as subsidiaries of, or were absorbed by, the People's Bank of China. Based on the Soviet model, the People's Bank of China controlled almost all financial assets and served as both the central bank and the only commercial bank for practically all financial transactions. Its main role was to provide the cash flow necessary to fulfill the production plan of the central planner, and it had direct control over credit aggregates. The main business of banks was to provide short-term loans to state-owned firms, since long-term investment was funded by the government in accordance with the production plan.

China's banking reform has consisted of four phases: 1978–1992, 1993–2001, 2002–2012 and 2013 onwards. In the first period, the banking system experienced institutional restructure, with the establishment of a two-tier banking system. From 1979 to 1983, the three aforementioned banks were reformed and promoted, each specializing its operations in a specific sector: the rural sector (Agricultural Bank of China), import-export and other foreign market activities (Bank of China) and the construction sector (Construction Bank of China). These initial reforms did not produce any fundamental changes since there was still no competition, the main objective being to enlarge the size of the financial sector. The reform of 1984 was important since the remaining commercial banking functions of the People's Bank of China were passed on to the newly established Industrial and Commercial Bank of China. From then on the People's Bank of China was to focus on its role as central bank; however, it did not become independent from the government. These four original banks remain the dominating players of the banking sector today, and are usually referred to as the "big four". After 1985, sectoral restrictions were eliminated and these four state-owned banks were allowed to compete with each other. Also, an increasing number of small and medium-sized banks were created; however, competition remained very limited since the new banks were also state-owned and remained small in size.

In the second phase (1993–2001), the first true attempt to create competition through commercialization of the banking system took place. First, although the banking sector remained heavily regulated, the central bank was given more independence. State-owned banks were further reformed to separate them from policy lending and turn their focus towards commercial lending. The big four were re-capitalized and restructured to reduce inefficient branches and staff (see Box 2.1). To encourage greater competition, medium-sized banks were turned into national joint-stock commercial banks in 1993. However, the banking reform during this period is considered to have been unsuccessful. The big four's domination was not challenged, since private banks did not obtain enough capital and bank regulations ruled out price competition. Fu and Heffernan (2007) investigate the cost x-efficiency[9] of Chinese banks over the period 1985–2002 and argue that x-efficiency declined between 1993 and 2002. Fu (2004) finds the average cost efficiency of the developed economies to be roughly 85%, and that of the emerging markets to be around 17% less on average.

The third phase began in 2002, after China joined the WTO in December 2001 and agreed to open up banking, financial services and insurance to foreign investment. A five-year WTO interim period was initiated and China's banking reform was accelerated so as to increase flexibility and successfully manage the challenges of foreign banks. China introduced a new set of reforms to strengthen the stability of the sector while increasing efficiency and competition. The most ambitious reform was a process of partial privatization of the big four through the adoption of an IPO strategy from 2003 to the present day. The Agricultural Bank of China was the last of the big four to be listed on a stock exchange (2010). However, the level of foreign ownership remains small. Other banks have followed suit, offering their own IPOs on the stock exchange. Likewise, domestic banks have attracted foreign strategic investors to improve their governance and acquire know-how. The government has injected capital into the big four and the national joint-stock commercial banks to strengthen them.

The introduction of foreign banks was the most important reform of this period. It would increase the efficiency of the banking industry by gradually increasing competition with foreign banks. Although foreign banks were allowed to carry out foreign currency business with Chinese and foreign enterprises, they were initially only allowed to offer local currency business to foreign enterprises and individuals in specific cities. The latter restrictions were gradually released, with the number of cities increasing every year. Eventually, they were also allowed to provide local currency business to domestic Chinese enterprises and individuals. Since 2006, foreign banks have been treated the same as domestic banks.

The evidence suggests this period was successful in terms of efficiency. Hsiao et al. (2015) measure the cost and profit efficiency of 107 Chinese commercial banks from 2007 to 2012. They use the performance of foreign banks as the benchmark since they have experience of intensive competition in the international market, more advanced technologies and better know-how; however, competition in China's banking sector is mainly assessed in terms of non-price measures, which puts foreign banks at a disadvantage. The authors find that, although foreign banks were still the most cost efficient, domestic banks had gradually caught up to the cost advantage with them due to the increased competition. On the contrary, the initial profit advantage of the domestic banks over the foreign banks was widening. However, it is expected that this latter competitive advantage of the domestic banks will be reduced by the gradual deregulation of rates since 2013.

The main purpose of the last stage of reforms since 2013 has been to further increase competition by deregulating commercial financial services. Although successful in improving efficiency, the 2002–2012 reforms did not change the level of concentration of the banking sector by much. After their IPOs, the big four became among the largest banks in the world, and most medium-sized banks still lacked the strength to compete with them. Their large number of branches nationwide gave them a large advantage in collecting deposits in a market without price competition. However, the new reforms have introduced market-based interest rates and deregulated cross-border capital transactions. The new policies include the removal of lending rate floors (2013), the relaxation of loan-to-deposit ratio regulations (2014), the removal of deposit rate floors (2015) and the establishment of a deposit insurance scheme (2015). However, the increase in competition has been more gradual than this suggests since, even following the liberalization of interest rates, the central bank has continued to announce benchmark rates and suggest that commercial banks should follow them.

Liberalized interest rates were first introduced by the rising shadow banking sector.[10] Acharya et al. (2016) find the rise of shadow banking in China to have been fueled by the large stimulus plan implemented after the 2008 global financial crisis. Banks have provided a large component of the new shadow banking services[11] through the issuing of Wealth Management Products (WMPs). The size of the shadow banking sector began to increase in 2012, when WMPs saw tremendous growth (see Acharya et al. 2016). With heavy regulation of interest rates, capital ratio requirements and loan-to-deposit ratio limits, banks developed financial assets that were not regulated, such as WMPs, in order to compete, offering higher interest rates than for deposits.

Price competition reforms have been successful. With interest rates liberalized, the competition among the banks, and also from shadow banking, has forced banks to increase their deposit rates. Likewise, loan interest rates have decreased due to market pressure from growing competition. At the same time, the size of non-performing loans (NPLs) has increased since 2012 due to the large amount of loans spurred by the public-sector stimulus plan. However, the new context may have provoked a structural change in the financial results of banks, with declining profit margins since 2015. Okazaki (2017) shows that lower interest rate income and larger impairment losses were the causes of these lower profits. The trend in NPL is particularly alarming since it may increase the likelihood of systemic risk.

For further discussion regarding the new developments in financial reform in China, not only of the banking sector but also the growing equities markets and bond markets, see Tobin and Volz (2018). For a cross-country comparison of the financial sector of China, see Chapter 3.

2.5.1 Access to finance

The financial sector serves as the intermediary between households and enterprises, allocating financial resources where they can be more productive. Financial inclusion, defined as the use of formal financial services, is an important dimension of the financial sector. Households with access to the financial markets may invest in property and education. Businesses with access to finance are not constrained by internal funds when pursuing investment plans. The literature on institutions and economic growth, and the importance of financial development as a facilitator of growth and poverty reduction in particular, has investigated the importance of access to finance. However, China is usually considered a counter-example in cross-country studies. The Chinese financial system remains underdeveloped, while its economy is growing at a remarkable pace.

Using the World Bank Global Findex database, Demirgüc-Kunt and Klapper (2013) analyze the use of financial services across 148 countries, including ownership of current and savings accounts and use of credit. They examine individual and country characteristics associated with these three indicators of financial inclusion. They conclude that differences in income among countries (and among individuals) affect the level of financial inclusion. Regarding China, Fungáčová and Weill (2015) find that households do have access to bank accounts, and that exclusion is mostly voluntary. However, this is not the case for firms' access to credit in the financial sector. Compared to other BRICS nations, credit from the formal financial sector is less developed in China.

According to previous studies, access to finance is among the top concerns for small and medium-sized enterprises (SMEs) in China. Using the World Bank Enterprise Survey of China 2012, Regis (2018) finds that, although Chinese firms seem not to be constrained by lack of access to a bank account,[12] only around 31% of the firms surveyed in 2012 obtained access to credit. According to Regis (2018), credit constraints are significant factors in investment decisions. Together with size, access to credit is the firm characteristic that has the greatest impact on the likelihood to invest. Ayyagari et al. (2010) make use of the 2003 China Enterprise Survey and find that China is a fast-growing economy, with a banking sector serving only a small proportion of its SMEs. Access to bank credit is associated with faster growth, whereas financing from the informal financial sector is not. They also find that firms with access to bank credit grow faster than other firms, even after controlling for corruption and firm self-selection. However, Hallward-Driemeier et al. (2006) do not find a significant relationship between access to finance and the performance of Chinese firms.

Figure 2.9 shows Chinese SMEs' perceptions of the main obstacles to their business activities in 2002, 2005 and 2012 (see Box 2.2 for more details). Access to finance has gained importance for firms, doing so especially between 2002 and 2005. In 2002, most of the other obstacles shown were considered more important than or as important as access to finance. By 2005, access to finance had become the major obstacle according to firms. In 2012, it still features in the top three, just behind tax rates and the informal sector. Further, when firms were specifically asked about the biggest obstacle to their business, access to finance remained the top obstacle. This suggests that the financial sector should remain high on the agenda of economic policy.

Box 2.2 Business environment and obstacles to the firm

The success of the Chinese economy relies on its dynamic private sector, which consist mostly of Small and Medium-Sized Enterprises (SMEs). SMEs have become the main source of job creation. Although firm-level data from official sources on SMEs is scarce, the World Bank Enterprise Survey for China is available in several years. It covers many characteristics of the firm related to infrastructure, corruption and bribery, crime, financing and credit, competition and informality, land and permits, business government-relations, etc. The sample is intended to be representative of the country's private sector small and medium-sized enterprises. The main objective of the survey is to ascertain characteristics of the business environment, including access to finance.

Figure 2.9 presents information regarding the most important obstacles to SMEs based on the surveys carried out in 2002, 2005 and 2012. First, firms were presented with a set of obstacles from the business environment and were asked to rate how severe each is, on a scale ranging from 0 (no obstacle) to 4 (very severe obstacle). The bar plots present the average response of the firms. Second, firms were asked to select only the single most important among all obstacles. The tables show the top four choices as well as the proportion of firms which have selected them. Although comparability is affected by the subjectivity nature of these indicators and the fact that the items labeled as obstacles have changed over time (e.g. tax rates were considered to be very important both in 2002 and 2012 but were not included in 2005), we can distinguish some clear patterns.

Access to finance was not among the top priorities in 2002 but became very important in 2005 and 2012 when it was identified by 24.5% and 21% of the firms (respectively) as the most important obstacle to their business. However, the plots show a decline in the average intensity of access to finance, from 1.36 in 2002 and 1.40 in 2005 to just 0.81 in 2012. It seems that firms consider the magnitude of the access to finance as obstacle to have been decreasing. Still, this suggests that further reforms in the financial sector to facilitate access to credit would have a larger impact on SMEs than other reforms. In comparison, customs and trade regulations have not been considered an important constraint by SMEs in any of the three surveys. Therefore, the incremental effect on SMEs of further reforms to the exports sector may be limited.

The decline of this indicator (i.e. the importance of the lack of access to finance) is part of a more general trend in the business environment in China. The average aggregate intensity of all obstacles decreased from 1.44 in 2002 to 0.86 in 2005 and then to just 0.5 in 2012. Since 2002, important structural changes in the country have transformed the private sector and its SMEs into the most dynamic

2012

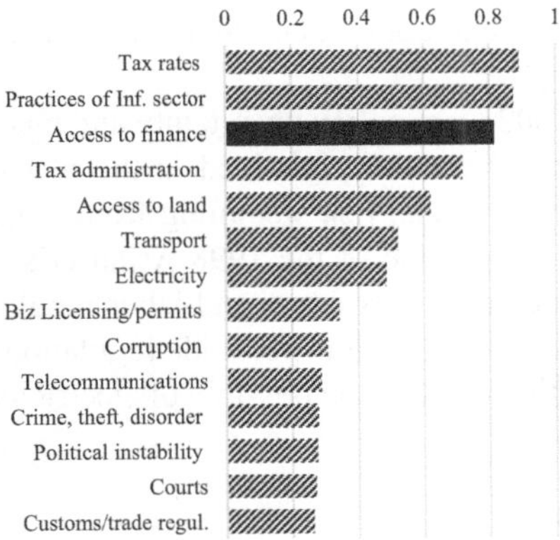

Top four obstacles in 2012 (%):

Access to finance	21.0
Worker's skills/education	16.1
Practices of the informal sector	15.8
Tax rates	15.6

2005

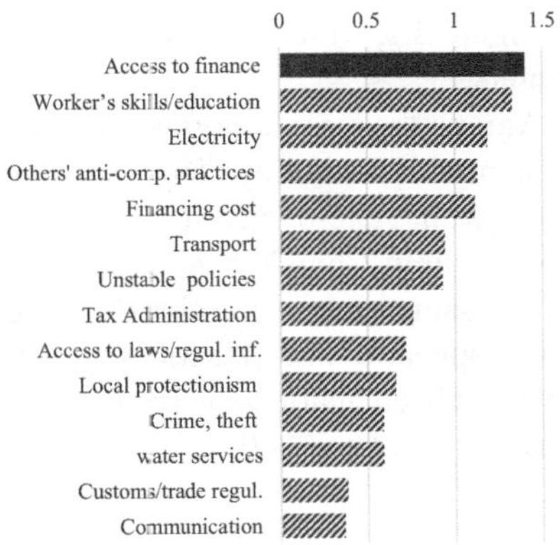

Top four obstacles in 2005 (%):

Access to finance	24.5
Electricity	17.3
Workers' skills/education	13.6
Others' anti-competition practices	11.2

2002

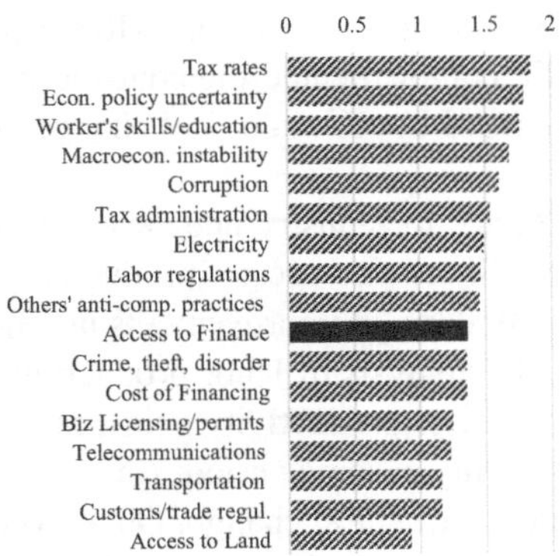

Top four obstacles in 2002: not available.

Figure 2.9 Obstacles to the business of the firm

Source: The World Bank Enterprise Survey of China in 2002, 2005 and 2012 (www.enterprisesurveys.org). The data were collected for the year preceding the survey: 2001, 2004 and 2011, respectively. The 2003 survey is excluded because the two relevant questions were not included (see notes). There is no other recent survey for China.

Notes:

1 The bar plots measure the intensity of each obstacle. They represent the average response of firms to the question "to what degree is an obstacle to the current operations of this establishment?" In answering, firms choose the degree of difficulty from 0 (no obstacle) to 4 (very severe obstacle).
2 The "Top four obstacles" refer to the percentage of firms that chose each obstacle, in response to the question "What is the biggest obstacle from the business environment?". The answer to this question is not available for 2002.
3 However, the comparability of results over time is limited by the fact that the questions have been revised. For example, "tax rates" was the obstacle with the highest intensity in both the 2002 and 2012; however, it was not included as an obstacle in 2005.

part of the Chinese economy. SMEs form the main share of private firms, as seen in Figure 2.7, which have led the outstanding generation of employment in urban centers.

Among the most important obstacles in 2002 were policy uncertainty and macroeconomic instability. This was due to the uncertainty involved in the recent move from state-owned to private firms, the financial risk stemming from large NPLs within China's banking system and the residue of the 1998 Asian crisis. At the same time, institutional obstacles (including corruption and labor regulations) appear to have faded away. Infrastructure and customs & trade regulations have not been major concerns for SMEs, with the exception possibly of electricity between 2002 and 2005.

2.6 Conclusions

The economic performance of the Chinese economy has shown astonishing gains in terms of GDP. In particular, growth has accelerated significantly since the economic reforms beginning in 1978. A simple growth accounting exercise for the period 1952–2015 shows the economy to have grown by 8% per year on average. In the period 1952–1978, growth was mostly provided by capital accumulation, while labor grew by around 1–1.5% per year and TFP was very close to zero. In the second period of market-oriented reforms, the effect of the one-child policy meant that the contribution of labor to growth was almost nonexistent. However, in this period growth was stronger because TFP complemented the contribution of capital accumulation. This period is characterized by technological change as a new source of growth.

Employment has moved from the primary sector to industry and services. It is expected that this relocation of employment will provide greater productivity. This is a potential new source of economic growth through improvements in efficiency. However, regarding structural change, the analysis of labor productivity shows most growth to have originated in within-sector productivity gains, rather than gains in efficiency due to labor reallocation. Only in some periods (the 1980s and 2000s) have there been efficiency gains due to structural change. On a more positive note, the post-reform period shows that it is not only industry (and manufacturing in particular) that have gained in productivity but also the service sector.

The dynamics of urban employment show the transformation of the productive sectors from an economy dominated by SOEs to a market-oriented economy with the largest proportion of firms belonging to the private sector. Urban employment has grown and diversified as well, based on labor market mechanisms. In 1978, more than 99% of employment was provided by state-owned companies and cooperatives. By 2016, 55% of total employment was generated by private firms, with an additional 20% provided by self-employment. It is the market-oriented reforms that have made possible the creation of so many jobs in an economy moving away from the rural sector. Among the remaining challenges to the Chinese economy is the normalization of the informal sector, which still represents a large share of the economy.

Among the top priorities of the economic reforms has been the increasing opening up of the economy. The economic integration into the global market has transformed China from a minor player specializing in food-related products and a small amount of manufacturing into the largest exporter in the world. The transformation of its manufacturing sector has made China very competitive in a large number of new products. The strongest sector is the clothing industry, which shows the largest revealed comparative advantage. Machinery and electronics is another sector in which China is highly competitive. It is also the largest sector in terms of volume, contributing almost half of Chinese exports.

The financial system is one of the key sectors requiring further reform. First, there are signs of systemic risk, with the recent increase in NPLs and shadow banking. Although reforms have introduced market-oriented practices, the stimulus plan after 2008 may also have pushed banks too fast. At the same time, financial stability is also threatened by the feeling that state ownership and the size of the balance sheets of the largest banks make them "too big to fail". Second, firm-level data suggest that access to finance is one of the dimensions of the business environment requiring improvement. SMEs in particular show relatively low levels of access to credit. Therefore, reforms aimed at increasing access to finance would improve the performance of the real economy.

Notes

1 BS309, Business Building, Xi'an Jiaotong Liverpool University, 111 Ren'ai Road, Dushu Lake Higher Education Town, SIP, Suzhou 215123, P.R. China. email: paulo.regis@xjtlu.edu.cn, tel: +86 (0)512 8816 1705
2 Chapter 10 presents some discussion about the rising Gini coefficients of inequality over time of both rural and urban sectors.
3 This type of function is usually named the Cobb-Douglas.
4 The linear relationship can be obtained from the Cobb-Douglas production function of differentiation with respect to time.
5 Here public firms group mostly state-owned enterprises and collectives; and also share-holding cooperatives ad joint ownership firms (i.e. firms with public sector participation). The importance of the latter two types of firms is rather small.
6 Private firms include: limited liability firms, share-holding firms, private enterprises and foreign owned firms.
7 An RCA of 2 indicates China exports twice as much of that product proportional to the country's total export than the average country.
8 Although rural credit cooperatives also existed, they were gradually absorbed into the Agricultural Bank of China.
9 X-inefficiency is the difference between the most efficient behavior of a firm (bank, in these studies) given the technology and their observed behavior in practice usually caused by a lack of competition. It only considers the output that is produced with the given inputs utilized by the firm.
10 Shadow banking groups activities of financial intermediaries that provide services related to commercial banking (such as accepting deposits and providing loans) but outside normal banking regulations.
11 Banks may contribute to the shadow economy by developing off-balance sheet financial products that are not under the regulation of the monetary authority.
12 95% of firms declare having a check or savings account.

References

Acharya, V. V., J. Qian, and Z. Yang (2016), "In the Shadow of Banks: Wealth Management Products and Issuing Banks' Risk in China," Working Paper, New York University.

Ayyagari, M., A. Demirgüç-Kunt, and V. Maksimovic (2010), "Formal versus Informal Finance: Evidence from China," *Review of Financial Studies* 23:3048–3097.

Bai, C., and Z. Qian (2010), "The Factor Income Distribution in China: 1978–2007," *China Economic Review* 21: 650–670.

Cai, F. (2004), "The Consistency of China Statistics on Employment: Stylized Facts and Implications for Public Policies," *Chinese Economy* 37(5): 74–89.

Cai, F. (2005), "Exploring the Fair Distribution Mechanism in Accordance with Economic Development," *People's Forum*, 17 October (in Chinese).

Cai, F. (2006), "Maximum Employment is the Economic Base of Social Harmony," *Wen Wei Po* (in Chinese).

Cai, F. (2012), "The Coming Demographic Impact on China's Growth: The Age Factor in the Middle-Income Trap," *Asian Economic Papers* 11(1): 95–111.

Demirgüc-Kunt, A., and L. Klapper (2013), "Measuring Financial Inclusion: Explaining Variation in Use of Financial Services Across and within Countries," *Brookings Papers on Economic Activity* 44(11): 279–340.

Desmarchelier, B., P. J. Regis, and N. Salike (2018), "Product Space and the Development of Nations: A Model of Product Diversification," *Journal of Economic Behavior and Organization* 145:34–51.

Fabricant, S. (1942), *Employment in Manufacturing, 1899–1939: An Analysis of Its Relation to the Volume of Production*, New York: NBER books, National Bureau of Economic Research.Feenstra, R. C., R. E. Lipsey, H. Deng, A. C. Ma, and H. Mo (2005), "World trade flows: 1962–2000," *NBER Working Paper* No. W11040.

Fu, X. (2004), *Efficiency and Competition in China's Banking Sector*, PhD Thesis, Cass Business School, City University, London.

Fu, X., and S. Heffernan (2007), "Cost X-efficiency in China's Banking Sector," *China Economic Review* 18: 35–53.

Fungáčová, Z., and L. Weill (2015), "Understanding Financial Inclusion in China," *China Economic Review* 34: 196–206.

Gaulier, G., and S. Zignano (2009), "BACI: International Trade Database at the Product-level the 1994–2007 Version," *CEPII Working Paper* 2010–23.

Hallward-Driemeier, M., S. Wallsten, and L. C. Xu (2006), "Ownership, Business Climate and Firm Performance: Evidence from Chinese Firms," *Economics of Transition* 14: 629–647.

Holz, C. A., and Y. Sun (2018), "Physical Capital Estimates for China's Provinces, 1952–2015 and Beyond," *China Economic Review*, forthcoming. Available at: https://doi.org/10.1016/j.chieco.2017.06.007.

Hsiao, C., Y. Shen, and W. Bian (2015), "Evaluating the Effectiveness of China's Financial Reform – The Efficiency of China's Domestic Banks," *China Economic Review* 35: 70–82.

Hsueh, T., and Q. Li (1999), *China's National Income, 1952–1995*, Westview Press.

Lewis, W. A. (1954), "Economic Development with Unlimited Supplies of Labor," *Manchester School* 22(2): 139–191.

Li, D. K., L. L. Liu, and H. L. Wang (2009), "The U Curve of Labor Share in GDP during Economic Development," *Economic Research Journal* 1: 70–82 (in Chinese).

Luo, C. Y., and J. Zhang (2009), "The Economic Explanation of Decrease of Labor Share – the Empirical Analysis based on China's Provincial Panel Data," *Management World* 5: 25–35 (in Chinese).

National Bureau of Statistics (2007), *Data of Gross Domestic Product of China: 1952–2004*, Beijing: China Statistics Press.

Okazaki, K. (2017), "Banking System Reform in China: The Challenges to Improving its Efficiency in Serving the Real Economy," *Asian Economic Policy Review* 12: 303–320.

Regis, P. J. (2018), "Access to Credit and Investment Decisions of SMEs in China," *Review of Development Economics*, forthcoming. https://doi.org/10.1111/rode.12366.

Rodrik, D. (2006), "What's So Special about China's Exports," *China and the World Economy* 14: 1–19.

Shao, M., and J. L. Huang (2010), "Foreign Investment and the Labor Share in China: An Empirical Study based on Industrial Level Panel Data," *China Economic Quarterly* 4: 1189–1210 (Chinese).

Timmer, M. P., G. J. de Vries, and K. de Vries (2015), "Patterns of Structural Change in Developing Countries," in: J. Weiss and M. Tribe (eds.), *Routledge Handbook of Industry and Development*, Routledge, pp. 65–83.

Tobin, D., and U. Volz (2018), "The Development and Transformation of People's Republic of China's Financial System," *ADBI Working Papers* 825, Asian Development Bank Institute.

Wang, Z., and S. J. Wei (2010), "What Accounts for the Rising Sophistication of China's Exports?" in: R. C. Feenstra and S. J. Wei (eds.), *China's Growing Role in World Trade*, University of Chicago Press, pp. 63–104.

Appendix

To measure the contribution of growth from the reallocation of workers across sectors, total productivity is usually decomposed considering sectoral data for employment shares and productivity levels (see Fabricant 1942). The change in aggregate productivity of the economy (Y) can be expressed as composed of three terms:

$$\Delta Y_t = \sum_{i=1}^{n} s_{i0}\,\Delta y_{it} + \sum_{i=1}^{n} \Delta s_{it}\, y_{i0} + \sum_{i=1}^{n} \Delta s_{it}\,\Delta y_{it} \qquad 2.3.$$

Where s_i is the share of sector i in total employment, y_i is the labor productivity of sector i, "0" refers to the value at the beginning of the period (period 0), t is the end period and delta is the "difference" operator (i.e. the change between the initial period 0 and the end period t). In total, there are ten sectors ($n = 10$). The change in total productivity is decomposed into the within-sector productivity gain (i.e. the first term of the equation) and the productivity gain due to reallocation of employment. The latter consists of two effects, static and dynamic reallocation effects (second and third terms), and it is associated to structural change since it requires a change in the structure of employment across sectors. The static structural change (second term) is the gains in productivity by changes in labor shares if productivity were the same than at the beginning of the period. The dynamic structural change is driven by both changes in employment shares and changes of intra-industry productivity.

The within-effect is the weighted (by initial labor shares) average change in labor productivity levels across sectors in the first term. It is positive if weighted labor productivity increases during the period. Technological change and new physical capital that would improve labor productivity in the same fashion across all sectors would be absorbed in this term. The second term, the static reallocation effect, is the contribution to productivity of labor reallocation across sectors. It is positive if labor moves from less to more productive sectors. The third term, known as the interaction term, is the joint effect of changes in employment shares and changes in productivity levels across sectors. It is positive when workers are moving to sectors that are experiencing an increase in productivity. This is the gain in labor productivity because some sector is increasing its productivity more than other sectors. Therefore, there is either an increase in TFP or the capital stock of sector i, which is stronger than other sectors.

3 The rise of China

Shiwei Hu[1]

3.1 Introduction

> China is a sleeping lion. Let her sleep, for when she wakes she will shake the world.
>
> – Napoléon Bonaparte

In the age of industrial revolution, agricultural China was seen as a sleeping lion by many Western nations due to its self-isolation and conservatism. Nearly two centuries later, this lion is not only awake, but also roaring. Sustained growth since the economic reform has drastically improved the living standard of billions of Chinese and contributed to the world economy. The rise of China is a peaceful one as its increasing political influence benefits the stability and prosperity of the international community. No one disagrees that China's rise will undoubtedly be one of the great events of the 21s century.[2] In this chapter, we make comprehensive analysis of the rise of China.

We start in section 3.2 by providing some background to China's reform and present some evidence of China's success in economic growth compared with a control group of a few advanced economies, India and the world. We then decompose the story of economic success into three parts, trade, FDI and finance, in sections 3.3, 3.4 and 3.5, respectively. We go through the contemporaneous history of China and show how China found the correct way to develop. The three stories of trade, FDI and finance may serve to understand why China succeeds. To illustrate the story, we rely on the data of the China Statistical Yearbook and World Development Indicators from the World Bank. Finally, in section 3.6 we analyze the rise of China's political power and global influence. The combination of rises in economic size and political power may complete the picture and provide a landscape for the readers to understand the miracle of China's rise.

3.2 China's economic growth since 1978

After the communist revolution, China gradually established a centrally planned economy. Misallocation of capital, labor and natural resources in the planned economy impeded economic growth in China. Therefore, China's living standard remained low compared to OECD countries with market economy.

Since 1978, when new leadership came to power, the government was determined to reform. The aim was to shift the social welfare function from ideology to economic performance by establishing a market-oriented economy. At that time, most Chinese worked in the large agricultural sector. Thousands of communal farming groups showed distorted incentive schemes and low efficiency in agricultural production as most of the output was "taxed" and few products were left to the peasants. As a result, hundreds of millions of peasants were trapped hopelessly in deep poverty in the planned economy. To resolve the crisis in the agricultural sector, China initiated the first reform and reshaped the rural economy by establishing the household responsibility system. Namely, every household worked for themselves instead of for the commune and were allowed to retain most of the output as surplus. This fundamental reform incentivized peasants to put effort into agricultural production (McMillan et al. 1989). Consequently, more input in the agricultural sector and higher productivity significantly improved the crop production and hence the living standard of millions of rural residents (Lin 1992).

The reform for state-owned enterprises (SOEs) was another vital agenda item. Under the centrally planned regime, SOEs operated inefficiently under the soft budget constraint (Kornai 1980; Kornai et al. 2003). To cope with the incentive distortion, the reform empowered the management team with greater operational autonomy and incentive compatible contracts. Some distressed SOEs were privatized or acquired by private peers. The rest of the SOEs were consolidated to form large conglomerates. Consequently, the surviving SOEs were large, competitive and vibrant, dominating in several strategic industries such as oil production, finance, airlines and so forth. Additionally, SOEs actively invested overseas and expanded their business to every corner of the world. The size of SOEs grew massively over the past four decades. In 2017, 23% of Fortune Global 500 companies came from China and 10% were large Chinese SOEs.

Furthermore, China has increased openness to the international community since the reform. We will discuss international trade and foreign investment in sections 3.3 and 3.4, respectively. Reforms in the financial system that changed the banking sector and stock markets will be covered in section 3.5. The market-oriented reform stimulated economic growth in China. In addition, the positive spillover effect of Chinese development contributed to world development.

In the past four decades, China's output has been expanding. In the early days of reform and opening-up (1978–1980), China's economic growth reached 7.7% (see Table 3.1a), well above the world average level of 3.1%. When the dividend for reform and opening-up was further released, China's annual GDP growth rate reached 9.8% in the 1980s. The Golden Age of China's growth was undoubtedly the two decades of the 1990s and 2000s, when its GDP growth rate exceeded an unprecedented 10%. To see the impressive growth of China, we take the US and Japan as benchmarks. In the same period, the annual growth rates of GDP in the US were 3.8% and 1.7%, respectively, while Japan's GDP growth rates fell to 1.1% and 0.7%, respectively. Although China's economic growth has slowed down since 2000, its growth rate remains far above the world average. Throughout the whole period of 1978–2016, China's annual GDP growth rate was 9.6%, substantially higher than the world level 2.9%. At the same time, China's economic growth was faster than some developed economies, for example Japan (2.1%), the EU28 (1.9%) and the US (2.6%). India, another rising star in emerging markets, has been rapidly growing in the past few decades. Nevertheless, India's growth rate is much below that of China.[3]

The contribution of the Chinese economy to the world economy also rose steadily. At the beginning of the economic reform (1978–1980), China's contribution to global economic growth was merely 2.9%, far lower than other developed economies (see Table 3.1b, Japan 14.2%, EU28 28.8% and US 11.4%). When the reform sped up, the role of the Chinese economy also strengthened. China's contribution to the global growth rate rose from 4.9% in the 1980s to 11.5% in the 1990s. As the contribution continued to increase, China eventually became the top contributor to global growth. During 2011 to 2016, roughly one-third of global economic growth was driven by China. Let us take a look at other economies. In the past few decades, the contribution rate of Japan and the EU28 has fallen sharply. The contribution of the US peaked at 31.7% in the 1990s and declined afterwards. Despite the ascending trend, the contribution of India to the global economic growth has been at a relatively low level. In the past four decades, China's average contribution rate was 18%, very close to 18.5% of the EU28 and 20.6% of the US.

Figure 3.1 illustrates the share of the five economies in the world GDP. In 1978, the EU28 and the US accounted for 33.5% and 24.2% of the world GDP, respectively. Note that the sum of the two accounted for more than half of the world GDP. At that time, China's share was only 1.1%, slightly above India's share

Table 3.1 GDP growth rate and contribution to the growth of world GDP in selected economies, 1978–2016

	1978–1980	*1981–1990*	*1991–2000*	*2001–2010*	*2011–2016*	*1978–2016*
a. GDP growth rate						
China	7.7	9.8	10.6	10.8	7.3	9.6
India	0.6	5.5	6.1	7.8	6.9	6.0
Japan	4.1	4.7	1.1	0.7	1.2	2.1
EU28	2.6	2.7	2.3	1.3	1.1	1.9
USA	1.5	3.4	3.8	1.7	2.1	2.6
World	3.1	3.3	3.0	2.9	2.6	2.9
b. Contribution to the growth of world GDP						
China	2.9	4.9	11.5	24.5	30.2	18.0
India	0.2	1.9	2.9	5.4	7.5	4.3
Japan	14.2	16.6	4.4	2.2	3.8	6.5
EU28	28.8	26.8	24.0	12.5	10.3	18.5
USA	11.4	24.9	31.7	14.2	17.8	20.6
World	100.0	100.0	100.0	100.0	100.0	100.0

Source: Calculations based on the data of GDP (constant 2010 USD) from the World Development Indicators.

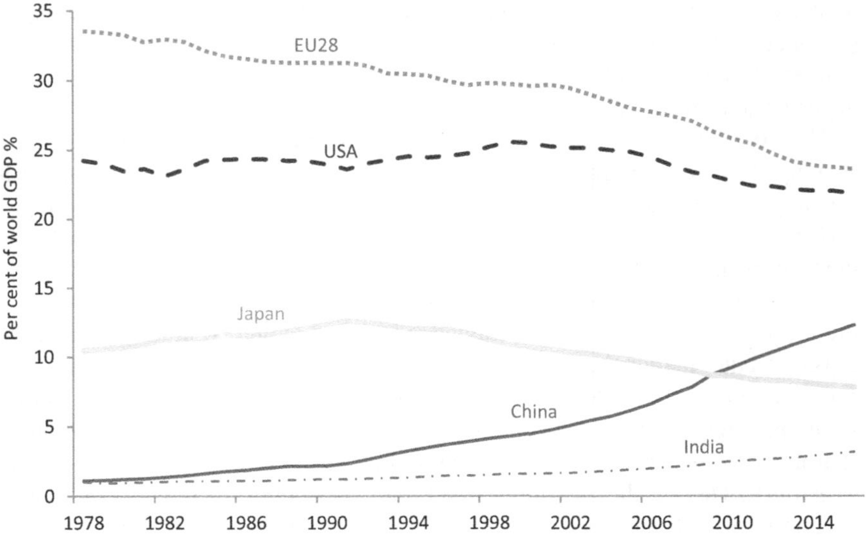

Figure 3.1 Per cent of world GDP in selected economies, 1978–2016

Source: Calculations based on the data of GDP (constant 2010 USD) from the World Development Indicators.

of 1%. But shares of both the EU28 and the US have been shrinking since then. The share of the EU28, in particular, fell from 33.5% in 1978 to 23.6% in 2016. The rise of Japan is not monotonic as it reached a peak in 1991 at 12.6% and then started to fall. In 2016, Japan's GDP accounted for only 7.8% of the world's total GDP. By contrast, the shares of China and India had been rising steadily. In particular, India's share had tripled from 1% in 1978 to 3.2% in 2016. More strikingly, China saw a 10-fold increase in its share of world GDP from 1.1% in 1978 to 12.3% in 2016. A milestone for China is year 2010, when China's GDP surpassed that of Japan and became the world's second largest economy. All these stylized facts show the increasingly important role of the Chinese economy in the world.

Meanwhile, China has been upgrading its economic structure over time. In 1978, on the one hand, agriculture was the most important industry in China (see Figure 3.2b), the output of which accounted for 43.4% of GDP. On the other hand, industry and services sectors were fairly underdeveloped. Over the past four decades, it is striking that China has become a major manufacturing power. The industry output has risen from 0.09 trillion in 1978 to 4.44 trillion in 2016 (see Figure 3.2a). In addition, China's service sector has also grown rapidly, from 0.1 trillion in 1978 to 4.34 trillion in 2016. On the contrary, the role of agriculture has been less important. The share of agriculture in GDP fell from 43.4% in 1978 to 7.7% in 2016 (see Figure 3.2b), while the share of industry and services' sectors have risen continuously. By 2016, the shares of the latter two sectors were 46.7%

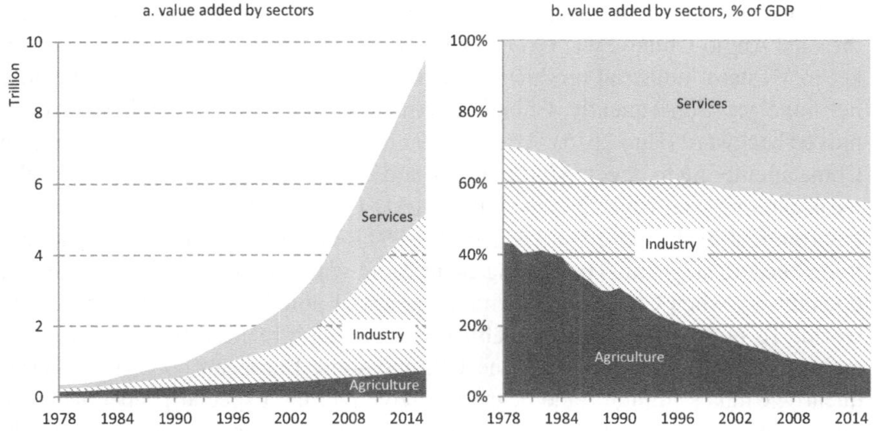

Figure 3.2 Value added by sectors in China, 1978–2016

Source: Authors' calculations based on data from the World Development Indicators; Agriculture, value added (constant 2010 USD), Industry, value added (constant 2010 USD), Services, etc., value added (constant 2010 USD).

and 45.6%, respectively. Therefore, the focus of China's economic structure has shifted from the traditional agricultural sector to the modern industry and services' sectors. The upgrading economic structure in part stemmed from physical capital accumulation, technological progress and also the rural-urban income gap amid China's economic reform, as hundreds of millions of peasants were encouraged to search for jobs in the urban areas in industry and services' sectors. The labor migration and flow continuously fueled the industrialization and urbanization in China (Zhang and Shunfeng 2003). We will mention in Section 3.3 (see Figure 3.4) that China has become a world factory in the manufacturing sector since the share of China's exports of high-tech products in China's total exports has been rising.

Since the economic reform, China's economic growth and increasing influence were inevitably related to its policy. In addition, China's policy had an influential impact on the development of China's international trade and FDI, which will be covered in detail in the next two sections.

3.3 Trade development in China

In this section we focus on trade development in China since 1978. China has a long history of international trade dating back to the era of the Silk Road 2,000 years ago. Tons of silk, porcelain and tea were continuously exported to the Middle East and Europe through the ancient network of trade routes. Apart from the original Silk Road, China had been actively expanding its maritime trade routes as well. The extensive international trade flourished for hundreds of years until the late Qing Dynasty (AD 1644–1911) when China's original economic order was disrupted by drastic changes in the international environment. After the First Anglo-Chinese war (AD 1839–1842), China was forced to open its market to Western industrial products, which turned China from a net exporter to a net importer. Consequently, China's international trade became stalled, or even moved backward (Huo 2015). After the communist revolution (AD 1949), despite China attempting to develop its economy and revive trade, it was restricted by the weak economy destroyed by the civil war (AD 1945–1949) and the tough external environment of the Cold War (AD 1947–1991). Therefore, China's international trade became stagnant. The turning point came with the inception of reform and opening-up, when China implemented a series of policies to open to the outside world. To boost trade, China established diplomatic relationships with several major countries, such as Japan, the US, and some European countries. Consequently, China's foreign trade began to revive rapidly. Especially since its entry into the WTO, sharp tariff cuts and more open policies helped China to gradually become an important player in international trade. In particular, China's export value exceeded the US in 2013, becoming the largest exporters in the world. In 2015, the sum of Chinese imports and exports reached 4.5 trillion USD,[4] getting close to 5.1 trillion USD in the US.

Table 3.2 illustrates the growth rates of export and the contribution to the growth of world exports for China, India, Japan, the EU28 and the US over the past four decades.[5] During 1978–2016, China's export trade grew at an annual rate of 17.2%, twice the export growth rate of the world. In all periods except

Table 3.2 Growth rate of export and its contribution to the growth of world exports in selected economies, 1978–2015

	1978–1980	*1981–1990*	*1991–2000*	*2001–2010*	*2011–2015*	*1978–2015*
a. Growth rates of exports (%)						
China	28.8	14.8	17.9	21.4	4.9	17.2
India	14.9	7.8	11.5	22.4	–1.5	11.1
Japan	15.9	7.0	4.4	7.7	–4.2	5.4
EU28	20.3	8.9	4.9	8.9	–1.4	6.7
USA	22.6	6.8	7.0	6.8	1.8	7.0
World	23.5	7.2	6.5	10.5	–1.3	7.4

	1978–1980	*1981–1990*	*1991–2000*	*2001–2010*	*2011–2014*	*1978–2014*
b. Contribution to the growth of world exports (%)						
China	0.6	1.8	5.8	11.8	35.4	11.2
India	0.3	0.6	1.1	2.8	1.4	2.1
Japan	4.8	7.4	4.8	3.7	–4.7	3.3
EU28	36.9	50.8	30.9	31.2	28.2	32.8
USA	11.9	12.3	14.6	7.3	18.4	9.8
World	100.0	100.0	100.0	100.0	100.0	100.0

Source: Calculations based on the data of exports of goods and services (current USD) from the World Development Indicators.

2001–2010, China had been the fastest growing exporter in the world. Even in the post-crisis period when international trade was severely hurt by the global financial crisis, China maintained a growth rate of 4.9% in export in 2011–2015, outperforming other major economies.

In addition, China has contributed to the growth of global exports. Although the contribution of China's export to the world export was only 0.6% (see Table 3.2b) in the early years of reform and opening-up (1978–1980), trade value has continued to climb since then. The contribution rate of China's exports increased to 11.8% during 2001–2010, surpassing the US and becoming the most important country for world export growth. Specifically, the contribution rate of China's exports reached 35.4% over 2011–2014, exceeding the EU28. In other words, more than one-third of the world's incremental exports came from China.

In the past four decades, China has had a rising share inworld exports, from 0.5% in 1978 to 11.4% in 2015 (see Figure 3.3). Especially after China's accession to the WTO in 2001, the proportion of China's exports expanded rapidly. This is largely driven by the permanently granted most-favored-nation treatment to China by other WTO members with whom China had normalized a relationship. In addition, several trading partners had eliminated many of their restrictions on imports from China. Due to accession to the WTO, China benefited from easier access to foreign markets, which boosted China's exports in many sectors (Blancher and Rumbaugh 2004). In 2013 as the ratio rose to 10%, China became the world's largest exporter, surpassing the US for the first time. China's share even increased to 11.4% in 2015. At the same time, the export shares of EU28 and Japan had been declining since the 1990s. Moreover, India's export share remained below 2% of the world as a whole.

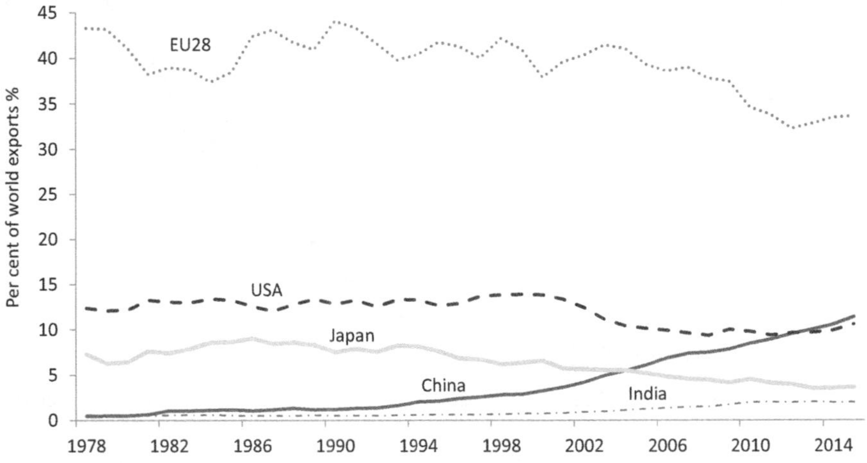

Figure 3.3 Percent of world exports; selected economies, 1978–2015

Source: Calculations based on the data of exports of goods and services (current USD) from the World Development Indicators.

The changes come not only from trade value and shares, but also the dynamics of the Chinese exports' structure. In the 1980s, China's exports of primary goods and manufactured goods were similar.[6] But since the 1990s, the exports of manufactured goods saw faster growth than that of primary goods (see Figure 3.4). From 1990 to 2016, primary goods' exports rose from 15.9 billion USD to 105.2 billion USD. By contrast, the exports of manufactured goods soared from 46.2 billion USD to almost 2 trillion USD. Therefore, manufactured goods were the dominant exports of China over the past two decades. Figure 3.5 decomposes the four categories of manufactured goods. In 1980, *Light Textile Industrial Products, Rubber Products, Minerals and Metallurgical Products* were of the most importance, accounting for 44% of all manufactured goods' exports. Starting from a low volume, the exports of *Machinery and Transport Equipment* grew rapidly. The exports of *Machinery and Transport Equipment* became the largest share of manufactured goods' exports by 2001 and accounted for almost half of the manufactured goods' exports (49.4%) in 2016. In a nutshell, China's exports successfully upgraded its structure from natural resource-intensive products to labor-intensive products, and eventually to high-tech products.

The upgrade of China's industrial structure was in part driven by the tremendous R&D expenditures. According to the World Bank, China's R&D expenditure over GDP had increased from 0.56% in 1996 to 2.07% in 2016 at an annual rate of 7.1%.[7] Moreover, China surpassed the EU28 (2.05%) in 2015. Although the R&D intensity of China is still lower than Japan (3.28%) and the US (2.79%),

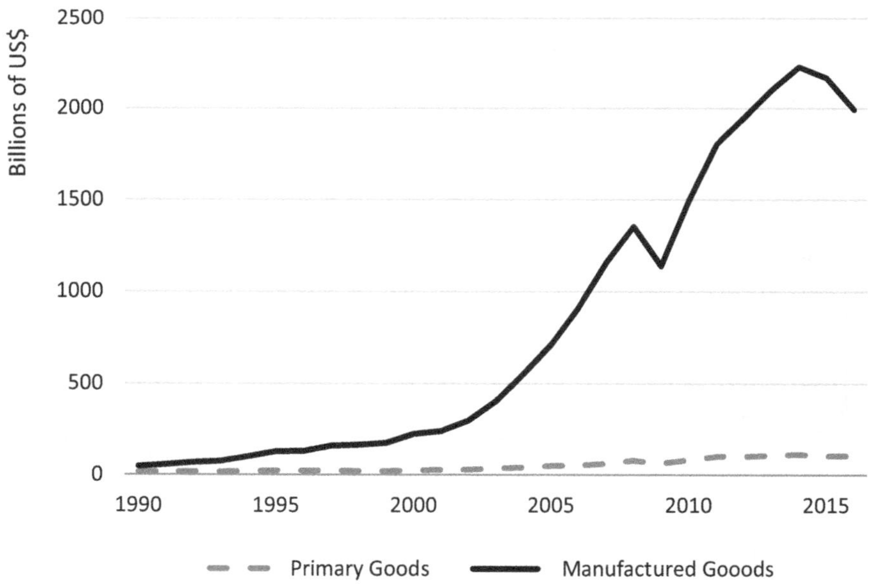

Figure 3.4 Exports value by category of goods, 1990–2016

Source: China Statistical Yearbook (2016, 2017), exports value by category of goods.

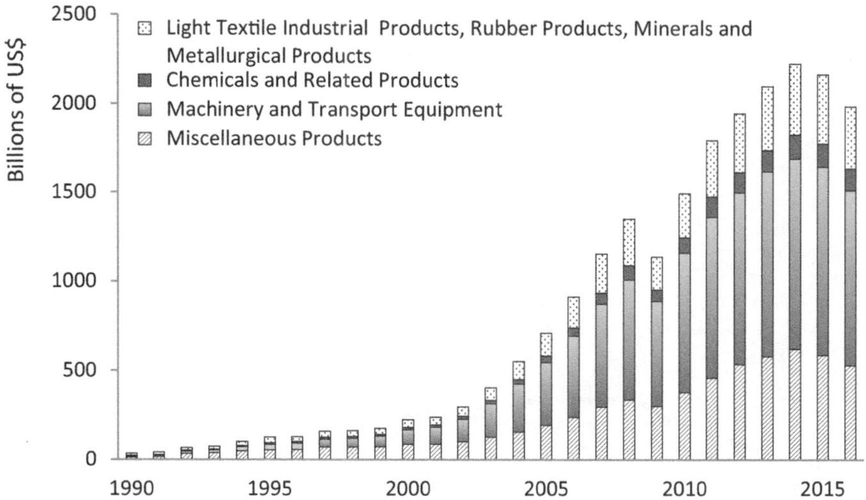

Figure 3.5 Exports value by category of manufactured goods, 1990–2016

Source: China Statistical Yearbook (2016, 2017), exports value by category of goods.

the gap is getting narrower. In addition, the productivity spillover from trade and FDI had a positive and significant effect on Chinese firms' productivity, which played an important role in improving the quality of China's exports (Chuang and Hsu 2004).

To sum up, since the economic reform in the late 1970s, China's international trade has been developing very rapidly. The increasing contribution of China's exports to the world's incremental exports shows a pivotal role of China in the development of global trade. At the same time, the structure of China's export products has been escalating, shifting from exports of primary and labor-intensive products in the past to the high-tech exports of today. That is to say, both the quantity and quality of Chinese exports have been improving. China's entry into the WTO marks a new stage of China's engagement in economic globalization. At the same time, China has also been actively developing bilateral free trade areas. By 2016, China had signed bilateral free trade agreements with 13 countries, including China-South Korea Free Trade Area, China-Australia Free Trade Area, China-ASEAN Free Trade Area, China-Switzerland Free Trade Area, China-Singapore Free Trade Area, and so forth.[8] In the trend of globalization, China has been and will continue to be an active participant in international trade.

3.4 FDI development in China

The inception period of the economic reform and opening-up was described as a tough period when China had a shortage of capital and technology. Low FDI

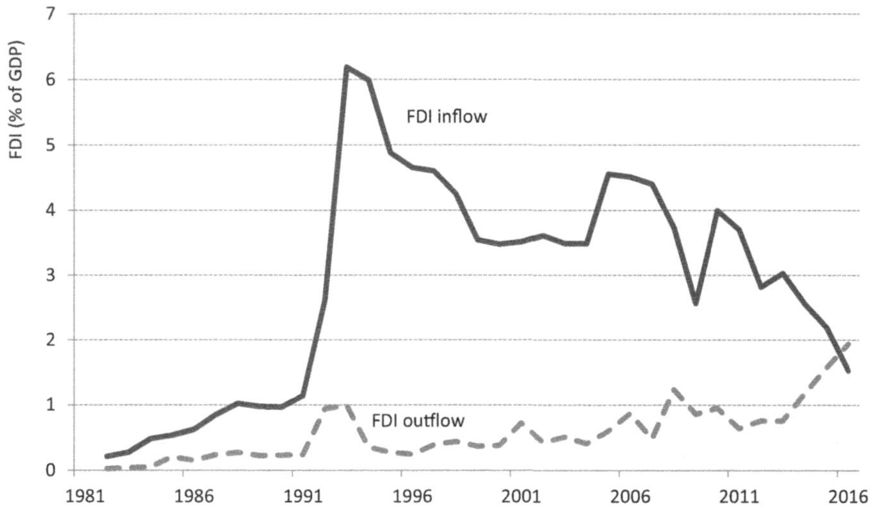

Figure 3.6 FDI inflows and outflows (% of GDP) in China, 1982–2016

Source: Based on the data of FDI from the World Development Indicators, foreign direct investment, net inflows (% of GDP), foreign direct investment, net outflows (% of GDP).

inflow became a particular financial constraint. In 1982, the FDI inflow to China accounted for 0.2% of GDP only (see Figure 3.6).[9]

To improve the attractiveness of the Chinese market to foreign investors, the Chinese government implemented a "Bring In" policy, targeted at foreign capital and advanced technology. Combined with its own advantages of a cheap labor force and a continuous improvement in infrastructure, China has observed a rapidly surging FDI inflow, especially since the 1990s. The statistics suggest China's FDI inflow over GDP reached a record high of 6.2% in 1993. Jobs and technology spillover along with FDI contributed to the economic and social development in China. Despite the decline in the ratio of FDI to GDP in later years, the average level of 3.8% remains significant over the period of 1994–2016. In addition, the stagnancy of FDI inflow suggests that China has attempted to lower the dependence on foreign capital and hence rely on domestic capital as an alternative. Having accumulated a large amount of savings, the major source of domestic investment, China gradually relied on internal capital to stimulate economic growth (Tang et al. 2008). This has been confirmed by the fast-growing stock market, expanding bond market and bank loan market discussed in the next section.

In addition to the open policy of 1978, the ample labor forces in China are one of the key reasons for China's success in attracting large amounts of FDI. Figure 3.7a illustrates the working-age population in some of the most populous regions in the world, including China, India, Sub-Saharan Africa and Southeastern Asia, where most labor-intensive products in the world are manufactured.

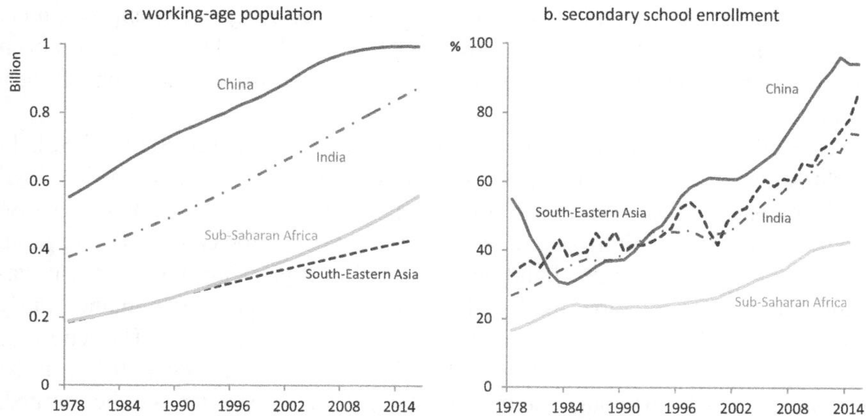

Figure 3.7 The quantity and quality of labor force in China, 1978–2016

Source: Based on data from the World Development Indicators, population ages 15–64, total, school enrollment, secondary (% gross).

Specifically, China has the largest group of working-age population, accounting for 20.1% of the world working-age population in 2015, while India ranked second with 17.8% of the world working-age population. Crucial for labor-intensive products, abundant labor workers in China attracted tremendous investment from multinational firms. In addition, compared to other populous regions, the quality of China's labor force is another advantage. Figure 3.7b plots the trend and level of secondary school enrollment in these regions. Except the short period of 1985–1995, the educational level proxied by the secondary school enrollment in China outperformed all other regions. In particular, the educational attainment in China has improved substantially since the mid-1990s, leading India and other peers. In 2015, the secondary school enrollment achieved 94.3%, suggesting fundamental improvement in human capital. High quality labor could be more productive and lower the cost of training. As a result, multinational firms prefer to establish manufacturing units in China and to hire well-educated employees to lower production cost. In sum, the good quantity and quality of labor forces are attracting the large inflow of FDI to China.

Fast expansion of infrastructure is another driver for FDI inflow. In principle, good infrastructure lowers the cost of production for manufacturing firms. In the next subsection, we will cover three aspects of infrastructure. First, China has made great progress in energy development and variety. We take electricity output for an example (see Figure 3.8a). In terms of absolute number, China's electricity output rose from 0.4 trillion KWH in 1985 to 5.8 trillion KWH in 2015. It is hard to believe that over the past three decades, electricity output increased by 14.5 times. Meanwhile, methods of generating electricity also became diversified. In 1985, thermal power was the primary method, accounting for 77.5% of total electricity output. In 2015 other types of electricity generation, such as hydropower, nuclear power and wind power became increasingly important for China, despite the large bulk of thermal power. As a state policy, clean energy has been given priority nowadays in China, in an aimed to take over the positions of thermal power.

Second, transportation has been modernized in China (see Figure 3.8b). In 1980, highways were the dominant means of transportation. Since the 1990s, civil aviation entered the boom period in which its length of transportation routes rose to be comparable to highways. In recent years, civil aviation continued to expand, exceeding highways in 2014 and became the fastest growing type of transportation. Unlike civil aviation, the length of waterways in operation remained fairly stable during 1980–2016, largely due to the fixed river capacity. The length of railways in operation doubled from 0.05 million kilometer in 1980 to 0.12 million kilometer in 2016. Although the increment in length of operation is rather limited, the improvement in operation speed is considerable. One typical example is the high-speed train in China. The breakthrough of high-speed technology and manufacturing capacity since 2008 have enabled China to boost the length of operation of its high-speed train network from 672 kilometer to an impressive number of 22,980 kilometer in 2016 (see Table 3.3). In addition, the ratio of high-speed train to overall railway operation has increased from 0.8% to 18.5%. The operation of high-speed trains has tremendously expanded the operational capacity of the China railway system as well as overall transportation capacity.

Finally, China also made great achievements in telecommunications. At the beginning of the Chinese economic reform, fixed telephone subscriptions were rare, as China accounted for 0.7 % of worldwide subscriptions in 1978 (see Figure 3.9). Like other types of infrastructure, fixed telephone subscriptions have grown rapidly since then. In 2006, the development of China's fixed telephone

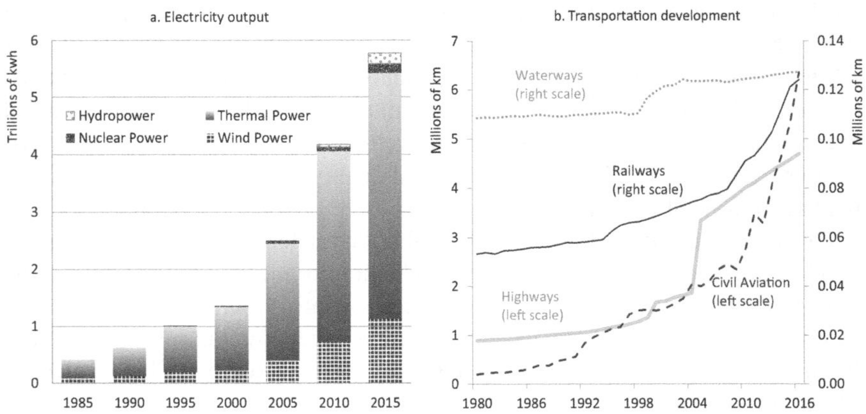

Figure 3.8 Development of electricity and transportation in China

Source: China Statistical Yearbook (2017), Electricity Balance Sheet, Length of Transportation Routes

Table 3.3 Development of high speed railway in China, 2008–2016

Year	*2008*	*2009*	*2010*	*2011*	*2012*	*2013*	*2014*	*2015*	*2016*
Length in operation (km)	672	2699	5133	6601	9356	11028	16456	19838	22980
% of railways	0.8	3.2	5.6	7.1	9.6	10.7	14.7	16.4	18.5

Source: China Statistical Yearbook (2017), Basic Statistics of High Speed Railway

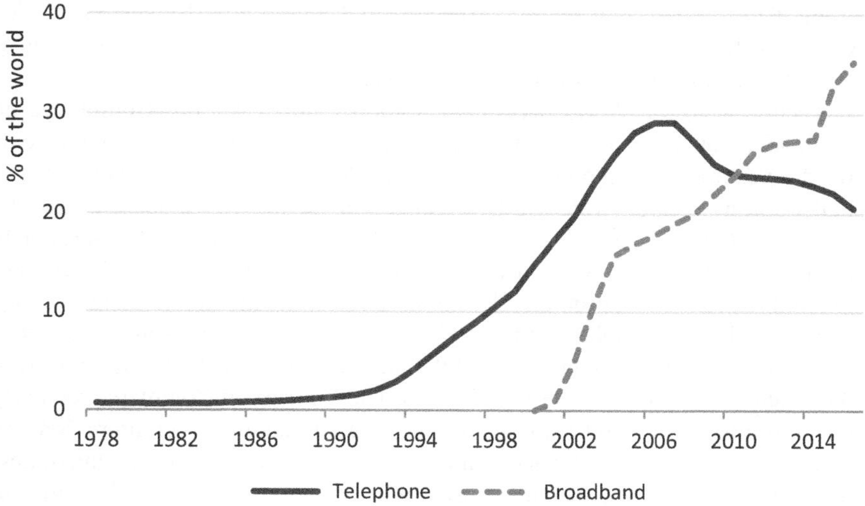

Figure 3.9 Telecom development in China, 1978–2016

Source: Calculations based on data from the World Development Indicators, fixed telephone subscriptions, fixed broadband subscriptions.

subscriptions reached a peak at a share of 29.2% in the world market. It declined afterwards due to the crowding-out effect of mobile phone subscriptions. In addition, the revolution of the Internet since the late 1990s and early 2000s changed the model of telecommunication and highlighted the central role of the network. Not a bystander of this Internet revolution, instead China was an active participant. Despite low initial fixed broadband subscriptions of 0.9% in 2001 (see Figure 3.9), China saw an incredibly high growth rate in the following years. High growth rate of fixed broadband subscriptions and a large domestic market contributed to the improvement of China's share of fixed broadband subscriptions in the world from 0.9% in 2001 to 35.2% in 2016. In a nutshell, the development of telecommunications in China enhanced the attractiveness of China as a destination for foreign investment.

Having attached importance to inward foreign investment, the Chinese government also initiated the "Going Global" strategy to encourage firms to invest and expand in the international market. The programs launched by the Chinese Government together with the China Council for the Promotion of International Trade set a couple of goals, including an increase of Chinese FDI abroad, higher product diversification, improvement in the level and quality of the projects, expansion of financial channels with respect to the national market, and better brand recognition of Chinese companies in the EU28 and the US markets. Despite stagnant growth of outward FDI at the beginning of the economic reform, FDI outflow increased since the 1990s. The ratio of FDI outflow to GDP rose from 0.2% in 1996 to 1.9% in 2016 with modest volatility over time (see Figure 3.6). Surging from 2014 to 2016, FDI outflow exceeded FDI inflow in 2016, suggesting that China has become a net exporter of capital. Both OECD countries and emerging markets are looking forward to Chinese investment now.

According to the World Investment Report (United Nations Conference on Trade and Development, 2016) and the Report on development of China's outward investment and economic cooperation (2016), the top three economies of FDI outflow in 2015 were the US, China and Japan, with a share of 20.4%, 9.9% and 8.7%, respectively. China has become the second largest investor in terms of outward FDI. This is driven by the active investment of the private sector, and is also in part prompted by the Chinese government's favorable policy. For example, the People's Bank of China called on multiple sources of funding for outward investment, initiated the internalization of RMB, and improved the efficiency of cross-border transactions. The Ministry of Commerce regularly released information and outlooks for outward investment in certain regions. In case of emergencies (civil wars, conflicts, or terrorist attacks in investment destination), the Chinese government usually intervenes and takes quick actions to protect investment overseas. For example, during the Libyan civil war in 2011, the Chinese government pulled back deployed workers and investment on a large scale.

Most of China's outward investments flow to emerging economies. In 2015, the investment to emerging markets accounted for 70.9% of total FDI outflow. In terms of industry, the manufacturing sector attracted the largest flow of Chinese investment, accounting for 25.2% of total FDI outflow. Information, communication and technology (ICT), and finance were hot targets as well, while mining and resource extraction had a low share. All of this is consistent with the global capital flow, suggesting that China FDI outflow improved in both quantity and quality.

To conclude, cheap labor, well-developed infrastructure, and the "Bring In" strategy successfully stimulated inward FDI to China. This has led China to overtake the US as the largest FDI recipient in the world. The large amount of capital inflow as well as technology and management spillover fueled the rapid growth of the Chinese economy. In turn, China has become the second largest economy in the world and started to export capital reversely to the international markets, both emerging markets and high-income economies. In particular, driven by the "Going Global" policy, Chinese firms have been actively investing in a range of sectors in overseas' markets. Both inward and outward FDI offers China an opportunity to leverage its economic influence on the globe.

3.5 Financial development in China

A financial system is the core of any modern economy. Prior to the reform, China was financially underdeveloped. In addition to the functions of a central bank, the People's Bank of China (PBoC) was also in charge of industrial and commercial credits and savings' business in the centrally planned economy. Most banks did not operate as commercial banks in the market, while stock markets did not even exist. The outcome was inefficient capital allocation in the economy. Since reform and opening-up began in 1978, the reform of the Chinese financial system was listed as one of the main agendas. In particular, China has carried out a series of significant reforms in its banking system to make PBoC a professional central bank and to allow commercial banks to compete in the market. In addition, China established two stock exchanges in Shanghai and Shenzhen. As a result, the financial sector started to grow and expand over the years. Since the development of financial intermediaries, markets and institutions are a critical and inextricable part of the growth, it is expected that China would benefit from this development (Levine 1997; Beck et al. 2000; Beck and Levine 2002).

The reform of 1994 allowed PBoC to focus on its role as a central bank to set monetary policy and commercial banks to focus on business activities. The Commercial Banking Law that mandates banks as market players instead of policy vehicles for the government took effect in July 1995. As a result, the Big Four (Industrial and Commercial Bank of China, Bank of China, China Construction Bank and Agricultural Bank of China) started to expand their businesses. Furthermore, the government established three policy banks, National Development Bank; the Agricultural Development Bank of China; and Export and Import Bank of China.[10] In addition, the private investors were able to obtain charters for banks. One typical example is a private national bank, China Minsheng Banking Corporation, which was opened in 1996 as a joint-stock bank. The entry of new banks raised competition and made the loan market vibrant.[11]

Credit to GDP is a widely adopted indicator in the literature of financial development (Beck et al. 2000; Beck and Levine 2002). Figure 3.10 presents the credit to GDP ratio of major economies along with the world average. It is evident from the figure that there was rapid growth of credit in China in the 1990s. Excessive credit fueled the economic growth, but the state-owned banking sector soon accumulated large scale of non-performing loans that made the Big Four banks technically insolvent in the early 2000s. To avoid a banking crisis, the regulator established four large non-performing asset management companies (AMC) in the late 1990s and early 2000s to deal with the toxic assets on the balance sheet of the Big Four banks.[12] In addition, the department of Treasury injected capital into the Big Four until they met the capital requirement of the Basel Accord I. Further, China reformed the regulatory framework by establishing the China Banking Regulatory Commission in 2003 to supervise banks on behalf of the central government. Over the period of 2003–2016, the banking sector expanded massively. In 2007, foreign banks were allowed to do business with local currency. Hundreds of new city commercial banks, rural commercial banks, and credit unions entered

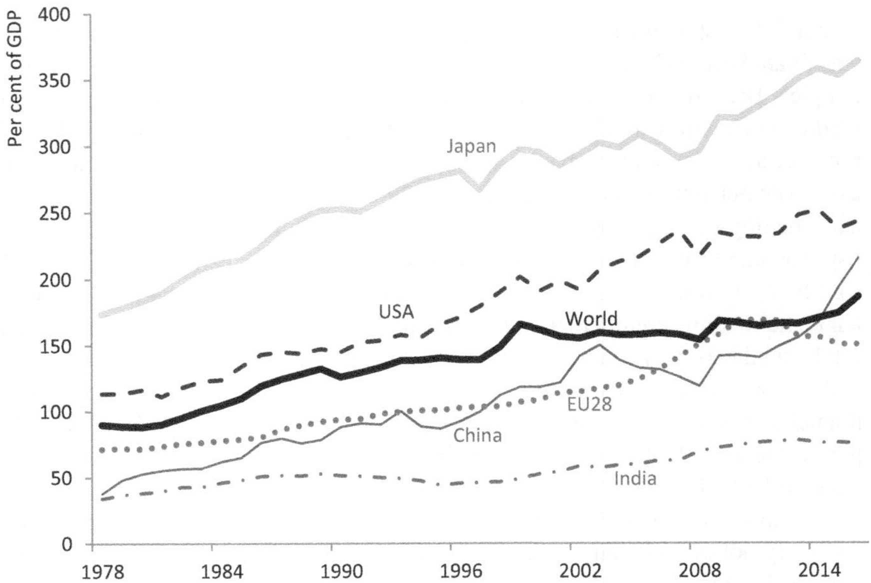

Figure 3.10 Domestic credit provided by financial sector (% of GDP) in China, 1978–2016

Source: Based on data from the World Development Indicators, domestic credit provided by financial sector (% of GDP).

the market, expanding credit supply. The credit to GDP, our primary indicator for financial development suggests in Figure 3.10 that China had greater financial development, as its credit to GDP had surpassed the EU28 in 2014 and the world average in 2015.

In 1990 and 1991, China set up two stock exchanges in Shanghai and Shenzhen, respectively. The initial goal was to help distressed SOEs but soon the listed firms included both SOEs and private companies. Figure 3.11 shows the trend and pattern of stock traded over GDP, another major indicator for financial development (Beck et al. 2000; Beck and Levine 2002). The Chinese market was rather small in the early 1990s when few firms were listed and few people were trading in the market. It did not take a long time before the market expanded, as more and more ordinary people became aware of stock and started to invest in the market. In addition, firms tended to go public and raise funds from direct finance. The market went bullish in 2007 and 2008 but soon turned into a sudden crash. Millions of investors made huge losses. Having being the majority of the market participants, individual investors speculation in 2015 again made another crash featured as leveraged fire sales. Overall, the Chinese stock market shows similar cyclicality with other major markets in the world. But due to the dominance of individual investors, Chinese markets show larger volatility. Nevertheless, the growth of stock markets has supported many financially constrained firms, which

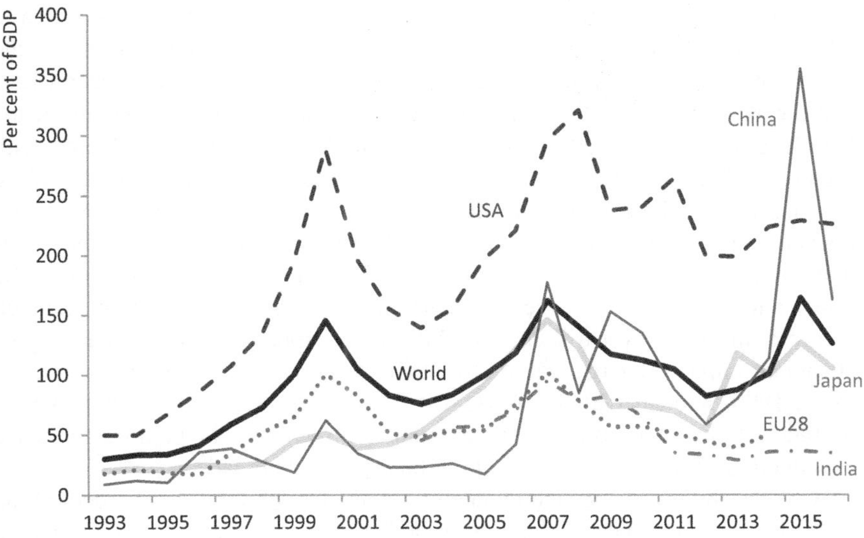

Figure 3.11 Stocks traded, total value (% of GDP) in China, 1993–2016

Source: Based on data from the World Development Indicators, stocks traded, total value (% of GDP).

now have access to the equity market and raise funds. Therefore, the development of the stock market is expected to be beneficial to the real economy.

To conclude, China's financial sector has undergone profound reforms in the right direction. The re-organized financial institutions, newly established stock markets, and market-oriented practices promote financial development. Like in many other countries where financial development of a better functioning financial system leads to an increase in long-term growth, China is not an exception. In addition, China has the potential for balanced growth once further reforms, liberalization and deregulation are in place.

3.6 Political power of China

The prior sections have discussed the rise of Chinese economic power since 1978. That's not the end of the story. In principle, the rise of political influence is often parallel to the economic expansion. Since the communist revolution, the pattern of China's global political power tends to be cyclical.

From 1950 to 1958, China's global political power rose, as China's military power and its domestic and international capabilities of political mobilization were strengthened during the Korean War (Yan 2006). From 1959 to 1966, flawed policies like the Great Leap Forward and the People's Commune destroyed the productivity greatly and impaired China's global political power. Moreover, Sino-Soviet relations began to deteriorate in 1959. The joint pressure from both the US and the Soviet Union in harsh international relations, together with the Cultural Revolution that created disorder, chaos and loss of productivity, forced China to retreat from the combat with both the US and the Soviet Union. To resolve the crisis, Chairman Mao decided to rebalance and ease the tensions between China and the Western world. In 1971, China resumed permanent membership of the UN Security Council. Furthermore, China established diplomatic relations with Japan in 1972, suggesting that China was attempting to connect to the rest of the world. Since 1978 the new leadership in China initiated the economic reform and opened up to the international community. In 1979, China normalized the diplomatic relationship with the US. Since the 1980s, China focused on its domestic issues and chose to be passive in international affairs. But still, China resumed membership in the World Bank and IMF. In addition, China was expanding its economic impact by large exports to OECD countries and emerging economies in the 1990s and early 2000s. Accession to the WTO eventually enabled China to trade freely and access the huge international markets. The political influence expanded as Chinese products and investment flowed abroad.

As the second largest economy and one of the five permanent members of the UN, China has become a global power, both economically and politically. China has been a stakeholder and constructive participant in global affairs, from North Korea, Iran and South Sudan, to global warming, HIV and clean energy. More importantly, the international community came to realize that any vital issued cannot be effectively dealt with without China's engagement (Bergsten 2008). In the Asia-Pacific region, China plays a pivotal role in its effort on regional issues of cooperation and stability. Not a single proposal or policy would work in Asia, if not taking into account China's response and strategy (Bergsten 2008).

First of all, China has been a constructive participant in resolving international conflicts. To deal with the nuclear crisis of North Korea, China hosted a series of Six-party talks that involved North Korea, the US, China, Russia, Japan and South Korea in Beijing over the period of 2003–2007, aiming to find a peaceful resolution. The crisis started in 2002 when North Korea announced its intention to develop nuclear weapons and intended to negotiate bilaterally with the US. The request was turned down as the US believed the talks should involve all stakeholders in the region. Eventually, both sides compromised and agreed to hold a Six-party talk in Beijing. In spite of some preliminary progress after six rounds of talks, North Korea quitted the talks. Although the talks were abandoned, China's endeavor to maintain peace and stability received applause from the international community. Likewise, China was also an indispensable stakeholder in the Syrian crisis and the Iranian nuclear talks and contributed to the peaceful resolution. In particular, China deployed special ambassadors to be involved in the negotiations.

Second, China has been active in multilateral cooperation schemes. China has been an important part in APEC (Asia-Pacific Economic Cooperation), which was established in 1989 to facilitate economic cooperation among the 21 economies in the Asia-Pacific region. As a leading member, China also initiated the BRICS, an association of five major emerging economies that discuss development affairs. Moreover, China has been actively engaging in a number of multilateral, regional cooperation schemes. These schemes include Shanghai Cooperation Organization (China, Russia and some Central Asian countries), ASEAN+3 (Association of Southeast Asian Nations and China, Japan and South Korea), and ASEAN+6 (ASEAN+3 and India, Australia and New Zealand). All these multilateral schemes foster the cooperation between counties in international affairs, defense, trade, finance and culture.

In addition, China plans to build close ties with Northeast Asia, Southeast Asia, Central Asia and South Asia through large-scale infrastructure projects of highways, railways, airports, dams and so forth. The vehicle for the large amount of investment is the recently launched Asian Infrastructure Investment Bank (AIIB), a multilateral development agency for Asian countries. It is established to promote the interconnection and economic integration in Asia, and it is aimed to strengthen cooperation between China and other Asian countries.

On top of infrastructure projects, China put forward the Belt and Road Initiative (BRI) that attempts to reshape global trade. There are two parts of the strategy to connect China with Eurasian countries, the belt and the road. The belt is the railway and highway transportation along the ancient Silk Road, which takes one from China all the way to Europe. The road is actually the maritime Silk Road of shipping lanes from China through Asia and Africa. The belt and road of business routes cover about 65% of the world's population, about one-third of the world's GDP, and about a quarter of all the goods and services the world moves. It has the potential to be the world's largest platform for regional collaboration.

Third, having provided generous aid to underdeveloped countries, especially the least developed countries, in poverty reduction and improvement in living standards, China qualifies as a responsible member in the international community. One feature of Chinese aid is no prerequisite, which has deep roots in China's faith of non-interference, equality, and mutual benefit. In addition, China fully respects the development models, history and culture of the aid recipients. By 2012, China provided a total amount of 345.63 billion RMB in helping other countries.[13] China provides aid funds in three forms: free assistance, loans that bear no interest, and loans with favorable rates. The last form is widely used in foreign aid programs such as economic infrastructure (including transportation, communication and electricity infrastructure), industry and so on (see Figure 3.12a). As a policy bank, China Ex-Im Bank provides cheap funds to foreign recipients at the rates in the range between 2% and 3%. Moreover, aid recipients include developing countries in Africa, Asia, Latin America and the Caribbean, and Oceania, showing little evidence of geographic bias in China's aid overseas (see Figure 3.12b). In particular, Asia and Africa shared almost 80% of China's aids. With regard to economic and social effects, China's foreign aid supports infrastructure projects, which can effectively promote agricultural development and physical capital accumulation. In addition, China's aid attempts to improve the level of education, medical and health conditions and hence contributes to human capital accumulation.

Fourth, China has been an increasingly important peacekeeper of the world. In 1988, China entered the special committee in the UN on peacekeeping operations.

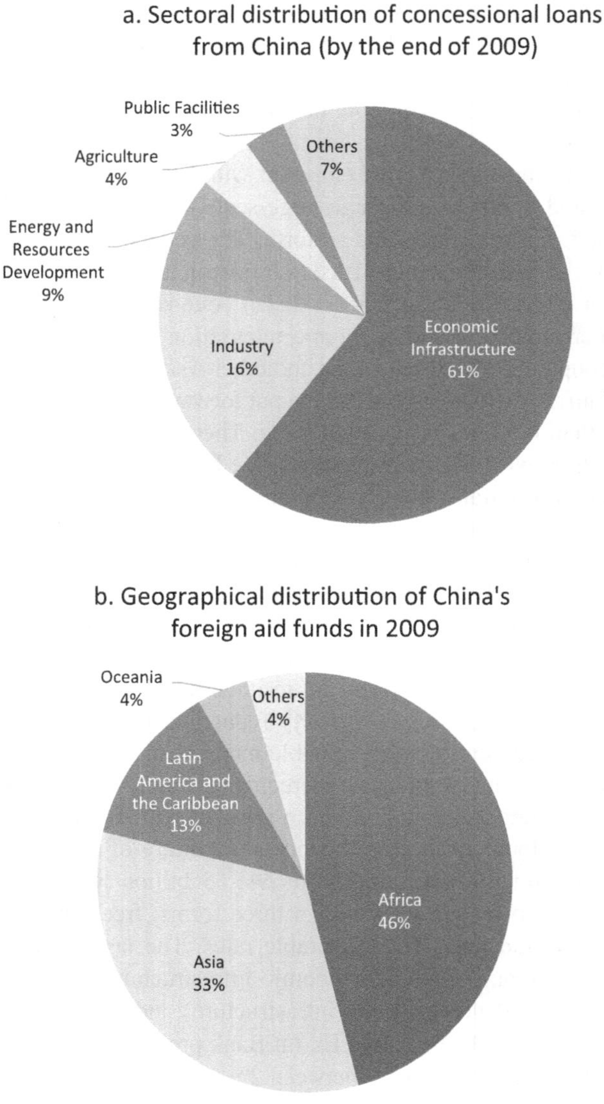

Figure 3.12 Foreign aid from China

Source: China's Foreign Aid 2011

In 1992, China sent its first company of engineers to Cambodia. The Chinese troops in the peacekeeping operations substantially expanded and China's soldiers became an active component of the UN peacekeeping forces. For example, according to the Ministry of Public Security's International Cooperation Bureau, 2,000 Chinese "blue helmets" are currently carrying out tasks in 12 different missions in a total of 15 current peacekeeping operations. Over the past two decades, China participated in more than 20 missions dispatching 20,000 troops and military observers. Africa, as the most unstable continent that suffers from civil wars, diseases and coups, received the most peacekeeping forces from China out of the five permanent members of the UN Security Council. Most observers acknowledge that their impressions of the Chinese peacekeeping troops have changed from threat to trust.

The Chinese navy has been part of the safety net along with the international community on the Aden Gulf to protect bulk carriers from pirates' harassment, kidnap and attacks. Thousands of bulk carriers pass through the busy shipping lanes under the international maritime cooperation against piracy, in which Chinese warships work closely with Indian and Western counterparts in anti-piracy missions. This is crucial for regional safety and the prosperity of international trade. Therefore, China provides public good to the international community and gains friendship from counterparts.

Last, China has contributed to global issues such as global warming. As the largest developing country and a newly industrial economy, China believes that climate change is a global challenge. Hence, China is willing to take responsible actions. For example, China has ratified the Paris climate change agreement and promised to cut greenhouse gas emissions. The Chinese leader is fully aware that the economy needs to be more efficient in its use of energy and resources, and that it is urgent to upgrade its capacity to produce advanced, higher value technologies. More importantly, clean energy has been given priority for China's future. According to the United Nations Environment Programme's annual report on global trends in renewable energy, in 2015 China invested 102.9 billion USD in renewable energy, or 36% of the world total, and installed half of the world's new wind power. Its coal consumption has peaked and begun to decline, to be replaced by renewables such as solar, hydro, and nuclear power. In sum, China has shown enough commitment to take a responsible role in clean energy.

3.7 Conclusions

This chapter reviews the rise of China's economic and political power since 1978. During it initial economic boom, China's story was split into economic growth, development of international trade, FDI and finance, relative to the world. China has been growing at an unprecedented rate, outperforming major developed countries and emerging markets. The economic success is closely tied to international trade, foreign investment, and financial development. First of all, both the volume and structure of Chinese exports have made remarkable progress. Consequently, China has become the biggest trading nation in the world by the total of imports and exports of goods. Second, China attracted a steady flow of foreign investment, which fueled business formation and expansion. Meanwhile, Chinese firms started to seek investment opportunities abroad. Last, financial development is an indispensable part of China's miracle as the improved function and resilience of the financial system better serve the real economy. Our arguments rely on data analysis and presenting stories. We aim to show experiences and lessons of China that may inspire policymakers and academia to come up with constructive ideas for development.

To complete the story, we examine another dimension of the rise of China, namely, the expanding political power and its impact on the international community. We show evidence that it is a peaceful rise for collaboration and prosperity, as China has been contributing to the international conflict resolution, multilateral cooperation schemes, aid programs, peacekeeping and global issues. We present several cases and examples in history for our arguments and confirm China's constructive role in the international community.

The rise of China is an event that attracts extensive attention. China's experiences suggest that its success stemmed from the opening-up and the rules and institutions of the current international system, namely free trade, frictionless investment, financial development and stable international relationships. The rise of China does not have to trigger tensions but could create opportunities for cooperation and prosperity.

"Today, the lion has woken up. But it is peaceful, pleasant and civilized," said Chinese President Xi Jinping in a meeting in Paris in 2014.

Notes

1 Beijing Foreign Studies University, International Business School, No. 2 North Xisanhuan Road, 100089, Beijing, P.R. China. Email: hushiwei@bfsu.edu.cn. I thank Nimesh Salike for useful comments and suggestions. Any errors are my own. This work is supported by the Fundamental Research Funds for the Central Universities (2015QD008).
2 Donald Winchester, China and the Future of the World, Society and Culture in Vision, Summer 2016, www.vision.org/global-economy-china-and-the-future-of-the-world-4621
3 This chapter compares the economic data for China, India, Japan, EU28 and the US. I choose these economies since China and India are the two biggest emerging markets in the world, while Japan, EU28 and the US are import advanced economies. The sum of GDP in the five economies accounted for 68.7% of the world GDP in 2016 (see Figure 3-1).
4 World Bank: the World Development Indicators; Exports of goods and services (current USD); Imports of goods and services (current USD).
5 In this section we focus on the exports from China, which is a good barometer for the rise of Chinese economy and trade.
6 Not shown in Figure 3.4 due to missing data from the 1980s.
7 World Bank: the World Development Indicators, research and development expenditure (% of GDP).
8 http://fta.mofcom.gov.cn/
9 Data on FDI to China was not available before 1982, and we believe the size of FDI to GDP should be even lower.
10 The Big Four are the four largest commercial banks in China by total assets, conducting businesses in deposit taking and extending loans to corporations and households. By contrast, the three policy banks are development finance institutions created by the Chinese central government. Policy banks provide financing for the projects aimed at economic development, rather than stockholders' value maximization.
11 For more details of Chinese banking reform, please refer to Chapter 2.
12 The four AMCs are China Great Wall Asset Management for the Agricultural Bank of China, China Orient Asset Management for the Bank of China, China Huarong Asset Management for the Industrial and Commercial Bank of China and China Cinda Asset Management for China Construction Bank.
13 Source: China's Foreign Aid 2011 & 2014. www.scio.gov.cn/zfbps/ndhf/2014/Document/1375014/1375014.htm www.scio.gov.cn/zfbps/ndhf/2011/Document/896982/896982.htm

References

Beck, T., R. Levine, and N. Loayza (2000), "Financial Intermediation and Growth: Causality and Causes." *Journal of Monetary Economics* 46: 31–77.

Beck, T., and R. Levine (2002), "Industry Growth and Capital Allocation: Does Having a Market- or Bank Based System Matter?" *Journal of Financial Economics* 64: 147–180.

Bergsten, C. F. (2008), *China's Rise: Challenges and Opportunities*, Peterson Institute.

Blancher, M. N. R., and M. T. Rumbaugh (2004), "China: International Trade and WTO Accession." No. 4–36, International Monetary Fund.

Chuang, Y. C., and P. F. Hsu (2004), "FDI, Trade, and Spillover Efficiency: Evidence from China's Manufacturing Sector." *Applied Economics* 36(10): 1103–1115.

Huo, J. (2015), *History of Chinese Foreign Trade*, Beijing: China Commerce and Trade Press.

Kornai, J. (1980), *Economics of Shortage*, Amsterdam: North-Holland Press.

Kornai, J., E. Maskin, and G. Roland (2003), "Understanding the Soft Budget Constraint," *Journal of Economic Literature* 41(4): 1095–1136.

Levine, R. (1997), "Financial Development and Economic Growth: Views and Agenda." *Journal of Economic Literature* 35: 688–726.

Lin, J. Y. (1992), "Rural Reforms and Agricultural Growth in China." *American Economic Review* 34–51.

McMillan, J., J. Whalley, and L. Zhu (1989), "The Impact of China's Economic Reforms on Agricultural Productivity Growth." *Journal of Political Economy* 97(4): 781–807.

Tang, S., E. A. Selvanathan, and S. Selvanathan (2008), "Foreign Direct Investment, Domestic Investment and Economic Growth in China: A Time Series Analysis." *The World Economy* 31(10): 1292–1309.

United Nations Conference on Trade and Development (UNCTAD, 2016), *World Investment Report 2016*. Geneva: United Nations.

Yan, X. (2006), "The Rise of China and Its Power Status," *The Chinese Journal of International Politics* 1(1): 5–33.

Zhang, K. H., and S. Shunfeng (2003), "Rural-urban Migration and Urbanization in China: Evidence from Time-series and Cross-section Analyses," *China Economic Review* 14(4): 386–400.

References

Part II

Geographical connections

4 China and geography

Steven Brakman[1]

4.1 Introduction

It is well-known that economic activity is unevenly distributed over space. Production and consumption tend to concentrate in cities. China is no exception. Eyeballing the map of China reveals that activity is concentrated in the eastern part of the country, especially along the coast. In between these clusters of activity there is lots of empty space. The western part of China is relatively empty, but pockets of emptiness are visible in the eastern part and in between cities. This distribution is difficult to explain using standard economic techniques that rely on perfect competition and the absence of any barriers to trade. Relatively recently a convincing model has been developed by Paul Krugman (1991) to explain why clustering of economic activity arises and under what conditions this happens. He received the Nobel Prize in Economics for this work in 2008.

Key in Krugman's model is that firm production is characterized by economies of scale and imperfect competition and that supply is subject to trade barriers. Consumers are characterized by a 'love of variety', implying that all products are consumed by all consumers. Finally, both firms and workers can select a location. The consequence of this model is that it can endogenously determine the size of economic activity in different locations in a general equilibrium framework. The basic model has been extended in different ways to include elements from international economics, industrial organization, economic geography, spatial economics, urban economics and endogenous growth. The crucial characteristic remains that location choices are endogenously determined and that agglomeration of economic activity in various locations is a general equilibrium outcome. For a country like China, the model provides interesting elements. China is rapidly industrializing, making agglomeration of economic activity beneficial (see Chapter 5). Furthermore, the Chinese government is reducing restrictions on migration of workers within China. So, workers can increasingly follow economic incentives and choose an optimal place to work, possibly stimulating further clustering of economic activity.

In this chapter we first illustrate the basic model as it was developed by Krugman and then apply it to China by analysing what could happen with further reductions in migration restrictions. We indicate that economic activity will further stimulate economic agglomeration in China.

4.2 An example

The model developed by Krugman can most easily be illustrated by means of an example.[2] Suppose there are two regions (or countries), North and South, and two sectors of production, manufacturing and agriculture. The manufacturing industry produces varieties, that is differentiated products, under internal economies of scale. The cost per unit of output therefore falls as a firm expands its production level. As a result, each firm produces only one variety. A firm can reside either in North or South and has to decide where to produce. This location decision essentially differentiates the example from New Trade Theory.

Total demand for each variety of manufactures in the example is exogenous. We assume that each firm sells four units to workers in the manufacturing industry and six units to the farmers. Total demand for each variety is therefore 10 (= 6 + 4). The production of agriculture, and hence the demand it generates, is location-specific. Its spatial distribution is exogenously given; we assume that four units are sold in the North and two units in the South. The location of the workers in the manufacturing sector, and hence the four units they demand at that location, is not exogenous. The role of the immobile workers is important as they ensure that there is always positive demand in *both* regions. Finally, transport costs between North and South is 1 euro per unit. The firms choose location to minimize transport costs. We are now able to determine the location decision of each firm.

First, we can calculate the regional sales of each firm, given the location of the other firms. In Table 4.1, three possibilities are given; all firms in the North, all firms in the South, or 25% of all firms in the North and 75% of all firms in the South. Sales in each region are equal to the sales to the workers in manufacturing plus the sales to the farmers. Take, for example, the last row in Table 4.1. The firm sells five units in the North, namely four to the farmers located in the North plus 1 (= 25% × 4) unit to the manufacturing workers located in North. Similarly, the firm sells five units in the South, namely two units to the farmers located in the South plus 3 (= 75% × 4) units to the manufacturing workers located in the South.

Second, using Table 4.1 we can construct a decision table, by calculating transport costs as a function of the firm's location decision, given the location of the other firms (see Table 4.2). Suppose, for example, that all firms are located in the North. Table 4.2 indicates that transport costs for a firm located in the South will then be 8 Euro, namely 4 for sales to the farmers in the North and 4 for sales to all workers in manufacturing located in the North (abstracting from sales to

Table 4.1 Geography of sales

	Sales in North	*Sales in South*	*Total sales*
All firms in North	4 + 4 = 8	0 + 2 = 2	10
All firms in South	0 + 4 = 4	4 + 2 = 6	10
25% firms in North 75% firms in South	1 + 4 = 5	3 + 2 = 5	10

Table 4.2 Transport cost decision table

	If location in North	*If location in South*
All firms in North	0 + 2 = **2** (to farmers in South)	4 + 4 = 8 (to workers & farmers in North)
All firms in South	4 + 2 = 6 (to workers & farmers in South)	0 + 4 = **4** (to farmers in North)
25% firms in North 75% firms in South	3 + 2 = 5 (to workers & farmers in South)	1 + 4 = 5 (to workers & farmers in North)

its own workers). Similarly, if the firm was located in the North, transport costs would be only 2 for the sales to the farmers in the South. Since transport costs are minimized by being located in the North, if all other firms are located in the North, the firm decides to also locate production in the North. As Table 4.2 shows (second row) a firm will locate to the South if all other firms are also located there, whereas (last row) the firm is indifferent between locating to the North or South (since transport costs are the same if the firm locates in either region) if 25% of the firms are located in the North and 75% in the South.

On the basis of this example, we can illustrate a few distinctive characteristics of the Geographical Economics approach.

First, the concept of *cumulative causation*. If, for some reason, a location has attracted more firms than the other location, a new firm has an incentive to locate where the other firms are. Take the first row in Table 4.2. If all firms are located in the North, a firm, minimizing transport costs, should also locate there to minimize transport costs. Similarly, for the second row in Table 4.2, the firm will locate to the South.

Second, Table 4.2 illustrates the existence of *multiple equilibria*. Agglomeration of all firms in either the North or the South is an equilibrium. However, we cannot determine beforehand where agglomeration will occur. This depends critically on initial conditions, that is, the previous location decisions of other firms.

Third, an equilibrium might be *stable or unstable*. The bold entries in Table 4.2 are both stable equilibria; if a single firm would decide to relocate, this decision would not influence the location decisions of the other firms. The last row in Table 4.2 describes an unstable equilibrium. If a single firm decides to relocate, the new location will immediately become more attractive for all other firms. This will trigger a snowball effect: all firms will follow the pioneer. In this example only agglomeration is a stable equilibrium.

Fourth, we note that a stable equilibrium can be *non-optimal*. If all firms are located in North transport costs are only 2. If all firms are located in South transport costs are 4, see the bold entries in Table 4.2. Thus, transport costs for the economy as a whole are minimized if all firms agglomerate in the North, whereas agglomeration in the South is a stable equilibrium.

Fifth, the tables illustrate the *interaction of agglomeration and trade flows*. With complete agglomeration, that is all manufactures are produced in a single region, trade between regions will be of the inter-industry type (food for manufacturers). In fact, this equilibrium also reflects the so-called *home-market* effect; the combination of economies-of-scale and transport costs is responsible for the clustering of all footloose activity in a single location. Due to this combination, transport costs can be minimized. The large region ends up with a large market for manufacturing goods, which can be sold without incurring transport costs. The consequence is that this region becomes the exporter of manufactured goods; large regions tend to become exporters of those goods for which they have a large local market, hence the term *home market-effect*. If the manufacturing industry is located in both regions, as described by the last rows in the tables, trade will also be of the intra-industry type. Besides trading manufactured goods for agricultural products, different varieties of the differentiated manufactured products will be traded between both regions.

The example is useful as it illustrates some important aspects of Geographical Economics. But an example is just an example, and it is not a substitute for a well-specified model. What is missing in the example?

First of all, the interaction of transport costs, price-setting behaviour and location choice is missing. We simply assume that the demand each firm faces is a given independent of price-setting behaviour and transport costs. In fact, prices are completely lacking in the example. There is no analysis of the market structure. In reality, prices, wages and transport costs will determine the purchasing power of consumers. One might guess that this interaction drives the location decisions of consumers and producers. The next section illustrates that this is indeed the case.

Furthermore, it is a partial equilibrium model in the sense that firms do not worry about the necessary labour; wherever they decide to locate labour availability is not the problem. However, assumptions with regard to functioning of the labour market are important, as our illustration of China will show.

Mathematically one can proceed by developing a model that deals with all the aspects previously mentioned. We will not present the model in mathematical detail but only highlight a few key aspects in the next section: general structure, demand (section 4.3.1), supply (section 4.3.2) and equilibrium (section 4.3.3).[3]

4.3 Geographical economics

This section gives a non-technical overview of the structure of the geographical economics model, as illustrated in Figure 4.1 (with so-called 'callouts' a-g).[4] There are two regions (1 and 2) and two sectors in the economy (food and manufactures). Consumers in region 1 consist of farm workers and manufacturing workers. Similarly, for region 2. The farm workers earn their income by working for the farmers in their region. If they own the farm, it is as if they hire themselves. They then play a dual role, as both farmers and farm workers. The income stream of the farm workers is part of a bilateral transfer: they receive an income from the farmer (the farm wage rate) and in return they supply labour services to the farmer. All such bilateral transfers are indicated with double-headed arrows in Figure 4.1. The closed-headed arrows refer to the direction of money flows, that

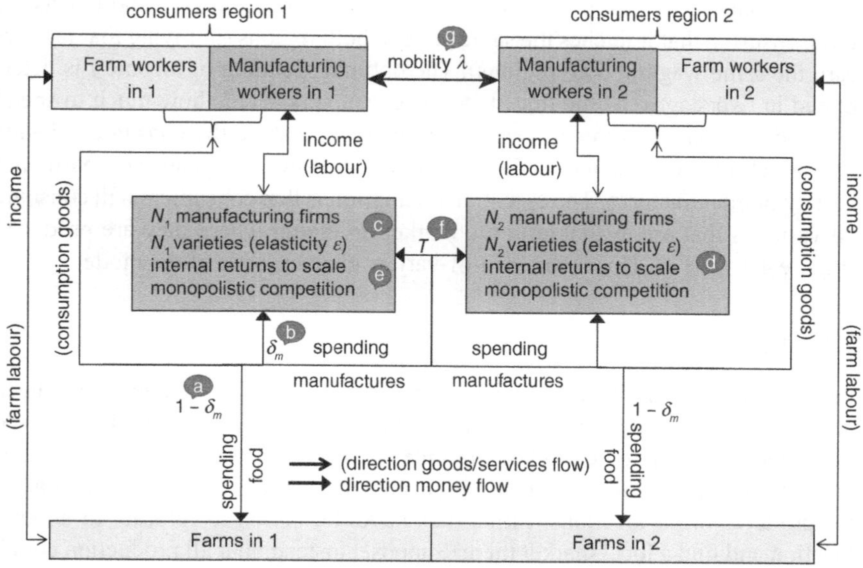

Figure 4.1 Structure of the geographical economics model

is of income and spending. What the flow represents exactly is indicated along the lines connecting the arrow heads. The open-headed arrow refers to the direction of goods flows. These are indicated in parentheses along the lines connecting the arrow heads. The farmers in region 1 use the labour services of the farm workers from region 1 to produce food under constant returns to scale and perfect competition. They sell this food to the consumers, either in region 1 or in region 2. There are no transport costs for food.

The manufacturing sector consists of N_1 firms in region 1 and N_2 firms in region 2. Each manufacturing firm produces a differentiated good; that is, it produces a unique variety of manufactures, using only labour under internal economies of scale. This implies that the firms have monopolistic power, which they use in determining the price of their product. There are transport costs involved in selling a manufactured good in another region. These costs do not arise if the manufactured good is sold in the region in which it is produced. As a result of the transport costs involved in exporting manufactured goods firms will charge a higher price in the other region than at home. The manufacturing workers earn their income (the manufacturing wage rate) by supplying labour to the firms in the manufacturing sector of their region.

4.3.1 Demand

Consumers spend their income on agriculture (food) and manufactures (Figure 4.1, parts a and b). Assuming that the production of food is characterized by constant returns to scale, and food is a homogenous good, consumers do not care if it is produced in region 1 or in region 2. Also, there are no transport costs for food, ensuring that it fetches the same price in both regions (implying that farmers earn the same wage in both regions). The optimal spending of income I is determined in two stages. At the first stage the consumers decide how much to spend on food and manufactures in general. In the second stage the consumers decide how much of their income, dedicated to manufactures, is spend on a particular variety of manufactures. The essential assumption is that consumers will consume all varieties that are available in the market no matter where they are produced (Figure 4.1, part c). This is the love-of-variety characteristic of the model.

4.3.2 Supply

Food production is characterized by constant returns to scale and is produced under conditions of perfect competition. Workers in the food sector, which is used as numéraire, are assumed to be immobile. This is an important assumption (see the example in section 4.2) because it ensures that there is always a local market for products in all locations. Firms thus have the option to relocate to another location and find a local market there. Suppose, instead, that all production could, hypothetically, be concentrated in a single location, then it would be optimal to concentrate all production there; this would avoid any transportation costs and the relocation option no longer makes sense. The immobile sector thus makes the model interesting by giving firms the option to relocate.

Production in the manufacturing sector is characterized by internal economies of scale such that $l_i = f + mx_i$, where l_i is the amount of labour necessary to produce x_i units of variety i. The parameters f and m are the fixed and marginal labour input requirements. The increasing returns assumption is crucial (Figure 4.1, parts e and d). Firms with a large sales volume have lower unit labour cost of production than firms with a smaller sales volume. The smaller firms will be driven out of the market by the larger firms that can set a lower price. In the end each firm produces a unique variety and has to decide where to locate. Once it has made a location choice it will export its unique variety to the other location (because of the love-of-variety effect there is always demand for its product in all locations).

Exporting is costly. Producers add transportation costs to the price. Usually in these types of models, transport costs are of the *iceberg* type; the parameter $T \geq 1$ denotes the number of goods that need to be shipped to ensure that one unit of a variety of manufactures arrives per unit of distance. Suppose $T = 1.1$, then 1.1 units have to be shipped to ensure that one unit arrives at the destination (0.1 units melt away in transit). The advantage of this, admittedly unrealistic, type of transport costs is that one does not have to include and model a separate transportation sector.

4.3.3 Equilibrium

Equating demand to supply on the commodity and labour markets gives the equilibrium prices and wages that allow us to calculate the real wage in each location.

In the previous example we analyzed three situations and discussed the consequences. All three were equilibria. But how is equilibrium reached? Workers and firms in the manufacturing sector are mobile and can choose a location. Workers choose a location where they can earn the highest (real) wage. If they migrate they become employed by firms that start producing a new variety at the new location.

If the real wage for manufacturing workers is, for example, higher in region 1 than in region 2 we expect manufacturing workers to move from region 2 to region 1. If the real wage is higher in region 2 than in region 1, we expect the reverse to hold. We let the parameter γ denote the speed with which manufacturing workers react to differences in the real wage and use a simple dynamic system:

$$\underbrace{change\ workers\ region 1}_{migration} = \gamma \underbrace{\left(w_1 - \bar{w}\right)}_{wage\ difference}; \quad \bar{w} = \underbrace{\lambda_1 w_1 + \lambda_2 w_2}_{average\ real\ wage} \qquad 4.1.$$

Note that $\bar{w}$ denotes the average real wage in the economy. A similar equation holds for region 2. This process continues until real wages are equalized and workers no longer have an incentive to relocate. This migration equation describes how workers react to real wage differences (Figure 4.1, part g). It assumes that a positive difference between the real wage in a region relative to the rest of the economy immediately results in migration. It is easy to model restrictions on migration. One can assume, for example, that migration only takes place if the difference between the real wages and the rest of the economy has to be at least 10%, or any other percentage that describes (simulated) reality better. In the simulations to follow, various assumptions are made with respect to migration policies and how it affects migration.

4.4 Stelder illustration

A nice illustration of the geographical economics model is developed by Dirk Stelder (2005) to see to what extent the model can be used to predict the location of European cities. Stelder defines a large grid of square locations on a truncated map of Europe. The distance between two locations is in principle calculated as the shortest path (that is 1 for horizontal and vertical neighbours, $\sqrt{2}$ for diagonal neighbours). Stelder's grid of Western Europe has more than 2,800 locations. Sea transportation is made possible at a few places, which are part of the network but do not act as potential locations for cities. The model allows for specific costs for transportation across land, across sea, and in hubs where (un)shipping can take place. The grid is also extended with a third dimension (height) to take the extra transportation costs into account when goods have to cross mountains.

The Stelder model starts with a flat initial distribution in which all locations on the grid are of equal size. The model simulations then calculate the re-distribution of economic activity based on differences in real wages. The location and size of the cities which emerge in the equilibrium depend on the chosen parameter values in the model and on the geographical shape of the economy. Figure 4.2 shows what happens if workers migrate to cities with the highest real wages.

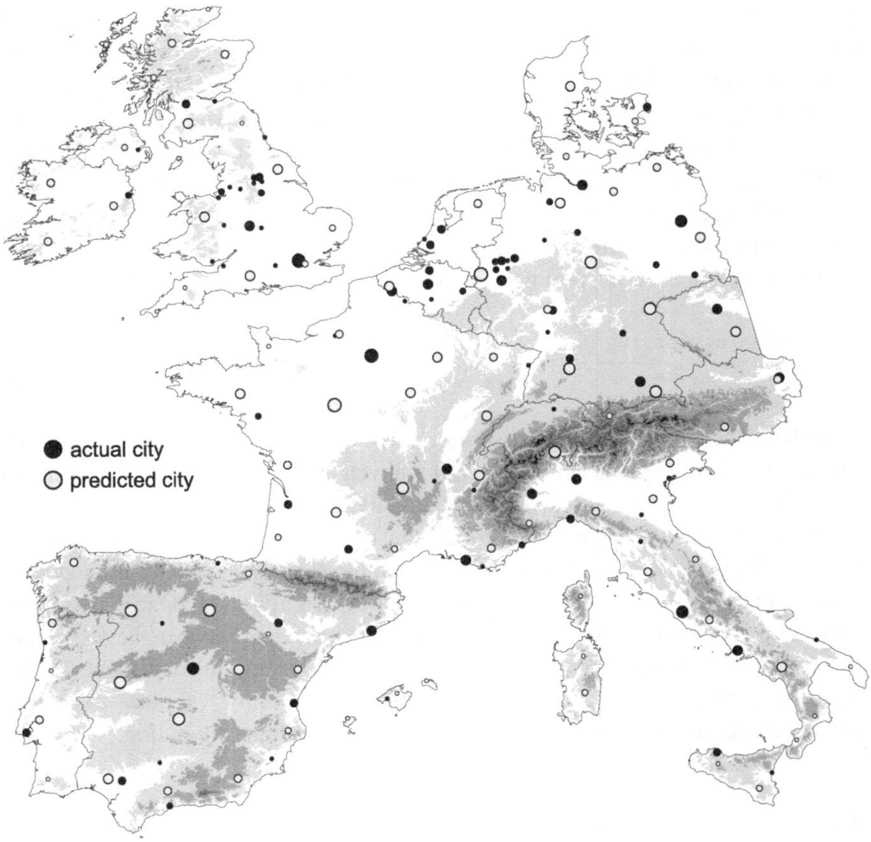

Figure 4.2 Simulated model of European cities

The open circles are the simulated outcomes and the closed circles the 94 largest actual cities in 1996. The model predicts too many large cities in Spain and too few cities in the UK, the Netherlands and Belgium. The results are nevertheless relatively good for Germany where the Rurhgebiet, Bremen, Berlin, Frankfurt, Stuttgart and Munich are not far from the right place. Vienna is on target, and in the periphery of various countries some cities also appear correctly, like Lille, Rouen, Nantes, Bordeaux and Nice in France, Lisbon in Portugal, and Seville and Malaga in Spain.

Stelder points out that these model results of course *should be* wrong, because the model is a simplified version of reality. One of the objectives of the model is to clarify to what extent pure economic factors have contributed to the city formation process in Europe. He concludes that even a basic model can produce city hierarchies if applied in spaces closer to geographic reality. This is also the reason why it is interesting to look at China from the viewpoint of this model.

4.5 Urbanization in China

Today more than half of the world population lives in cities, but this is a relatively recent phenomenon. We provide a more detailed discussion of urbanization in Chapter 5. Here we briefly focus on urbanization in China and (for comparison purposes) India (see Figure 4.3). Panel *a* of the figure provides the urban population as a percent of the total population and panel *b* in millions of people. In 1960 the degree of urbanization was substantially below the world average in both countries and slightly lower in China than in India, namely 16% vs 18%. In India the developments are stable: the urban population share rises steadily every year and reaches 33% in 2016. In China the developments are much more dramatic. Initially the urban population share rises from 1960 to 1964, but then it declines until 1972 and slowly crawls back until 1977 (to 17.5%). From 1978 onwards, the urban population share starts to rise quickly and reaches 57% in 2016.

As panel b of Figure 4.3 shows, the urban population is always larger in China than in India, although the gap narrows until the end of the 1970s and starts to widen again thereafter. In India the urban population rises from 83 million to 439 million, an increase of 358 million people. In China the urban population rises even more dramatically, from 108 million in 1960 to 783 million in 2016, an increase of 675 million people or almost half of China's current population. The Chinese hukou system, which limits mobility through a system of migration permits from rural regions to the city, is partly motivated to handle these enormous migration flows towards cities (see the next section and Chapter 5), and thus keep Chinese cities smaller than they would have been with unrestricted urbanization.

Figure 4.4 illustrates the degree of over- or under-urbanization in China and India since 1960, using the methodology of Brakman et al. (2016). We use a simple measure; for each year a regression line between the log of income per capita (in constant 2005 USD) as the dependent variable and the degree of urbanization (urban population as percent of the total population) as the independent variable

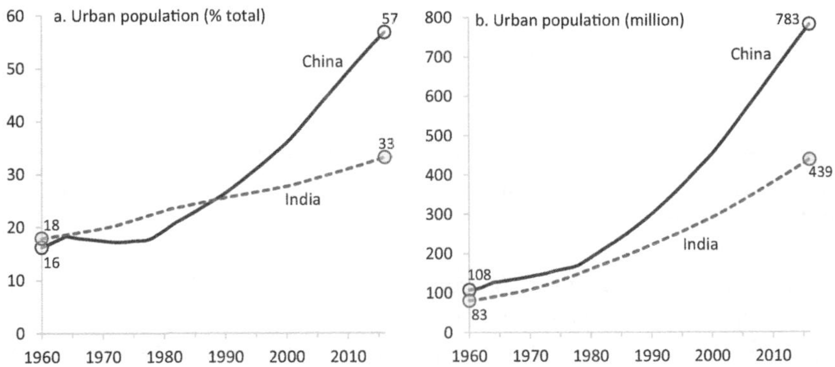

Figure 4.3 Urban population in China and India, 1960–2016

Source: Created using World Bank Development Indicators online; urban population in per cent of total (panel a) and million people (panel b).

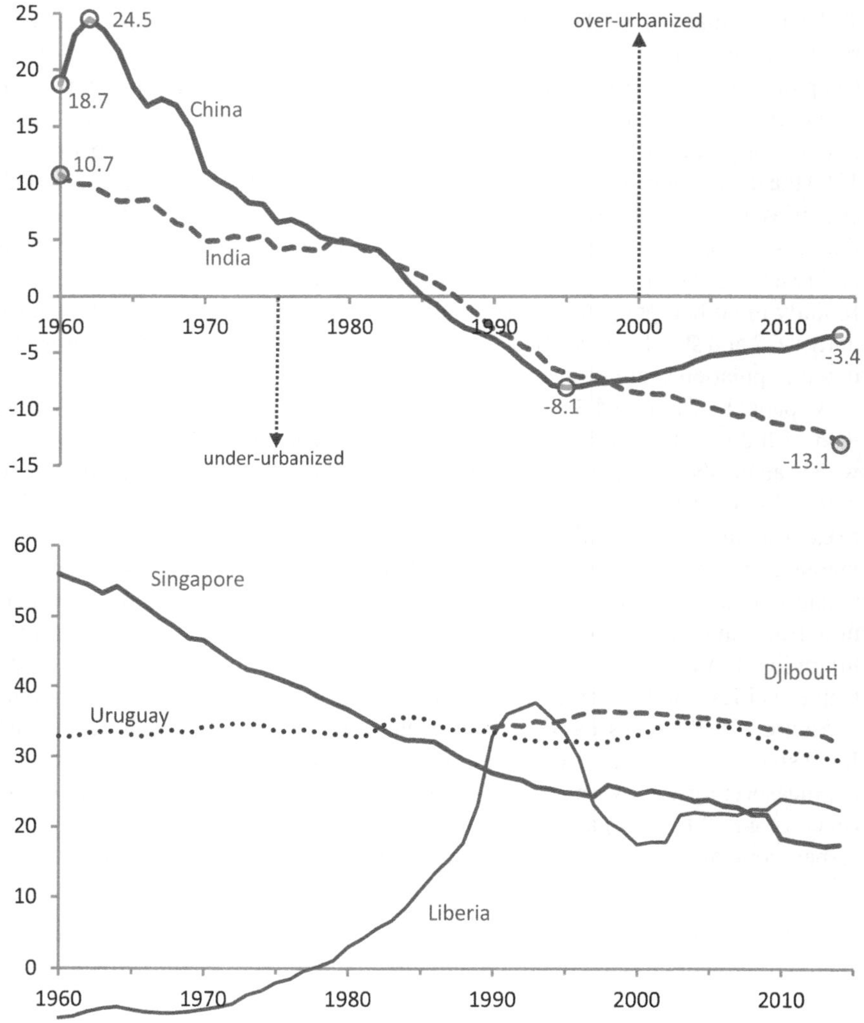

Figure 4.4 Deviation of urbanization for China and India, 1960–2014

Source: Under- or over-urbanization in terms of the deviation (in percentage points) of the cross-section regression line in any given year (see also main text).

for 186 countries is calculated (a cross-section regression). Countries below the regression line are called under-urbanized since urbanization levels are lower than expected based on income per capita (using the regression line for that year; see also Chapter 5 on the link between urbanization and economic development). Countries above the regression line are called over-urbanized. We repeat the exercise for all years. The degree of urbanization is shown for China and India in the period 1960–2014 in Figure 4.4.

This suggests that China's recently high-lighted under-urbanization (with a smaller share of the population in cities than what can be expected on the basis of its income per capita level) is a recent phenomenon, starting only in 1986. Before 1986 China was actually over-urbanized, with a higher share of the population in cities than what could be expected on the basis of its income per capita level. The degree of over-urbanization reached a peak of 24.5 percentage points in 1964 and rapidly declined since then (although it remained substantial throughout the 1960s and 70s). The 1964 peak level of over-urbanization was 24.5 percentage points, as illustrated in Figure 4.4. China's maximum level of under-urbanization occurred in 1995, with 8.1 percentage points fewer people living in cities than what could be expected on the basis of its income level. Since 1995 China's degree of under-urbanization has declined substantially, to 3.4 percentage points in 2014.

The under-urbanization in China since 1985 has raised the question of why this is the case. Recent growth in China has been accompanied by migration from the country side to cities. As a result, and illustrated by Figures 4.3 and 4.4, China's urbanization rate has steadily risen since 1985. Recent research argues that Chinese cities are still (too) small (see Au and Henderson 2006a, 2006b). This is the consequence of restrictions on migration that are imposed through the so called *hukou* system (see Zhao, 2005; Chan and Buckingham, 2009). Compared to other industrializing countries at comparable stages of economic development, China has a relatively even distribution of cities (Fujita et al. 2004, 2955). The hukou system is an internal visa arrangement that aims to regulate migration. The system limits migration flows from rural to urban areas, but also restricts inter-urban migration flows (see Zhang and Zhao 2013). Without such a visa, a Chinese citizen has only limited rights to local (government) services. Those rights are tied to one's official place of residence. It can only be changed if (local) authorities hand out a (new) visa or permit for the actual place of residence (if different from one's official place of residence).

The general view is that the *hukou* system is still restrictive.

> all these restrictions sharply reduce the benefits and raise the costs of migration, particularly into large cities. Migration is limited and most migration is short-term, or "return" migration. (. . .). Overall the hukou system holds hundreds of millions of people in locations where they are not exploiting their earnings potential.
>
> (Fujita et al. 2004, 2957)[5]

However, there is some evidence that the *hukou* system has become less restrictive over time (Chan and Buckingham 2008; Brakman et al. 2017) and that migration flows increasingly are determined by market forces instead of visas. This raises the question: what would happen to Chinese cities if the *hukou* system is no longer in action? The model introduced in this chapter might be helpful to illustrate what could happen in China.

4.6 Simulating China: relaxing the *hukou* system

As with all simulations the results are not necessarily aimed to give a precise prediction, but only to illustrate in what direction agglomeration in China might be moving if the hukou system is relaxed.[6] In practice, real world complications most likely interfere with the stylized results of a model that ignores such possible complications. Bosker et al. (2012) use the geographical economics model, introduced by means of an example in section 4.2 and like the structure explained in section 4.3, and add congestion effects to yield less extreme agglomeration outcomes than illustrated in the example in section 4.2; with congestion, locations of various sizes can be an equilibrium outcome of the model.

One way of including congestion is by adding an additional non-tradable service called housing. If workers relocate to another region the price of housing in that location rises to make the location less attractive. In addition, workers can change occupation from manufacturing to agriculture and vice versa, which equalizes wages in a region. The inclusion of housing implies that the real wages as used in Equation 4.1 also include the price of housing. Using various assumptions for restrictions on migration it is possible to simulate and predict what could happen in China once authorities relax the *hukou* system and stimulate interregional labour mobility. The key-parameters of the model are estimated, using regression analyses and some calculations based on data from the Chinese Statistical Yearbooks. These estimates are used to calibrate the model to mimic the actual situation for China in 2000. The next step is to analyse how the geography of China changes under various (hypothetical) migration rules. The basic calculation is based on (variants) of Equation 4.1. The exercise is, in principle, done for 264 prefecture cities (data restrictions reduce the number of prefecture cities in some applications), capturing some 86%.

Figure 4.5 illustrates the actual situation in 2000 with regards to population. The darker the shading, the larger the population shares of that particular area. Eyeballing the figure, it is clear that the eastern part of China is home to the largest share of the population. This includes cities like Beijing, Shanghai and Guangzhou. What is also visible from the shading is that it is not exclusively the coastal areas where the population concentrates. Large concentrations can also be found in non-coastal provinces like Hunan, Hebei, Anhui, Jiangsu and Shandong.

The model provides estimates of wages and prices, and together they determine real wages that allow us to simulate how workers move across space. Migration results in more spatially equalized real wages. The prediction of the model is straightforward; those areas with high real wages see an inflow of workers. This reduces nominal wages and increases the price of housing and as a consequence real wages decline. The opposite takes place in the cities where workers originate.

The most extreme scenario is a *no-hukou* case; all restrictions are dropped. Small real wage differences attract workers from all over China. The agglomeration shadow of high real wages is felt everywhere. The resulting equilibrium spatial distribution of the population can be expected to be more concentrated.

Such an extreme scenario is unrealistic. Even without the Chinese *hukou* system some migration hurdles remain (see also Chapter 5 on provincial borders);

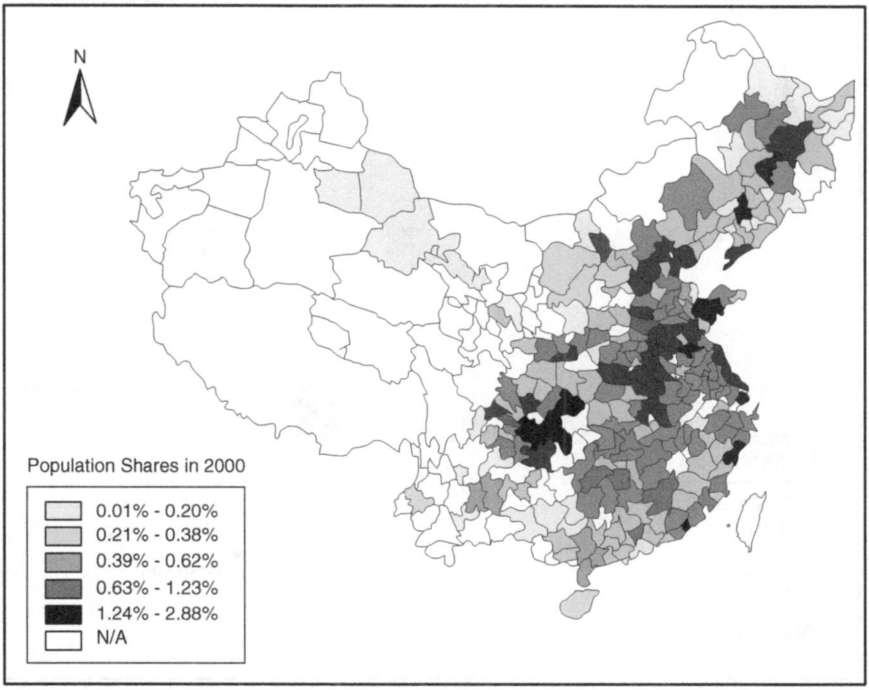

Figure 4.5 Distribution of people across prefecture cities in 2000

Source: Bosker et al. 2012; N/A = not available and/or not a prefecture city.

these are sunk costs that are always present when one relocates to another place to live. In the scenario depicted in Figure 4.6 a 15% real wage threshold is assumed. Only if real wage differences are larger than 15% of people start to migrate. Figure 4.6 illustrates the simulated outcome of this (hypothetical) scenario. It reflects a *Hukuo* system that has become more liberal. Visual inspection immediately reveals that agglomeration is now working more forcefully; compared to the actual situation in 2000 (see Figure 4.5) the simulated outcome shows that the population is concentrated in a few large areas (in fact only 52 out of 264 prefecture cities 'survive' in the sense that economic activity takes place). One can calculate Herfindahl index (HI) for the prefecture population distribution as an indicator for the degree of agglomeration; one for the actual situation in 2000 and one for the simulated distribution. In 2000 the HI was 0.004, and in the simulated situation 0.047, which is more than 10 times larger than the actual situation in 2000, indicating strong concentration. Some of the population concentrates in the usual suspects: Beijing, Guangzhou and Shanghai, but also in Chongqing; the heartland of China is attractive and is able to attract a lot of economic activity. Market and supplier access are high in these initially already large agglomerations. As a result, they can offer relatively high wages and profits that attract

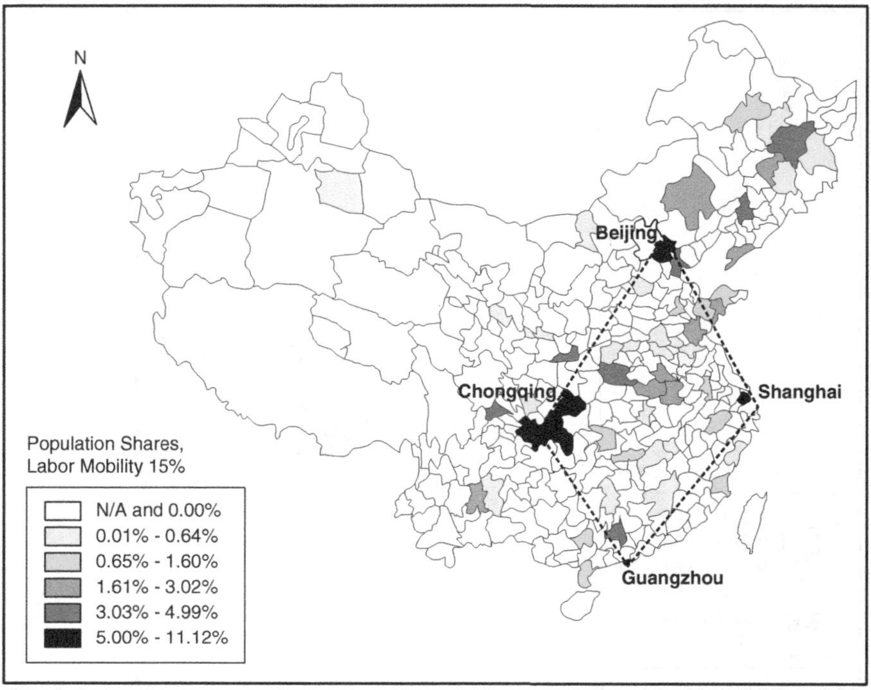

Figure 4.6 China's economic geography: relaxing *hukou*

Source: Bosker et al. (2012); compare with Figure 4.5 for changes.

workers and firms alike. The simulation is consistent with the findings of Zhang and Zhao (2013), who note that the four cities named in Figure 4.6 are also today's top four migration destinations in China.

The case illustrated in Figure 4.6 is of course an extreme scenario; migration barriers are small. In practice, the relaxation of the *hukou* system will take place more gradually. This can be modelled by allowing for decreasing migration thresholds in variants of Equation 4.1. Instead of a 15% real wage threshold one can use a smaller real wage threshold of 10%, which results in even stronger agglomeration because migration is easier (only 23 of the initial 264 prefecture cities survive). For a larger threshold of 20% the number of surviving cities is larger (120 to be precise).

What have we learned by applying a geographical economics model that is calibrated on the actual Chinese situation in 2000? The *hukou* system has a strong impact on the distribution of economic activity. Relaxing the restrictions results in strong agglomeration. The reason is – according to this type of model – that agglomerations that are initially already large offer agglomeration rents that makes them more attractive. Allowing migration makes these markets even larger and offers (local) consumers and firms further agglomeration rents. A limit to this process could be that congestion effects become stronger in large cities; however, there is a limit to city growth.

4.7 Conclusions

Even a casual look at maps reveals that economic activity is unevenly distributed over space. Neo-classical models cannot explain these characteristics. Constant returns to scale imply that production can become small without affecting the price of goods. In the presence of transportation costs, concentration is not required; one can produce all goods necessary in one's own backyard (this is why these models describe, what is sometimes called, backyard capitalism).

Modern theoretical developments summarized under the name 'geographical economics', can explain why uneven spatial distributions of economic activity can be an equilibrium outcome. Key characteristics of these models are imperfect competition, labour mobility and transportation costs. If certain locations offer high(er) real wages, workers will relocate to those locations. Real wages are higher in larger agglomerations because they have large local markets – so firms and consumers can avoid paying transport costs – and can supply more peripheral regions from there. In this way, large agglomerations benefit from agglomeration rents. Some of the key characteristics of this model are explained by using a stylized example that already shows what type of equilibria are possible and illustrates some of the characteristics of these equilibria.

These theoretical models can be applied to real world situations. The case of China is interesting because the Chinese government is restricting migration by using a system of internal visas, the so-called *hukou* system. One of the consequences is that migration to cities is relatively difficult for those workers that do not have the correct visa for a particular city. Recently the Chinese government is making this system more liberal. What could happen to China is answered by a scenario analysis.

The main findings show that a slackening of the restrictions on labour mobility will lead to more pronounced core-periphery outcomes. In the resulting more uneven city-size distribution, Beijing, Shanghai, Guangzhou and Chongqing will further strengthen their dominant position in the Chinese urban hierarchy. However, besides these 'Big Four', other cities remain as well. Two groups of cities can be distinguished: those in the populous heartland of China offering preferential access to China's internal market, and several more peripheral cities that survive because their distance from China's main population centres shields them from competition with China's largest population centres.

Notes

1 Steven Brakman: Faculty of Economics and Business, University of Groningen, The Netherlands, PO Box 800, 9700AV, Groningen, The Netherlands; s.brakman@rug.nl. I would like to thank Charles van Marrewijk for useful comments and suggestions and the construction of some graphs.
2 This example is taken from Brakman et al. (2009).
3 See for a detailed derivation Brakman et al. (2009).
4 This section is based on van Marrewijk (2017, Chapter 16).
5 For an instructive account of the *hukou* system see http://chunzhu.wordpress.com/2008/04/22/understanding-the-hukou-system/.
6 This section is based on Bosker et al. (2012).

References

Au, C.-C., and J. V. Henderson (2006a), "Are Chinese Cities Too Small?" *Review of Economic Studies* 73: 549–576.

Au, C.-C., and J. V. Henderson (2006b), "How Migration Restrictions Limit Agglomeration and Productivity in China," *Journal of Development Economics* 80: 350–388.

Bosker, M., S. Brakman, H. Garretsen, and M. Schramm (2012), "Relaxing Hukou: Increased Labor Mobility and China's Economic Geography," *Journal of Urban Economics* 72: 252–266.

Brakman, S., H. Garretsen, and C. van Marrewijk (2009), *The New Introduction to Geographical Economics*, Cambridge: Cambridge University Press.

Brakman, S., H. Garretsen, and C. van Marrewijk (2016), "Urban Development in China," *Cambridge Journal of Regions, Economy, and Society* 9: 467–477.

Brakman, S., H. Garretsen, and Z. Zhao (2017), "Spatial Concentration of Manufacturing Firms in China." *Papers in Regional Science* 179–205.

Chan, K. W. (2009), "The Chinese *Hukou* System at 50," *Eurasian Geography and Economics* 50(2): 197–221.

Chan, K.-W., and W. Buckingham (2008), "Is China Abolishing the Hukou System?" *The China Quarterly* 195: 582–606.

Chandler, T. (1987), *Four Thousand Years of Urban Growth: An Historical Census*, St. David's University Press.

Fujita M., T. Mori, J. V. Henderson, and Y. Kanemoto (2004), "Spatial Distribution of Economic Activities in Japan and China," in: J. V. Henderson and J.-F. Thisse (eds.), *Handbook of Regional and Urban Economics, volume IV*, North Holland, Amsterdam: Elsevier, pp. 2911–2980.

Krugman, P. R. (1991), "Increasing Returns and Economic Geography," *Journal of Political Economy* 99: 483–499.

Marrewijk, C. van (2017), *International Trade*, Oxford: Oxford University Press.

Stelder, D. (2005), "A Geographical Agglomeration Model for Europe," *Journal of Regional Science* 657–679.

Zhao, Z. (2005), "Migration, Labor Market Flexibility, and Wage Determination in China: A Review," *The Developing Economies* 43: 285–312.

Zhang, J., and Z. Zhao (2013), "Measuring the Income-Distance Tradeoff for Rural-Urban Migrants in China," IZA Discussion Papers 7160, Institute for the Study of Labour (IZA).

5 Industrialisation, urbanisation and migration in China

Charles van Marrewijk[1]

5.1 Introduction

After analysing the general links between geography, location, and the economy in Chapter 4, this chapter looks more closely at the relationships between industrialisation, urbanisation, and migration. To do so, we start in section 5.2 with a general overview in 2016 for all countries in the world of the connections between economic development and the share of income generated in agriculture (falling), services (rising), and industrialisation (first rising then falling). We continue in section 5.3 with an analysis over time in the period 1970–2016 of structural changes in China and India. These two countries are similar in size (in terms of population) and had a similar initial level of income per capita. Moreover, both countries embarked on a process of rapid economic development during this time period. We will see that the relative peak in industrialisation occurred in 2006 in both countries, but at a much higher level in China than in India. This is indicative of the difference in economic development strategies.

The remainder of the chapter focuses on the role of industrialisation and associated migration flows in economic development. We start in section 5.4 with a general overview of urban development in history, followed in section 5.5 with more recent (since 1960) urban development for the world as a whole. We continue in section 5.6 with an analysis of the link between urbanisation and income per capita of the world as a whole and a discussion of the changes over time in this respect in China. Section 5.7 concludes with a brief discussion of the size, direction, and structure of rural-urban migration flows, also regarding wage inequality. Section 5.8 concludes.

5.2 Economic development and structural change

During the rapid expansion of the Chinese economy after the Economic Reform process started in 1978 (see Chapter 3), the structure of the economy also changed (see Chapter 2). Countries are, of course, always adjusting the structure of the economy in response to changes at home and in the rest of the world. During periods of rapid economic development these changes are faster and more fundamental. At a highly aggregated level we can distinguish three main types of economic activities: agriculture, industry (or manufacturing), and services. We illustrate changes at this level of aggregation in two steps. First (in this section), we provide a cross-section analysis of the level of economic development and the structure of the economy in 2016. Second (in section 5.3), we analyse changes over time since 1960 for a selection of countries.

For the cross-section analysis in this section, we gathered information from the World Bank Development Indicators online in 2016 regarding the share (in percent) of income (value added) created in agriculture, industry, and services for all countries (see also van Marrewijk, 2017).[2] The sum of these shares is, of course, equal to 100% for each country. As a proxy for the level of economic development we use income per capita, corrected for price differences (GNI PPP in current international dollars using a log scale). As a visual indicator for the importance of a country we use the size of the population. The analysis in this section is based on information from 170 countries, together accounting for almost 7.2 billion people, or 97% of the world population. This includes the countries of the European Union (EU) separately. However, for ease of reference, we also include and identify the EU average in Figures 5.1–5.3. In addition, we identify the three main countries in terms of total population, namely China, India, and the US. Taken together, these four observations account for more than 3.5 billion people, or 49% of the total population included in the figures (48% of the world population).

For thousands of years, most people used to work in agriculture in a struggle to put enough food on the table to feed the family. By 2016, however, the population-weighted average share of agriculture in total income has fallen to 12.6%. The share of agriculture is above 50% for Sierra Leone (59.4%, income per capita US$ 1320) and Tchad (50.1%, income per capita US$ 1950). The share of agriculture is below 0.1% for Singapore (0.0%, income per capita US$ 85,020) and Hong Kong (0.1%, income per capita US$ 60,090). These examples suggest that the share of income generated in agriculture falls as the income level rises. Figure 5.1 shows that this is indeed quite generally the case by using a scatter diagram with bubbles proportional to a country's population level. The dashed line in the figure is a regression line. It has a slope of −8.593 and explains 68.7% in the variation of the share of income generated in agriculture. This means that if the income per capita level rises by 10%, then the share of income generated in agriculture falls by about 8.6 percentage points. The figure shows that India, China, and the EU are close to the regression line. The share of income generated in agriculture for these countries is therefore about equal to what you should expect based on their level of economic development. For the US this share is a little bit higher (1.1%) simply because it cannot be negative, as the regression line would predict based on the high level of income per capita in the US (see also later in this section).[3]

We now move to the relationship between economic development and the share of income generated in the services sector. It is clear from Figure 5.2 that nowadays (in 2016) services are the most important component of production as the population-weighted average share of services is more than 57%. The share of services in output is below 36% for Sierra Leone (33.7%) and Tchad (35.1%).

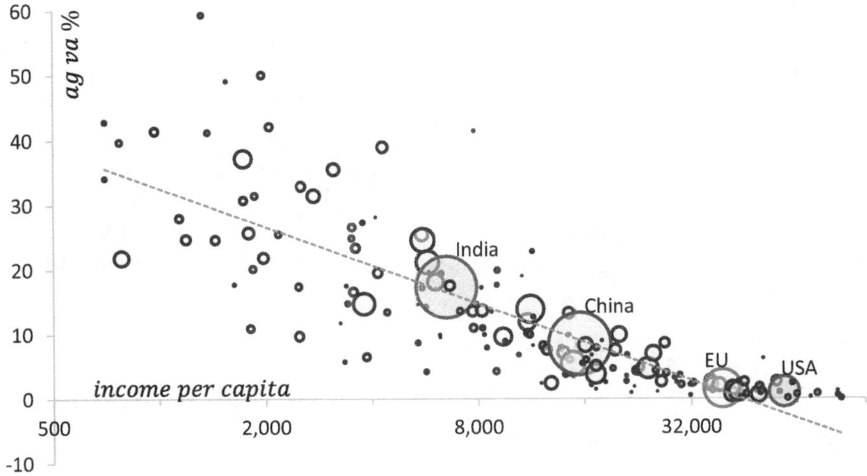

Figure 5.1 Agriculture value added (% of GDP) and economic development, 2016

Source: Created using World Bank Development Indicators Online data; income is GNI per capita PPP (current international dollars); ag va % = agriculture value added (% of GDP); bubbles proportional to size of population; data in 2015 is used if 2016 is not available; 170 countries plus EU included; dashed line is a regression line.

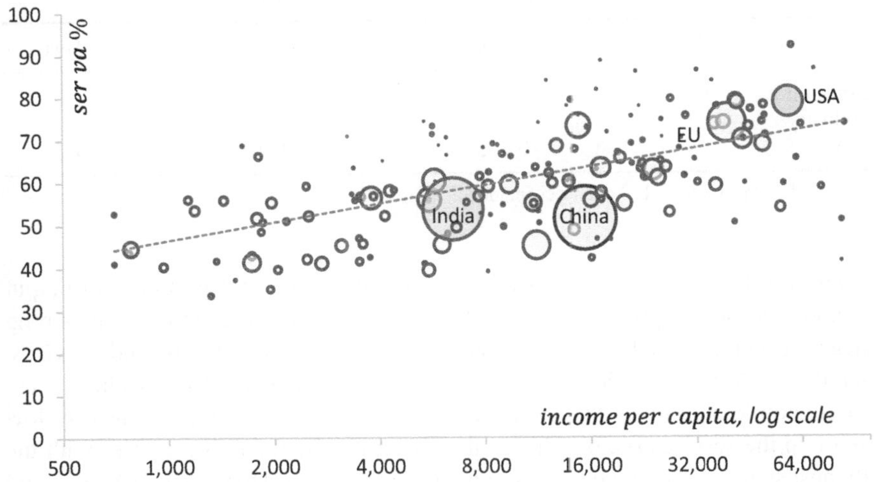

Figure 5.2 Services value added (% of GDP) and economic development, 2016

Source: Created using World Bank Development Indicators Online data; income is GNI per capita PPP (current international dollars ser va % = services, etc. value added (% of GDP); bubbles proportional to size of population; data in 2015 is used if 2016 is not available; 170 countries plus EU included; dashed line is a regression line.

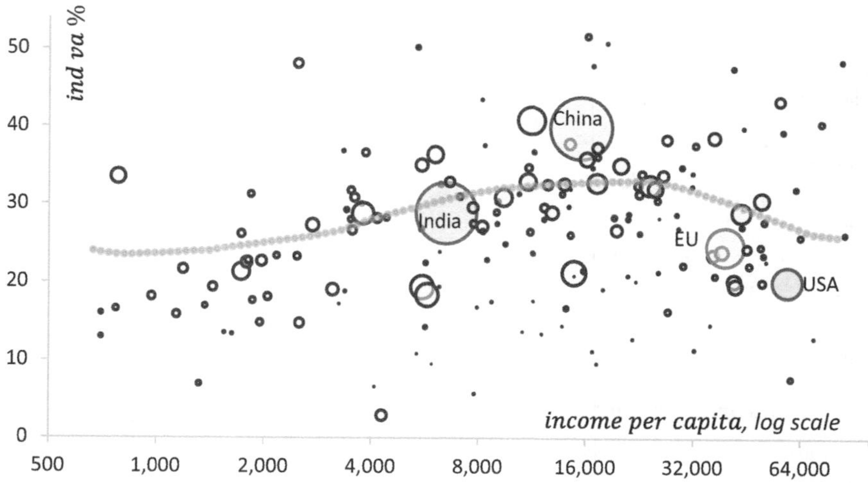

Figure 5.3 Industry value added (% of GDP) and economic development, 2016

Source: Created using World Bank Development Indicators Online data; income is GNI per capita PPP (current international dollars); ser va % = services value added (% of GDP); bubbles proportional to population; data in 2015 is used if 2016 is not available; 170 countries plus EU included; dotted line is smoothed (Technical Note 5.1).

Table 5.1 Correlation between value added shares of GDP, 2016

Component of GDP	*Agriculture*	*Industry*	*Services*
Agriculture	1		
Industry	−0.378	1	
Services	−0.675	−0.428	1

Source: See this section; 170 countries included.

These are the same two countries for which the share of agriculture in output is above 50% (see previous figure). These examples are indicative of the strong negative correlation between the share of output in agriculture and services, namely −0.675 (see Table 5.1). In general, therefore, if a country has a high share of economic activity in the agricultural sector it tends to have a relatively low share in the services sector. This is also illustrated by the two countries with the highest share of output generated in the services sector: Hong Kong (92.2%) and Barbados (88.9%), where the share of output generated in agriculture is low (0.1% and 1.5%, respectively).

Since the share of output generated in agriculture is negatively related to economic development (see Figure 5.1) and negatively related to the share of output generated in services (see Table 5.1), we should expect the share of services to be positively related to the level of economic development. Figure 5.2 shows that this is indeed the case. The dashed line in the figure is again a regression line. It has a slope of 6.242 and explains 34.1% in the variation of the share of income generated in services. This means that if the income per capita level rises by 10%, then the share of income generated in services rises by about 6.2 percentage points. It also means that the connection between economic development and the share of output generated in services is less strong than for the share of output generated in agriculture (where the share of explained variance is twice as high). Figure 5.2 shows that, given its level of economic development, the share of output generated in the services sector is relatively low in China as this observation is located far below the regression line. The other main countries identified in the figure are much closer to this line, with India slightly below, the EU slightly above, and the US somewhat further above.

To conclude our analysis in this section, we continue with the relationship between economic development and the share of income generated in industry (or manufacturing). In this case, however, the relationship is more complicated. This is already clear by combining the information provided earlier with the information in Table 5.1. On the one hand, we see that the share of income in industry is negatively correlated with the share generated in agriculture (correlation coefficient −0.378), which (as we saw for services) would suggest that the relationship between economic development and the share of industry is *positive*. On the other hand, we see that the share of income in industry is also negatively correlated with the share generated in services (correlation coefficient −0.428); since the share in services is positively related to economic development, this suggest that the relationship between economic development and the share of industry is *negative*. Which part of these conflicting suggestions should we believe? Both suggestions are correct, as we will now explain.

The relationship between the share of income generated in industry and economic development is shown in Figure 5.3 using a bubble diagram. Instead of a regression line (as in Figures 5.1 and 5.2), we include a smoothed, population-weighted moving average line to indicate the link between the share of industry and economic development, see Technical Note 5.1 for details on how to construct this line. The reason for this is simple: a regression line would not do justice to the connection between industrialisation and economic development.[4] The smoothed line indicates that this relationship is non-monotonic. At the early stages of economic development, industrialisation tends to rise as the economy develops. This process reaches a peak of about 33% of GDP for income levels of about US$ 18,000 to US$ 25,000. For even higher income levels, industrialisation falls as the economy continues to develop. China clearly stands out in Figure 5.3 as a country with a high level of income generated in industry (40%) compared to its level of economic development. India, Europe, and the US are below the smoothed line, indicating that the share of income generated in industry is somewhat lower than expected, in particular for the US (20%).

5.3 Structural change in China and India

After the cross-section analysis in section 5.2, it is now time to analyse structural change in China over time. Such an analysis requires, of course, a proper benchmark for comparison purposes. At the end of this section, we will use developments relative to the world as a benchmark. We start this section, however, by evaluating Chinese developments relative to developments in India, the only other country in the world with a similarly sized population that has also witnessed a rapid transition process.

To get an indication of the speed of economic development in China and India, Figure 5.4 provides information on income per capita relative to the US (in percent) from 1970 to 2016. The 1970 starting year was chosen because income per capita levels are quite similar in India and China initially, namely around 5.2% of American income levels in the period 1970–1975, and it pre-dates the starting years of the economic reform process leading to rapid economic development in both countries. Regarding the latter, the Indian economic reform process, moving from autarkic policies to liberalisation, deregulation, privatisation, and reduced controls, started in the early 1990s, whereas the more impressive Chinese economic reform process ('more impressive' in terms of subsequent gains in economic growth) started earlier (in 1978). In terms of economic development (measured by income per capita) China has been ahead of India for about half a century. According to the Maddison Project data shown in Figure 5.4, China surpassed India in terms of income per capita in 1970.

The India average relative to the US for the period is 5.3%, rising from 5.3 in 1970 to 11.2 in 2016. As Figure 5.4 shows, Indian relative income is mostly declining initially, particularly from 1975 to 1985, and strictly rising since 1986. The low point for India is thus reached in 1985 (3.1%) and since then rises by 0.26 percentage points on average per year to reach 11.2% in 2016. The Indian

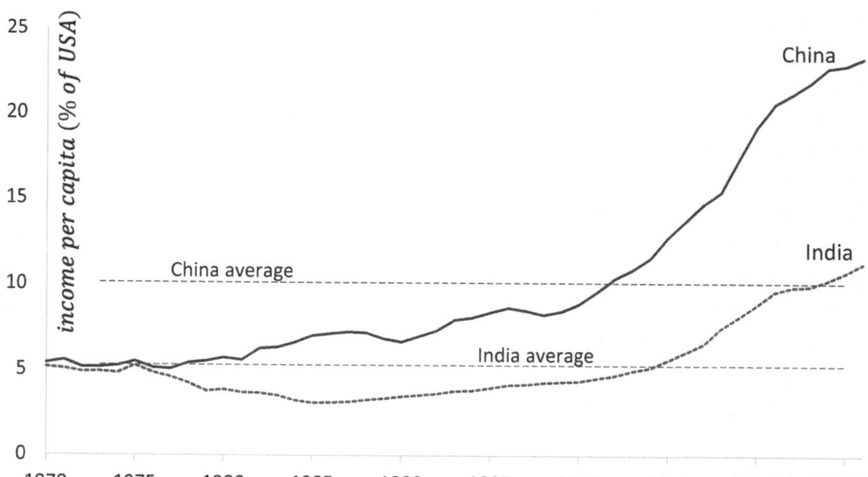

Figure 5.4 Income per capita in china and India relative to the US (%), 1970–2016

Source: Created using Maddison Project Database (2018); cgdppc relative to US (in percent) in relevant year.

economy has thus grown more rapidly than the American economy on a per capita basis for more than two decades. The China average for the period is 10.1%, rising from 5.4 in 1980 to 23.2 in 2016. Chinese relative income is stable initially and then rises rapidly. The low point for China is reached in 1977 (5.0%); since then Chinese relative income rises on average by 0.47 percentage points per year to reach 23.2% in 2016. Relative Chinese income is rising since 1977 for most years, except for the protest period 1988–1990 and during the Asian crisis in 1997–1998. The Chinese economy has thus grown more rapidly than the American economy on a per capita basis for about four decades.

Figure 5.5 illustrates the development of the share of income generated in agriculture (as a per cent of GDP) in China and India from 1970 to 2016. As we should expect based on our discussion in section 5.2 (see Figure 5.1), the importance of agriculture in total production is rapidly declining for both countries. Also in line with our expectations (since China is mostly economically more advanced than India), the importance of agriculture in total production is lower in China than in India (about 7.5 percentage points on average for the period as a whole). For India, the highest share of agriculture in total income is generated in 1973 (45%) and the lowest share in 2016 (17.4%). For China, the highest share of agriculture is generated in 1970 (35%) and the lowest share also in 2016 (8.6%).

Figure 5.6 illustrates the development of the share of income generated in services (as a percent of GDP) in China and India from 1970 to 2016. Based on our discussion in section 5.2 (see Figure 5.2), we expect the share of income generated in services to generally rise as an economy develops. This is the case in India, where the lowest point in the share of services is reached in 1973 (31.0%),

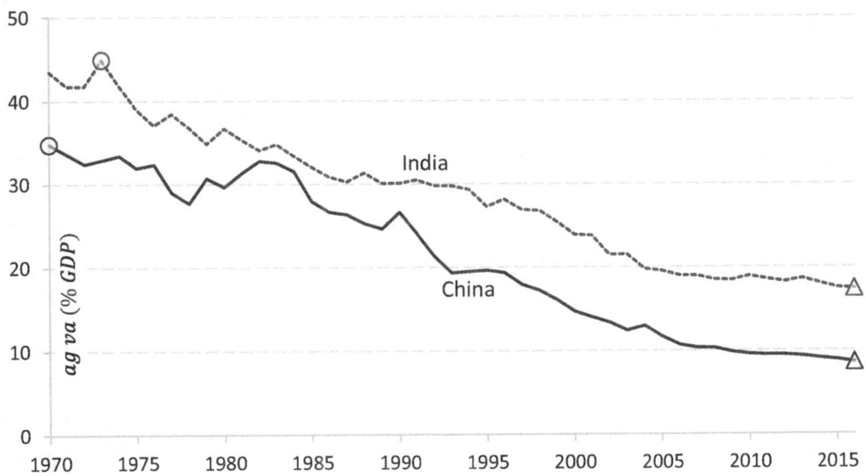

Figure 5.5 Agriculture value added in China and India; % of GDP, 1970–2016

Source: Created using World Bank Development Indicators Online data; circle = highest value; triangle = lowest value; ag va = agriculture value added; see main text for details.

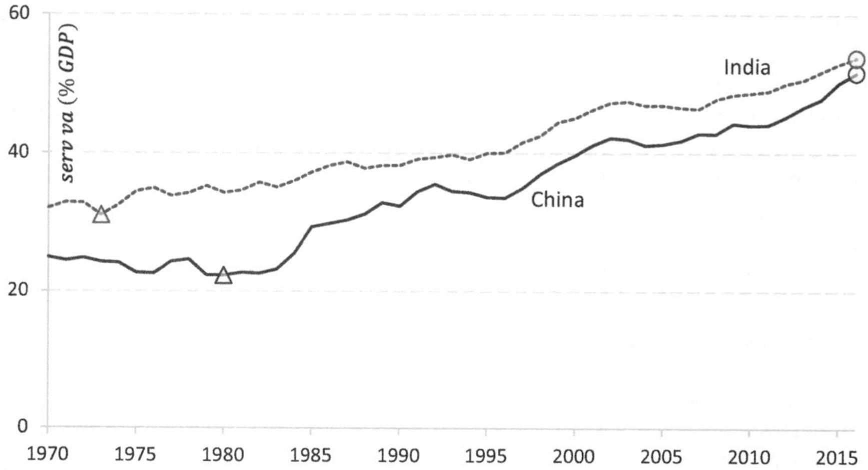

Figure 5.6 Services value added in China and India; % of GDP, 1970–2016

Source: Created using World Bank Development Indicators Online data; circle = highest value; triangle = lowest value; serv va = services value added; see main text for details.

while its highest point is reached in 2016 (53.8%) and the trendline in the share of services rises by about 0.4 percentage points per year. It is not the case initially in China, where the share of services is declining until 1980 (to reach 22.3%) because the share in industry is rising before it starts rise to the highest point (of 51.6%) in 2016. Since 1980, therefore, the share of services in income has been rising in China by about 0.8 percentage points per year, or about twice as fast as in India. Please note that the share of services generated in income is still lower in China than in India, although China is economically more advanced than India. Based on the discussion in section 5.2 we would expect the opposite ordering of the countries in this respect. This is a first indication of the different development strategies in the two countries, where the production and export of services (information technology services, business outsourcing services, and software workers) plays a more important role in India.

To conclude the first part of this section, Figure 5.7 provides an overview of the share of industry in value added (as a per cent of GDP) in China and India since 1970. It is, of course, the part not covered by the developments in agriculture and services in Figures 5.5 and 5.6 as the total shares must sum to 100%. Since China's share in agriculture *and* services is below that of India its share in industry must be higher. As indicated in Figure 5.7 this is indeed the case, and substantially so. China's average share of income generated in industry is about 45% in the period. This is substantially higher (15 percentage points, or about 50%) than the 30% average share generated in industry in India. Manufacturing activities have thus played a much more important part in China's development process than in

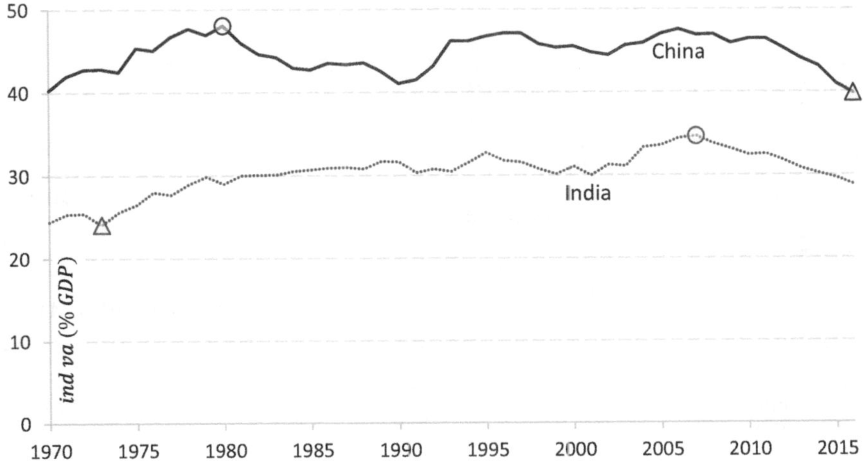

Figure 5.7 Industry value added in China and India; % of GDP, 1970–2016

Source: Created using World Bank Development Indicators Online data; circle = highest value; triangle = lowest value; ind va = industry value added; see main text for details.

India's. For both countries we observe a (weak) rise-and-decline process in the share of income generated in manufacturing, although at different relative scales and with China ahead of India. The lowest point of the share of income generated in industry in India is reached in 1973 (24.1 %) and the highest point in 2007 (34.7%). India's share in industry has been declining rapidly since the peak in 2007 (by almost 6 percentage points) to 28.8% in 2016. In China, in contrast, the share of income generated in industry seems to hover around the average of 45% for most of the period in Figure 5.7, although there is a clear rise at the beginning of the period (1970–1980) and a clear decline at the end (2011–2016). In line with this pattern, China's highest share of income generated in industry is in 1980 (48.1%) and its lowest share in 2016 (39.8%).

The previous discussion on the changes over time of the share of income generated in agriculture, services, and industry is insightful, but lacks a proper benchmark of performance relative to other countries and relative to the level of economic development. We conclude this section therefore with a discussion that does just that by measuring the degree of industrialisation relative to the world average and the level of economic development relative to the US (see Figure 5.8). Industrialisation is calculated as follows. First, we compute a population-weighted world average share of income generated in industry for all countries with data available in each year. Second, to smooth out small fluctuations over time, we calculate the five-year world moving average located at the end (so 2016 is the moving average over the years 2012–2016, and so on). Third, we determine a nation's degree of industrialisation relative to the world

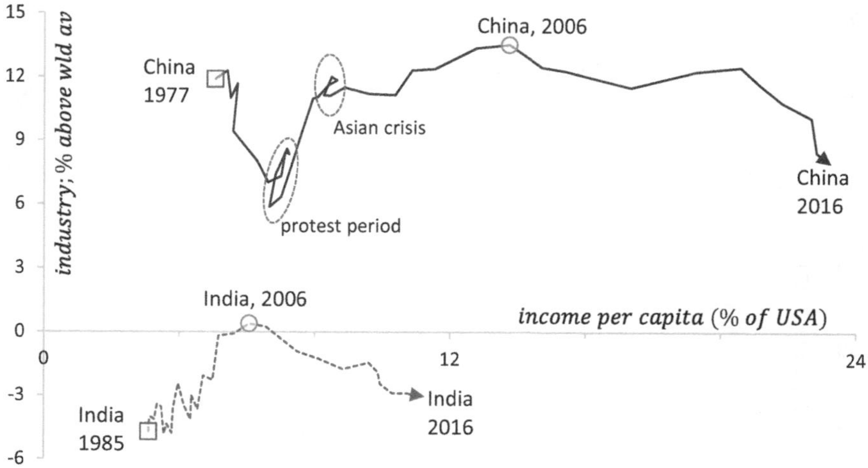

Figure 5.8 Industrialisation and economic development in China and India, 1970–2016

Source: Created using World Bank Development Indicators Online data and Maddison Project Database (2018); income per capita = cgdppc relative to US (in percent) in relevant year; wld av = world average; industry value added (% of GDP) in percentage points above the world five-year average for that year, see main text for details.

by calculating the share of income generated in industry minus the five-year world moving average. The level of economic development relative to the US was already discussed at the beginning of this section. For completeness, we also calculated the level of economic development relative to the world, which is available for a shorter time and leads to similar conclusions, see Technical Note 5.2.

Figure 5.8 shows the relationship between economic development (horizontal axis) and industrialisation (vertical axis) for China and India since 1970. To avoid cluttering the diagram, the observations start at the lowest level of income per capita relative to US in the 1970–2016 period, which is 1977 for China and 1985 for India. Since then relative economic development has been monotonically rising for India, so we move from left-to-right in the figure as time passes by for India. This is generally also the case in China, although there are brief periods of reverse movement as well, namely during the protest period (1988–1990) and the Asian crisis (1997–1998), as indicated in the figure. For India we observe a clear, but modest rise-and-decline movement in industrialisation, with a relative peak in 2006 of 0.4 percentage points above the world average. Industrialisation has thus played only a modest role in India's economic development process. For China we observe a similar, but much more pronounced rise-and-decline movement at a much higher level of industrialisation and a higher level of economic development from the end of the 1980s up to 2016. The relative peak in industrialisation in China is also in 2006, namely a remarkable 13.5 percentage points above the world average. Industrialisation has thus played a key role in China's economic development process and the country has been highly successful in this respect as it is closing the gap with the US at a much higher speed than India. To enable this industrialisation process, which largely occurred in big cities, a massive number of people moved from rural areas to the city. Before discussing this point in more detail, we start with an overview of urban development.

5.4 Urban development in history

Recent evidence shows that our Neanderthal ancestors were already engaged in human building projects as long as 175,000 years ago, when they created large mysterious cave structures about 300 metres from the cave entrance (Jaubert et al. 2016).[5] It is, of course, a long way to go from these early structures to something that we would now call a city. There is an ongoing debate about what constitutes a city (involving trade, self-sufficiency, and plumbing) and what is thus the world's oldest city, either continuously inhabited, or not (see Compton 2015, also for the discussion later). It is clear, however, that city development is related to the agricultural revolution, which started in the Fertile Crescent around 8500 BC. The oldest city is thus located somewhere in the Fertile Crescent. Familiar names are Damascus (Syria) and Jericho (Palestine), with early settlements dating as far back as 9000 BC (but not continuous settlements). Less familiar is Byblos (Lebanon), founded in 7000 BC, with continuous habitation since 5000 BC. Or possibly Aleppo (Syria), with settlement dating back only to 6000 BC, but evidence of wandering nomad domestic camps up to 5000 years earlier.

Another issue that creates occasional controversy is the question: what is the largest city in the world? Various sources arrive, of course, at slightly different answers, but we will base our review on the influential work of Chandler (1987), who uses a range of methods to estimate the size of a city and includes the surrounding suburban or urbanised area. Figure 5.9 illustrates the evolution of the size of the largest city for the past 5000 years using a log scale. Memphis (Egypt) was probably the largest city in 3000 BC, with a modest population (according to modern standards) of 30,000 inhabitants. Ur (Iraq) took over some 1000 years later with a population of around 65,000 people, followed by Babylon (Iraq) around 600 BC with 200,000 people.[6] Figure 5.9 shows that the size of the world's largest city started to rise particularly fast after 1200 AD. There are five Chinese cities in Figure 5.9, starting with Xi'an (or Chang'an, Shaanxi province), followed by Kaifeng (Henan province), Hangzhou (Zhejiang province), Nanjing (Jiangsu province), and Beijing. The latter was the first city to cross the one million threshold. Beijing was first replaced by London (the first city to reach five million), then by New York (the first city to reach 10 million), and ultimately by Tokyo (the first city to reach 20 million and 30 million).

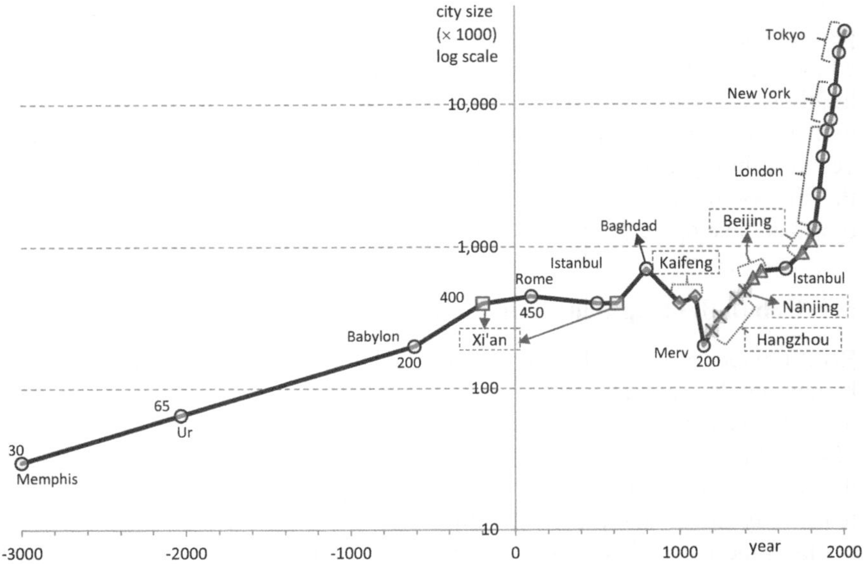

Figure 5.9 The world's largest city since 3000 BC

Source: Based on data from Chandler (1987), updated for Tokyo metropolis in 2015; Chinese cities in dotted boxes with larger text size and different markers; non-Chinese cities with circular markers.

5.5 Recent urban development

Today more than half of the world population lives in cities, but this is a relatively recent phenomenon. In 1960 about 34% of the world population lived in cities, rising to 53% in 2014 and crossing the 50% threshold only in 2011 (see Figure 5.10). As one might expect, there is a high positive correlation between the share of the rural population and the share of income or employment generated in agricultural activities. Since the latter is negatively correlated with general development levels (as measured by income), there is a positive correlation between income levels and urbanisation. This is illustrated in Figure 5.10 for the high-income OECD member countries, where the share of the urban population was 64% in 1960 (almost twice the world average), rising to 81% in 2014 (28 percentage points higher than the world average).

Figure 5.10 also depicts urbanisation developments in China and India, by far the two largest countries in terms of total population, and in Latin America (LAC) and Sub-Sahara Africa (SSA; referred to as Africa in the discussion later). In 1960 the degree of urbanisation was similar and substantially below the world average in China, India, and Africa, namely around 15–18%. It was substantially higher in 1960 in Latin America, about 45% (which is higher than the world average).

The developments over time are rather diverse. Latin America almost closes the gap with the OECD countries as the urban population share rises steadily to

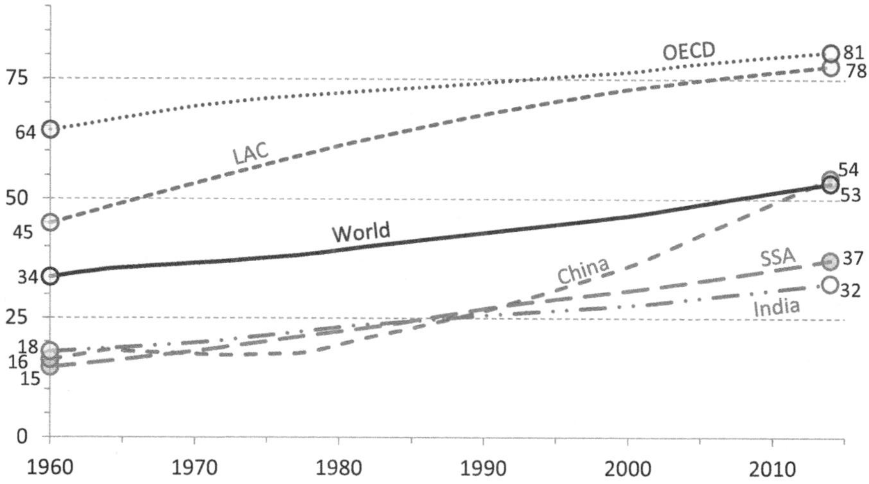

Figure 5.10 Urbanisation since 1960

Source: Based on data from World Development Indicators online; urbanisation: urban population (% of total); OECD = high income Organization for Economic Cooperation and Development countries; SSA = developing Sub-Sahara Africa; LAC = developing Latin America and Caribbean.

78% in 2014. In India the developments are stable: the urban population share rises steadily every year and reaches 32% in 2014. In Africa the urbanisation process is also relatively stable, but urbanisation is more rapid than in India: the urban population share more than doubles to 37% in 2014. The urbanisation rate is higher in Africa than in India from 1985 onwards. In China the developments are much more dramatic. Initially the urban population share rises from 1960 to 1964 (from 16.2 to 18.3%), but then it declines until 1972 (to 17.2%) and slowly crawls back until 1977 (to 17.5%). From 1979 on the urban population share starts to rise quickly (more than 0.7 percentage points per year) and even stronger from 1996 onward (more than 1.0 percentage points per year), reaching 54% in 2014 and surpassing the world average in 2013.

Figure 5.11 shows the impact on the absolute number of people living in cities (panel *a*) and in rural areas (panel *b*). For the high-income OECD countries, the urban population rose by 86% or 400 million people in the period 1960–2014 (from 463 to 863 million), while the rural population declined by 20% or 50 million people (from 257 to 207 million). A similar process is observed in Latin America, where the urban population rose rapidly from 80 to 408 million and the rural population is almost stagnant (a slight increase only of 19 million people). The Indian urban population also rose rapidly, by 420% or 339 million people (from 81 to 419 million). In contrast to the OECD countries and Latin America, however, the rural population also increased rapidly, by 137% or 507 million people (from 369 to 876 million). In absolute terms, the population increase in India

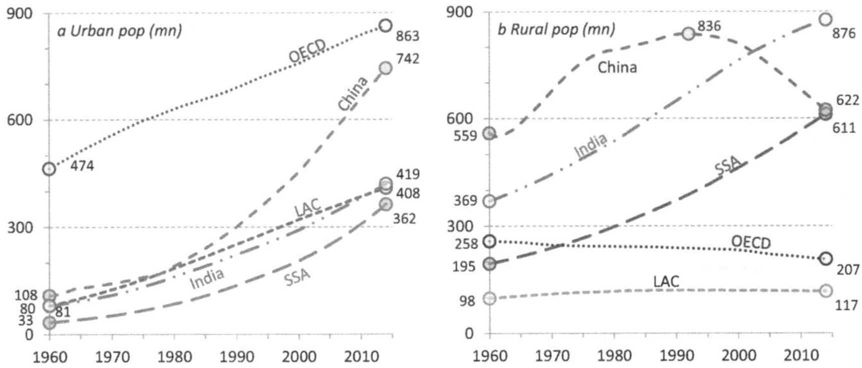

Figure 5.11 Urban and rural population since 1960, million

Source: See Figure 5.10.

is thus larger in the villages than in the cities. Similar observations hold for Africa, where the urban population rose by 329 million (about a 10-fold rise) and the rural population even more, namely by 416 million people (from 195 to 611 million). Together India and Africa are responsible for 69% of the worldwide increase in the rural population (of 1.4 billion people), while taking care of only 23% of the rise of the worldwide urban population (of 2.9 billion people).

China is responsible for the most spectacular urbanisation process, as it takes care of the largest urban population increase in this period, namely by 587% or 634 million people (from 108 to 742 million). The increase in the number of people living in Chinese cities is thus higher than the total population of the European Union in 2015 and about twice the population of the US in 2015. In the Chinese rural areas, the population increased only by 11% or 63 million people (from 559 to 622 million). Those numbers are distorted, however, by the fact that there was a peak of 836 million people in the Chinese rural population in 1991 (meaning an increase of 50% or 277 million people in the period 1960–1991) and a substantial decline since then (a fall of 26% or 215 million people in the period 1991–2014). Under the simple assumption that the Chinese population growth is the same in the cities and the rural areas, the implied migration flow from the villages towards the cities in China is 461 million people in the period 1960–2014.[7] If the population growth rate is higher in the rural areas, the implied migration flows are even larger.

5.6 Urbanisation and income per capita

As briefly suggested in section 5.5, the degree of urbanisation tends to go hand in hand with rising levels of income per capita. The World Bank collects information on urbanisation, income, and population. The degree of urbanisation is then measured as the share of the population living in urban areas.[8] The relationship between urbanisation and income per capita in 2016 is illustrated in Figure 5.12.

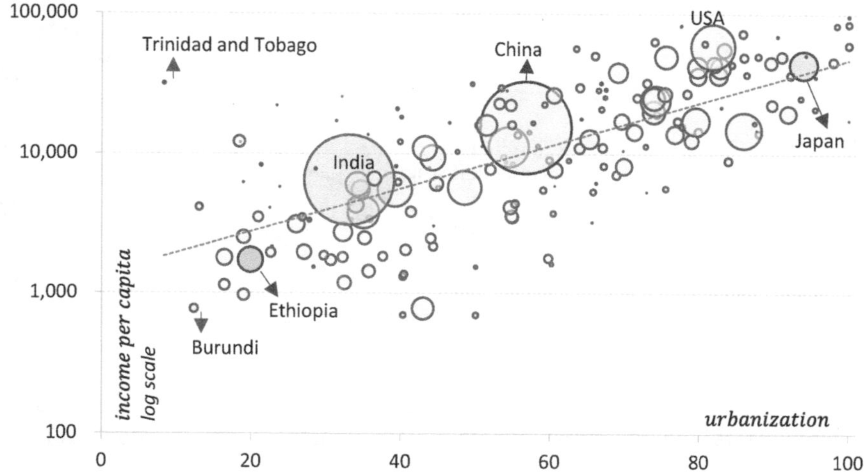

Figure 5.12 Urbanisation and income per capita, 2016

Source: Created using World Bank Development Indicators online; income per capita: GNI PPP (current international dollar); urbanisation: urban population (% of total); bubbles proportional to size of population; 180 countries included.

The lowest degree of urbanisation (8.4%) is reached in Trinidad and Tobago, with a fairly high level of income per capita (US$ 31,770) and a small population (1.4 million). The second-lowest degree of urbanisation (12.4%) is reached in Burundi, with a low level of income per capita (US$ 770) and a population of 10.5 million. The lowest urbanisation rate (19.9%) for the first 'sizeable' country (above 100 million people) is Ethiopia, with a low-income level of US$ 1,730.

There are four countries in Figure 5.12 with 100 per cent of the population living in cities, namely Nauru, Hong Kong, Singapore, and Macao. The average population for these four countries is 3.4 million and the population-weighted average income level is US$ 72,000.[9] The first 'sizeable' country with a high urbanisation rate (93.9%) is Japan, with an income level of US$ 43,540 per capita.

The previous examples suggest that highly urbanised countries tend to have higher levels of income per capita. Using recent data for 180 countries, Figure 5.12 shows that this is indeed the case. Examples of large countries identified in the figure are: India (population 1,324 million, urbanisation 33.1%, and income per capita of US$ 6,490), China (population 1,379 million, urbanisation of 56.8%, and income per capita of US$ 15,470), and the US (population 323 million, urbanisation 81.8%, and income per capita of US$ 58,700). The regression line in Figure 5.12 suggests that a one percentage point higher degree of urbanisation is associated with about 3.55% higher income per capita levels. The line explains about 49% of the variation in log income per capita.

We conclude this section with a brief discussion of economic development in China and urbanisation. To do so, we measure income per capita in China as a per cent of the US in that year using the Maddison Project data (see section 5.3) and

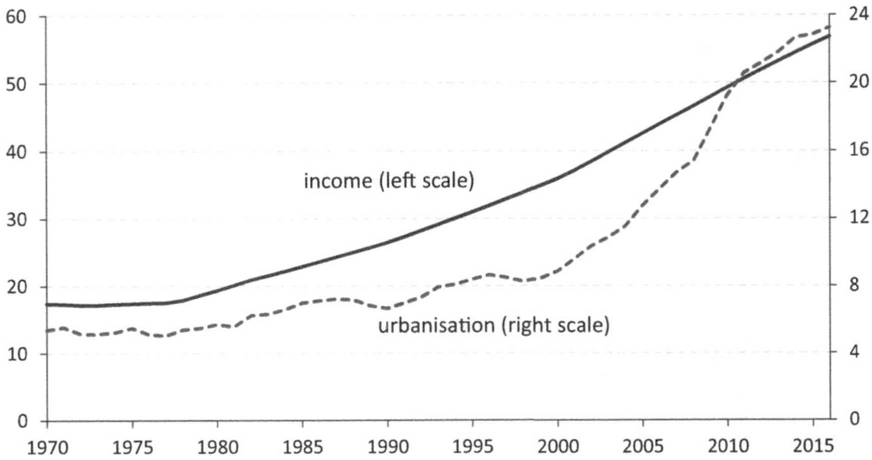

Figure 5.13 Urbanisation and income per capita in China (relative to US), 1970–2016

Source: Created using World Bank Online data for urbanisation (urban population, % of total) and Maddison Project Database (2018) for income per capita (cgdppc as % of US in relevant year).

urbanisation using the World Bank data (urban population as a percent of the total population). The results for the period 1970–2016 are provided in Figure 5.13. There is a clear positive association between urbanisation and economic development in China in this period. Initially, in the period 1970–1978, urbanisation fluctuates around 17.4% and income per capita around 5.3% of that in the US. From 1978 onwards, at the start of the Economic Reforms, relative income per capita starts to rise from 5.4% of the US in 1978 to 23.2% in 2016. At the same time the degree of urbanisation also starts to rise (with some fluctuations) from 17.9% in 1978 to 56.8% in 2016. Associated with the rapid development process in China is thus an equally impressive process of rapid urbanisation to facilitate the development process. The urbanisation process, in turn, required a massive movement of people from rural areas to the city, as the next section analyses.

5.7 Labour migration

We indicated in section 5.5 that there has been an enormous migration of people in China from rural areas to the city. We argued in section 5.6 that urbanisation and economic development go hand in hand, such that the migration flows which enabled the urbanisation process were necessary for China's economic development process. In general, people mainly migrate for one of two reasons. In China there is a third aspect to take into consideration.

- First, fighting and other violence associated with (civil) war, persecution of minorities, drugs trade, and so on may force people to leave their homes and seek safety and shelter elsewhere. This type of migration is low in China.

- Second, there may be differences in the reward to specific types of labour in different locations. This creates an incentive for people to migrate from locations with low real wages to locations with high real wages. Almost all labour migration in China is of this type.
- Third, there is a China-specific aspect to take into consideration in our discussion, namely the household registration system known as *hukou* which limits labour mobility.[10]

Before the Economic Reform process started in 1978 there was hardly any migration from rural areas to the city since the strict state control of necessities (jobs, food & clothing, housing, and medical care) simply did not make it possible. The first relaxation in 1980 immediately led to people from the countryside searching for jobs in nearby cities; this was largely intra-provincial migration (Chen 2012). Labour migration flows increased more rapidly and became more inter-provincial at the end of the 1980s and early 1990s. Large flows of low skilled migrants (see Table 5.2) were attracted to jobs for the export-oriented sectors along the east coast, in particular to the Pearl River Delta (Shenzhen, Guangzhou [or Canton], and neighbouring cities near Hong Kong) and the Yang Tze River Delta (Shanghai and surrounding cities). Therefore, the share of inter-provincial migrants was larger than the share of intra-provincial migrants in the period 2000–2010.

In the new millennium, the proportion of migrants going to the Pearl River Delta and the Yang Tze River Delta has been declining, such that the share of intra-provincial migrants exceeds the inter-provincial migrants again since 2015. Su et al. (2018) analyse the driving forces for rural-urban migration and find that (p. 142): 'higher wage differentials, larger population size, higher GDP per capita, and faster employment growth are the attributes of a city that attract rural-to-urban migrants.' They also find that moving from one province to another province (inter-provincial migration) has a strong deterring effect on migration (like the border effect of trade flows), related to differences in culture, institutional barriers, and dialect.

Using data collected for 20 major Chinese cities in 2005, Han and Li (2017) analyse in detail the impact of labour migration on the wage structure in urban China. Keeping in mind that the workers migrate from the rural areas to the city

Table 5.2 Characteristics of residents and migrant workers; 20 cities, 2005

Characteristic	*Residents*	*Migrants*
Wage per month (RMB)	1609	978
Education		
• College and above (%)	35.9	1.9
• Highschool (%)	56.5	74.4
• Dropouts and below (%)	7.6	23.7
Average age	37.2	30.4

Source: Simple average of Table 5.1.b and 5.1.c, see Han and Li (2017).

to earn higher wages, it is remarkable how much lower the wages they earn in the cities is compared to the wages earned by residents (see Figure 5.14). In 2005 residents earn on average the highest wages in Shenzhen, namely 3252 RMB per month. This is much higher (167%) than the 1216 RMB per month migrant workers earn on average in Shenzhen. Similar observations hold for all 20 cities included in the figure: the average wage for residents is 65% higher than for migrants (1609 vs 978 RMB per month, see Table 5.2). The lowest resident mark-up is 25% in Shaoxing, followed by 31% in Tianjin. The highest resident mark-up is 167% in Shenzhen, followed by 100% in Beijing. The proportion of migrants in the workforce varies considerably between cities, ranging from 9% in Jinan to 65% in Shenzhen. The resident mark-up in monthly wages is highly correlated with the share of migrants in the workforce (correlation coefficient is 0.80). All of this can be taken as an indication that *hukou* restrictions are still important today.

Chapter 4 explains, using simulations in a geographical economics model, how lower restrictions on the *hukou* system, which eases labour mobility, allows firms and workers to go to places that offer higher wages (workers) or better market access (firms). The urbanisation characteristics described earlier fit into this picture. But there is more. Brakman et al. (2017) show that the relaxation of the *hukou* system leads to more agglomeration of firms. Specifically, they find that localisation tendencies are stronger for private firms and foreign owned firms. In

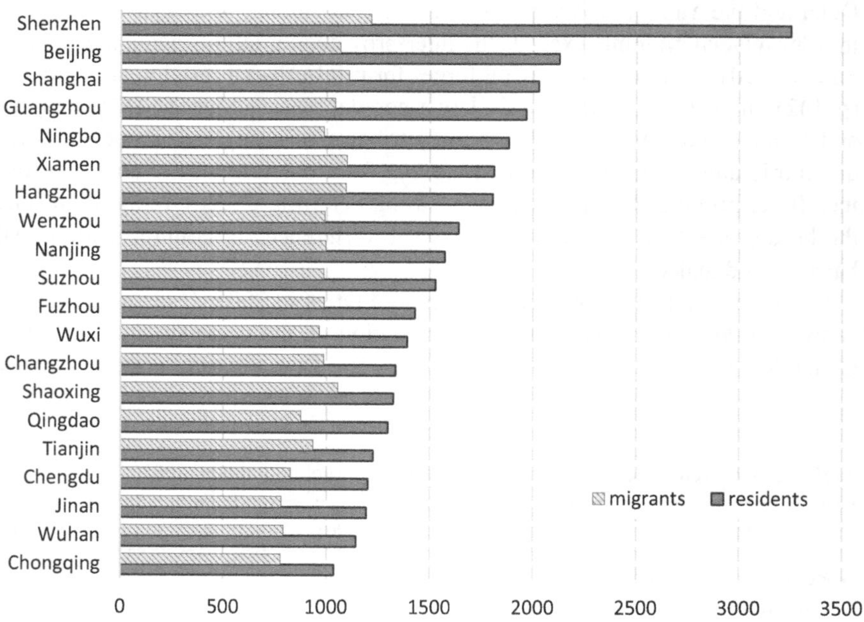

Figure 5.14 Monthly wages for residents and migrants; 20 cities, 2005

Source: Created using data from Han and Li (2017); average wage in RMB per month, ordered by wage of residents.

contrast, state- and collectively owned manufacturing firms are more dispersed. This indicates that once market forces are allowed to work, agglomeration takes place. In addition, Brakman et al. (2018), find that this process is accompanied by the sorting of high-skilled workers in skill-intensive industries, which explains the higher wages in the bigger cities.

When comparing the monthly wages in the 20 cities, we obviously must take labour characteristics into consideration as the migrant workers are younger and have on average much lower education levels (see Table 5.2). In a detailed analysis taking these differences into consideration, Han and Li (2017) show that there is a substantial residual effect of migration on inequality, which is related to the share of migrants. Migration has widened urban wage dispersion and increased the education premium. Job segregation and the low elasticity of substitution in jobs between migrants and residents due to *hukou* restrictions is therefore important for understanding Chinese urban labour markets.

5.8 Conclusions

We analysed the role of industrialisation and urbanisation in the economic development process of China. In general, the share of income generated in agriculture falls and the share generated in services rises as an economy develops successfully, whereas the share of income generated in industry first rises and then falls again. Although this is also the case in China, the role of industrialisation is much more important, and the role of services is less important than we would expect based on China's level of economic development in the past three decades. The peak of China's industrialisation process (relative to the world) occurred in 2006. Since then it has been declining fairly fast (and the share of services rising), bringing the structure of the Chinese economy more in line with its level of economic development.

Economic development goes hand in hand with urbanisation. To enable China's rapid economic development process therefore required equally rapid urbanisation and thus a massive flow of people from rural areas to the city. This process started in the early 1980s with the first relaxations of the *hukou* system and initially focused on intra-provincial migration. Towards the end of the 1980s and during the 1990s inter-provincial migration became more important. In recent years, intra-provincial migration dominates again. Empirical analyses show that *hukou* restrictions are still important for explaining rising wage dispersion and residual inequality (see also Chapter 10).

5.8.1 Technical note 5.1: smoothed population-weighted average

The dotted line in Figure 5.3 is constructed as follows. Let $J = \{1,..,170\}$ be the set of countries (this excludes the EU average) and let $\bar{y}$ be some level of income per capita. For $\ln(\bar{y}) = 6$ to 11.6 in steps of 0.05, determine the population-weighted average share of industry value added (in percent) for all countries $j \in J$ such that $abs\left(\ln(y_j) - \ln(\bar{y})\right) < 1$, where y_j is country j's level of income per capita.[11] The dotted line smooths the points (by taking the 21-point moving average) generated by this procedure and thus calculates a population-weighted average in the neighbourhood of $\bar{y}$). For reference, Figure 5.15 shows the results of a similar procedure for the share of agriculture and services value added as a percent of GDP. These dotted lines are reasonably close to the regression lines of Figures 5.1 and 5.2.

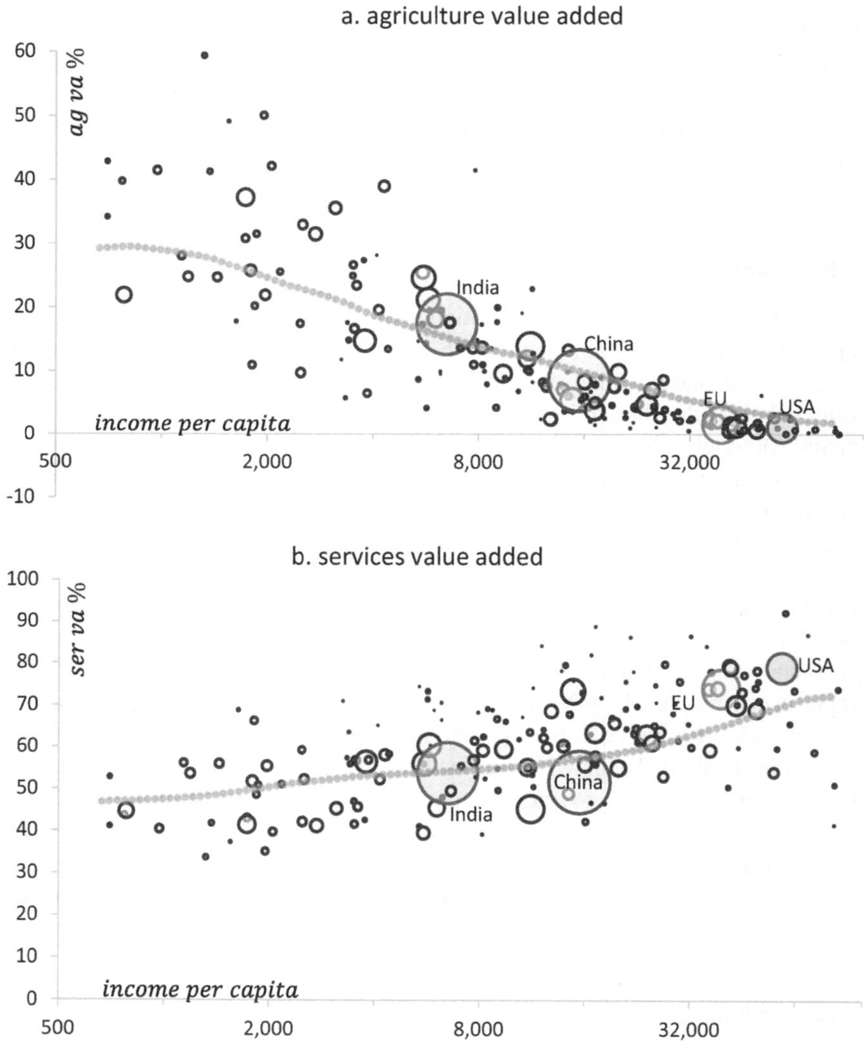

Figure 5.15 Agriculture and services value added (% of GDP) and economic development, 2016

Source: See Figure 5.2, and the explanation in Technical Note 5.1.

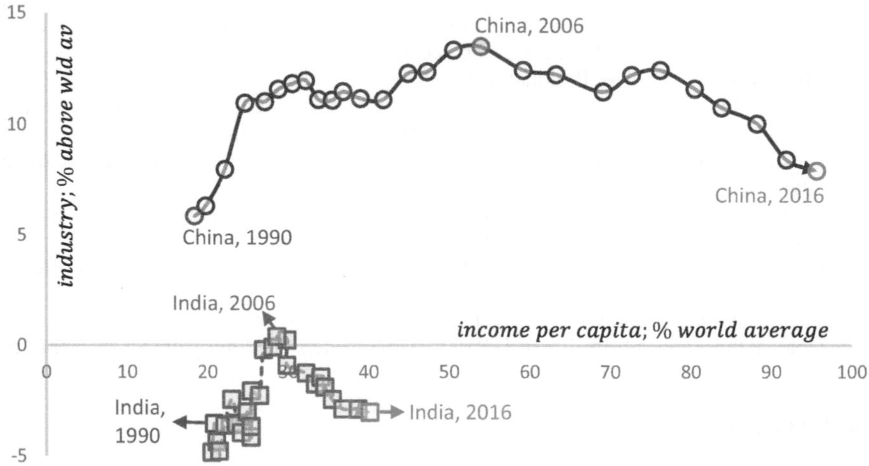

Figure 5.16 Industrialisation and economic development in China and India, 1990–2016

Source: Created using World Bank Development Indicators Online data; income is GNI per capita PPP (in current international dollars) as a percent of the world average in the relevant year; wld av = world average; industry value added (% of GDP) in percentage points above the world average for that year, see main text for details.

5.8.2 Technical note 5.2: industrialisation and economic development relative to the world

Section 5.3 analyses industrialisation relative to the world average and economic development relative to the US in the period 1970–2016. Alternatively, we can measure economic development relative to the world average instead of the US. To do so, we use income per capita corrected for purchasing power parity relative to the world average in the relevant year. Unfortunately, these data are only available since 1990. Figure 5.16 therefore shows the relative developments in the 1990–2016 period. The general pattern and major conclusions are like those discussed in Section 5.3 based on Figure 5.8.

Notes

1 Utrecht University School of Economics, Adam Smith Hall 2.10, Kriekenpitplein 21–22, 3584 EC, Utrecht, The Netherlands. Telephone: *31 30 253 7109. Email: j.g.m.vanmarrewijk@uu.nl. I thank Steven Brakman for useful comments and suggestions. Any errors are my own.
2 Information on the share of employment in agriculture, industry, and services is less widely available.
3 The regression line 'predicts' zero per cent income generated in agriculture at an income level per capita of about US$ 44,600 (GNI PPP, current international dollars) in 2016. There are 18 countries in the figure with a higher income level.

4 The regression line is almost horizontal and explains only 8% of the variance in industrialisation. In contrast, using a similar smoothed line procedure for the share of income generated in agriculture and services gives results quite like the regression lines of Figure 5.1 and Figure 5.2, see Technical Note 5.1.
5 This section is based on Brakman et al. (2016).
6 We are skipping a few cities in the first 2000 years of Figure 5.9 that took over the 'largest city' banner, but without clear information on the number of inhabitants.
7 This includes 'migration' of people for villages that pass the threshold of becoming a city.
8 Data is provided by national statistical offices (with varying definitions of urban areas), but collected and smoothed by the UN Population Division.
9 Lowest income is for Nauru (US$ 17,510 per capita) which has a population of only 10,000 people.
10 The discussion is based on Su et al. (2018), and see also chapter 4.
11 Note: $\overline{y}$ thus ranges from 403 to 109,089, rising in steps of slightly above 5% per step.

References

Brakman, S., H. Garretsen, and C. van Marrewijk (2016), "Urban Development in China," *Cambridge Journal of Regions, Economy, and Society* 9: 467–477.

Brakman, S., H. Garretsen, and Z. Zhao (2017), "Spatial Concentration of Manufacturing Firms in China," *Papers in Regional Science* 179–205.

Brakman, S., S. Hu, and C. van Marrewijk (2018), "Urban Development in China: On the Sorting of Skills," mimeo Available at: earlier version: www.cesifo-group.de/DocDL/cesifo1_wp5028.pdf.

Chandler, T. (1987), *Four Thousand Years of Urban Growth: An Historical Census*, Lewiston: Edwin Mellen Press.

Chen, Y. P. (2012), "Land Use Rights, Market Transitions, and Labour Policy Change in China (1980–84)," *Economics of Transition* 20(4): 705–743.

Compton, N. (2015), "What is the Oldest City in the World?," *The Guardian*, 16 February.

Han, J., and S. Li (2017), "Internal Migration and External Benefit: The Impact of Labor Migration on the Wage Structure in Urban China," *China Economic Review* 46: 67–86.

Jaubert, J., S. Verheyden, D. Genty, M. Soulier, H. Cheng, D. Blamart, C. Burlet, H. Camus, S. Delaby, D. Deldicque, R. L. Edwards, C. Ferrier, F. Lacrampe-Cuyaubère, F. Lévêque, F. Maksud, P. Mora, X. Muth, É. Régnier, J.-N. Rouzaud, and F. Santos (2016), "Early Neanderthal Constructions Deep in Bruniquel Cave in Southwestern France," *Nature* 435: 111–115.

Marrewijk, C. van (2017), *International Trade*, Oxford: Oxford University Press.

Su, Y., P. Tesfazion, and Z. Zhao (2018), "Where are the Migrants From? Inter- vs Intra-provincial Rural-urban Migration in China," *China Economic Review* 47: 142–155.

6 International trade and supply chains

Nimesh Salike and Willem Thorbecke[1]

6.1 Introduction

China followed the 'Flying Geese'[2] model of development, similar to several economies in the region. The basis of this model is the division of labor among East Asian economies based on dynamic comparative advantage. It states that the production of goods would move towards less advanced economies as the cost of production in the advanced economies grows over the time. This pattern was observed in the region as production from Japan was transferred to the Newly Industrialized Economies (NIEs) of Hong Kong, Singapore, South Korea and Taiwan during the 1980s and then to the Association of Southeast Asian Nations (ASEAN) economies, particularly, Indonesia, Malaysia, Philippines and Thailand during the 1990s. China followed this pattern starting in 2000. Since these economies in the region are heavily dependent on exports for their economic development, the flying geese pattern was detrimental to the production, trade and investment behavior in the region. China has gone through numerous changes and upgrading of the policies related to trade and investment to meet the demands for regional transformations. Actually, the policy changes were adopted much earlier, right after it opened up its economy in the 1980s. Nevertheless, the benefits of these changes were widely reaped later, in particular after China joined the World Trade Organization (WTO) in 2001.

There have been structural shifts in trade and investment patterns in East Asia over the years characterized by interactions between trade, foreign direct investment (FDI) and production networks. After the appreciation of the Japanese yen following the Plaza Accord of 1985, Japanese companies shifted production sites to other economies, in particular South Korea and Taiwan. However, with the increase of both wages and exchange rates in these economies, the locational advantage of producing labor-intensive goods in the NIEs declined. So, Japanese firms transferred production to the ASEAN economies. With the advent of the Asian Economic Crisis of 1997–1998, new Japanese FDI to ASEAN slowed down but the flow of intermediate goods (parts and components) from Japan to ASEAN continued for the existing factories. Then, there was a surge in FDI to mainland China, which helped China to become a part of the production and distribution networks. During the 1990s and early 2000s, South Korean and Taiwanese companies also adopted a similar strategy. These FDI flows have contributed to the rise of production networks among the East Asian nations by slicing up the value chain, thereby increasing trade in intermediate goods. This coincided with the opening up of the foreign investment policy of China and China became the largest recipient of regional FDI, either with branch offices or greenfield investments, and became a key player in the regional production network. As Figure 6.1 shows, China's inward FDI was merely 8.1 billion USD in year 1990. It then started to pick up and reached 100 billion USD by 2000. The growth was even more rapid in later years and peaked in 2015 with over 310 billion. USD In terms of percentage of total world FDI flows, China maintained a ratio of almost 12% from 1990.

China's international trade has expanded gradually over the years after its opening up. China's accession to the WTO has been one of the key turning points in the rapid promotion of its trade since 2001. Traditionally, the majority of China's trade has been with Asian counterparts as evidenced in Figure 6.2, followed by Europe and North America. It is essential to understand that China was heavily involved in the intermediate goods trade whereby it imports parts and components from different economies of the region, assembles them and re-exports the finished goods, particularly to the United States (US) and Europe. Since the investments in the region are closely linked with intermediate goods trade, exports and imports within the region also rose significantly over these years.

In the aftermath of the Global Financial Crisis (GFC) in 2007, the East Asian region was buffeted by a big drop in exports to its main markets, the US and

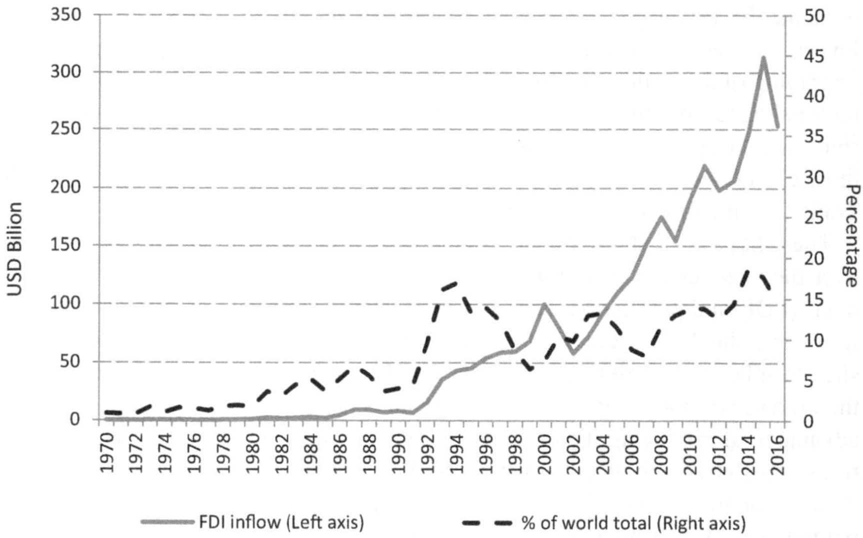

Figure 6.1 Inward FDI in China

Source: Created using UNCTAD Statistics online data, http://unctadstat.unctad.org/EN/

Note: Includes China, Hong Kong SAR, Macao SAR and Taiwan.

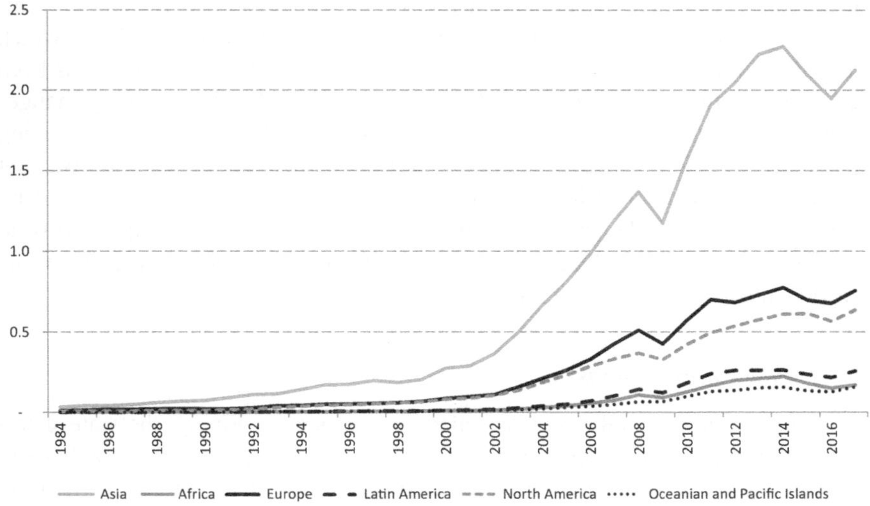

Figure 6.2 China's trade (export and import) with the world (USD trillion)

Source: Created using CEIC online database, www.ceicdata.com/en

Europe, as the purchasing power of the Western economies fell. China also suffered from this event and in order to cope with this, China went through structural changes that are reflected in its policy alternations. First, China increased its focus on the domestic market as the purchasing power of the Chinese people was going up over the years. Secondly, China geared up for increasing the innovation capabilities of its firms. This is a marked shift for China from a capital-oriented economy toward a knowledge-based economy.

The rest of the chapter is organized as follows. In Section 6.2, the opening up of China and its attempts at policy reform are discussed. Sections 6.3 and 6.4 focuse on the important phenomenon of production networking in the region, which explains the close relationship between trade and investment within participating economies. In Section 6.5 and 6.6, we discuss the role of China in the production network. Section 6.7 discusses the new challenges faced by China posed after the GFC and the policy changes adopted henceforth. We conclude the chapter in Section 6.8.

6.2 Policy reforms

China's economic growth over the past four decades can be attributed to the market-oriented reforms adopted by Deng Xiaoping since 1978. Trade and foreign direct investment were core elements of China's development strategy undertaken from that point onwards. Changes and upgrading of such trade- and investment-related policies have been very successful in bringing about reform.

China adopted an export-oriented development strategy in the 1980s and the trade and foreign investment strategies evolved step-by-step since then. The Chinese government has been prudent in amending its trade-related policies, which led China's trade regime to undergo a remarkable transformation. This has been even more effective since China's WTO accession in 2001. These policy changes were also induced by the regional production networking phenomenon taking place in the region. While development of the intermediate goods trade was not originally intended by Chinese policymakers, it was significantly affected by China's policies implemented over the years. Both exports and imports rose in tandem from the 1980s. The policy changes also led China to become one of the world's most attractive destinations for foreign investment.

6.2.1 Policy prescriptions[3]

In China, policy formulation takes place in two stages. Firstly, the state determines the national priorities and then policies are tried on an experimental basis in specific regions in order to reduce the risk of failure. Specialists from central government agencies draft the state policies and experiment with them in particular regions. And secondly, using lessons from experiment, the policy is implemented in the whole country. Three specific policies related to foreign trade and investment played an important role in the structural changes: foreign investment policies, foreign trade policies and technology-enhancing policies.

For promoting industrialization, policies on trade and foreign investment were instrumental in attracting much needed capital into the country. Also, technology policies promoted continual industrial upgrading. These policy changes affected how Chinese enterprises function. With deregulation policy, entrepreneurs and start-up companies were encouraged, which gave rise to small and medium enterprises. Further, joint ventures and foreign trade corporations were also encouraged under this policy. Selective policies towards certain activities, such as tax and tariff reduction, credit and foreign exchange access, etc. were also introduced.

These policies went through constant adjustments over the past three decades. For policy formulation and implementation, two administrative departments, the Foreign Investment Administration Commission of China (FIACC) in 1979 and the State Office for Import and Export of Machinery and Electronics Products (SOIEMEP) in 1993, played crucial roles on issues related to trade, investment and technology. The main mission of FIACC was to accumulate foreign trade surpluses and facilitate technological progress. Nevertheless, it also had a significant role in the development of trade, in particular intermediate goods trade. SOIEMEP was established, primarily with the objective of promoting the technological capabilities in Chinese enterprises. Its main role was to take charge of the coordination, administration, inspection and supervision of the import of machinery and electronics products, and to guide the regional and departmental administration of machinery and electronic products.

These two main bodies were then supported by the establishment of several other parallel offices at the ministry level and state-owned enterprises (SOEs).

For example, the Export-Import Bank of China (EIBC) was founded under the State Council of China in 1994 in order to improve the efficiency of the state's industrial, investment and trade policies. A nationwide semi-administrative organization, the China Chamber of Commerce for Import & Export of Machinery & Electronics Products (CCCME), was set up in 1988, which provided import- and export-related services (e.g., consulting, information, marketing, legal services, training and international cooperation promotion services) to its member enterprises. Under the guidelines and coordination of CCCME, more than 20 industry-level branches were responsible for promoting foreign trade and investment in areas such as automobiles, rail transport equipment, electrical elements, metal-working equipment and electric power equipment.

There were persistent and continuous efforts by the Chinese government in policy formulation and implementation to encourage foreign investment and trade as well as the promotion of technological capability. The 'Law on Chinese-Foreign Equity Joint Ventures' promulgated in 1979 allowed foreign firms to have joint-equity ventures with Chinese partners that helped to expand international economic cooperation. In 1986, the 'Provisions on the Encouragement of Foreign Investment' provided systematic preferential policies for FDI and exporting enterprises. Some of the facilities included priority of access to public utilities, loans and credits, income tax exemption or reduction, tax refund for reinvestment, free duties for intermediate goods and final products' exports, etc.

These two initiatives were turning points for attracting foreign investment into China. Several other supporting policies were also introduced by the government that helped to facilitate the entry of foreign capital into the country and also to increase foreign trade. These included the policy of deregulating barriers to investment and trade, the policy of encouraging foreign investment by offering factors of production, various tax discount policies, the policy of tariff exemption and duty reduction, the policy for easier credit and loan accesses, and the policy of deregulation of capital account control. There was a significant increase in foreign investment after the implementation of the 1986 Provisions, and most FDI was concentrated in special economic zones (SEZs).[4] The scope of the coverage of investment sectors were further encouraged by 2004 constitution amendments.

The 1979 Law was also crucial in supporting advanced technology in order to accelerate industrial upgrading. Foreign firms with advanced technology were given tax benefits. This has helped China to achieve structural change in manufacturing production.

Machinery and electronic products were prioritized as key exporting items in 1985 by the State Council. The 1985 Provision for the Collection and Refund of Product Tax and Value Added Tax on Import and Export Products helped to integrate trade in intermediate goods, in sectors such as machinery and electrical & electronics products. Firms that exported machinery and electronic products were given priority access to raw materials, intermediate goods, fuels, energy, packing stuffs and transportation. Correspondingly, sub-national governments allocated resources to increase the export of machinery and electronic products under the state policy. Also, discounts on export bills were given to encourage research and development (R&D). This policy was amended and extended in 1994, 1999, 2001 and 2006 in almost every national Five-Year-Plan. The latest effective version was updated in 2011. These efforts resulted in China's trade development in machinery and electronic products.

6.2.2 Regional experiments

Regional experimentation is one of the key policies that the Chinese government has undertaken during the process of reform. Some of the early successfully undertakings were in the fields of land reform, encouragement to private sector development, and, importantly, setting up special economic zones (SEZs) from the viewpoint of trade and investment. A SEZ is a specified geographical region within a national boundary that is set up with the specific goal of attracting foreign investment with the rules, laws, regulations and governance only applicable to that specific region. These include policies related to finance, taxation, customs, trading, quotas, labor, etc. It is a designated experiment to evaluate if such an environment could be successful for the targeted goal and if successful could be implemented throughout the country. Typically, SEZs are aimed to achieve one or more of these four policy objectives: attracting FDI; helping to alleviate large scale unemployment; supporting wider economic reform; and acting as an experimental laboratory for broader use in future (Zeng 2015).

Chinese policymakers were determined to set these up and established five SEZs in the coastal region: Shenzhen (1980), Zhuhai (1980), Xiamen (1980), Shantou (1981) and Hainan (1988). These SEZs were established primarily to target market-oriented reforms and to spur economic growth. Following the initial success of these SEZs, the second round was expanded to another 14 coastal cities, including Shanghai, Tianjin, Dalian, Qingdao, Guangzhou, Ningbo, Wenzhou and other economically developed cities. They were successful in marshalling global capital, technology and management knowhow. With the successful operation of these zones, further expansion of SEZs took place to a number of other provinces including the capital cities of inland provinces and autonomous regions that were principally targeted towards regional development. SEZs in China vary in their scope and function depending on the specific economic needs. For example, some of them are based on geographical space, management style, local government initiative, international cooperation or industry cluster as detailed in table 6.1 (World Bank 2015).

The SEZ experiment was vital in achieving China's economic transformation toward a market economy. It provided good prospects for foreign investors to operate their business with market-driven economics. Policies and practices such as access to ports for trade, tax holidays and exemptions, and access to a suitable labor force in the zone helped China to become one of the most attractive destinations for FDI. This also played a crucial role in the evolution of the East Asian regional production networks that helped China to develop into the 'factory of the world'. Further, SEZs have also spurred technology and

Table 6.1 Types of special economic zones in China

Administrative areas	Based on existing administrative regions Newly established administrative regions run as SEZs
Geographical areas	Based on geographical features and resources
International cooperation	Economic or industrial cooperation areas established with another country
Local industrial parks	Industrial and specific industry parks designated by local governments
Industry clusters	Established to support the development of certain industries Clusters of industries
Corporate SEZs	Industrial parks established by enterprises with their own supply and market chains

Source: World Bank (2015)

innovation that aided China to upgrade its technological level. Among other things, SEZs have contributed significantly to national GDP, employment, exports, and foreign investment and new technologies, as well as adoption of modern management practices (Zeng 2015). In spite of the positive benefits of SEZs, concerns were raised in later years that have fueled discussions on the viability of the continuation of SEZs. One of the major concerns with regard to the negative impact of these SEZs is the growing economic inequality in China, which is prevalent primarily amongst the rural residents and farmers. Also, further opening up of China with the entry to the WTO has potentially diminished the initial benefits of SEZs (Curtis et al. 2006).

Against this backdrop, another experiment initiated by the Chinese government related to trade is the creation of free trade zones within the country. The China (Shanghai) Pilot Free Trade Zone (SPFTZ) is the first such zone, established in 2013 with the objective of trade facilitation and capital account liberalization, and it is aimed to be a symbol for the new development model in the following decades. It targets the generation of institutional innovation and focuses on taking the core responsibilities of implementing pilot schemes, exploring governance systems, modernizing system capabilities and furthering reform. It is facilitated with financial and foreign exchange services; special tax policies for the firms operating in the zone that promote investment and trade development; investment management with further opening up of the sectors for investment such as financial services, shipping services, commercial services, professional services, cultural services and social services. It also facilitates in other areas such as customs, legal aspects and government function (EY 2014). The most significant new institutions lie in four areas: the implementation of a 'negative list' model for foreign investment management; the more efficient operation of new trade supervisory institutions for trade execution; the beginning of financial reform experiments on capital account convertibility and in financial services; and the cutting of red tape in administration (Yao and Whalley 2015).

The second round of expansion took place in 2016 with the launching of free trade zone (FTZ) in three coastal regions: Guangdong, Tianjin and Fujian. The government announced the reform and opening up of these FTZs with the focus on high-quality development, supply side structural reform, institutional innovation and risk prevention. These FTZs are given bigger decision-making power in reforms to help make new ground in pursuing opening up on all fronts, improve government management and foster new growth drivers and competitiveness (SCIO 2018). In 2017, the practice of FTZ was further expanded in other provinces including inland regions in Liaoning, Zhejiang, Henan, Hubei, Chongqing, Sichuan and Shaanxi.

6.3 Trade and FDI nexus

The key source of international trade, as suggested by the traditional explanations of the Ricardo and Heckscher-Ohlin models, emphasize the comparative advantage of participating countries due to the differences in technology and factor endowments. Other trade models based on differentiated products and monopolistic competition were viewed as providing an alternative account of international trade; nevertheless, they are also consistent with the traditional explanations of comparative advantage.

Furthermore, the tendency of a firm to get engaged and operate in a foreign country depends upon its OLI (Ownership, Location and Internalization) configuration (Dunning 1988). Ownership refers to the advantages that the firm receives that are not available to the host country. Internalization refers to the fact that it is in the best interest of the firm that possesses ownership specific advantages to transfer them to other countries within their own organization rather than to sell them. This could be done through licensing, joint ventures or managerial contracting. With regard to the location, firms would engage in foreign production where they perceive it is their best interests to use the abundantly available factor of production. The particular economic determinant of FDI depends on whether the FDI falls into any of these three categories: Market-seeking FDI; Resource- or asset-seeking FDI; or Efficiency-seeking FDI.

The interactions between FDI and trade could generate either 'Trade-oriented FDI' or 'Anti-trade-oriented FDI'. If foreign investment is complementary to product trade, it creates or expands the opportunity to import one product and to export the other product. Thus, this kind of foreign investment is trade-creating or trade-oriented (Kojima 1975). Some of these trade-oriented FDI are natural-resource-based industries and labor-intensive industries investments. Natural-resource-based investments are trade generating because they result from the investing country's desire to increase imports of its comparatively disadvantageously produced or domestically unavailable commodities. With regard to labor-intensive industries, as the wage rate in the advanced economies start to increase, the traditional labor-intensive industries from advanced economies tend to transfer to low wage countries where cheaper labor costs prevail and then import back. A high level of tariffs would lead to the substitution of exports of final products towards the export of intermediate goods, intermediate materials, machinery, equipment and technology necessary to the production of final goods from the investing country. These types of FDIs are also called vertical FDI. Japanese multinational enterprises (MNEs) seem to have been involved more in this trade-oriented FDI and therefore they generate more trade in the region. Since Japan has the disadvantages of limited availability of natural resources and high labor costs, Japanese FDI has concentrated in industries such as textiles, clothing, steel processing, motor vehicle assembly, and the production of intermediate goods for electrical and electronic goods.

Anti-trade-oriented FDI has the opposite consequences. MNEs involved in this type of investment are active in relatively new industries that are based on capital and knowledge and become domestic market-oriented. These are mainly firms from the US; therefore, US FDI has concentrated in industries such as chemicals, machinery, transportation and scientific instruments, which are associated with innovation and oligopoly. This framework was supported by Mundell's work that showed that capital movement occurs from a capital-abundant country to a capital-scarce country in search of a higher marginal rate of return (Ozawa 2007). These types of FDIs are also called horizontal FDI. This implies that this type of activity would require MNEs to operate, produce and sell goods and services directly to the consumers of the host country.

In Mundell's framework, capital always flows from locations with low marginal capital productivity to those with higher marginal productivity in search of allocative efficiency (Ozawa 2007). In contrast, Kojima (1975) recognized that the main role of FDI is to transplant superior production technology through the training of labor, management and marketing, from the advanced industrial country to lesser developed countries. The basis of these frameworks is helpful in understanding the activities leading to regional production networks in East Asia. Baldwin and Okubo (2014) termed this type of activity as 'networked FDI', which is more complex in nature and incorporates the ideas of horizontal FDI, vertical FDI and export-platform FDI. They observed that Japanese MNEs include both 'vertical-ness' and 'horizontal-ness' in almost all sectors and countries they operate in. This creates more opportunities for trade, compared to North American counterparts who are more horizontal in nature.

6.4 Advent of East Asian production networks

Fragmentation of the production process across national boundaries, which began in the 1990s, is the key feature of the East Asian production structure. 'Fragmentation' refers to a splitting up of a previously integrated production process into two or more components, or 'fragments'. One of the major consequences of the process of fragmentation into more simple production blocks is that new firms can spring up to take over some such blocks and to supply a number of other competing firms with its output. Thus, further economies of scale are generated and demand for the block can exhibit greater stability than would be the case if separate firms all performed identical processes (Jones and Kierzkowski 2001).

The difference in factor prices and factor intensities across different countries are the prime motivations for firms to fragment their production process. In the multiple stages of production leading to a final product, a country will engage in the production of the range of intermediate goods in which it has comparative advantages, in the sense of Ricardo or Heckscher-Ohlin (Cheng et al. 2001).

The effect of production fragmentation could be understood from Figure 6.3. The cost of production without fragmentation increases rapidly with output while the cost of production with fragmentation increases more slowly. However, fragmentation includes an initial investment represented by the intercept OA in Figure 6.3. Whether fragmentation would be beneficial or not depends on the service link cost (intercept OA) and the marginal production cost represented by the slope of total cost curves (Kimura and Ando 2005). Service link cost refers to the cost associated in linking separated production sites, both in terms of managerial capability and geographical distance. Therefore, reductions of these costs is crucial for success of fragmentation strategy. Some of the ways to lower these costs include strengthening infrastructure like physical (highways, ports), institutional (legal system, contracts) and technological (information communication) (Thorbecke and Salike 2016). Baldwin and Okubo (2014) noted that advancements in information and communication technology have helped MNEs to successfully locate to production sites with attractive production costs.

The fragmentation strategy of the firms, in particular that of Japanese firms, has given rise to production networks in the region and this network of supply chain became the hallmark for the trade and investment pattern for the economies in the region. Trade and FDI have a close relationship with a significant amount of trading being conducted among the affiliates of an MNE, which promote linkages between FDI and foreign trade, particularly within industries (Kawai and Urata 2004). An MNE may export capital goods and intermediate goods from its

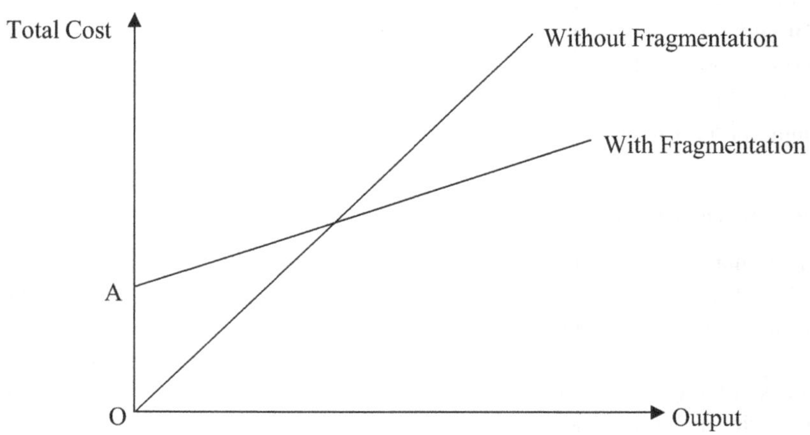

Figure 6.3 Cost reduction in fragmentation

Source: Adapted from Kimura and Ando (2005)

home office to its overseas affiliates to assist them in the production of finished products and may import products from them as well to serve its home market. Therefore, fragmentation is more likely to occur when there is an incentive to move intermediate goods production to the low cost region. According to Dunning's OLI theory, firms tend to internalize their specific assets under their ownership. Therefore, it is important for the host countries to realize trade gains from fragmentation-based specialization and focus on eliminating restrictions on FDI.

In East Asia, the breaking up of production processes among various economies started in the 1990s. Consequently, trade in intermediate goods within East Asian economies increased thereafter and expanded more rapidly than the conventional trade in final goods. Intra-firm, cross-border fragmentation exploits differences in locational advantages, particularly low wages, backed up with lowered service link costs (Kimura and Ando 2008). This is mainly due to the relatively more favorable policy setting for international production, agglomeration benefits arising from the early entry into this new form of specialization, considerable inter-country wage differentials in the region, lower trade and transport costs, and specialization in products exhibiting increasing returns to scale. Figure 6.4 shows the trend in FDI inflow and the intermediate goods trade in East Asia. It is evident from the figure that both FDI and trade increased in tandem in the region. Among the three key industries, where the majority of the production networking took place in the region, it is the electronics industry that has led, with little disruption during 2008–2009 due to the GFC. Therefore, production fragmentation played a pivotal role in the trade integration in the region (Athukorala and Yamashita 2006).

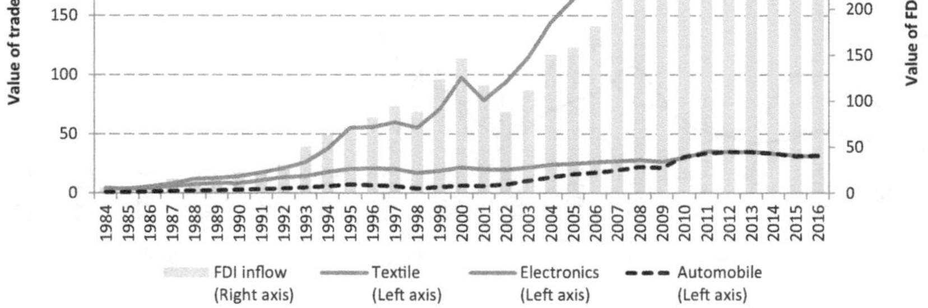

Figure 6.4 Intermediate goods trade and FDI inflow in East Asia

Source: Created using CEPII-CHELEM database

Note: Includes China, Hong Kong SAR, Taiwan, Japan, Korea, Malaysia, Philippines, Singapore, Thailand and Vietnam.

International production and distribution networks are more advanced and distinctive in East Asia than in other parts of the world (Kimura and Ando 2005). It is significant due to the coverage of economies and the significance of each economy in the region, and also, the varying levels of technological sophistication in the economies. Petri (2012) argued that the technology factor in FDI supports Akamatsu's (1962) 'flying geese' model of trade in Asia. The transfer of technological knowhow to less advanced economies from the advanced ones has helped these economies to move up the technology ladder. This has been done by investing in technologically less advanced areas by Asian firms, especially that of NIEs, then graduating to more advanced production and eventually exporting their own technology. The degree of dependence on this new form of international specialization is proportionately larger in East Asia than in North America and Europe.

6.5 China in the production network

Japanese MNEs played an important role in the development of East Asian production and distribution networks by expanding the fragmentation of production process overseas, particularly after the Plaza Accord of 1985. Japanese FDI continued to grow over the years in the region with the largest share occupied by China as a single country. As can be seen in Figure 6.5, China experienced a steady growth in Japanese FDI and is at par with both the other groups (NIEs and

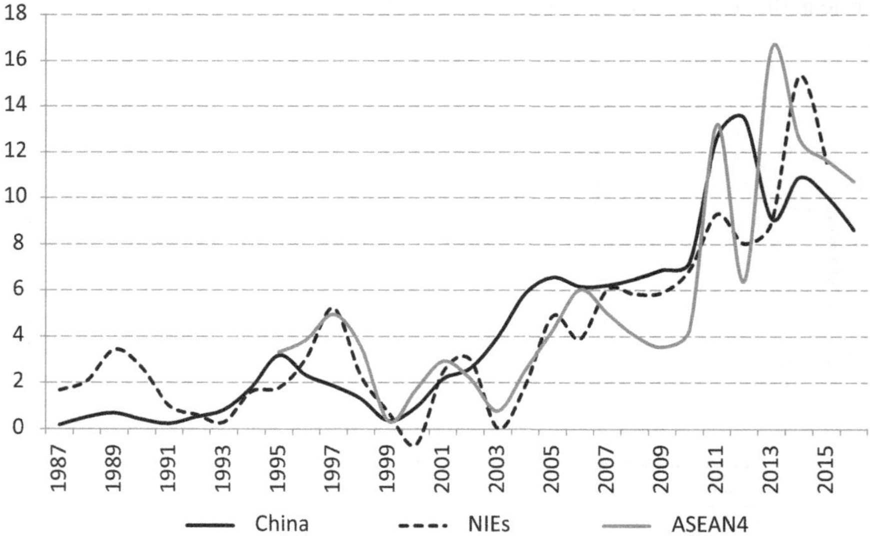

Figure 6.5 Japanese FDI in Asia (USD billion)

Source: Created using JETRO: Japanese Trade and Investment Statistics, www.jetro.go.jp/en/reports/statistics/

Notes: NIEs include Hong Kong SAR, Taiwan, Korea and Singapore. ASEAN4 includes Thailand, Indonesia, Malaysia and Philippines.

ASEAN4), which included four economies each of the region. The fluctuation of Japanese FDI was mainly due to the changes in the composition of manufacturing industries. After the 1997 Asian Financial crisis, Japanese FDI was diverted to China though it maintained its existing investments in Southeast Asian nations. This nature of Japanese FDI was instrumental in the successful undertaking of regional production networks.

The phenomenon of production networking in the region coincided with the opening up of the foreign investment policy of China, which helped China to become the largest recipient of regional Japanese FDI. Therefore, China became the important player in the regional production network by joining other economies in the region. Japanese companies established branch or Greenfield investment in these places. China's SEZ experiment was an important institutional pillar in the East Asian regional production networks and played a crucial role in the success of these networks particularly, as the production or assembly hub for the participating economies.

In 1988, China and Japan signed a bilateral investment treaty (BIT), a first such treaty by China with a foreign country. Despite the fact that the treaty was lacking investor protection, (see Hadley 2013), the treaty helped to increase Japanese investment in China, which was particularly focused on SEZs. Japanese FDI continued to grow during the 1990s and 2000s, which was largely concentrated in the electrical, electronics and automobile sectors. Machinery, electrical equipment, and transportation equipment together accounted for about 70% of total Japanese FDI in manufacturing (Huang et al. 2017). The inward FDI made a crucial contribution to the development of China's manufactured exports. This is also due to the impressive absorption capacity of China, which is associated with the country's FDI policy, human capital, R&D, and infrastructure quality (Tang and Zhang 2016). The growing knowledge base in China has facilitated the transfer of technology from FDI firms and the progress towards higher value added tasks within the value chain (see Kiyota et al. 2006).

The economic integration of China has deepened production fragmentation in East Asia and further intensified intra-regional trade (Thorbecke and Salike 2016). As can be seen in Figure 6.6, total trade of China with its Asian counterparts increased rapidly, especially after 2002. Japan, Hong Kong and Korea are three major economies where China does most of the trade, followed by Taiwan. A larger share of this intra-regional trade is in the form of intermediate goods trade and some specific industries like machinery, electrical and electronics, and automobile. For example, China imported 153 billion USD worth of electrical products in 2016 from the region, an increase of 32% compared to 2010. This figure was merely 13.4 billion USD in 2000.

Along with the important role played by Japanese FDI in establishing production networks in East Asia, China's own efforts at trade liberalization within the region also helped to further strengthen the networks. For example, there have been trade creation effects in the region due to ASEAN–China Free Trade Agreement (ACFTA), particularly in the machinery and transport sectors (Yang and Martinez-Zarzoso 2014). The Chinese government was also successful in shifting

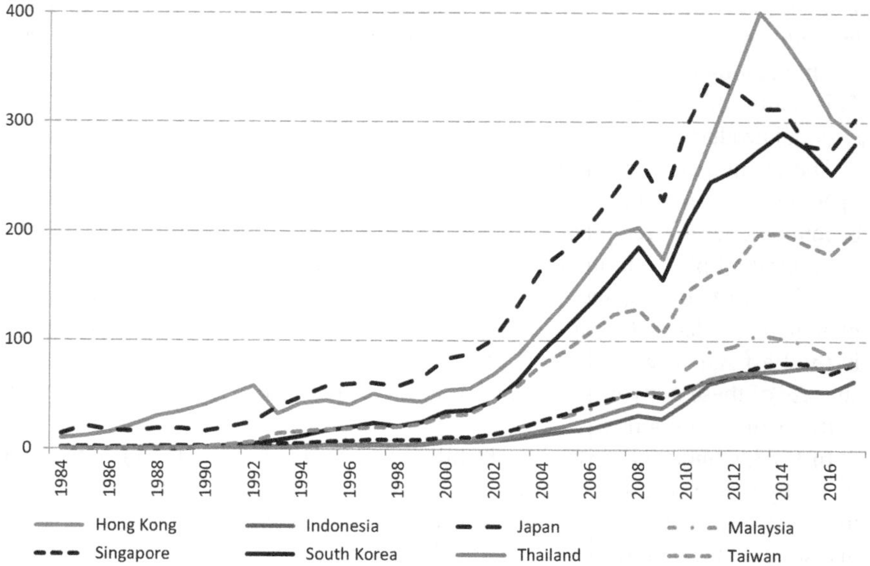

Figure 6.6 China's trade (export and import) with Asia (USD billion)

Source: Created using CEIC online database, www.ceicdata.com/en

low technology-intensive industries to medium technology-intensive industries and there is a further push to move towards high technology-intensive industries (Huang et al. 2017). China's involvement in the international division of labor and its consequences on the process of regional economic integration in East Asia is significant. Production sharing, FDI and high-tech trade are the main areas of focus of China's economic integration process. Trade data in East Asia show that firms in the region have contributed to China's exports and technological advancement over the years. However, the prospects of China's technological catch-up will depend on its ability to disseminate foreign technology into the local industrial sector and to develop its own innovative capacities (Gaulier et al. 2005).

6.6 China's processing and ordinary trade

Examining China's two main customs regimes, processing trade and ordinary trade, could further shed light on China's evolving role in East Asian production networks. Processing trade refers to the imports made by a country that are primarily intermediate goods and are used to produce final goods. They are imported duty free and are not allowed to enter the Chinese domestic market. They can only be used to produce goods for re-export (processed exports). Alternatively, ordinary imports are either intermediate goods or capital goods that can be used to produce other goods or final goods destined for Chinese consumers. Ordinary exports are produced using local factors or using imported inputs. The nature and pattern of these two types of trade are discussed later in separate figures.

Figure 6.7 plots China's processing imports and processed exports. Imports for processing are largely electronic parts and components and processed exports are largely final electronic goods. The figure shows that the difference between processed exports and imports for processing has increased. This implies that less of the value added of China's processed exports comes from imported inputs, and more comes from the China itself. Thus, the upgrading policies discussed earlier are bearing fruit.

The detailed breakdown of the processing trade by region is provided in appendix Table A6.1. In 2015, 310 billion USD in parts and components for processing came from East Asia (top panel). This figure includes more than 70 billion USD of 'imports' that are produced in China and then sent out and back in to benefit from tax breaks (Xing 2012). South Korea and Taiwan are the two leading sources of imports for processing. In 2015, imports for processing from Korea equaled 86 billion USD and imports from Taiwan equaled 70 billion USD. Japan shipped 48 billion USD of imports for processing to China and ASEAN-4 shipped 34 billion USD. The US and Europe both sent less than 25 billion USD in imports for processing to China in 2015. The US received 186 billion USD of processed exports and Europe received 108 billion USD from China in 2015. South Korea only received 47 billion USD and Taiwan only 16 billion USD (Middle panel of appendix Table A6.1). Parts and components for processing came largely from East Asia and not the West, whereas final goods go disproportionately to the West

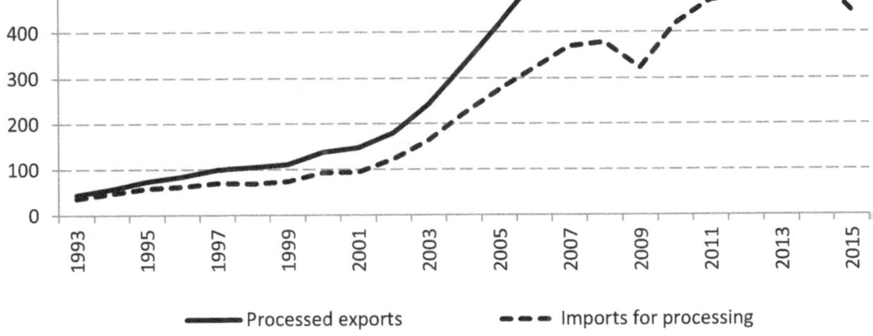

Figure 6.7 China's processing trade (USD billion)

Source: Created using China Customs Statistics database, www.chinacustomsstat.com/

(refer to appendix Table A6.1). It is indicated from the fact that China runs a deficit with South Korea and Taiwan, together worth 93 billion USD, in processing trade in 2015. Conversely, China had surpluses with the US and Europe worth 162 billion USD and 86 billion USD, respectively in 2015.

Figure 6.8 plots China's ordinary imports and exports. The figure shows that both ordinary exports and imports have grown rapidly. Before the GFC, processed exports exceeded ordinary exports but later ordinary exports became increasingly higher than processed exports. This also reflects the fact that more of the value added of China's exports now comes from China's domestic factors rather than from imported parts and components. Figure 6.8 also shows that ordinary imports fell in 2015. The fall is due to the drop in prices of crude oil and other commodities and to China's crackdown on giving luxury imports to government officials (Qian and Wen 2015).

Appendix Table A6.2 decomposes China's ordinary trade by region. Most of the ordinary electronics imports came from South Korea and Taiwan, particularly starting from 2010 (top panel). China also imports a lot from Japan, Germany and the US. These imports include automobiles and sophisticated capital goods. The top portion also shows that China imports a lot from Australia and Brazil. These are mainly primary inputs such as iron ore and coal. The middle panel of this table shows China's ordinary exports, which implies that the main markets for its exports are the US and Europe. In 2015, these exports accounted for over 200 billion USD in the US and over 185 billion USD in Europe. The bottom panel

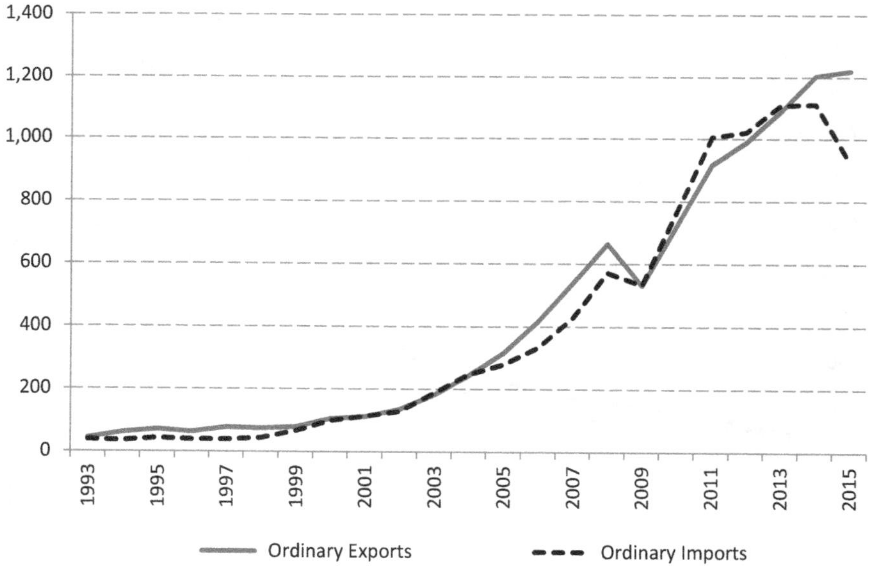

Figure 6.8 China's ordinary trade (USD billion)

Source: Created using China Customs Statistics database, www.chinacustomsstat.com/

of appendix Table A6.2 shows that overall China runs surpluses in ordinary trade with the US, Europe – excluding Germany – and ASEAN. It then runs deficits with advanced Asia, Germany, Australia and Brazil.

The data in this section indicate that China runs deficits with East Asian economies supplying parts and components, and large surpluses with Western economies that purchase final goods. China's contribution to the value added of goods produced within these global value chains has also increased steadily.

6.7 Changes after the global financial crisis

The 2007–09 GFC originated in the West and Asian economies were not directly impacted with losses from holding toxic assets. However, Asian economies, including China, were hit hard by the downturn in exports due to falling demand in the West. There have been concerns in Asia about overdependence on external markets and therefore calls for Asian economies to rebalance their production and marketing. Rebalancing could be achieved by boosting the productivity of the firms engaged in the production network and by producing higher value-added products rather than simply focusing on producing relatively cheap products.

6.7.1 Policy shift

The macroeconomic performance of China in the past decade reflects high domestic investment, high dependence on the foreign market and low domestic consumption. Following about four decades of high growth and the occurrence of the GFC, China's economy is experiencing an era of slower growth. Starting from 2011, the economy is growing by around 7% on average compared to double digit growth in the previous period. These circumstances exposed China to new challenges, which led Chinese policymakers to carry out major policy shifts. The rebalancing of the Chinese economy requires policy reforms in industrial structure and institutional arrangements that would facilitate a new pattern of growth (Deer and Song 2012). The rebalancing in China was adopted taking into consideration two main imperatives: increasing domestic demand and promoting innovation.[5]

Following the sluggish external demand after the crisis, China had a shift in its economic policy from being outward looking to inward looking and made domestic consumption the main driver of economic growth. This policy is undertaken as a long-term policy, as China realized that overdependence on the external market may not be fruitful over the long run. Furthermore, in order to deal with the demand problem during 2008, the Chinese government introduced a massive fiscal stimulus amounting to RMB 4 trillion (586 billion USD), which was 12.5% of the 2008 Chinese GDP (Fardoust et al. 2012). This fiscal stimulation package covered public expenditure in infrastructure construction (e.g., railway, road and airports, rural public service), social services development (e.g., public housing, health, education and culture) and environmental projects (e.g., energy saving, industrial pollution treatment, ecological recovery). Further efforts have been put in place to realize this objective. There has been tightening of lending to certain traditional industries such as labor-intensive manufacturing. China has expressed its commitment towards environmental protection both inside and outside of the country. Also, other fiscal and monetary macro policies were undertaken such as expanding the size of the fiscal deficit, implementing structural tax cuts, maintaining favorable interest rates and monitoring the real sector development.

After entering the so-called 'new normal[6]', China seeks to promote innovation as the engine of growth in the coming decades. As more and more Chinese firms are becoming global, it has been necessary for them to be innovative to remain competitive in the global market, particularly so for firms that participate in global supply chains in information technology, computing and telecommunications. Also, in the domestic market, Chinese companies have had to innovate in order to compete with foreign companies at the high end (Yip and McKern 2014). China's R&D expenditure accounted for 2 trillion USD in 2015, which is about 21% of the world's total and second only to the US. The average growth rate of this spending is 18% per year between 2010 and 2015.

Yip and McKern (2014) noted that China possesses several innovation enablers on both the supply and the demand sides. In terms of supply, the availability of relatively cheap high-quality human resource is a key factor for spurring innovation. The government is very supportive in providing specific funds and infrastructural assistance for startups and potential inventors. Also, the high level of information technology development has played a positive role in stimulating innovation-related traits in the minds of the people. On the demand side, there is a huge market in China, particularly the middle-income group of people. This has led to potential innovation in several areas such as cheap products, better quality, good service, etc.

The Chinese government is keen on promoting firm innovation by inducing the development of technology-intensive industries. In this regard, in 2009, 10 key industries were selected for 'restructuring and revitalization', including steel, automobile, shipbuilding, equipment, ICT, and non-ferrous metals, *etc*. Further, a national plan called 'Made in China 2025' was introduced by the State Council in 2015 that aims to transform China into a leading manufacturing power focusing on improving manufacturing innovation, fostering Chinese brands, enforcing green manufacturing, advancing restructuring of the manufacturing sector, etc. The 10 key sectors are new information technology, numerical control tools and robotics, aerospace equipment, ocean engineering equipment and high-tech ships, railway equipment, energy saving and new energy vehicles, power equipment, new materials, biological medicine and medical devices, and agricultural machinery. 'Made in China 2025' will focus on five major projects, including establishing a manufacturing innovation center. The motivation behind this is to promote technological upgrading and indigenous innovation with the purpose of substituting imported intermediate products with the one produced by local suppliers.

6.7.2 Emergence of Chinese outward investment (OFDI)

Another aspect of the rebalancing that China is targeting, is to be a net exporter of capital, rather than an importer of capital. On this front, there has been a major shift in the overseas' investment scenario after the GFC. Chinese outward FDI (OFDI) began to take place from 2005 but it was only after 2010 that Chinese OFDI took a big leap forward. It was a mere 5.5 billion USD in 2004; started to pick up in 2005 and grew rapidly after 2010, with an annual average growth rate of 19% from 2010 to 2016. As can be seen in Figure 6.9, China's outward FDI amounted to over 260 billion USD in 2016, which is over 16% of global outward FDI flows, and in the same year China's OFDI surpassed its own inward FDI, becoming a net capital exporter. The distribution of Chinese OFDI in the world is diverse, though mostly concentrated in Asia. For example, in 2015, about 70% of Chinese OFI went to Asian economies, followed by North America, Latin America, Europe and Oceania.

Although being a relatively new player in the area of OFDI, China has gathered much attention due to its rapid increase in investment size and the political sensitivity surrounding SOEs. Several studies have tried to explain the behavior of Chinese OFDI. Huang and Wang (2013) argue that Chinese OFDI has some specific characteristics that make it different from Japanese (efficiency-seeking) or American (market-seeking) types of FDI. For example, the main purpose of Chinese OFDI is to strengthen domestic production rather than moving factories abroad. Chinese firms tend to acquire foreign firms that have higher technology than the parent firms, and then use this superior technology and well-established brand names to gain access to the market channels. Therefore, Chinese OFDI is

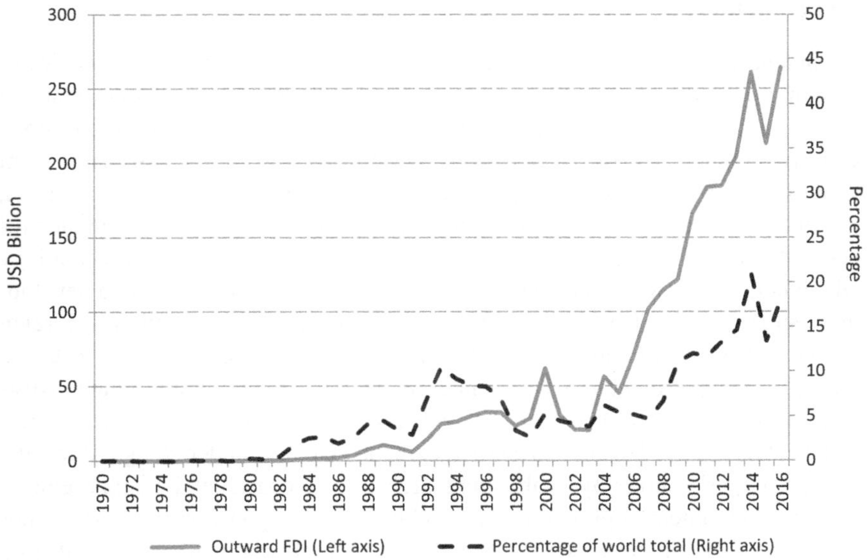

Figure 6.9 Chinese outward FDI

Source: Created using UNCTAD Statistics online data accessed on 2018/0312, http://unctadstat.unctad.org/EN/

Note: Includes China, Hong Kong SAR, Macao SAR and Taiwan.

technology-seeking in nature. Moreover, domestic market size is one of the key factors for Chinese firms to make investment in developed economies (Kolstad and Wiig 2012). Apart from the large market size, Buckley et al. (2007) also found that Chinese OFDI is attracted to countries with high levels of political risk and with greater culture and geographic proximity.

Yao and Wang (2014) investigated whether China as a major foreign investor has undermined the importance of Western economies, especially that of the OECD and found that there is indeed such crowding-out behavior. However, unlike the common impression, China does not seem to displace OECD countries' FDI in resource-abundant host economies located in Africa or Latin America. The displacement is found mainly in less resource-abundant, higher income host countries and those located in Asia, Europe and North America. The authors argued that the Chinese government needs to adopt more transparent OFDI policy and more government level cooperation in order to reduce anxiety about Chinese OFDI on the world stage. This is especially important as the backlash against Chinese FDI in Germany, the US and other places is reaching a fever pitch (see Chazan 2018).

In general, the existing studies have found evidence that availability of natural resources is a significant determinant of Chinese OFDI. In addition, an increasing number of studies also provide evidence in support of other determinants, such as market size and the technology level of the host economy.

6.8 Conclusion

We analyzed the patterns of international trade and investment during the development process of China thereby highlighting the phenomenon of supply chain in the region. We argue that China's connection to the outside world through trade and investment is a result of both push and pull factors. Major push came from Chinese government through the opening up policy of 1978. Several state level, province level or city level administrative institutions were established in the process. Major policy reforms took place in the fields of trade, FDI and technology which helped China to excel in these areas. Whereas the export-oriented development strategy made China open up its border for trade, liberalization in foreign capital was led by several investment friendly policies and practices. For instance, the regional experiment of SEZ was hugely successful in attracting foreign investment into the country. These developments were coincided with China's accession to WTO in 2001 which further strengthened China's undertakings. Recently, China is experimenting by establishing FTZs in both coastal and inland regions.

The development of production networking in the region was one of the major pull factors for China to get associated in the supply chain where in FDI goes in hand with trade. China became one of the important players of this network as China emerged as one of the most attractive destinations for Japanese FDI. Whereas Japanese MNEs were practicing production fragmentation strategies in the region, China's own policy reforms was instrumental to reap benefits of this development to get successfully integrated in this supply chain. China's competence as an assembly hub for the products produced in the region became a major advantage for the growing nexus of trade and investment. Looking at the Chinese custom data of processing trade, China has been increasingly using domestically produced goods for assembly of final goods.

The occurrence of GFC led China to take another turn of policies. Comprehending to the risk of overdependence in external markets, China is rebalancing the economy with more emphasis on the domestic market and focus on innovation. On this front, China is also emerging as an important player in the outward FDI market. Most of the Chinese OFDI is aimed at resources, market size and technology.

Notes

1 Nimesh Salike, International Business School Suzhou, Xi'an Jiaotong-Liverpool University, South Campus, 8 Chongwen Road, Dushu Lake Science and Innovation District, Suzhou Industrial Park, Jiangsu, China 215123. Telephone: + 86 512 8816 1713. E-mail: nimesh.salike@xjtlu.edu.cn.

Willem Thorbecke, Research Institute of Economy, Trade and Industry, 1–3–1 Kasumigaseki, Chiyoda-ku, Tokyo, 100–8901, Japan. Telephone: 81–3–3501–0230. E-mail: willem-thorbecke@rieti.go.jp. Center for International Development, Harvard University, 79 JFK Street, Cambridge, MA 02138, USA. E-mail: willem_thorbecke@hks.harvard.edu.

2 Akamatsu (1962).
3 This sub section is based on Huang et al. (2017).
4 More discussion on SEZs is made in subsequent sections.
5 It is noteworthy that China's exports and imports have stabilized, particularly after 2014 (refer to Figure 6.2); however, it is too early to come up with specific conclusions without more data.
6 'New normal' refers to the Chinese government's attempt to rebalance the economy to slower but more sustainable economic development.

References

Akamatsu, K. (1962), "A Historical Pattern of Economic Growth in Developing Countries," *Journal of Developing Economies* 1(1): 3–25.

Athukorala, P. C., and N. Yamashita (2006), "Production Fragmentation and Trade Integration: East Asia in a Global Context," *The North American Journal of Economics and Finance* 17: 233–256.

Baldwin, R., and T. Okubo (2014), "Networked FDI: Sales and Sourcing Patterns of Japanese Foreign Affiliates," *The World Economy* 37(8): 1051–1080.

Buckley, P. J., L. J. Clegg, A. R. Cross, X. Liu, H. Voss, and P. Zheng (2007), "The Determinants of Chinese Outward Foreign Direct Investment," *Journal of International Business Studies* 38: 499–518.

Chazan, G. (2018), "Backlash Grows over Chinese Deals for Germany's Corporate Jewels," *The Financial Times*, March 14.

Cheng, L., Q. Larry, and T. Guofu (2001), "Foreign Direct Investment and International Fragmentation of Production." in: S. W. Arndt and H. Kierzkowski (eds.), *Fragmentation: New Production Patterns in the World Economy*, New York: Oxford University Press.

Curtis, T., S. Hill, and C. C. Lin (2006), "Special Economic Zones (SEZs): Chinese, Russian, and Latin American Cases and the Use of SEZs as an Economic Development Tool," Prepared for the International Economic Development Program, Ford School of Public Policy, University of Michigan.

Deer, L., and L. Song (2012), "China's Approach to Rebalancing: A Conceptual and Policy Framework," *China & World Economy* 20(1): 1–26.

Dunning, J. H. (1988), "The Eclectic Paradigm of International Production: A Restatement and Some Possible Extensions." *Journal of International Business Studies* 19(1): 1–31.

EY (2014), "Insights of China (Shanghai) Pilot Free Trade Zone," EY China (Shanghai) Pilot Free Trade Zone Publications Series Inaugural Issue. Ernst & Young, China.

Fardoust, S. F., J. Y. Lin, and X. Luo (2012), "Demystifying China's Fiscal Stimulus," Policy research Working Paper 6221, The World Bank.

Gaulier, G., F. Lemoine, and D. Ünal-Kesenci (2005), "China's Integration in East Asia: Production Sharing, FDI & High-Tech Trade," CEPII, Working Paper No 2005–09, Paris.

Hadley, K. (2013), "Do China's Bits Matter-Assessing the Effect of China's Investment Agreements on Foreign Direct Investment Flows, Investors Rights, and the Rule of Law," *Georgetown Journal of International Law* 45: 255–341.

Huang, Y., N. Salike, and F. Zhong (2017), "Policy Effect on Structural Change: A Case of Chinese Intermediate Goods Trade," *China Economic Review* 44: 30–47.

Huang, Y., and B. Wang (2013), "Investing Overseas Without Moving Factories Abroad: The Case of Chinese Outward Direct Investment," *Asian Development Review* 30(1): 85–107.

Jones, R. W., and H. Kierzkowski (2001), "A Framework for Fragmentation," in: Sven W. Arndt and Henryk Kierzkowski (eds.), *Fragmentation: New Production Patterns in the World Economy*, New York: Oxford University Press.

Kawai, M., and S. Urata (2004), "Trade and Foreign Direct Investment in East Asia," in: Riyana Miranti, and Denis Hew (eds.), *APEC in the 21st Century*, Singapore: Institute of Southeast Asian Studies.

Kimura, F., and M. Ando (2005), "Two- dimensional Fragmentation in East Asia: Conceptual Framework and Empirics," *International Review of Economics and Finance* 14: 317–348.

Kimura, F., and M. Ando (2008), "Fragmentation in East Asia: Further Evidence," Discussion Paper Series DP 2006–23 (KUMQRP).

Kiyota, K., T. Matsuura, S. Urata, and Y. Wei (2006), "Reconsidering the Backward Vertical Linkages of Foreign Affiliates: Evidence from Japanese Multinationals," *World Development* 8: 1398–1414.

Kojima, K. (1975), "International Trade and Foreign Investment: Substitutes or Complements," *Hitotsubashi Journal of Economics* 16(1): 1–12.

Kolstad, I., and A. Wiig (2012), "What Determines Chinese Outward FDI?" *Journal of World Business* 47: 26–34.

Ozawa, T. (2007), "Professor Kiyoshi Kojima's Contributions to FDI Theory: Trade, Structural Transformation, Growth, and Integration in East Asia," *The International Economy* 11(1): 17–33.

Petri, P. (2012), "The Determinants of Bilateral FDI: Is Asia Different?" *Journal of Asian Economics* 23: 201–209.

Qian, N., and J. Wen (2015), "The Impact of Xi Jinping's Anti-Corruption Campaign on Luxury Imports in China," Working paper, Yale University. Available at: http://aida.wss.yale.edu/~nq3/NANCYS_Yale_Website/resources/papers/QianWen_20150403.pdf

SCIO (2018), "China Unveils Plans to Deepen Reform, Opening-up in FTZs," The State Council Information Office, The People's Republic of China. Available at: http://english.scio.gov.cn/topnews/2018-05/24/content_51510661.htm

Tang, Y., and K. H. Zhang (2016), "Absorptive Capacity and Benefits from FDI: Evidence from Chinese Manufactured Exports," *International Review of Economics and Finance* 42: 423–429.

Thorbecke, W., and N. Salike (2016), "Understanding FDI and Production Networks in East Asia," *Asian-Pacific Economic Literature* 30(2): 57–71.

World Bank (2015), "China's Special Economic Zones: Experience Gained," Handout: The Investing in Africa Forum: Partnering to Accelerate Investment, Industrialization, and Results in Africa, held in Addis Ababa, Ethiopia.

Xing, Y. (2012), "Processing Trade, Exchange Rates, and China's Bilateral Trade Balances," *Journal of Asian Economics* 25: 540–547.

Yang, S., and I. Martinez-Zarzoso (2014), "A Panel Data Analysis of Trade Creation and Trade Diversion Effects: The Case of ASEAN – China Free Trade Area," *China Economic Review* 29: 138–151.

Yao, D., and J. Whalley (2015), "The China (Shanghai) Pilot Free Trade Zone: Background, Developments and Preliminary Assessment of Initial Impacts," Working Paper 20924, National Bureau of Economic Research.

Yao, S., and P. Wang (2014), "Has China Displaced the Outward Investments of OECD Countries?" *China Economic Review* 28: 55–71.

Yip, G., and B. McKern (2014), "Innovation in Emerging Markets – The Case of China," *International Journal of Emerging Markets* 9(1): 2–10.

Zeng, D. Z. (2015), "Global Experiences with Special Economic Zones Focus on China and Africa," Policy Research Working Paper 7240, World Bank.

Appendix

Table A6.1 China's processing trade, 2010–2015

	Korea (1)	*Taiwan (2)*	*Japan (3)*	*ASEAN- 4 (4)*	*US (5)*	*Germany (6)*	*Rest of Europe (7)*	*Australia & Brazil (8)*	*Rest of the World (9)*	*Total (10)*
	Imports for processing (USD billion)									
2010	71.1	70	61.6	42.1	21.7	6.7	13.2	3.1	127.9	417.4
2011	79.6	71.9	64.9	44.7	21.9	7.3	15.6	3.9	160	469.8
2012	83.9	68.5	62.8	38.2	19.8	6.4	13.5	4.6	183.5	481.2
2013	87.1	72.5	56.4	36.2	21.6	7.4	14.9	4.8	196.1	497
2014	98.7	76.2	55.6	35.2	24.8	8.2	15.2	5.3	205.3	524.5
2015	86.5	70.2	48.0	34.3	23.4	6.8	14.2	2.4	161.7	447.5
	Processed exports (USD billion)									
2010	34.9	15	65.5	25.2	162.6	33.2	94.1	18.1	291.7	740.3
2011	39.6	17.7	75.2	28.6	175.6	34.2	101.4	21.7	341.5	835.5
2012	46.1	16.2	78.6	32	184.6	29.7	93.8	22.8	359	862.8
2013	47.2	16.6	75.9	31.7	186.7	26.0	88.2	22.8	365.4	860.5
2014	47.8	18.3	73.5	31.8	194.8	27.6	91.6	22.0	376.9	884.3
2015	47.0	16.2	65.1	27.5	186.2	25.6	82.2	19.6	329.5	798.9
	Balance in processing trade (USD billion)									
2010	–36.2	–55.0	3.9	–16.9	140.9	26.5	80.9	15.0	163.8	322.9
2011	–40.0	–54.2	10.3	–16.1	153.7	26.9	85.8	17.8	181.5	365.7
2012	–37.8	52.3	15.8	–6.2	164.8	23.3	80.3	18.2	175.5	381.6
2013	–39.9	–55.9	19.5	–4.5	165.1	18.6	73.3	18	169.3	363.5
2014	–50.9	–57.9	17.9	–3.4	170.0	19.4	76.4	16.7	171.6	359.8
2015	–39.5	–54	17.1	–6.8	162.8	18.8	68	17.2	167.8	351.4

Source: China Customs Statistics, www.chinacustomsstat.com/

Notes: ASEAN 4 includes Indonesia, Malaysia, the Philippines, and Thailand. Rest of Europe includes Austria, Belgium, Denmark, Finland, France, Greece, Ireland, Luxembourg, the Netherlands, Italy, Portugal, Spain, Sweden and the United Kingdom.

Table A6.2 China's Ordinary Trade, 2010–2015

	Korea (1)	*Taiwan (2)*	*Japan (3)*	*ASEAN- 4 (4)*	*US (5)*	*Germany (6)*	*Rest of Europe (7)*	*Australia & Brazil (8)*	*Rest of the World (9)*	*Total (10)*
	Ordinary imports (USD billion)									
2010	45.3	29.2	89.4	49	63.8	57.9	56.7	91	286.0	768.3
2011	55.9	34.2	100.5	67	81.4	73.5	70.8	122.4	401.9	1007.6
2012	56.8	36.1	88.7	68	90	72.3	70.4	122.6	416.9	1021.8
2013	62.6	42.2	82.9	71.8	94.9	73.5	75.5	139.5	467.0	1109.9
2014	63.6	48.8	83.8	68	96.4	81.9	81.3	134.6	451.5	1111.1
2015	59.2	47.6	72.2	61.6	89.9	68.4	71.4	102.3	351.4	924.0
	Ordinary exports (USD billion)									
2010	30.1	12.4	51.1	46.5	107.5	31.8	105.7	29.9	305.7	720.7
2011	38.6	15.2	66.5	61.3	135.6	39.4	127.4	39.6	393.4	917.0
2012	36	15.4	66.4	78.8	151.3	36.2	121.1	43.3	439.5	988.0
2013	38.4	17.2	67	92.7	162	37.4	128.2	45.7	498.9	1087.5
2014	46.1	20.1	69	97.4	179	40.7	145	46.6	559.9	1203.8
2015	46.9	19.9	63.5	100.4	201.7	39.5	145	32.7	571.0	1220.6
	Balance in ordinary trade (USD billion)									
2010	–15.2	–16.8	–38.3	–2.5	43.7	–26.1	49	–61.1	19.7	–47.6
2011	–17.3	–19	–34	–5.7	54.2	–34.1	56.6	–82.8	–8.5	–90.6
2012	–20.8	–20.7	–22.3	10.8	61.3	–36.1	50.7	–79.3	22.6	–33.8
2013	–24.2	–25	–15.9	20.9	67.1	–36.1	52.7	–93.8	31.9	–22.4
2014	–17.5	–28.7	–14.8	29.4	82.6	–41.2	63.7	–88	108.4	93.9
2015	–12.3	–27.7	–8.7	38.8	111.8	–28.9	73.6	–69.6	219.6	296.6

Source: China Customs Statistics, www.chinacustomsstat.com/

Notes: ASEAN 4 includes Indonesia, Malaysia, the Philippines, and Thailand. Rest of Europe includes Austria, Belgium, Denmark, Finland, France, Greece, Ireland, Luxembourg, the Netherlands, Italy, Portugal, Spain, Sweden and the United Kingdom.

Part III

Policy connections

7 Chinese institutions

Yanghua Huang

7.1 Introduction

In the eyes of the outsiders, the modern China is still a country of contradictions and complexity. On the one hand, the unprecedented growth has turned China from an economically backward country into the world's second-largest economic power. According to various predictions and estimations, China is already or going to be the biggest economic power in the coming years (Stiglitz 2015; Center for Economic and Business Research 2015). In less than four decades, about 800 million Chinese people escaped the poverty trap. China updates a new target to move 30 million people out of absolute poverty by 2020. Although certain undesirable consequences remained, such as income inequality, regional disparity, ecological and environmental deterioration, China shows higher stability and resiliency. It seems that Chinese institutions are functioning well in governing those issues. On the other hand, Chinese institutions are not only exceptional to the West in many aspects, but they also violate the model of "good governance" of standard economic theory. In recent years, China is making efforts to strengthen the whole nation's confidence in institutions and China's path toward modernization. China is also actively sharing its institutional model[1] with other developing countries.

How do we understand the Chinese administration and economic institutions? How have they evolved? How do Chinese institutions impact modern economic development? In this chapter, we are going to explore these issues from a historical perspective. The key message is that China has been a unitary state for more than 2200 years, which is quite different from the Western nation states that emerged after Medieval times. In this long-term evolution, Chinese key players have been persistently making investments in shaping, reinforcing and adapting Chinese institutions to govern one of the world's biggest countries and ancient civilizations. Due to path dependency (David 1985; North 1991), Chinese institutions have been evolving along a different trajectory of historical foundations laid out in early Imperial China. After being challenged by external civilizations in the 19th century, China started to institutionally modernize to redefine its position in the dynamic world system, by melding its traditional and imported institutions.

In the literature of modern economics or political science, institutions are generally defined as human-created constraints that structure political, economic and social interactions (North 1991). There are two types of institutions, organizations and rules that govern behavior. The economic function of institutions is to provide basic and stable mechanisms that govern the incentives of agents and coordinate activities in major political and economic games (Xu 2011). Nowadays, most researchers have reached a consensus that the institution is the fundamental determinant of long-term economic performance (Acemoglu et al. 2005; Acemoglu and Robinson 2012). However, some researchers emphasize the "macro" institutions that reduce transaction costs of the whole society or allocate resources from one social group to another as the most important factor for economic growth, such as constitutional arrangements, political organization, ideology or the national development strategy (North 1981; Landes 2006; North and Weingast 1989; Weingast 1995; Ekelund and Tollison 1997; Murphy et al. 1991, 1993; Lin et al. 1996; Chang 2011). Others suggest that "micro" institutions are crucial to economic development under given macro institutions. Among others, institutions that affect the cost of contracting and the allocation of property rights are highlighted to determine the efficiency of different types of organizations (Coase 1960; Williamson 1985; Grossman and Hart 1986; Hart and Moore 1990). The state, like the firm, is an alternative institution to the market system. Within the state, agents are not coordinated by market transactions or the price mechanism, but by direct orders. The major role of the state is to define the structure of property rights with its exclusive power of controlling violence (North and Thomas 1976; North 1981). Once the incentive of property rights is the most important determinant to long-term growth, stagnation or decline, then the state is the ultimate factor. Olson (1965, 2000) provides a model of the state with the theory of collective action. He assumes that the self-interested ruler (the "bandit") maximizes tax revenue from the robbed (Olson 2000). For the roving bandit, the incentive is to collect short-term taxes from a region, stealing and destroying the long-term growth potential; on the contrary, the stationary bandit has the incentive to provide essential public goods, such as securing property rights and providing protection from other bandits and to secure long-term economic development that generates expected tax revenue. The move from roving bandit to stationary bandit is the origin of the state. This is a process of civilization that favors the long-term economic development.

This chapter studies the broad Chinese institutional changes, with particular attention on the linkages between the ancient and modern institutions that impacts China's modern economic development. We will mainly follow the macro approach of institutions. More specifically, we focus on the fundamental institutions of governance of China and explain how the historical state and ideology impact modern institutions and development. What makes Chinese institutions different lies in China developing a unitary state much earlier than most modern countries. The role of the state was vital to Chinese institutional architecture, including reinforcing the bureaucratic governance structure, unitary ideological control, state monopolism, talent allocation and public infrastructure provisions.

7.2 Origins of Chinese institutions as a unitary state

As one of the oldest countries, China started institution building earlier than most modern countries. The Xia Dynasty (the 21st—16th century B. C.) is proposed to be the first documented ancient hereditary state. The founder of Xia succeeded in governing the floods of major agrarian areas and then controlled tribes located nearby. Since then, China adopted feudalism. This was much earlier than Europe. By the 8th century BC, after the political and military rises of a few big states, the *de facto* controls of the central state (East Zhou) were significantly weakened. China entered a statute of separation that lasted for centuries, from the Spring and Autumn Period (770–476 BC) to the Warring States Period (475–221 BC).

Military rivalry between regional states urged institutional experiments to secure competitiveness. By 221 BC, when the remote Western state of Qin conquered the six big states with its magnificent military superpower, China became a centralized unitary state.[2] It is generally believed that the institutional reforms of Qin made this geographically remote state rise to be the superpower and unifier. After Qin's conquest and further territorial expansion, its local institutions were transplanted across China. China became an empire rested on a centralized political system, in which the authority of the state was the fundamental mechanism for all other institutional arrangements. The institutional prototype formed in the era of Qin-Han evolved in the coming 22 centuries, generating a long-lasting influence even on today's Chinese institutions. To fully understand their origins, it is necessary to review the major institutional reforms and ideology since Qin.

Qin's institutional reformed could be dated back to the 4th century BC Shang Yang (390–338 BC), a Chinese Legalist (*fa jia*) intellectual and reformist, started to implement an overall institutional reform since 359 BC (Table 7.1) with the support of Duke Xiao Gong of Qin (381–338 BC) (Bodde 1986, 34–38). Chinese Legalism was one of the ancient schools of statecrafts, which highlighted the philosophy of "enriching the country and strengthening the military power" (*fuguo qiangbin*). In the Legalist doctrine, the human is self-interested and adaptive to external incentives. The state must set up institutions to guide people's decision-making in line with the state's ambitions. So, they emphasized the importance of the statute law in reinforcing the state power, rather than arbitrary orders of monarchs. In the warring time, the strategic goal of Qin was to reinforce its power against the other states. To this end, Shang Yang made a set of institutional reforms based on written rules to encourage agricultural production and military growth. They also advocated for state monopoly and mercantilist policies to accumulate national wealth.

Legalist reforms promoted domestic market integration that led to significantly reduced transaction costs, restriction of unproductive social groups and acceleration of information and knowledge diffusion that were important to productivity growth. Those institutions empowered China to take advantage of huge potential of the integrated market far earlier than the other countries.[3] After reunification, the state of Qin became an empire. In the first place, the relationship between the central and subnational governments was the fundamental institution. There were

Table 7.1 Institutional reforms of the Legalist Qin

Category	*Institutional reforms*
Political institution	governance by the rigid system of statute laws, rather than the arbitrary lords
	replace the traditional feoffment system with counties based on populace
	abolish the power and the hereditariness of the noble class
	dispatch salaried bureaucrats in charge of regional administration
	reform the household register system, each neighborhood covers five–10 families; the whole neighborhood would be punished for any inhabitant's guilt; reward delating and group punishment of harboring
	separate big families, extra head tax for families with more than two male adults (father and grown-up sons, or adult brothers)
Military institution	"farming-warfare" complex
	reward the title of nobility to civilians based on progressive military exploits (number of decapitations of the enemy)
	demote the idle nobility class
	prohibit private violence, arms
Economic institution	emphasize the importance of agriculture at the expense of commerce
	abolish the old fixed and tenured landholding system, privatization of the land and permission of land transactions to alter the social status of peasants;
	state monopoly in salt and iron production and sales
	improve the canal and irrigation system
	draft corvees for public projects and infrastructures
Social institution	standardize the system of measurement
	unify the norms of roads, track gauge
	adopt the single standard script

Source: Yu (2016, 223); Bodde (1986, 35); Harrison (1972, 88).

two options for the emperor: traditional feudalism or bureaucracy. Qin accepted the Legalist prime minister's design of bureaucracy, which was the prototype of China's modern governance.

At the central administration, the emperor system deified the supremacy of the emperor, upon which political and social orders were rearranged. The executive central administration was institutionalized to operate state affairs.[4] The typical system was the "Three Lords and Nine Ministers" (*sangong jiuqing*), which later formalized as "Three Provinces and Six Ministries" (*sansheng liubu*). It is an institution of separation of powers, even the emperor was bounded legally. The central administration drafted state policies, and local administrations were subjected to implement them. At the subnational level, the prefecture-county system (*jun-xian zhi*) replaced the traditional hereditary fief system. The empire was initially partitioned into 36 prefectures and then subdivided into a number of counties. There was a standard administration for each prefecture and county, consisting of a civil governor (*jun shou*), a military commander (*wei*) and an imperial inspector (*jian*

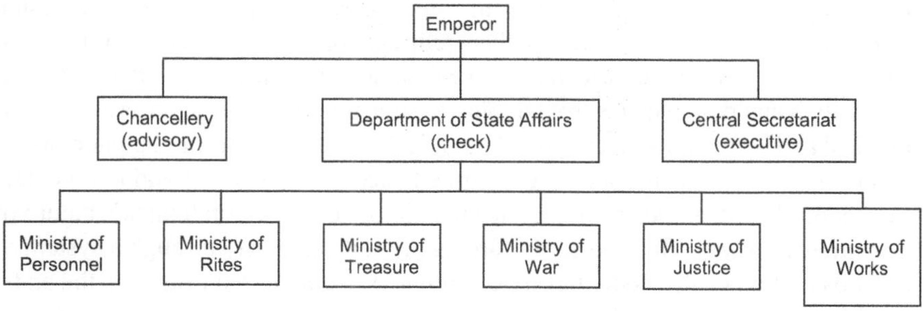

Figure 7.1 Stylized central government of Imperial China

yu shi) who was the immediate representative of the emperor (Bodde 1986, 54).[5] Local bureaucrats were centrally selected and appointed to manage their jurisdictions based on the unified statute laws. The administrative division of labor between the central and local governments could be described as "the central manages bureaucrats and the local manages residents". The prefecture-county system was the footstone of the unitary China and lasts till today.

In the light of the contract theory, Imperial China's governance structure is a multiple principal-agent model. The emperor was the principal, central bureaucrats were the first tier of agents and local bureaucrats were the second tier of agents. Suppose all the players are rational, then the emperor seeks to secure his rule and benefits of being the ruler, and bureaucrats maximize their benefits from posts. Information asymmetry and conflicts of interests between players cause the "agency dilemma". Bureaucrats may violate the emperor's interest, such as hiding local information about outputs, taxes, finance and rebellions, or even fostering local armed forces that threatened the throne. To alleviate the "agency dilemma", supporting institutions to the bureaucracy and prefecture-county system were set up. Some of which are still effective in modern China. First, bureaucrats were subject to recall, and their posts were not hereditary, in order to prohibit the formation of interest groups. Second, an assessment system on the capability and performance of the bureaucrats was founded to align their efforts with the emperor's interests. Third, China kept improving a vertical information collection system by dispatching inspectors to each level of the administration. Last, but most importantly, the unified China employed the ideological device to reduce the cost of information and opportunistic behaviors of the bureaucrats and common people. Ideology, in turn, strengthened Chinese institutions and shaped the social value system and then the economic outcomes.

Ideologies underlie the subject frameworks for the individual to receive and interpret information, which are important institutional arrangements to reduce transaction costs of the whole society (North 1981, 1991). To reinforce the bureaucracy, Chinese rulers adopted social values as the orthodoxy ideology. As mentioned earlier, Qin adopted Legalism as the ideology of state building.

In order to aggrandize Legalism, Qin Shi Huang, the first emperor of the unified China, approved his Legalist prime minister's proposition of severe suppression of other ideas in 213 BC.[6] Rather than religions or superstitions, the Qin advocated "learning from the officials". Since then, general education and works were officially banned or even destroyed; only technical knowledge, such as agronomy, medical and botany, was accessible, but under the control of technobureaucrats. In this obscurantist system, people got limited access to education and knowledge. In general, Legalism designed the incentive structure based on human's nature of self-interest. It was effective in reinforcing the state authority through a system of rewards and a penalty code, but it accumulated dissatisfaction towards the state, resulting in widespread rebellions that destroyed the newly founded empire.

The alternative, Confucianism, put the human goodness by nature and harmonious relationships between people as the cornerstone of its value system, rather than the self-interest of the Legalist. Instead of harsh control, Confucianism advocates "good governance" that prioritizes moral education of people to follow codes of ethics.[7] Confucianism suggested rebuilding all social relationships by restoring family ties grounded on filial piety (*xiao*), a virtue of respect for one's parents and elders. The relationship between ruler and its subjects was in the familistic way, the people were the children and the emperor was the father (Callis 1959, 48), then the society would be in harmony.

Learnt from Qin's collapse, Emperor Wu Di (157–87 BC) of the Han Dynasty converted to a synthetist value system around 134 BC, in the name of "the promotion of Confucianism to the disparagement of all other schools". This new ideology combined Confucianist codes of ethics, Taoist doctrine of state's responsibility for the livelihood of the populace and Legalist anti-mercantilism, state monopoly and the reliance on the penalty code to discipline the governed (Huang 1997, 43). The synthetist ideology made Imperial China "the Confucian-Legalist State" (Zhao 2016), rested on formal Legalist institutions and informal Confucianism ideology. The essence of Confucianism is the idea of benevolence, which could be popularized through moral education, so the installation of Confucianism developed a national public educational system that consisted of higher education institutions and an elementary system. The ascending Confucianism also reinforced the central-local relationship. After ideological restoration, Wu Di selected and appointed Confucianist scholars to civil posts. Since then, imperial bureaucrats must learn Confucianist classical works and follow the Confucianist doctrine of governance. This ideological device reinforced personnel control and became a key solution to the agency dilemma of the central-local relationship. First, imperial civil servants shared the common value system, and violators would be removed from posts. This personnel institution was further formalized during the Sui Dynasty (581–619). The emperor Sui Wen Di initiated the Imperial Civil Examination (*ke ju*) in 587. Since then, all imperial officials were selected by their knowledge of Confucianist classical works. Only few qualifiers of progressive triennial examinations were appointed to civil posts.[8] Competence in the examination could only be assured through years of laborious education, for which Chinese families had to invest a considerable sum. The Confucianist doctrine of "good governance" also served as a counter force to the emperor system. The emperor was the personification of a Confucianist saint and the role model of the people. Once an emperor failed to obey the mandate of good governance, he lost his legitimacy. Successive emperors, either substitutes from the imperial family, rebellious leaders or even nomadic invaders,[9] had to allege to follow Confucianism in order to gain legitimacy and the support from the people, especially from the scholar-bureaucrats. Being ideologically locked-in enabled the empire to be a hyper-stable society for more than 2000 years.

7.3 Incentive and performance in Imperial China

Imperial China's institutions had comparative advantages in providing large-scale public infrastructures and necessary standards for economic transactions. Major institutions also affected the allocation of talents and social resources that led to economic take-off in the year of agricultural civilization, but they were reluctant to embrace innovation and industrialization.

First, the centralized political system was the institutional foundation for the public infrastructure provision. The unitary state had a stronger capability in mobilizing mass resources for infrastructure improvement and cutting cross-regional coordination costs, which were important to avoid the collective action dilemma. In pre-modern times, agricultural production was the primary source of output and taxation, of which the public irrigation system was the vital part of the infrastructure. As early as the Qin-Han era, the state tamed the Yellow River, the major grain production zone, by preventing floods, trenching canals to connect rivers into a stable water network and developing an advanced irrigation system consisting of kanats, canals and shafts. The unified state was also able to allocate large-scale resources to provide pivotal defense against the robbing nomads from the north and the west. For example, the magnificent defense works like the Great Wall[10] could only be completed by the unified state. Emperor Han's defeat of the Huns in the 120s BC provided long-term security for the making of the ancient Silk Road that connected trade, commodities, culture, knowledge and technology between China and the West.[11] China also developed long-range canals and a post communication system, which facilitated market integration. Stable agricultural production and national defense ensured the empire's long-term population growth and economic prosperity.

Second, the institution-based allocation of talents was vital to long-term performance (Baumol 1990; Acemoglu 1995; Murphy et al. 1991). In ancient China, the formal social ladder was defined as a four-tiered hierarchy following Confucianism. The first tier was the educated scholars. They were politically privileged and exempt from taxes and corvée. The scholar was followed by farmers and artisans, and the lowest was merchants. The institution of the imperial civil examinations (*ke ju*) provided incentive for social mobility, by which only the educated scholars were eligible to get access to state power and wealth. This shaped people's value system. It encouraged Chinese families to make significant investments in education. For the privileged and rich families, their social status would only be sustained by descendants' success in *ke ju*, while education was the most important pathway to change the social status and living conditions of the poor. Once the *ke ju* became an industry (*ju ye*), the scholar-bureaucrat class formed. The scholar-bureaucrat tradition was of great importance to the intellectual's career orientation. Under the value pressure of "scholarship pursuing surmounts all other occupations", a great number of educated social elite were devoted to unproductive activities like public administration, intellectual endeavors and art. Even the educated took over state affairs; they operated mainly based on moral management rather than mathematical management, which, though it is the essence of modern governance, was underdeveloped (Huang 1997). This scholar-bureaucrat class was looked unfavorably upon by other social classes like artisans, engineers and merchants. The routine of anti-merchants and the depression of conspicuous consumption resulted in an undeveloped spirit of entrepreneurship and the rise of the merchant class to power in China (Yu 2016, 213).[12] Therefore, when the market economy started to grow in the late stage of the empire, the role of the entrepreneur was not as active as their Western counterparts, which is suggested as one of the basic causes of the failure of Chinese scientific development, or the "Needham's Grand Issue". The *ke ju* was abolished in 1905 for its incapability of selecting bureaucrats to manage modernization and globalization. Though the modern education system was introduced afterwards, the state still adheres to the custom of selecting graduates to government posts. The Chinese family's preference in investing in education has sustained as well.

Third, since the making of the empire, wealth was viewed as a pillar of state authority which must be under state control.[13] Not only was folk commerce depressed and businessmen held in contempt in the lower social order, but the state also built up a monopolist system to control staple commodities of strategic importance since the Han Dynasty.[14] However, state monopolism was mainly for luxury and military ends, rather than market demand and foreign trade. Although ancient China achieved a high level of industrial production and quality, the non-market-orientation hampered the development of the market economy and modern production mode.[15] Moreover, a great share of craftsmen were from hereditary lines, and their entrepreneurship was depressed. The state-running routine in Imperial China is one of the institutional origins of modern state-owned enterprises (SOEs).

Fourth, the unitary state supplied essential institutions to reduce transaction costs of economic activity, such as the single currency, the universal measurement and script system and standardized transportation, etc. Those institutions facilitated domestic market integration and the social division of labor, which boosted productivity by sophistication of specialization (Smith 2000; Young 1928; Yang 2000). The state set up a macroeconomic management system for stabilizing unexpected market fluctuations.[16]

In sum, Imperial China's institutions and ideology were favorable to agricultural production. However, the super-stable institutional structure was cautious toward innovations that may have threatened the ruling group and established social orders (Acemoglu and Robinson 2012). Although China reached a very high level of agricultural civilization during the Han Dynasty, agricultural technology stagnated for 1000 years. China developed sophisticated skills in many handicrafts, but they were not generalized into scientific laws and could not provide support for industrial innovation and sustainable productivity improvement. China's fleet of advanced treasure ships that explored the Maritime Silk Road in the 15th century, earlier than the geographical discovery,[17] was suddenly ceased by the imperial injunction of "close the door and lock the country". The world's largest international trade network degraded to a narrow tributary system. Compared to the rise of the West after the Industrial Revolution through institutional change (North and Weingast 1989; Mokyr and Nye 2007), Chinese traditional institutions were the fundamental cause of its economic underdevelopment when the industrial civilization came. In this regard, China's modern economic development was reached by reforms in the rigid traditional institutions.

7.4 Legacy of Chinese traditional institutions

Chinese institutions underwent significant changes as a response to social, economic and cultural transformation, especially after being challenged by Western industrialization since the 19th century. In general, China's modernization is a process of re-balancing indigenous and imported institutions. We can trace the path dependency of traditional institutions in modern China.

7.4.1 Modern Chinese unitary governance structure

Although there are many differences, the governance structures between imperial and modern China share similarities. Foremost, the central-local governance structure remains in the center of modern institutions. Figure 7.2 presents the Chinese historical governance structure. The prefecture-county system has been the solid foundation of Chinese governance since its establishment in Qin Dynasty, regardless of how ruling groups and ideologies change. As to demographic, social and economic developments, the central government faced increasing challenges in processing local information, with increasingly sophisticated governance and administration levels extended upon the basic prefecture-county system. When

Table 7.2 Development of Chinese township and village enterprises since reform

	Number (million)	*Employment (million)*	*Value added (billion yuan)*	*Total output (billion yuan)*	*Revenue (billion yuan)*
1978	1.52	28.3	20.8	51.4	43.1
1983	1.35	32.3	40.8	101.9	92.9
1988	1.89	95.5	174.2	750.2	662.0
1992	20.9	106.2	448.5	1788.0	1639.0
1998	20.0	125.4	2218.6	9669.4	8935.1
2002	21.3	132.9	3238.6	14043.5	12976.0

Source: China Township and Village Enterprise Statistics (1978–2002).

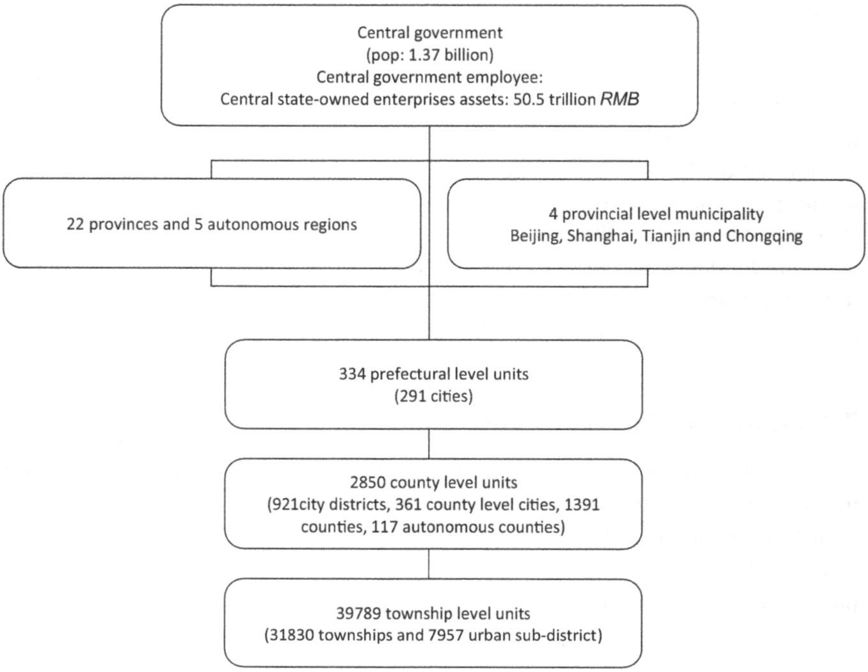

Figure 7.2 Regional governance structure of contemporary China

Source: Xu (2011), NBS.

the empire collapsed at the turn of the 20th century, China experimented with various governance structures, including constitutional monarchy, republicanism, presidency, cabinet responsibility, provincial autonomy, etc.[18] However, each resulted in China's political and military fragmentation and incapability to secure sovereignty and improve people's living conditions. Hence, the People's Republic of China (PRC) restored the centralized administration tradition to maintain unification, and it started a new wave of state building in changing global settings.[19]

Since the founding of the PRC in 1949, the central government has been updating national strategies at different stages of development. Ensuring that the subnational governments implement national plans is fundamental to China's modernization. The contemporary governance structure is a five-tiered administrative system, extended from the prefecture-county system. The solution to solve the agency dilemma was the extension of the traditional personnel control system. Officials are appointed, assessed and supervised by the superior administration according to their capability, effort, integrity and performance in implementing the central authority's strategy. Since the civil servant market is a closed market, almost all payments to and welfare of an official is bonded to his post; the personnel assessment system is the crucial incentive structure to the officials (Li and Zhou 2005). In this unitary state, the change in the personnel assessment system would make a difference in economic performance. For example, when the central authority decided to make economic construction the central task since 1980, the whole country worked as a machine to pursue economic growth through reforms up to today.

7.4.2 Modern ideology

Ideology still plays an important role in modern China. As discussed previously, ideological unity has been an essentially informal institution to China's unitary governance. It provided a common belief to the ruling group and the people. The disadvantage of China's ancient ideology was that ethics dominated and were incapable of embracing innovations that may have caused shocks to the social order. Modern China's ideology inherits the routine of unitary ideology, but it keeps on updating according to the progress.

China's orthodoxy ideology is the "Socialism with Chinese Characteristics", which means Marxism-Leninsm adapted to Chinese circumstances for a present stage. It was created by Deng Xiaoping and is now the guiding principle of the Communist Party of China (CPC). It includes the socialist path and a theoretical system with Chinese characteristics. The socialist path with Chinese characteristics is an ideology about what the meaning of modernization and the path of modernization that fits China best truly is. As social and economic progress, the meaning of modernization is subject to being updated, and then the path keeps on being improved, then the theoretical system developed. Now, the theoretical system includes the theories, ideas and thoughts of Chinese leaders since Deng Xiaoping. In general, socialism with Chinese characteristics is a very pragmatic philosophy. It concentrates on the real circumstances of China and is subject to being updated according to socio-economic dynamics, which defines the practical path of China's modernization.

Chinese central authority keeps on identifying the "primary contradiction" of the society and then finds the fundamental conceptual solution and long-term development strategy to deal with it. For example, the CPC had been claiming that China's major development contradiction lies in backwards social production and the people's ever-growing demand for material and cultural products since 1987. Increasing social output through high-speed economic growth to increase the quantity of supply has been the key solution to this contradiction. Since then, China has been putting economic growth rates and the improvement of people's basic needs as the top priority, even at the expense of protections of labor and environment, tremendous resource consumption and enlarging social inequality. After 30 years of pursuing it, China is now a middle-income country.

The CPC's 19th National Congress, held in November 2017, declared that China faced the new primary contradiction between unbalanced and inadequate development and the people's ever-growing needs for a better life, which includes economic, political, cultural, social and ecological needs, etc. The change of the social primary contradiction indicates a new era of socialism with Chinese characteristics. But China is still at the primary stage of socialism and the world's largest developing country, so the mission of the CPC is to lead and unite the Chinese people of all ethnic groups into fulfilling the central task of economic development, to uphold the "Four Cardinal Principle", continue to Reform and Open-up, and strive to build China into a great modern socialist country that is prosperous, strong, democratic, culturally advanced, harmonious and beautiful.

As a response to the characteristics of the new era, China's latest ideology, or modern Marxism for the 21st century, is the "Xi Jinping Thought on Socialism with Chinese Characteristics for a New Era", which was unveiled in the 2017 CPC National Congress and has been added to the CPC Constitution and Constitution of the PRC. The thought is based on the five new development concepts, which was put forward in 2015 and features innovative, coordinated, green, open and shared development. This new ideology shifts China's development path from high-speed development to high-quality development. At present and in the period to come, high-quality development is the fundamental requirement for making economic policies and conducting macroeconomic regulations. For example, since December 2017, China has been adopting targeted approaches and specific measures to ensure victory in "three critical battles" against potential risk, poverty and pollution that are important for decisively bringing to completion the building of a moderately prosperous society in all respects. It demonstrates that the economic growth rate is no longer the top priority of Chinese authorities; macroeconomic stability, social equality and environmental protections are the well-defined new priorities. In order to implement these policies, the CPC and the Chinese government made organizational reforms. Those changes are not merely in policy change itself, but they are also guided by ideological development. This updated ideology is important for public and market transformation, as it rebuilds social norms.

The custom of scholar-bureaucrat governance is also evolving. In modern China, bureaucrats are selected and promoted by their loyalty to the ideology and capability in fulfilling their duties. High ranking officials must have sufficient experience in lower posts.[20] They are also regularly selected to participate in systematic training programs in order to keep in line with the updated concept and strategy of development.

7.4.3 State-led development

Based on the latest ideology, the state development strategy is drafted in detail. The most important blueprint is the Five-Year Plan (FYP) of national economic and social development. FYP became a routine in 1953, and the latest version is the 13th FYP (2016–2020). A typical FYP covers developing guiding ideas, goals, key sectors and regions, major projects and policy deployments. With the guideline of the successive national FYPs, each ministry compiles departmental FYPs that guide the development of specific areas, such as agriculture, industry, commerce, science and technology, innovation and entrepreneurship, international trade and investment, SOEs reform, education, human resources, healthcare, infrastructure, environmental protection, sports, etc.

Under the guidance of national and ministerial FYPs, each provincial, prefectural or county administration makes a jurisdictional general FYP and specific FYPs. SOEs make firm-level FYPs as their business strategies, to redefine their functions in fulfilling state plans. FYPs are the guideline for the annual agenda. On the one hand, the FYP of China is a "manifesto" of public investment that affects market expectations. With Keynesian multiple effects, public investment from the government or public utility suppliers (normally SOEs) induces a greater magnitude of investment. On the other hand, the FYP generates investment that supports social and economic development, especially in the public sectors with strong externalities and generic technologies with strategic importance. In the first place, China's transportation and communication infrastructures have been developed consistently with accelerating FYPs, which are exceptional among developing countries and offer strong support to China's industrialization, urbanization and attraction of foreign capital.[21] Development of those sectors are still under the state control nowadays; their development plans are made by the central authority, investments are dominated by fiscal funds and key national projects must be approved by the state in advance.

Although there are many countries that have the FYP institution, China's FYPs are stronger in enforcement due to unitary governance. FYPs of Argentina lasted only eight years. Former socialist countries, like the Soviet Union, Romania and Ethiopia gave up FYP routines around 1990. The Republic of Korea's FYP existed from 1962 to 1996. FYPs of India and Nepal are not as strong as China's due to the rotating central administration and weak central-local ties. FYPs of Vietnam and Laos are influenced by China's FYPs. Also, the normal process of making the FYP is the CPC gives suggestions of development for the next five years to the Chinese central people's government (the State Council). The latter is responsible for preparing the draft for the legislative body (the People's Congress) for checking and approval.

7.4.4 Education and talent pipeline

Enthusiasm for education is still prevalent in modern China, both for family investment and the state that highlights the leading role of innovation in transforming the economic growth model. Influenced by traditional social values, the intellectuals are respectable in general in the Confucianist cultural realm. Even today, education is still one of the major channels for social mobility in China. Chinese families make intensive investments in education, even at the very early stages of schooling. The PRC has been persistently investing in general education for the public. According to World Bank statistics, China's lower secondary completion rate reached 98.6% in 2015, compared to 85.5% in India and 80% in South Africa, while the average of middle-income countries was about 80%.[22]

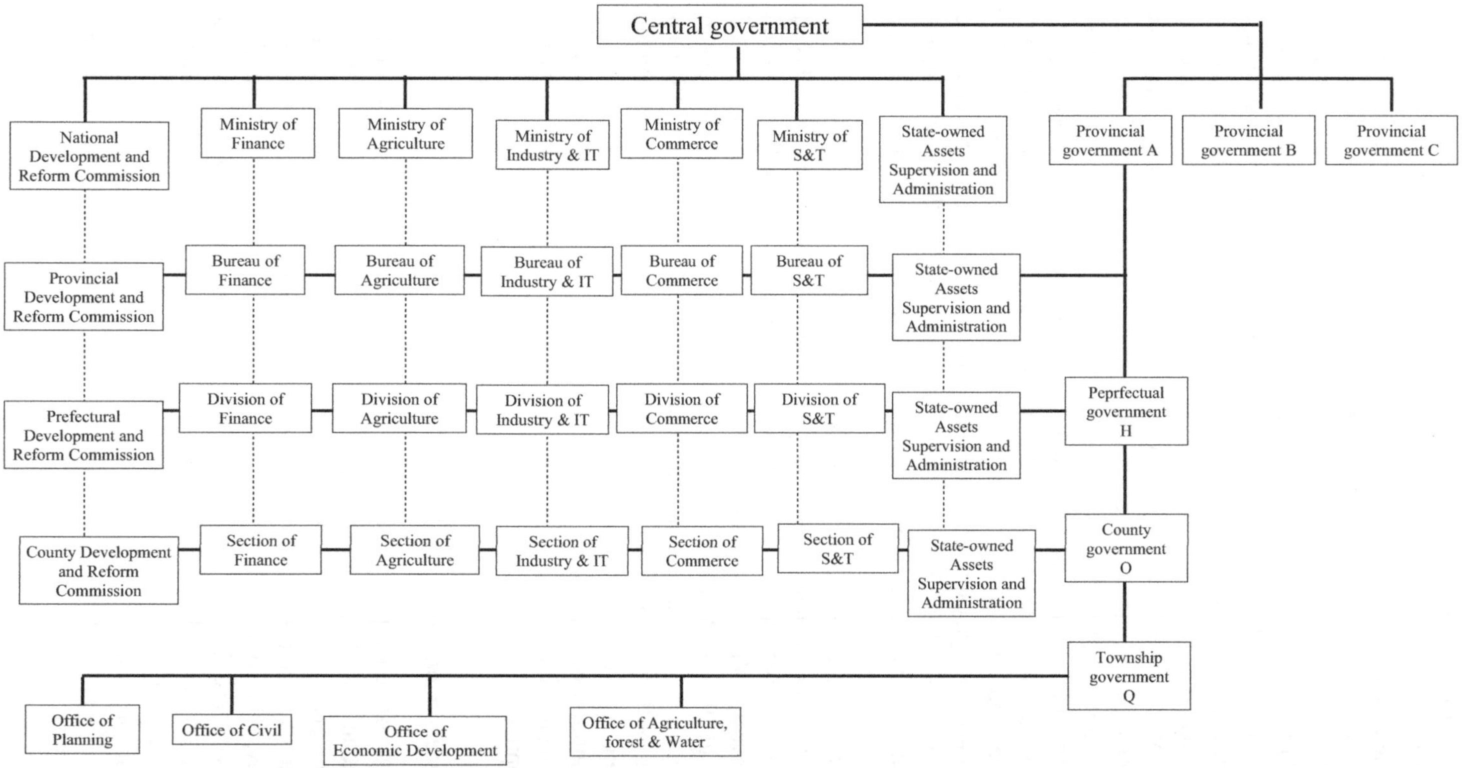

Figure 7.3 Economic governance structure of contemporary China

Source: Made by the author.

Notes: Solid line denotes administrative hierarchy; dot line denotes operational guidance.

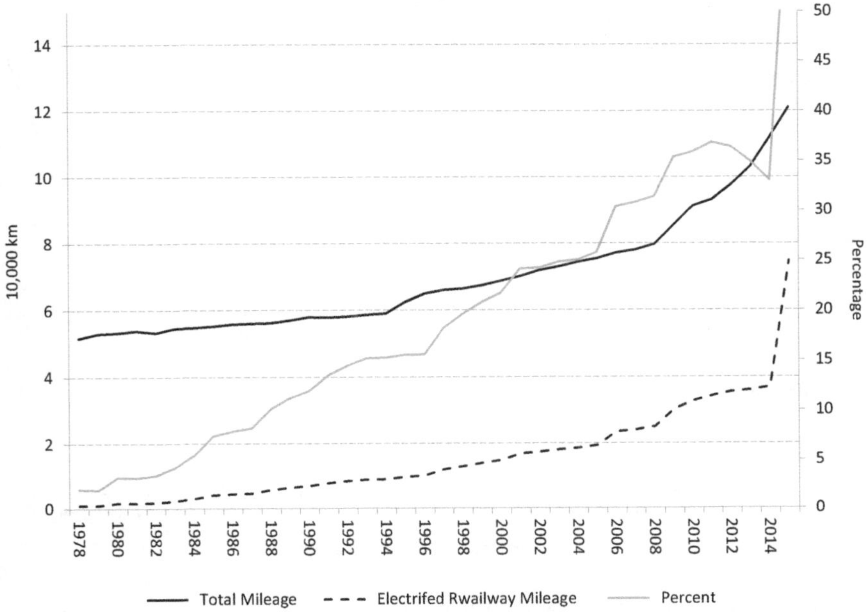

Figure 7.4 Railway mileage of China (10,000 kilometer)

Source: National Bureau of Statistics.

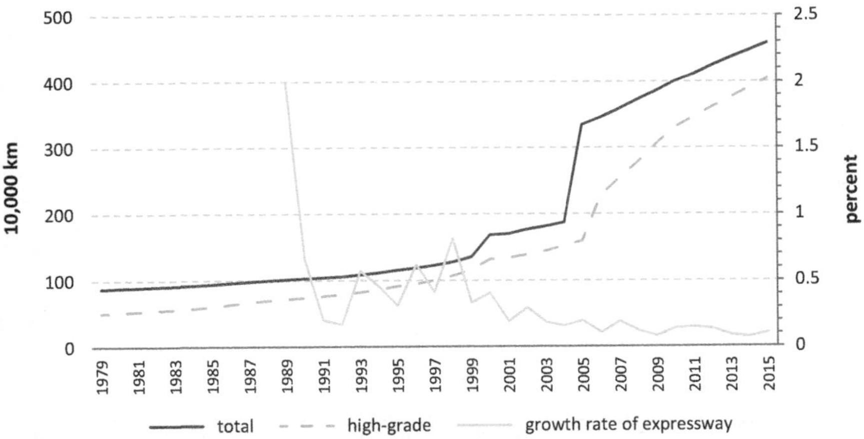

Figure 7.5 Road mileage of China (10,000 kilometer)

Source: National Bureau of Statistics.

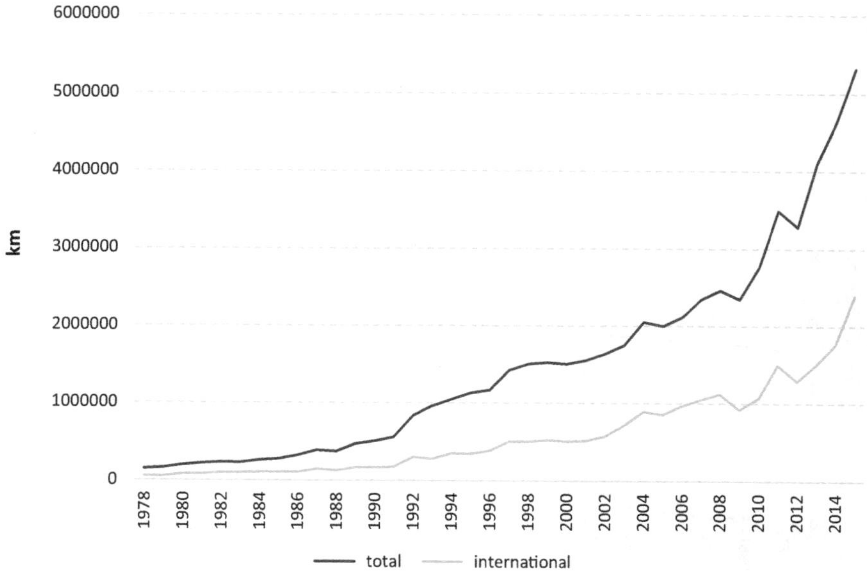

Figure 7.6 Schedule flight mileage of China (kilometer)

Source: National Bureau of Statistics.

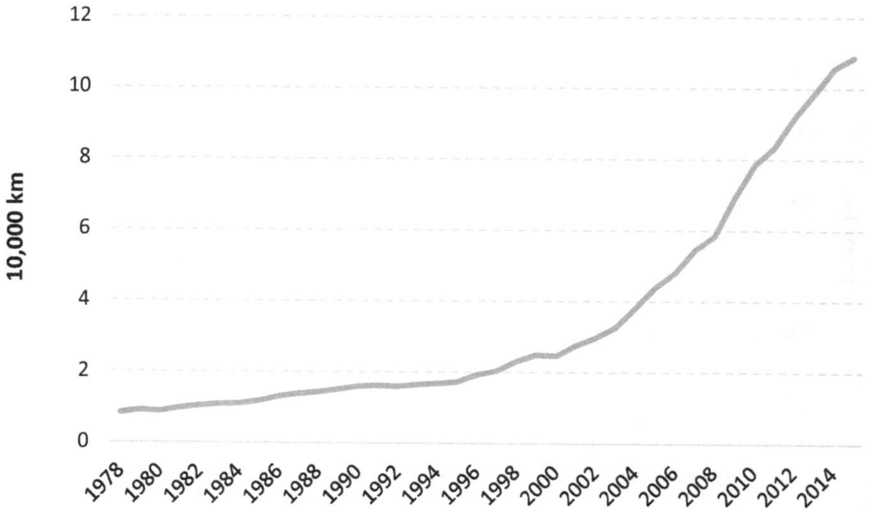

Figure 7.7 Oil pipeline of China (10,000 kilometer)

Source: National Bureau of Statistics.

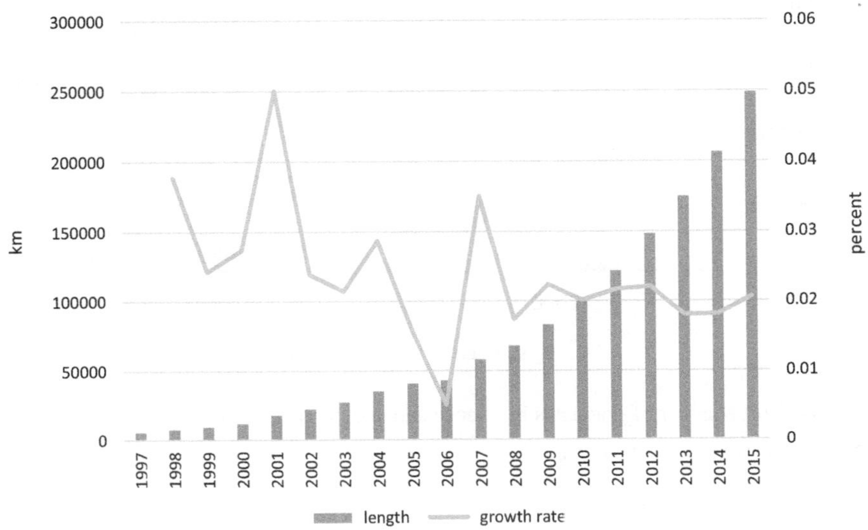

Figure 7.8 Length of optical cable of China (10,000 kilometer)

Source: National Bureau of Statistics.

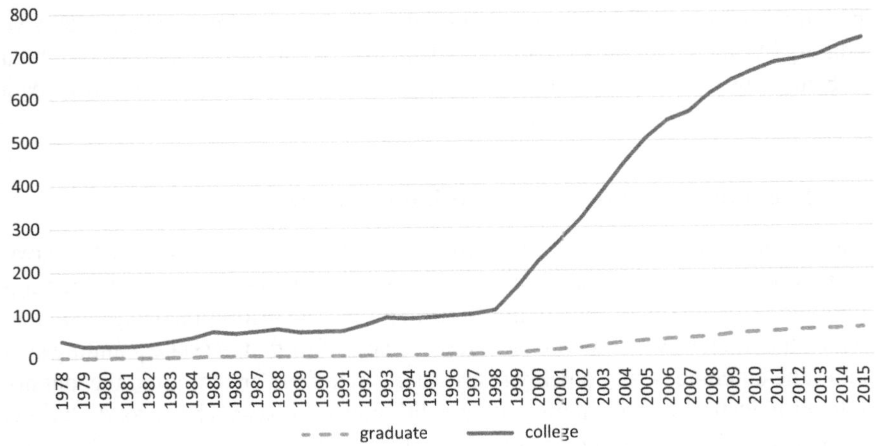

Figure 7.9 Number of graduate and college enrollment of China (10,000 person)

Source: National Bureau of Statistics.

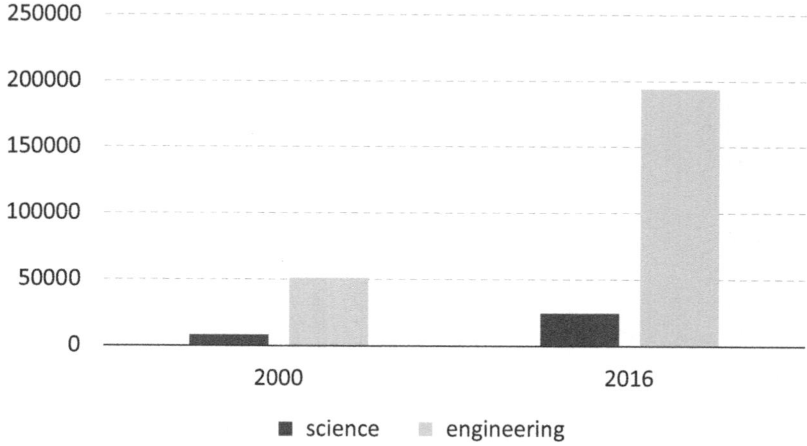

Figure 7.10 Number of graduates in science and engineering of China (person)
Source: Ministry of Education.

After the reform under the guideline of "enlargement of enrollment", the number of college graduates increased from one million in 1998 to nearly 740 million in 2015. In 2000, the number of science and engineering graduates (master's and doctoral degree holders in total) was 8,077 and 24,378, respectively. In 2016, there were 50,811 and 194,116 science and engineering graduates. Modern education transformed China from a labor-intensive country into a talent-intensive country. As the quantitative traditional demographic dividend fades away, China is benefiting from the qualitative demographic dividend and growing towards a prominent global innovation hub.

7.5 Economic institutional transition of the PRC

Chinese economic institutional modernization could be generally divided into two phases. The first is the planned economic system before the Reform and Opening-up (*gaige kaifang*) by the end of the 1970s. This was an institutional experiment in which the market system was almost replaced by a full-fledged state planning system. The outcome was to quickly restructure China from an agricultural economy into an industrialized economy with a solid industrial base. The second phase is market-oriented institutional reform, by which China seeks to exploit the "late-comer advantage" in the global economy. The outcome is the so-called "China puzzle" of economic development.

7.5.1 The centrally planned economic system (1949–1978)

The founding of the PRC was the beginning of a new socialist state. From 1952 to 1956, the state launched a nationwide "socialist transformation" of agriculture, handicraft and bourgeois industry and commerce.[23] The socialist transformation of the national economy eliminated the pillars of the market economy system, including essential private property rights and the market price mechanism. With socialist public ownership, the state took steady control of the economy.

Like many newly independent developing countries after the World War II, the PRC adopted the "catch-up strategy" and the "big-push industrialization" to recover the war-torn national economy. During the Cold War, China also sought to build an independent national economy (Rosenstein-Rodan 1943; Hirschman and Sirkin 1958; Gerschenkron 1962; Singer 1950; Prebisch 1959; Lin et al. 1996). Influenced by the Soviet Union's experience of industrialization, China implemented state-led industrialization and installed a centrally planned economic system. The pillar of the centrally planned economy was state monopolism. China launched the "156 major industrial projects"[24] and pursued a model of Heavy-Chemical Industrialization (HCI) since the 1st FYP (1953–1957). About 1,000 industrial projects were implemented, including defense industry, machinery industry, electronic industry, chemical industry and energy industry deployed nationwide. This was the beginning of China's substantial modern industrialization.

Correspondingly, a centralized industrial administration regime was built up. The principle of industrial management was "unitary leadership, hierarchical management" (*tongyi lingdao, fenji guanli*). For each sector, the state authorized one specialized ministry to practice vertical administrations of enterprises, projects, plans, raw materials, finance resources, employment and wages, etc. By the 1980s, there were more than 20 specialized industrial ministries.[25] The horizontal

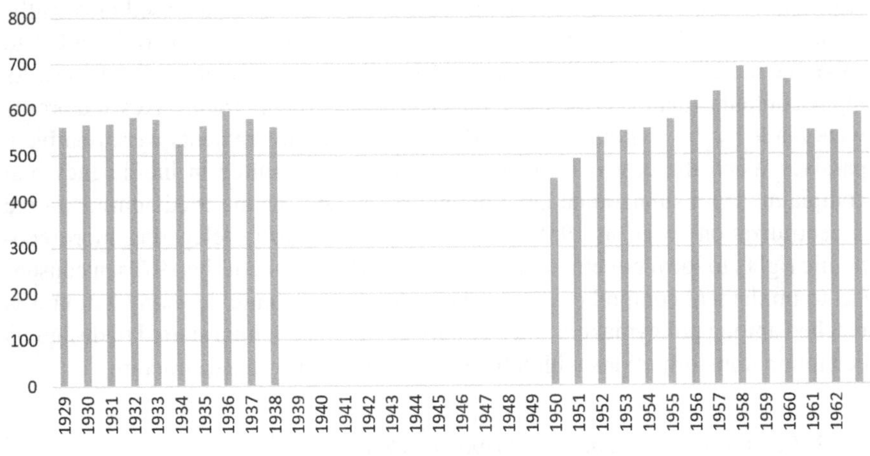

Figure 7.11 Historical GDP per capital of China (1990 international dollars)

Source: The Maddison-Project, www.ggdc.net/maddison/maddison-project/home.htm, 2013 version.

Notes: The Second Sino-Japanese War outbroke in 1931 and escalated into a full-scale war in July 1937. The 14 years of war brought huge destruction to China's economy. China's GDP per capita recovered to a level of 1937 in 1955.

industrial linkages were in the form of inter-ministerial administrative coordinations, which were ultimately controlled by the central planning authority. So, the interlaced state and ministerial planning fully replaces market transactions. The price mechanism was concealed.

In order to secure agricultural production and collect residuals to sustain industrialization inputs, the overall Household Registration (*hukou*) system was implemented in the 1950s by classifying all households into agricultural *hukou* and non-agricultural *hukou*. Rural residents of agricultural *hukou* were prohibited to migrate without formal urban jobs. The payments and consumption of non-agricultural *hukou*, urban residents and military servants, were strictly state allocated. The basic economic function of the *hukou* system is to support the high savings and investment development model.

In many respects, the PRC's centrally planned economic system is similar to the historical state-building regime as a unitary state, including state monopolism, productivity orientation, infrastructure provisions, farming-warfare complex, private property control, etc. Under unitary state monopolism, macroeconomic investment, production, savings, consumption and trade were decided by the state. As each specialized ministry functioned like a larger enterprise, ministerial SOEs were just sub-branches and could not be normal economic decision-makers. They took orders from superior planners, with very limited authorization, information and incentive to carry out independent operation. At the subnational hierarchies, provincial, prefectural, county departments controlled different tiers of SOEs. In short, the function of the market system was replaced by the state control.

According to firm theory (Coase 1937; Williamson 1985), this highly integrated system saves market transaction costs and supports the state to realize economic take-off in a short time.[26] However, as the industrial structure became sophisticated, the administration cost of the centrally planned economic system (e.g., the information cost and lack of economic incentive) increased drastically. Without the market system, the administrative decentralization trials failed to solve the deficiencies of information and incentives for economic distortions. As inputs, outputs, financial resources, big enterprises, foreign trade, taxes and profits were made by the central authority, the subnational governments were relatively passive. When the cost of economic centralization resulted in inefficiency and complaints from subnational governments and SOEs, China tried administrative decentralization twice in 1958 and 1970 by temporarily delegating more economic rights to local governments and SOEs.[27] By the end of the 1970s, a consensus to implement comprehensive market-oriented economic decentralization was reached among policymakers and advisory economists. China started to design its economic transformations within the bureaucratic governance structure.

7.5.2 Economic decentralization reform (1978–)

Inspired by the successful Household Contract Responsibility System[28] in the rural reform in the late 1970s, the contract responsibility system developed into China's economic decentralization since the 1980s. In a broad view, industrial and fiscal decentralization reforms are the mainline of overall market reform.

7.5.2.1 Industrial decentralization

Since the 1980s, SOEs started the market-oriented reform. As the first step, the Enterprise Contract Responsibility System was introduced, by which enterprises were authorized to share extra profits that exceeded the government target. This system partly solved the information and incentive problems but made limited progress to rectify the overlapping relationship between the state and SOEs. In the 1990s, all specialized industrial ministries were revoked and the only comprehensive ministry of industry was established.[29] Hundreds of materials and commodities that used to be under state plan were gradually allocated by the market mechanism through the invention of the double-track price system. In that system, there were two prices for the same product: one was the state pricing for the planned part, the other was the market price for the unplanned part. After a gradual transition, the double-track price converged to the market price, and the state price was eventually abolished. Price mechanism is now the dominant system for resource allocation for most of the markets, and only a few industrial products of strategic importance are kept under direct state control and pricing. Reforms in the prices of agricultural products and services are slower than industrial products.

Decoupling with parenting ministries made most SOEs become economic players of independent operation, accounting and financial responsibility. Moreover, after the enforcement of the Corporation Law in 1994, SOEs started ownership reform, then the modern stockholding system prevailed. Since the mid-1990s, under the principle of "restructuring the big and relaxing control over the small" (*zhuada fangxiao*), only a few big SOEs are remained in state administration. A great number of small and micro-sized SOEs were privatized in various ways. They became market players immediately. Township and village enterprises (TVEs) boomed after the deregulation. TVEs contributed to market development by increasing market supply and rationalizing market prices. Further trade deregulation of TVEs facilitated China's access to the world market.

Since the mid-1990s, the surge of privatization of a great number of SOEs and TVEs urged protection of private property rights. In the 2004 Constitution amendment, protection of lawful private properties was added; meanwhile the inventory of private property has been expanding. In order to utilize rural residual labors, rural residents were permitted to migrate to cities starting in 1978. Since then, the *hukou* restriction has been half-opened. The *hukou* system is under gradualist reform. In general, middle and small sized cities are abolishing *hukou* restriction in the coming year. But due to the insufficient supply of public services, there are still many social welfare benefits preferentially provided to local *hukou* holders. The complete abolishment of the *hukou* system is still on the way.

7.5.2.2 Regional decentralization and gradualist institutional experiments

Regional decentralization was implemented through the financial system reform and regional institutional experiments, which incentivized the subnational government to make institutional innovations to facilitate regional economic growth.

Table 7.3 Contribution of TVEs to Chinese export

	Total export (100 million yuan)	*Export of TVEs (100 million yuan)*	*Share of TVEs (%)*
1990	2985.8	485.6	16.26
1991	3827.1	669.9	17.50
1992	4676.3	1192.8	25.51
1993	5284.8	2193	41.50
1994	10422	3398.3	32.61
1995	12452	5394.6	43.44
1996	12576	6007.9	47.77
1997	15161	6826.5	45.03
1998	15232	6853.7	45.00

Source: China Township and Village Enterprise Statistics (1978–2002).

Table 7.4 Comparison of historical governance structure and economic institutions

		Governance Structure		*Economic institution*
		Central authority	*Regional decentralization*	
Pre-Qin		Weak	Strong	Rival local entrepreneurism
Imperial China Since Qin		Strong	Weak	Emperor monopoly
Modern China	Pre-reform	Strong	Weak	State planning
	Post-reform	Strong	Strong	State coordinated industrial/local entrepreneurism
England	Before the Glorious Revolution	Strong	Weak	Monarchical monopoly
	After the Glorious Revolution	Strong	Strong	State supported industrial entrepreneurism
United States	Before the Civil War	Weak	Strong	Economic regionalism
	After the Civil War	Strong	Strong	State supported industrial entrepreneurism
Eat Asia		Strong	Weak	State supported industrial entrepreneurism

Chinese regional decentralization is not in the typical form of fiscal federalism of the West (Weingast 1995), but within the established centralized political institutions. This institutional change is suggested to be the fundamental institution to explain the "China puzzle" (Xu 2011).

Before the reform, the central government adopted the Grand Fiscal Unification (*da yi tong*) system to control resources and invest in HCI. After the reform, rural and enterprise reforms fueled economic growth and increased fiscal revenue to the government. But most surplus of economic growth was collected by the central government, and subnational governments lacked incentive. In order to further encourage subnational governments, the "Revenue Sharing Contract System"

(RSCS) was introduced between central and subnational governments in 1980. Since then, subnational governments were permitted to keep surplus revenue over the target contracted with central government.[30] With this incentive, subnational governments requested higher authority to implement growth-boosting regional policies, such as cutting taxes or subsidizing for the local enterprises, even implementing regional protectionism.[31] The RSCS was formally replaced by the Tax-Sharing System (*fen shui zhi*, TSS) in 1994. The latter is a unified tax system that clarifies the tax division between the central and subnational governments. For example, the annual tax of a local government is T, and it shares $\alpha * T$ $(0 < \alpha < 1)$ and the central government shares $(1-\alpha) * T$. Under this system, both central and subnational governments are beneficiaries of regional economic growth. Therefore, the TSS provides a stable incentive mechanism for subnational government to be the "first mover" of institutional innovations to promote economic growth. Once their institutional innovations make both the central government and jurisdictional people better off, then it is likely to be approved.

In a unitary state, the up-to-bottom institutional changes would incur systematic risks and significant costs. Regional institutional experimentation became an important device to examine the quality of institutional changes. This is a process of variation and selection, which makes sure Chinese institutional transitions are stable and effective. There are two types of regional institutional experiments. First, some are made through the central decision-making process and implemented in selected regions. For example, the special economic zone (SEZ) is an effective regional treatment of new institutions and policy. The effects of regional institutional experiments would be evaluated and further generalized for nationwide implementation.[32] Second, some institutional changes are initiated by local authorities, neither violating the central government's prohibition nor approved by the central government before execution. If regional institutional changes are beneficial to regional economic growth without causing significant negative impacts on the national development plans, then the central government would authenticate and even spread them to the reset regions. This routine makes Chinese subnational governments function like entrepreneurs seeking business opportunities. There are two hypotheses to explain subnational governments' incentive to carry out institutional innovation. One is the market preserving fiscal federalism with "Chinese style" (Weingast 1995; Qian and Weingast 1996), which assumes the local government maximizes jurisdictional tax revenue (Qian and Xu 1993) by supporting local entrepreneurism. The other is the political tournament (Li and Zhou 2005), which assumes that higher economic performance is an indication of local officials' capabilities and a higher probability to get promotion. In short, the role of the Chinese government in economic development goes beyond the dichotomy of the invisible hand and the grabbing hand, instead acting as the "helping hand". Regional economic decentralization makes China different than the ancient time, when subnational governments were banned from making institutional innovations and lacked incentive to foster entrepreneurism. China's decentralization is also different from other smaller authoritative East Asian economies, where the local governments are not in direct economic competition.

Although there are many explanations for China's modern economic growth, the market-oriented decentralization reforms would be the most fundamental change of incentives. Decentralization formally rationalizes Chinese industrial and regional economic institutions, and the importance of the market institutions keeps on increasing. To further secure the market system, China improves market-enhancing institutions and a stable macroeconomic environment (Aoki et al. 2013), like private property protection, public investment in research and development (R&D), vocational training and human resource development, infrastructure development and financial market reform. As a result, economic reforms enabled the Chinese economy to grow at historically unprecedented rates by fostering investment, reallocation and technology adoption from abroad (Borensztein and Ostry 1996; Jefferson et al. 2000; Cao and Birchenall 2013; Zilibotti 2017; Zheng et al. 2017). However, the economic decentralization reform potentially develops industrial or regional interest groups, which threatens further reforms on the one hand and the function of the market system on the other. China is still seeking further institutional reforms to perfect the socialist market economy system.

7.6 Conclusion

In this chapter, we review the origins and evolution of Chinese institutions as a unitary state. To govern the unprecedentedly big country, China developed a centralized political system more than 2200 years ago. Upon this bureaucratic governance regime, economic and social institutions are arranged and evolved. Due to path dependency, many modern Chinese institutions have their historical origins. This means that Chinese institutions have been developing in a different trajectory with other countries.

Since the institutional reform at the end of 1970s, China has been carrying out industrial and regional decentralization within central authoritarianism for four decades.

The major advantages of Chinese institutions' economic growth include highly integrated domestic markets for industrial development and entrepreneurship, an efficient developmentalist state that coordinates resource allocation for strategic projects and prefers technological advances and an emphasis on education and social equality. There are also some imperfections in Chinese institutions. As advocated in China's latest strategy of development, China is going to make further economic institutional reforms to provide a fair ground for all market players, such as improving the property rights system and ensuring the market-based allocation of factors of production, improving the systems for managing different types of state assets, breaking administrative monopolies, creating a modern public finance system and reforming the budget system and taxation system.

Notes

1 In the rhetoric of "Chinese approaches" (*zhongguo fang'an*) or "Chinese knowledge" (*zhongguo zhihui*), especially when other developing countries choose their own paths of modernization.

2 There were seven big states in the Warring States Period, *Qin* (West), *Han* (Middle-South), *Zhao* (Middle-North), *Wei* (Middle), *Chu* (South), *Yan* (Northeast) and *Qi* (East).

3 The economic advantage of Chinese institutions was even recorded in Adam Smith's theory of the division of labor and the extent of the market (Smith 2000). In *Wealth of Nations*, Adam Smith admired the convenience of water transportation that linked regional markets. The expansion of domestic market promotes social division of labor, which is the source of national wealth creation.

4 Three lords were the Chancellery in charge of civil affairs, the Grand Commandant responsible for military affairs and the Imperial Secretary, who was the chief of inspection. Nine ministers comprised all the important ministers for the central government and the imperial house, such as justice, guards, treasure, agriculture, education, ceremonies, imperial clan, imperial household, etc.

5 Under the county, there were also grassroots public players participating in community public affairs. Those were not full-time posts, for they mainly relied upon the locals to carry out self-governance.

6 Including burned and banned classic works of other schools, and they buried alive hundreds of non-Legalist intellectuals.

7 Or the 'five constant virtues' of benevolence (*ren*), righteousness (*yi*), etiquette (*li*), wisdom (*zhi*) and fidelity (*xin*)

8 The typical imperial civil examination since the 14th century was the so-called 'three degrees and four examinations'. The lowest level of examination was the prefecture-county examination presided over by the local chief officials, where successful candidates were rewarded the degree of *xiu cai* (or Cultivated Talent, the basic requirement for a scholar-bureaucrat) and qualified to the provincial examination presided over by the governor. Qualifiers were rewarded the degree of *ju ren* (or Raised Man) and became candidates for civil posts. The highest level was the two imperial examinations, first held in the imperial capital city and then presided over by the emperor in the imperial palace. The successful candidates were rewarded the degree of *jin shi* (or Promoted Scholar) and became the honorary disciples of the emperor. All *jin shi* degree holders were immediately appointed to civil posts by the emperor. China's imperial examination institution spread to the East Asian countries of the Confucianist cultural realm, such as Japan, Korea and Viet Nam, and it officially terminated in 1905 when the Qing Dynasty implemented drastic modernization reforms. It is believed that contemporary China's civil examination is an updated version of the imperial civil examination institution.

9 For example, the Yuan Dynasty founded by the Mongols and the Qing Dynasty by the Manchus.

10 The Great Wall used to be the defensive battle line against the aggressive cavalry in the north.

11 China's recent "One Belt One Road Initiative" is partly inspired by the Ancient Silk Road tradition.

12 The rise of the merchant class was the social foundation of capitalist revolution in the West and political modernization (Acemoglu et al. 2005).

13 Following Legalist statecrafts, direct economic control was necessary to empower the state in a centralized country. The accumulation of wealth of merchants was viewed as a loss of the state treasure.

14 Since Sang Hongyang (155–80 BC), a finance minister of the Han Dynasty, salt, iron, alcohol and other necessities for consumption and production were under state monopoly, in order to enlarge the tax base, utilize scale economy and secure the supply of weapons.

15 For example, the Ministry of Works of the Tang Dynasty employed 12,000 to 20,000 craftsmen and a greater number of unskilled industrial labors in the 8th century (Zi 2015). In the Song Dynasty, there were 51 products under state administration, and 5000 state employed craftsmen in the capital city in 1003 BC In the early Ming Dynasty, there were more than 200,000 state employed craftsmen in 62 industries. By the late Ming, there were 12,000 full-time state employed craftsmen in the capital city solely, covering 188 professions. Till the end of the 19th century, when the Qing Dynasty adopted the modern industrialization, major industrial facilities were invested

and managed by state and local governments. A special administration and inspection office was set up in the Han Dynasty. Although an immediate cause of the state monopoly system was to finance the massive campaigns against barbarian tribes (*xiongnu*) in the north and west, the system remained after the military operations for 2600 years. In 2014, China formally abolished the state monopoly of salt.

16 For example, under the *ping-zhun* system, when the supply was in short, the state would undersell state reserves to rebalance. The Han Dynasty also set up the nationwide system of fiscal transfer (*jun-shu*), by which articles of tribute were delivered directly from one region to others where state support was needed.

17 During 1405–1433, one of Captain Admiral Zheng He's fleets included over 240 ships, carrying 27,400 crew members and visited more than 30 countries located to the West Pacific Ocean and Indian Ocean. Admiral Zhang's seven voyages provided safe passage for maritime trade.

18 As the constitutional monarchy in the late Qing Dynasty, parliamentary republic and semi-presidentialism in the 1920s and constitutionalism in the 1940s.

19 In Chinese history, from the First Opium War of the 1840s to the founding of the People's Republic of China in 1949, China was a semi-colonial and semi-feudal society. China was politically and economically separated and lost its sovereignty to the world industrial and military powers.

20 On average, a member of the Political Bureau of the Central Committee of Communist Party of China (CPC) has experience as governor of two provinces, or about 200 million people.

21 China's development experience in infrastructure is one of the most important causes of the "One Belt and One Road" Initiative. Chinese public financial provisions in infrastructure led to the launch of the Asian Infrastructure Investment Bank (AIIB) that targets on promoting social and economic development by investment in sustainable infrastructure.

22 This was of great importance before China's reform in education by the end of the 1990s, when the market demand for college graduates increased. Before the reform, higher education was the so-called 'elite education' and a great share of college graduates were recruited to civil posts or SOEs. In present China, the high and medium rank bureaucratic or management posts were dominated by college graduates in the 1970s and 1980s.

23 For agriculture and handicraft, cooperatives were set up; for industry and commerce, public ownership replaced private-ownership.

24 China got support from the former Soviet Union and other East European socialist countries. The preference of the state to the HCI was influenced by the international situation and domestic issues. First, the regional Korean War (1950–1953) and the international quarantine urged China to reinforce national defense, which led to a demand for military industry. Second, sustainable economic growth needs capital investment and technological progress that justified the HCI. Third, nationwide industrial plans were a solution to alleviate regional disparity. By the end of the first FYP, 146 projects were implemented out of the initial 156, four postponed and six canceled.

25 Such as Ministry of Machinery Industry, Ministry of Coal Industry, Ministry of Oil Industry, Ministry of Metal Industry, Ministry of Chemical Industry, Ministry of Textile Industry, Ministry of Light Industry, etc.

26 From 1952 to 1978, China's GDP increased from 67.9 billion to 364.9 billion *yuan*, steel production increased from 1.35 million to 31.78 million tons, agrarian production increased from 163 million to 304 million tons. From 1949 to 1978, the share of industrial output in national total output increased from 10% to 50%, and the total mileage of roads increased from 80,000 to 900,000 kilometers.

27 Including transferring most of SOEs to local governments, empowering local government's authority in making jurisdictional plans, reducing the number of centrally planned materials and sharing part of the excessive outputs.

28 It is a land leasing contract between the peasant family and the village collective economic organization. Peasants are permitted to keep most of the residual outputs and have stronger incentives to production. It was initiated by 18 peasants secretly in November 1978. After being authorized by the central authority, it is now the basic rural economic system.

29 Some of the old specialized industrial ministries were downgraded to sub-departments under the new ministry of industry or restructured from government units to enterprises or industrial associations providing public services.

30 A simple description of this fiscal reform between the central and local government is "cook and eat in separate ovens" (*fenzao chifan*).

31 Those local government's policy practices ran into the prisoner's dilemma at the expense of central government and social welfare. The progressive local tax cut weakened the state's capacity to provide public infrastructure and services, and the ability of macroeconomic control. Regional protectionism impeded national market integration that negatively affected market transaction efficiency.

32 In the broadest sense, SEZs encompassed the first group of municipal SEZs in the 1980s, and all the capital cities of inland provinces and approved autonomous regions in 1992, free trade zones, state-level economic and technological development zones, new areas, hi-tech and new industrial development zones, national bonded areas as well as border trade and cooperation regions. SEZ functions like a free port that provided the incentive for foreign investment and trade by decentralizing administrative authority, deregulating economic planning and facilitating the market process and providing the favorable supply of production factors. Since its initiative in 1980, exports and FDI in SEZ increased tremendously, with more than 90% of Chinese exports and FDI contributed by SEZs in 2005 (Xu 2011).

References

Acemoglu, D. (1995), "Reward Structures and the Allocation of Talent," *European Economic Review* 39: 17–53. Acemoglu, D., S. Johnson, and J. Robinson (2005), "The Rise of Europe: Atlantic Trade, Institutional Change, and Economic Growth," *American Economic Review*, 95(3): 546–579.

Acemoglu, D., and J. Robinson (2012), *Why National Fail: The Origins of Power, Prosperity, and Poverty*, New York: Crown Business.

Aoki, M., K. Murdock, and M. Okuno-Fujiwara (2013), "Beyond the East Asian Miracle: Introducing the Market-Enhancing View," in: M. Aoki (ed.), *Comparative Institutional Analysis Theory, Corporations and East Asia. Selected Papers of Masahiko Aoki*, Cheltenham: Edward Elgar.

Baumol, W. J. (1990), "Entrepreneurship: Productive, Unproductive, and Destructive," *Journal of Political Economy* 98(5): 893–921.

Bodde, D. (1986), "The State and Empire of Ch'in," in: D. Twitchett and M. Loewe (eds.), *The Cambridge History of China, Volume I: The Ch'in and Han Empires, 221 B.C.-A.D. 220*, Cambridge: Cambridge University Press, pp. 20–102.

Borensztein, E., and J. Ostry (1996), "Accounting for China's Growth Performance," *The American Economic Review* 86(2): 224–228.

Callis, H. (1959), *China: Confucian and Communist*, New York: Henry Holt and Company, Inc.

Cao, K., and J. Birchenall (2013), "Agricultural Productivity, Structural Change, and Economic Growth in Post-Reform China," *Journal of Development Economics* 104: 165–180.

Center for Economic and Business Research (2015), *World Economic League Table 2016*, Available at: https://cebr.com/reports/welt-2016/.

Chang, H. (2011), "Institutions and Economic Development: Theory, Policy and History," *Journal of Institutional Economics* 7(4): 473–498.

Coase, R. (1937), "The Nature of The Firm," *Economica, New Series* 4(16): 386–405.

Coase, R. (1960), "The Problem of Social Cost," *Journal of Law and Economics* 3(1): 1–44.

David, P. (1985), "Clio and the Economics of QWERTY," *The American Economic Review* 72(2): 332–337.

Ekelund Jr., R., and R. Tollison (1997), *Politicized Economy: Monarchy, Monopoly and Mercantilism*, College Station: Texas A&M University Press.

Gerschenkron, A. (1962), *Economic Backwardness in Historical Perspective*, Cambridge: Belknap Press of Harvard University Press.

Grossman, S. J., and O. D. Hart (1986), "The Costs and Benefits of Ownership: A Theory of Vertical and Lateral Integration." *Journal of Political Economy* 94: 691–719.

Harrison, J. (1972), *The Chinese Empire*, New York: Harcourt Brace Jovanovick, Inc.

Hart, O. D., and J. Moore (1990), "Property Rights and the Nature of the Firm," *Journal of Political Economy* 98: 1119–1158.

Hirschman, A., and G. Sirkin (1958), "Investment Criteria and Capital Intensity Once Again," The Quarterly Journal of Economics, 72(3): 469-471.

Huang, R. (1997), *China: A Macro History*, New York: M. E. Sharpe, Inc.

Jefferson, G., T. Rawski, L. Wang, and Y. Zheng (2000), "Ownership, Productivity Change, and Financial Performance in Chinese Industry," *Journal of Comparative Economics* 28(4): 786–813.

Landes, D. (2006), "Why Europe and the West? Why Not China?" *Journal of Economic Perspective*, 20(2): 3–22.

Li, H., and A. Zhou (2005), "Political Turnover and Economic Performance: The Incentive Role of Personnel Control in China," *Journal of Public Economics* 89(9): 1743–1762.

Lin, J. Y., F. Cai, and L. Zhou (1996), *The China Miracle: Development Strategy and Economic Reform*, Hong Kong: The Chinese University Press of Hong Kong.

Mokyr, J., and J. Nye (2007), "Distributional Coalitions, the Industrialization Revolution, and the Origins of Economic Growth in Britain," *Southern Economic Journal* 74(1): 50–70.

Murphy, K., A. Shleifer, and R. Vishny (1991), "The Allocation of Talent: Implication for Growth," *The Quarterly Journal of Economics* 106(2): 503–530.

Murphy, K., A. Shleifer, and R. Vishny (1993), "Why Is Rent-Seeking So Costly to Growth," *American Economic Review* 83(2): 409–414.

North, D. C., and R. Thomas (1976), *The Rise of the Western World: A New Economic History*, Cambridge: Cambridge University Press.

North, D. C. (1981), *Structure and Change in Economic History*, New York: Norton.

North, D. C. (1991), "Institutions," *Journal of Economic Perspectives* 5(1): 97–11.

North, D. C., and B. Weingast (1989), "Constitutions and Commitment: The Evolution of Institutions Governing Public Choice in Seventeenth-Century England," *The Journal of Economic History* 49(4): 803–832.

Olson, M. (1965), *The Logic of Collective Action: Public Goods and the Theory of Groups*, Cambridge: Harvard University Press.

Olson, M. (2000), *Power and Prosperity: Outgrowing Communist and Capitalist Dictatorships*, New York: Basic Books.

Prebisch, R. (1959), "Commercial Policy in the Undeveloped Countries," *American Economic Review* 49(2): 951–973.

Qian, Y., and B. R. Weingast (1996), "China's Transition to Markets: Market-Preserving Federalism, Chinese Style," *The Journal of Policy Reform* 1(2): 149–185.

Qian, Y., and G. Xu (1993), "Why China's Economic Reforms Differ: The M-Form Hierarchy and Entry/ Expansion of the Non-State Sector," *The Economics of Transition* 1(2): 135–170.

Rosenstein-Rodan, P. (1943), "Problems of Industrialization of Eastern and South-Eastern Europe," *The Economic Journal* 53(210/211): 202–211.

Singer, H. (1950), "Distribution of Gains Between the Lending and Borrowing Countries," *The American Economic Review* 40(2): 473–485.

Smith, A. (2000), *Wealth of Nations*, London: Electric Book Company.

Stiglitz, J. (2015), "The Chinese Century," Available at: www.vanityfair.com/news/2015/01/china-worlds-largest-economy 1/10

Weingast, B. (1995), "The Economic Role of Political Institutions: Market-Preserving Federalism and Economic Development," *Journal of Law, Economics, & Organization* 11(1): 1–31.

Williamson, O. (1985), *The Economic Institutions of Capitalism: Firms, Markets, Relational Contracting*, New York: Macmillan.

Xu, C. (2011), "The Fundamental Institutions of China's Reforms and Development," *The Journal of Economic Literature* 49(4): 1076–1151.

Xu, C. (2015), "Political and Economic Institutions of China and Their Influences," *Cato Journal* 35(3): 525–548.

Yang, X. Y. (2000), *Development Economics: Inframarginal versus Marginal Analyses*, Blackwell Publishing.

Young, A. (2000), "Increasing Returns and Economic Progress," *The Economic Journal*, 38(152): 527-542.

Yu, Y. S. (2016), *Chinese History and Culture (vol. 1): Sixth Century B.C.E. to Seventeenth Century*, New York: Columbia University Press.

Zhao, D. X. (2016), *The Confucian-Legalist State: A New Theory of Chinese History*, New York: Oxford University Press.

Zheng, L., M. Batuo, and D. Shepherd (2017), "The Impact of Regional and Institutional Factors on Labor Productive Performance – Evidence from the Township and Village Enterprise Sector in China," *World Development* 96: 591–598.

Zi, M. (2015), "The Boom of Industry and Commerce in Tang Dynasty and the Rise of Commercial Cities," *Journal of Literature and History* 1: 35–40 (in Chinese).

Zilibotti, F. (2017), "Growing and Slowing Down Like China," *Journal of the European Economic Association* 15(5): 943–988.

8 Macroeconomic policies in the People's Republic of China

Yang Chen, Ming He, and Simon Rudkin

8.1 Introduction

While clearly lagging behind the Eastern bloc countries and the former Soviet Union in political reform, China has made great achievement in pushing forward the economic realm reform (Oi 1992). Since the first wave of economic liberalization in late 1978, China has grown at an astonishing rate of almost 10% per year as of the end of 2017 (China Statistical Yearbook, 2017), raising 660 million people out of poverty (Yao, 2000). Per capita income increases from US$ 320 in 1980 to US$ 8,259 in 2016, and the number of people living on less than US$ 1.90 a day declines to 1.9% of the total population based on the international poverty line (the World Bank Poverty & Equity Data Portal). While the growth of national income should not be the only criterion for evaluating the success of economic policies, it is the first and most important indicator (Groves et al. 1994). Even though China's GDP growth has slowed down since 2012, and China remains a developing country with incomplete market reforms, the economic performance up to now is impressive by current global standards. This growth miracle on one hand is driven by waves of market-oriented micro-level economic reforms, and on the other hand shaped by the government-led macro-level economic policies.

In this chapter, we explore the targets, instruments and changes of three main macroeconomic policies, examine whether and to what extent these macroeconomic policies shape economic activities and reflect on the challenges of using these policies. Other important policies in China are also elaborated in the book. The industry policies are elaborated in Chapter 5; trade and public sector investment policies are mentioned in Chapter 6 and Chapter 9 respectively; population policy is discussed in Chapter 10; sustainability and environmental policies are analyzed in Chapter 11; Chapter 12 relates more to China's international policies. This chapter consists of five main sections. Section 8.2 presents the monetary policy targets, instruments, impacts on economic activities and the regime change. In Section 8.3, we illustrate China's institutional foundation as well as the center-local fiscal relation, provide an overview of fiscal revenues and expenditures and evaluate the sustainability of China's fiscal policy. Section 8.4 documents the status quo of China's trade development, the evolution of China's trade policy and reflects on the impacts of trade policy on environment. The last section concludes with brief discussions on other aspects of economic policies and future challenges that require significant policy adjustment.

8.2 Monetary policy

8.2.1 Monetary policy targets and instruments

The People's Bank of China (PBoC) transferred the regular commercial banking activities to four newly established commercial banks and has been established as the central bank of China since 1984. Since then, the central bank of China has started to play an important role in shaping and implementing the monetary policy and has experienced multiple changes in its institutional framework and operating procedures. One of the major changes took place in 1998. Before then, the PBoC implemented monetary policy mainly through the credit plan. Specific loan quotas were set and liquidity was provided through financial institutions mainly targeting government-supported sectors and projects especially state-owned industries. This quantity-based lending control led to a mismatch between credit demand and supply as well as a misallocation of resources and low production efficiency (Hsieh and Klenow 2009). From 1998 onwards, the PBoC shifted from direct credit control to an indirect market mechanism coupled with window guidance and established its market-oriented institutional framework and operating procedures.

The objectives of the central bank's monetary policy are defined in the People's Bank of China Act[1] as "to maintain the value of domestic currency to promote economic growth". The Act defines the relative independence of the PBoC from local governments, various levels of governments' agencies and other social organizations and specifies that the design and implementation of monetary policy should be under the leadership of the State Council. A major aim of the PBoC is to implement monetary policies in line with the growth target, which is set annually by the central government of China to guarantee an appropriate level of job creation so as to minimize unemployment. Along with this mandate, the PBoC also maintains price stability and actively participates in foreign exchange interventions to keep the Renminbi (RMB) exchange rate within its manageable floating range.[2] To maintain the value of the RMB, the PBoC adopts multiple policy instruments such as the open market operations (OMO) including issuing central bank bills and conducting conventional repos and reverse repo transactions (Figure 8.1), the benchmark deposit rates and lending rates of various maturities (Figure 8.2), the central bank lending and the central bank lending rate (Figure 8.2) and the required reserve ratios (Figure 8.3). Table 8.1 provides a summary of the multiple monetary policy instruments.

The three figures later on provide more details about the use of multiple policy instruments. Figure 8.1 shows the weekly amount of PBoC's injection and withdrawal of RMB in open market operations. The two trend lines depict the quarterly change of currency injection and currency withdraws. From the figure we find out three major episodes of the intensive use of open market operations.

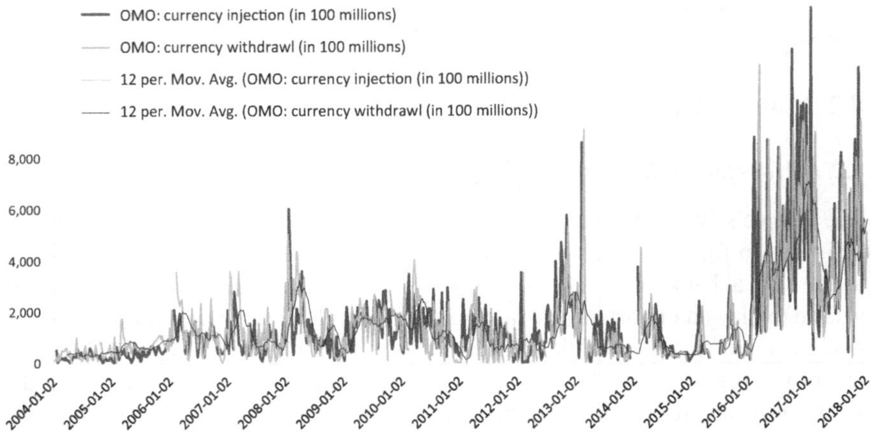

Figure 8.1 Open market operations of the PBoC (2004–01–02 to 2018–01–02)

Source: The data is sourced from the People's Bank of China, compiled using the Wind financial database.

Note: The two trend lines are plotted based on the 12-week moving averages based on the authors' calculations.

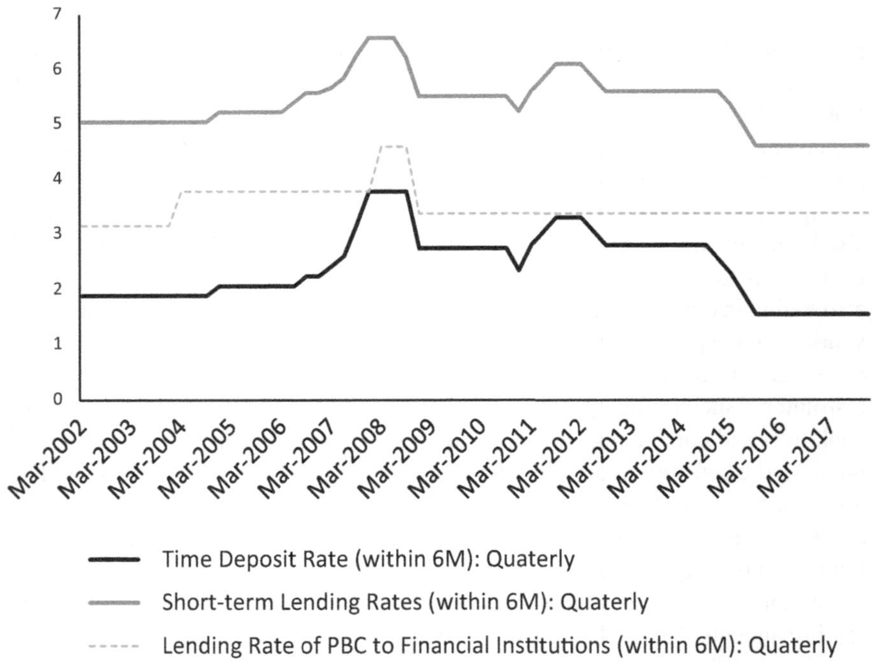

Figure 8.2 The benchmark rates and central bank lending rates (2002q1 to 2017q4) (%)

Source: The data is sourced from the People's Bank of China, compiled by the Wind financial database.

One takes place during the global financial crisis period from 2008 to 2009 and the second episode spans from 2012 to 2013. The third episode dates back to early 2016 and demonstrates the sharply increasing usage of open market operations up to early January in 2018 as an important means of liquidity management. Within the manageable floating exchange rate regime, the central bank of China

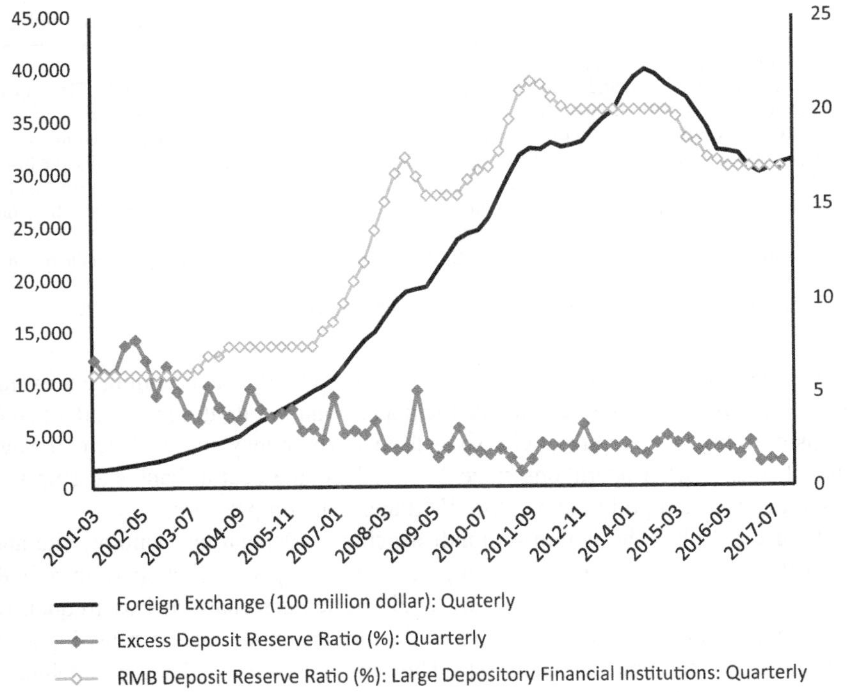

Figure 8.3 Reserve ratio and official foreign reserve (2001q1 to 2017q4)

Source: The data is sourced from the People's Bank of China, compiled by the Wind financial database.

Table 8.1 Monetary policy instruments of the People's Bank of China

Monetary policy instruments	
Open market operations	A quantity-based indirect tool which includes repurchases transactions[a], outright transactions and the issuance of central bank bills[b]. Since 2013, the short-term lending liquidity operation (SLO) and standing lending facility (SLF) is introduced into the monetary policy framework.
Interest rates	A price-based tool which includes various central bank base interest rates[c]. The deposit rate and lending rate of commercial banks are highly regulated.
Required reserve ratio	A discretionary and more direct tool.

(*Continued*)

Table 8.1 (Continued)

Specific credit policy instruments	
Specific central bank lending schemes	A discretionary tool. Under certain specific eligibility requirements, the PBoC provides special funds at a lower cost for particular groups of industries or regions
Window guidance[d]	An administrative tool in the form of "indirect pressure" through regular meetings with commercial banks so as to influence the quantity and the structure of bank lending.

Note: This summary is sourced from Table 8.2 in Sun (2013).

a Outright transactions include outright purchases and outright sales, through which the PBoC buys/sells securities directly from/to the secondary market to increase/decrease the base money.

b Central bank bills are short-term securities issued by the PBoC, which were introduced in 2002 to deal with the insufficient supply of government bonds. Through issuing central bank bills, the PBoC can effectively reduce the money supply. The PBoC has used them extensively to offset rises in liquidity in the banking system as a result of the PBoC's purchase of foreign exchange. Therefore, the central bank bills are often termed as sterilization bonds.

c They include the central bank lending rate, the rediscount rate, the interest rates paid on the required and excess reserves.

d The bank of Japan exercised this practice as well in the post-war era until the early 1990s.

commits itself to be actively engaged in foreign exchange intervention. For example, whenever the exchange rate hits the upper bound of floating range, the PBoC steps in to buy foreign currencies so as to increase money supply. The extensive use of open market operations since 2016 reflects the central bank's attempts to drain the excess liquidity due to the RMB appreciation pressure.

Figure 8.2 plots the within-6-month benchmark deposit and lending rate and the PBoC's official lending rate. Compared with the open market operations, both the benchmark rates and the official lending rates are changed less frequently. This implies that the PBoC relies less on the money market rates in affecting market liquidity and economic activities. The figure also shows that the benchmark rates and central bank lending rate rises consecutively from 2006Q1 to 2008Q3 indicating a tightening monetary policy stance in an attempt to cool down the over-heated economy to avoid high inflation. However, the occurrence of the global finance crisis shifts the monetary policy stance from being contractionary to expansionary as evidenced by falling money market rates and the rates at which commercial banks borrow from the central bank at the end of 2008. Though there are moderate increases of rates in 2011, the PBoC lowers these rates in 2012 and 2015 when the economic growth of China gradually slows down.

Figure 8.3 depicts the change of foreign exchanges and the reserve ratios from the period of 2001Q1 to 2017Q4. We observe a steady change of foreign reserve before the mid-2006 while the aggregate amount of foreign reserve at the end of 2017 is more than double that of mid-2006. This suggests a regime shift and the necessity to separate the policy analysis into two periods – before and after the mid-2006. The figure also illustrates that the RMB deposit reserve ratio is closely linked to the amount of foreign exchange. To understand this, we present in Table 8.2 the components of total asset and total liabilities in the balance sheet of central monetary authority of China. The rise of foreign exchange on the asset

Table 8.2 The components of the PBoC's balance sheet

Total assets	*Total liabilities*
1. Foreign assets	1. Reserve money
a. Foreign exchange	a. Currency issue
b. Gold	b. Deposit reserve of NFCs
c. Others	c. Deposit reserve of other FCs
2. Claims on government	d. Excess reserve of FCs and NFCs
a. Claims on central government	2. Bond issue
b. Claims on other depository corporations	3. Foreign liabilities
c. Claims on non-financial corporations (NFCs)	4. Deposits of government
	5. Own capital
3. Other assets	6. Other liabilities

Source: Authors' summary.

side leads to excessive liquidity which is contrary to the PBoC's target to maintain price stability. Therefore, the central bank of China has to absorb the excessive liquidity using three tools, namely, the repurchase transaction, the issuance of central bank bills, and the deposit reserve ratio (Sun 2015). The first two sterilize the effects of foreign exchange on the monetary base, while the last tool transforms assets into the form of liabilities. Before mid-2006, central bank bills are heavily used as sterilization bonds while after that it relies more on the deposit reserve ratio as a routine instrument. The highest reserve ratio reaches 21.5% in September 2011 and has declined to 17% most recently.

8.2.2 Evaluation of monetary policy

With the aforementioned policy instruments, does monetary policy really matter in China? A large strand of literature (Bernanke and Blinder 1992; Bernanke and Gerler 1995) find important roles of monetary policies in affecting output at least in the short run. However, only a few studies addressed such a question in a large transitioning and mixed economy like China (Dickinson and Liu 2007; Sun et al. 2010; Sun 2013, 2015; Xiong 2012). With an important role in implementing China's macroeconomic policies, the monetary policy institutions as described in the previous subsection and their operating model as mentioned in the next subsection have attracted great attention from the rest of world. However, the challenges of evaluating monetary policies on real economic activities lie mainly in two aspects.

First, a list of monetary policy tools that are jointly used in the implementation of China's monetary policy over the past decades and no single instrument can serve as an adequate representation of the monetary policy indicator. Some studies use the money aggregate and find that money supply is a more effective instrument in responding to both inflation and real output compared with interest rates in the backward-looking model (Fan et al. 2011). However, others argue that the growth of monetary aggregate is an endogenous indicator which includes not only information about money supply but also reflects the money demand. Interest rates also have limited role in measuring the monetary policy stance due to the segmentation of total credit market and the insensitivity of firms and individuals to the price of capital (Xiong 2012). Second, it is difficult to identify the causal relationship between monetary policy and economic fluctuations. A simple regression of any monetary instrument or the composite index of multiple tools on output, for example, is mostly likely to result in biased estimates because the causation may run in the opposite direction. Romer and Romer (2004) point out that fluctuation of economic activities as a result of exogenous policy movement should reflect the influence of monetary policy rather than other impacts. This calls for an evaluation exercise to isolate the exogenous components of policy changes from endogenous policy responses before analyzing their impacts on price stability (Figure 8.4) and the growth of the economy (Figure 8.5).

As a premise to analyze the role of monetary policy, a prerequisite is to break down the changes in policy instruments into three parts as suggested by Sun (2015). The three parts are the systematic responses to the state of the economy, the regime-dependent liquidity management, and exogenous components, among which only the third part is an effective indicator of monetary policy. Existing studies provide three approaches to address the measurement issues but there is still a lot of refinement needed in using any of them. The first direction is to adopt the narrative approach using the PBoC's quarterly monetary policy executive reports from 2001Q1 to 2017Q3 (Sun 2013, 2015; Xiong 2012). The second approach proposed by He and Pauwel (2008) and Xiong (2012) considers the PBoC's multiple instrument set. They examine changes in the set of instruments over time and assign a value to each of these changes. The recent approach proposed by Sun (2015) attempts to construct an overall policy index following Bernanke and Mihov (1998) in two stages. In the first stage, a VAR model including policy and non-policy variables is estimated. The policy-sector VAR residuals are disentangled from those in the non-policy block. In the second stage, those residuals are used in different model specifications that capture the PBoC's operating procedures and regime changes in an attempt to take the exogenous policy component out of the intervention into the foreign exchange market. The general findings along the three lines of research highlight that the PBoC's operating procedures have evolved over time and they are neither purely interest rate targeting nor purely reserves targeting but a mixture of both, but there is no consistent evidence confirming the persistent role of monetary policy in long-run economic activities.

With the two main monetary policy targets in mind, we present the growth of GDP, consumer price index, fixed asset investment and fluctuations of broad money supply (M2) in the next few figures which might motivate further studies to evaluate the contribution of monetary policy to real economic activities. Figure 8.4 illustrates the growth rate of the consumer price index, money supply and balance of loan in China (1992–2017). Since China initiated the market-oriented economic reform in 1992, there have been three major high inflation episodes. The growth rate of consumer price index peaks in 1994, 2008 and 2011. The

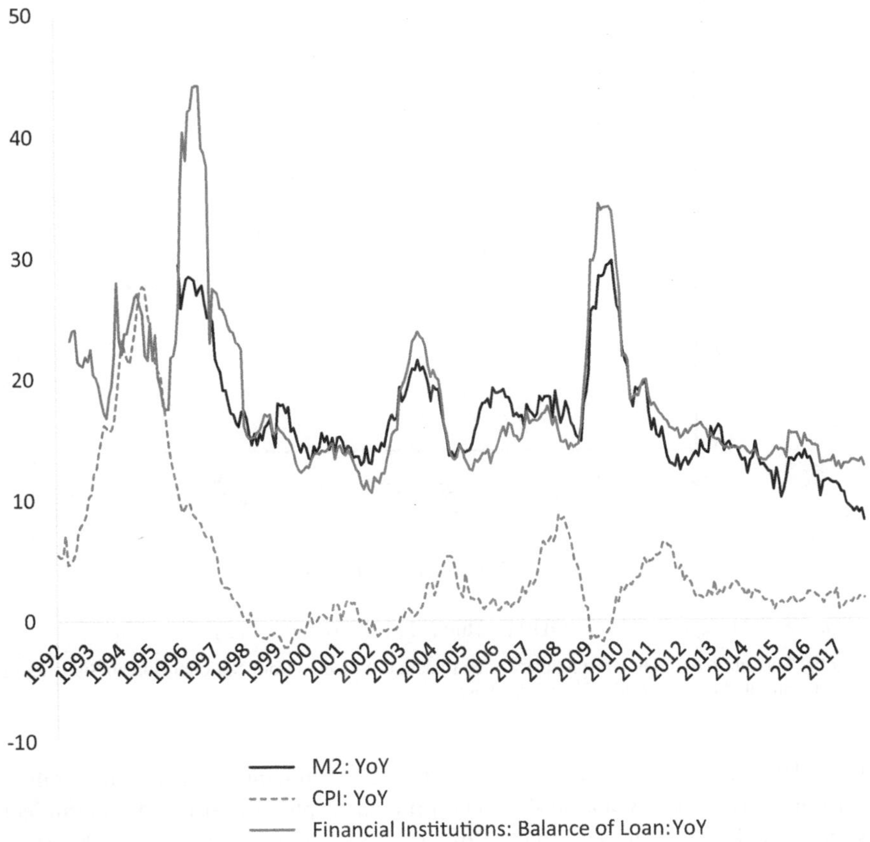

Figure 8.4 The growth rate of consumer price index, money supply and balance of loan in China (1992–2017) (% chg.)

Source: The monthly Consumer Price Index (CPI: YoY), M2 (YoY) and the balance of loan in financial institutions (YoY) are collected from National Bureau Statistics of China, compiled by the Wind financial database.

growth rate of CPI in year 1994 reaches a historical record of 27% after the 1992 reform due to multiple reasons. On the one hand, we can see from Figure 8.5 that the overall economy grows more than 12% from 1992 to 1993 as a response to the reforming and opening policy, which leads to excess aggregate demand and further increases the rising liability of the central bank of China due to the increased issuance of currency to the market. The rise of money supply and loan from financial institutions during 1993 does not lead to significant improvement in resource allocation and production efficiency. Instead, it is followed by insufficient supply resulting in hyper-inflation. Struggling with the misallocation of resources and low productivity coupled with the high level of government deficit,

Figure 8.5 The growth rate of GDP in China (1992–2017) (% chg.)

Source: The quarterly GDP constant prices (YoY) data is collected from National Bureau Statistics of China, compiled by the Wind financial database.

since 1994, the central government has started to implement the decentralization reform in fiscal policy and at the same time, attempted to reform the inefficient state-owned sector. The second peak of CPI growth appeared in March 2008 right in the wake of the global financial crisis, and it reached 10.8%. After that, there was a declining trend of this price index from August 2011 until most recently. The current CPI growth rate hovers at around 2%. To boost the economy and lift it out of recession, the broad money supply grows from 16% in November 2008 to 34% until September 2009. The Chinese version of quantitative easing does not lead to high inflation in consumer goods but results in excessive fixed asset formation (see Figure 8.6), especially in real estate, manufacturing and transportation, storage and postal service sectors. Based on data compiled from the Wind financial database, in 2015, the aggregate value of fixed asset formation in the real estate sector has reached 60997.7 billion RMB, which is much higher than that of manufacturing (35839.6 billion RMB) and is almost triple that of the transportation, storage and postal service sector (18248.9 billion RMB).

8.2.3 New macro-financial supervision and regulation framework

The quantitative easing adopted by most of advanced economies like the US, EU countries and Japan since the 2008 global financial crisis brings excessive

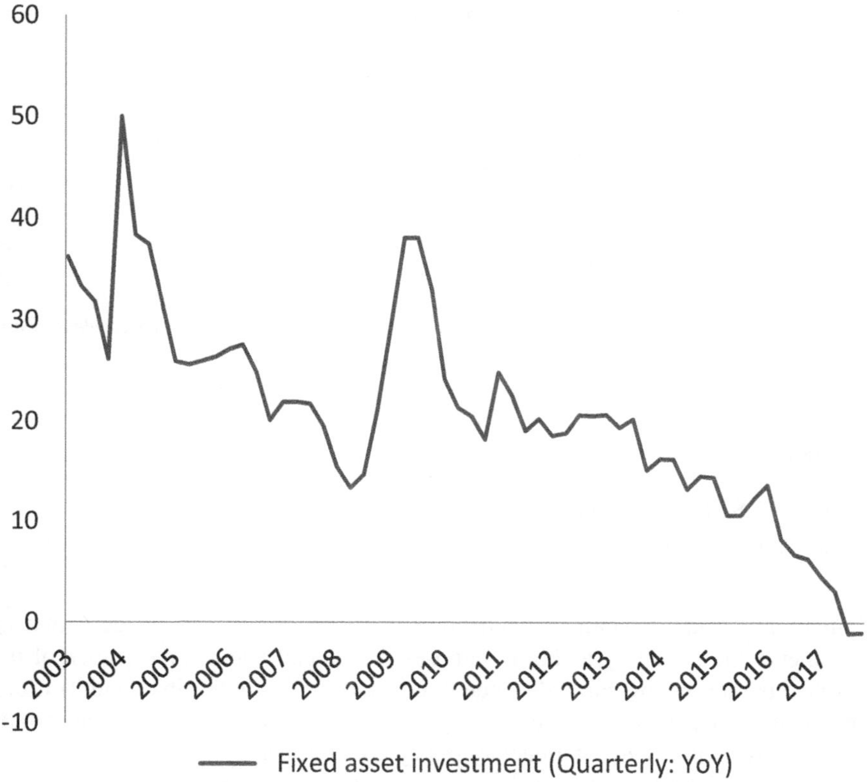

Figure 8.6 The growth rate of fixed asset formation (2003–2017) (% chg.)

Source: The quarterly fixed asset formation in YoY form is collected from National Bureau of Statistics of China, compiled by the Wind financial database.

liquidity and arbitrage transactions in the global financial market. This has made the capital flow more substantial within the traditional "Impossible Trinity" framework. Considering the importance of capital flow, Sun and Li (2017) transform the equilateral triangle into a scalene triangle, and this is first proposed in the literature as the "Scalene Impossible Trinity". They point out that the new development increases the relative importance of capital flow relative to the exchange rate regime and monetary policy independence. The freely floating exchange rate is not enough to contain capital flow and maintain an independent monetary policy.

Figure 8.7 illustrates the theory. Compared with the equilateral form ΔABC, the vertex A representing the combined choice of full capital control, fixed exchange rate and independent monetary policy, remains the same. However, vertex B moves to B' and C shifts to C'. This means that when capital flows freely, we cannot keep the exchange rate fixed as monetary policy is fully dependent on other countries (point B). Similarly, when capital flows freely, the floating exchange

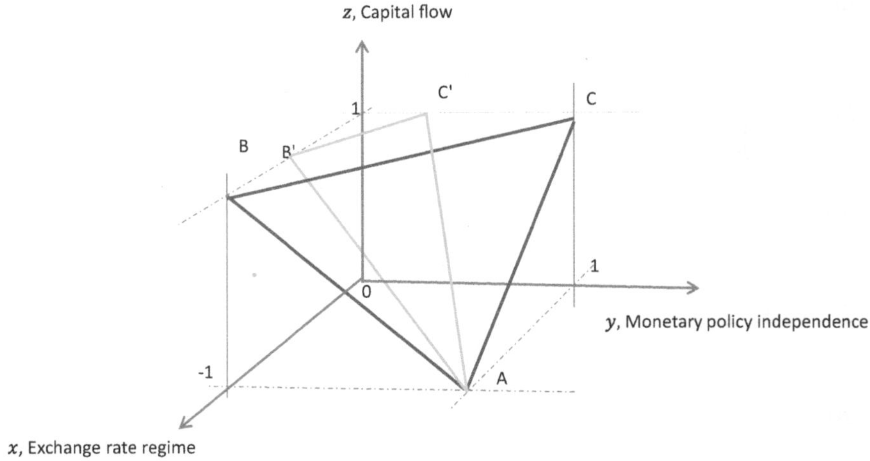

Figure 8.7 Scalene impossible trinity

Source: This figure is plotted by authors and is adapted from figure 3 in Sun and Li (2017).

rate regime cannot guarantee independent monetary policy. This suggests that 1) whenever the monetary authority chooses full capital control, the choice of fix exchange rate regime and independent monetary policy is feasible; and 2) if the monetary authority allows free capital flow, only a relatively stable exchange rate and relatively independent monetary policy could be achieved.

Full capital control comes with costs. It builds a barrier between the domestic and international financial market and distorts the market operation, which would lead to global trade imbalance. Instead of using full capital control, the PBoC introduces the dynamic adjustment mechanism of differentiated reserve requirements in 2011 and revises it further into the Macro-Prudential Assessment (MPA) in 2016. Since then, the monetary authority in China establishes its new macro-prudential supervision and regulation framework. The PBoC now mainly targets two kinds of capital flows: the substantial leverage financing including hedge funds from China and abroad, and the market speculation with retained funds conducted by financial institutions and enterprises.

To retain leverage, three regulation practices are adopted in the MPA framework. The first practice targets leveraging in the domestic foreign exchange market. In August 2015, the PBoC requires all financial institutions to deposit foreign exchange risk reserves equivalent to 20% of their foreign exchange short exposure to contain the speculative behavior. The second practice targets leveraging of domestic entities in external debt. As of April 2016, the PBoC has established the MPA mode of cross-border financing in four Free Trade Zones of Shanghai, Guangdong, Tianjin and Fujian. The third practice targets leveraging in the offshore RMB market. Since 25 January 2016, the PBoc has required that the normal reserve requirement apply to all foreign financial institutions which have

RMB deposits in domestic financial institutions (The Monetary Policy Executive Report,[3] 2016), hence, increasing the cost of speculative shorting of RMB and containing RMB outflows. Since August 2015, the PBoC has also used the price-based measures such as increasing the RMB trading fees to restrain the arbitrage behavior.

Putting the "Scalene Impossible Trinity" theory into practice, China not only strives to improve macro-prudential management of cross-border capital flow, but also endeavors to improve exchange rate flexibility by declaring that the mid-price quoting mechanism to be equal to the closing price from the last trading day plus the value change of the currency basket. In addition, within the context of financial market globalization, China actively participates in international monetary policy coordination to maintain macroeconomic stability. Future research on identifying China's monetary policy stance and evaluating its effectiveness and transmission to the real economy might take the new financial supervision and regulation framework into consideration.

8.3 Fiscal policy

8.3.1 Institutional foundation and the center-local fiscal relation

Before introducing the other major macroeconomic policy tool, we first briefly summarize China's institutional foundation, which distinguishes itself from that of most advanced developed countries in the world and offers an intriguing context for studying fiscal federalism. Bahl (1999) point out that China is a unitary, politically highly centralized while economically decentralized nation. Xu (2011) defines this system as "Regionally Decentralized Authoritarian (RDA)". Despite China's weak government institutions as reported from the conventional viewpoint of standard wisdom, this institutional foundation deeply shapes the policy-maker's incentives and behaviors, impacts society as a whole and brings about almost four decades of economic growth miracle.

Within the five-layer bureaucratic hierarchical framework beginning from the center, the province, to the prefecture city, county, and the lowest administrative level town and village, local governments at different levels are led by the State Council in Beijing and serve as the subordinate organs of the next higher-level administration. However, they have much freedom in making economic decision, and discretion to initiate, design, implement, negotiate and revise rules and regulations than many federal states. Determined by this institutional foundation, China's fiscal policy implementation and reform usually takes the step-by-step measure, proceeding by trial-and-error with frequent corrections and even reversals, and most of the time experimented from local region (provinces hereafter). Against this backdrop, the center-provincial fiscal relation goes through three stages: the pre-reform stage prior to 1979, the transitional stage from 1980 to 1993 and the post-1994 stage (Jin et al. 2005). The review of this evolving center-local fiscal relation helps us to gain a better understanding of the most recent tax reform in an attempt to build a modern fiscal system.

Before 1979, all tax revenues are uniformly collected and spent. The nickname "beating from one big pot" captures the essence of such a relationship. During the 1980–1993 period the fiscal contracting system governs the center-local fiscal relationship. The central budget revenues consist of two parts: the fixed revenue coming from customs duties, direct tax or profit remittance from the central-affiliated state-owned enterprises, and the variable revenues which are shared between the central and local governments according to the case-by-case negotiated pre-determined sharing schemes. The sharing scheme of fiscal revenues varies with local economic development. For example, Guangdong Province agreed to remit a fixed amount per year from 1980 to 1987, while Jiangsu province agreed to remit a fixed share to the central government. The *ex post* redistribution did not fully match the sharing scheme. In addition to the specified items written in the sharing scheme, the central government sometimes borrowed funds from provinces and transferred payments to provinces in the form of earmarked subsidies or matching grants on specific local programs or projects.

Using data reported by the National Bureau of Statistics of China (1978–2016), we plot in Figure 8.1 the sharing ratios of fiscal revenues and expenditures between the central and local governments. The red (blue) bar indicates the share of local (central) fiscal revenue; the purple (green) line depicts the local (central) share of fiscal expenditure. Before the 1994 fiscal reform, the annual average share of central fiscal revenue during 1978–1993 is around 30% while the local share is around 70%; the expenditure share is around 42% for the central and 58% for the local. During the 1978–1992 period, the state-owned sector experiences two rounds of reforms: one from 1978 to 1984 and the other from 1985 to 1992. Before 1978, Chinese government arranges funds and labor, allocates production inputs, determines production amount, and keeps all profits from the state-owned sector. During the 1978–1984 period, the state-owned enterprises are given more incentives and autonomy to make their own production plan, which significantly boosts productivity, profits and the central fiscal revenue. Since October 1984 until 1992, the state-owned sectors were not required to submit profits to the government anymore. Instead, they submit part of their profits in the form of taxes to the nation. At the same time, the right of management and ownership could be separated. Managers in the state-owned enterprises have more authority to make independent production decisions, especially in local-affiliated state-owned enterprises. We can see from Figure 8.8 that since 1985, local fiscal revenue share has started to increase and has gradually exceeded that of the center.

Since 1993, fiscal reform and ownership reform have been implemented together. The fiscal reform makes the tax burden more equitable across different sectors, reduces the practice of contracting tax rates with individual enterprises and clarifies the assignment of tax revenues to the center and the local, but it does not specify the assignment of expenditures. The reform ends the multi-year negotiation over revenue-sharing rates. The re-assignment policy clearly specifies that three quarters of value added taxes go to the center and one quarter of value added taxes plus most of income taxes belong to local governments. Central tax agencies are created as well to collect central taxes. In the meantime, the

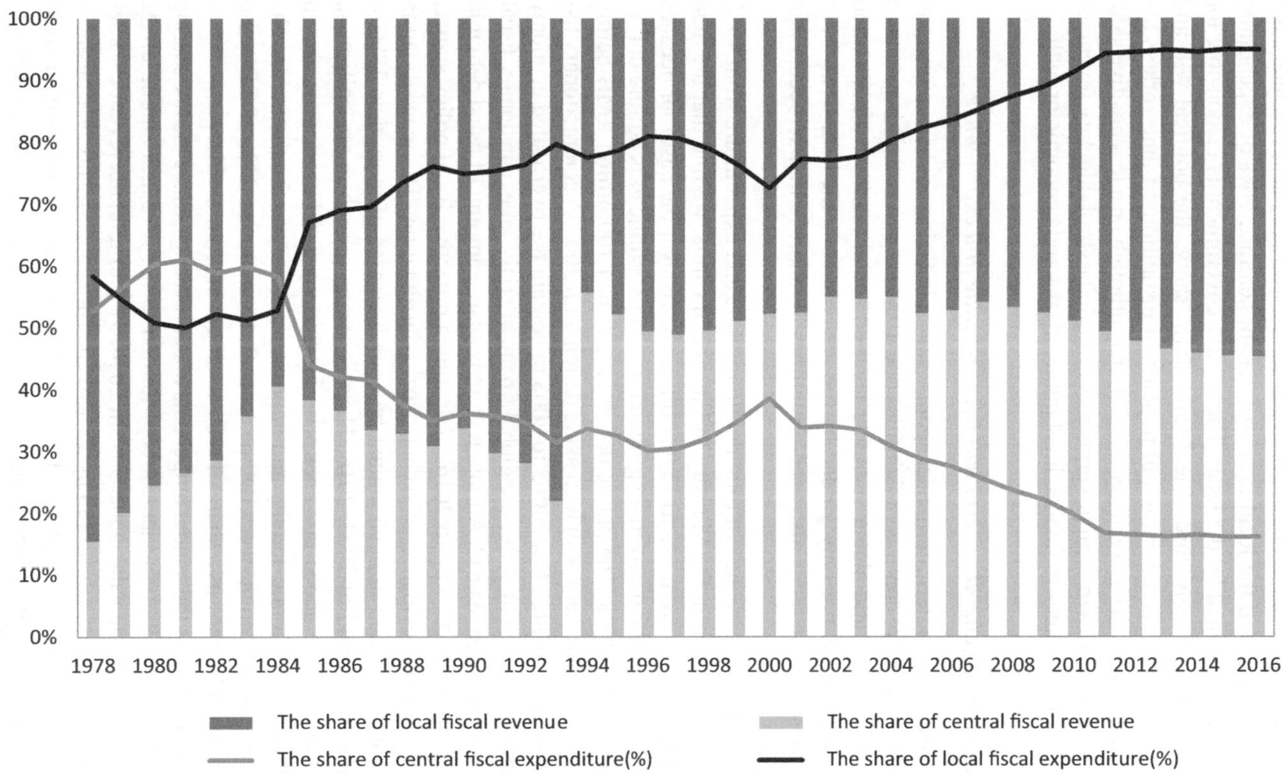

Figure 8.8 The center-local fiscal relation (1978–2016) (%)

Source: Data is collected from National Bureau Statistics of China.

central government endorses the ownership reform policy of "Grasping the Large and Letting Go of the Small". Many local-affiliated medium- and small-sized state-owned enterprises are either closed or privatized which further reduces the local fiscal capacity. From 1994 to 2016, the annual average fiscal revenue share between the central and the local is almost 1:1. In contrast, 76% of expenditure responsibility is assumed by the local. The central government is responsible for only 24% of fiscal expenditure. The fiscal reform shows the political will and authority of central government to put in place an institutional framework as the basis for predictable inter-governmental relations, although on a less positive side, it leaves more pressures to local governments to exploit extra-budgetary revenues, such as the land revenues to finance local public affairs and economic growth.

8.3.2 Overview of general government fiscal revenue and expenditure

In recent years, the midterm-term fiscal policy stance in China has been proactive, leaving room for future contingent liabilities due to the long-term banking sector's nonperforming loans and higher spending level on social security as population ages. Fiscal policy is not only guided by the government's medium-term focus on fiscal consolidation but is also used sometimes for short-term macroeconomic management.

There is a dramatic change of total public revenue and expenditure from 1978 to 2016. Using data from the Ministry of Finance of China, we find that the total public revenue grows from 113 to 15,961 billion RMB over the past four decades in nominal terms, while the average growth rate of total public expenditure during this period reaches 15%. The public deficit is less than 100 billion RMB before 1999, while after that there is an increasing deficit until 2002. A contractionary fiscal policy is implemented from 2003 to 2008 to contain the overheated economy and excessive investment. After the global financial crisis, an expansionary fiscal policy is implemented instead. Although there is a large amount of fiscal deficit in absolute terms from 2009 up to 2016, indicating a proactive fiscal policy stance, Figure 8.9 provides evidence of recent fiscal consolidation. This consolidation is mainly accomplished through annual revenue increases of more than 10% of GDP during the period of 2003–2016. There is strong growth in tax collection, in particular of value added tax, enterprise income tax and business tax driven by both buoyant economic activity and improvements in tax administration. The percentage of fiscal deficit over GDP peaks in 2015 at around 25% of GDP, and the annual fiscal balance as a share of GDP averages at around −2%.

Figure 8.10 presents the major components of tax revenues. Since the tax-sharing reform in China in 1994, the largest contribution to tax revenues among all 22 taxes has been from the value added tax. In 2016, 31% of total tax revenue comes from the value added tax, followed by 22% of enterprise income tax, 9% business tax and 8% of personal income tax. The contribution of enterprise income tax is closely linked with real economic activities, which peaks in 2008 and starts to decline in the following two years. However, the drop of enterprise income tax has been compensated by the rise of consumption tax during the same period. Although the contribution of value added tax in China dominates all the other

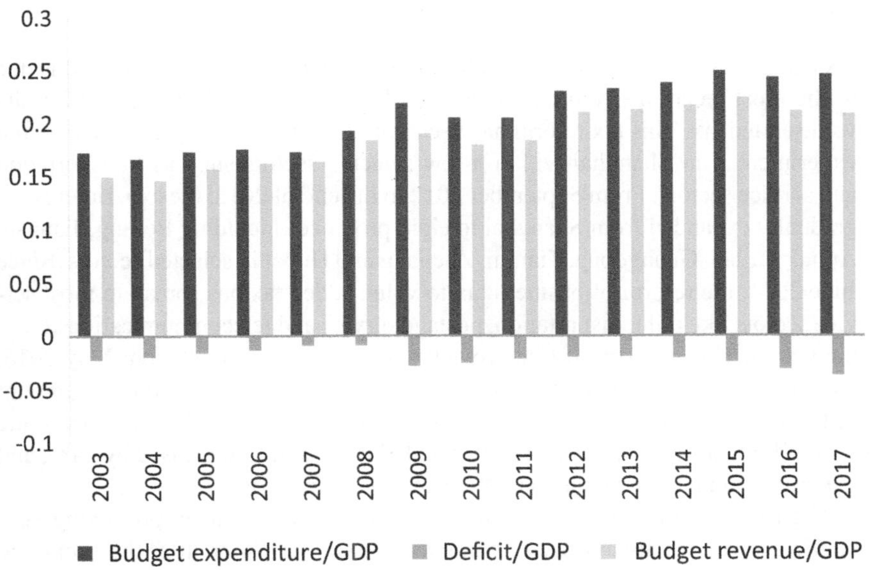

Figure 8.9 The share of budget fiscal revenue and expenditure over GDP (2003–2016) (%)

Source: Budget revenue and expense is sourced from the Ministry of Finance of China; GDP is collected from the National Bureau of Statistics of China.

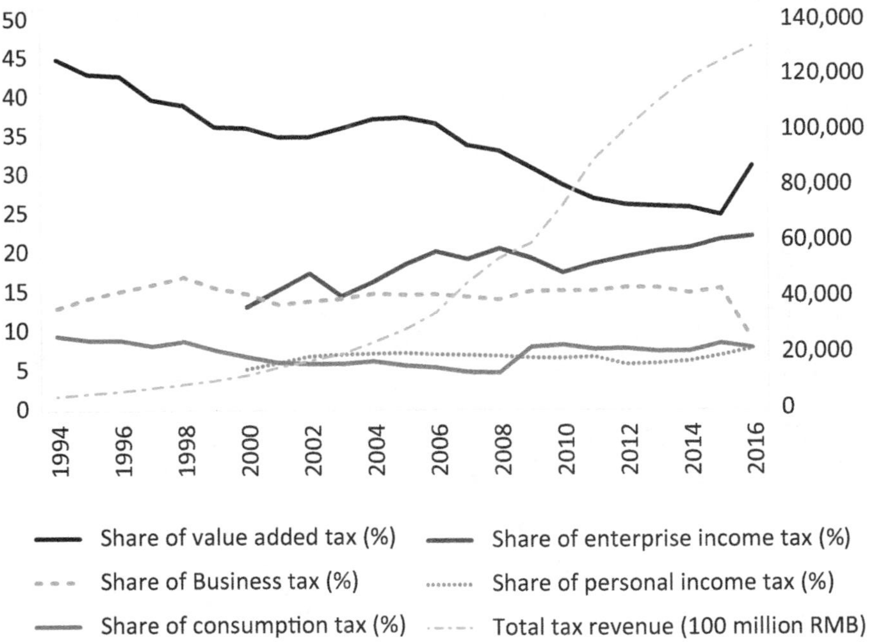

Figure 8.10 The composition of national tax revenue in China (1994–2016) (%)

Source: The shares of value added tax, income tax, business tax and consumption tax are calculated by authors using data sourced from the Ministry of Finance in China.

tax categories, there is a downward trend from 1994 until 2015. This trend is due to the most recent tax reform, which calls for the change of business tax to the value added tax. This tax reform has been initiated since January 2012 and is first experimented in Shanghai within a few selected sectors such as transportation and service sectors. From September 2012 to the end of 2012, the experiments are gradually expanded from Shanghai to eight provinces including Beijing, Jiangsu, Anhui, Fujian, Guangdong, Tianjin, Zhejiang and Hubei in selected sectors. Since June 2014, the reform of business tax to value added tax has spread to most service sectors like rail transportation, postage service and telecommunication across the nation. The Ministry of Finance announces that with effect from May 2016, the business tax would be formally revoked nationwide. As a result, the amount of business tax is reduced by 464 billion RMB from 2012 to 2016. However, the sum of both business tax and the value added tax has been increased by 24%, and the ratio of total tax revenue to GDP reaches 17% in 2016.

The role of public investment, infrastructure in particular, in promoting economic growth has always been an important issue for China after the economic reform. Why and to what extent do these public investments drive the economic growth? The answers help us to verify the appropriateness of the current infrastructure-led investment policies of the Chinese government and provide implications that might shape the size and composition of public expenditures. The link between public investment and economic growth will be explored in detail in Chapter 9. We now present the most recent public expenditure composition in China in Figure 8.11. The share of public expenditure on education,

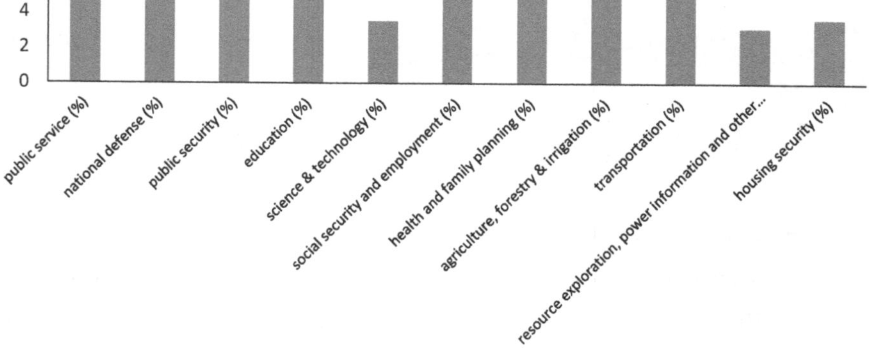

Figure 8.11 The composition of national fiscal expenditure in 2016 (%)

Source: The different categories of public expenditure data are collected from the Ministry of Finance in China. The shares are calculated by authors.

social security and employment, as well as on agriculture, forest and irrigation is 15%, 12% and 10%, respectively, and these three form the largest expense categories. This implies a shift in fiscal policy from supporting physical capital formation to building human and social capital as the demographic structure changes quickly (see Chapter 2 and Chapter 10). The Chinese authorities' attempts to shift spending away from capital to social projects are documented in a number of official documents since the 11th Five-Year Plan (2005–2010). Increased levels of expenditure on education, social security and health might also require the construction of infrastructure against the backdrop of a number of uncertainties and rigidities. Since the Global Financial Crisis, fiscal positions in many emerging market economies have weakened considerably and constrained the room for policymakers to utilize fiscal policy when shocks hit. Therefore, the Chinese government is now working on improving its budget systems towards transparency and sustainability, increasing monitoring and accountability and balancing the complex center-local relationship to reward local authorities in promoting social programs instead of concentrating on fixed capital investment.

8.3.3 Sustainability of fiscal policy

The previous two subsections describe the institutional foundation of fiscal policymaking, address the center-local government fiscal relation and give an overview of the trend and composition of the general government fiscal revenue and expenditure, but they do not account for the large amount of off-budget revenues and expenditures, especially for local governments. We provide more discussion here on extra-budgetary fiscal activities and point out the necessity of considering the long-run sustainability of fiscal policy.

Following the 1994 intergovernmental fiscal reform, the central government's fiscal revenues significantly increased from less than 30% before 1994 to around 55% in 2016. However, no significant changes are made in expenditure assignments between central and local governments. Governments of a higher hierarchical level have more flexibility to offload expenditure obligations than those of a lower hierarchical level. In 2016, local governments bear more than 85% total public expenditures. Most of these expenses are on infrastructure investment, service delivery and social spending. Local governments have little discretion over tax rates and tax policies, and this has caused a large amount of budget deficits, especially for less developed regions such as Tibet, Xinjiang, Qinghai, Hainan and Inner Mongolia (Table 8.3), and increased the dependence on central tax refunds and fiscal income transfers over time (Figure 8.12). As a means of compensation, the central government introduces complicated transfer system including general transfers, earmarked transfers or subsidies and tax funds. Figure 8.13, using data from the Ministry of Finance in China indicates the percentages of general transfers, earmarked transfers and tax refunds over the total fiscal income transfer from the center to the local. First, general transfers include a variety of fiscal funds for different redistributive purposes to narrow regional disparity. The amount of general transfer might be affected by local output, size of

Table 8.3 The top five provinces with largest per capita budget deficits

Provinces	*Budget deficits (Unit: Yuan)*
Tibet	–57,361
Xinjiang	–34,948
Qinghai	–21,742
Hainan	–19,522
Inner Mongolia	–8,333

Source: The annual average per capita budget deficit for each of the 31 Chinese provinces is calculated by authors based on budget revenue and expenditure data from 2010 to 2015 collected from the Ministry of Finance of China.

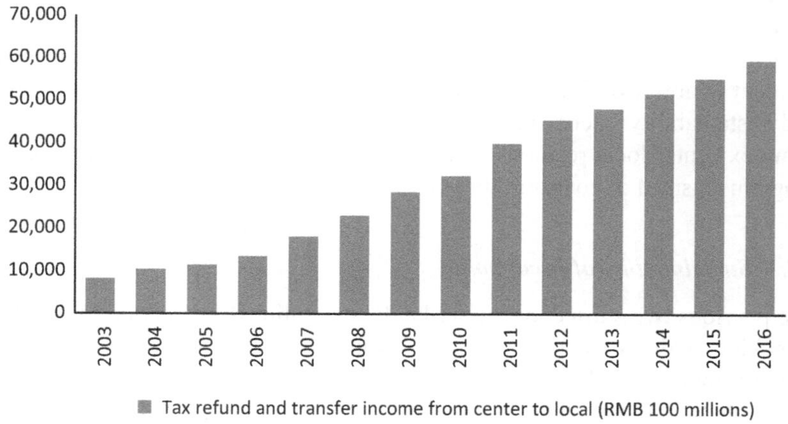

Figure 8.12 Tax refunds and fiscal income transfers from center to local (2003–2016)

Source: Data is sourced from the Ministry of Finance in China.

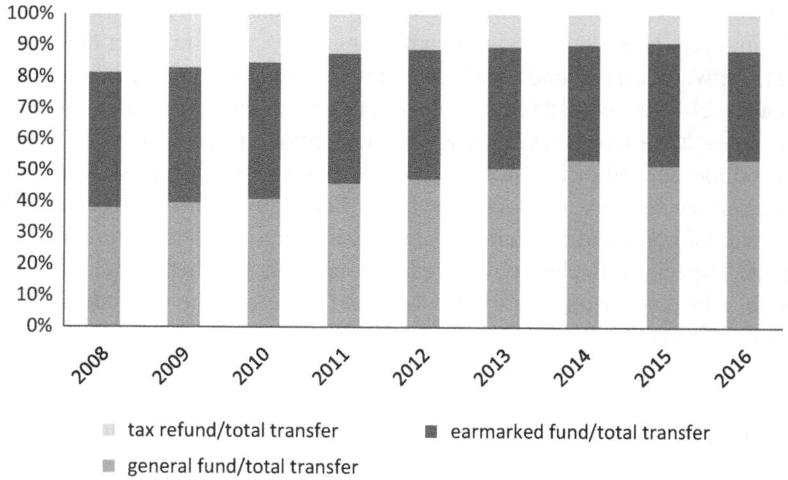

Figure 8.13 The percentage of tax refund, general transfer and earmarked transfer (2008–2016)

Source: Data is sourced from the Ministry of Finance in China.

government and population density. Although under-funded in 1995 with a share of only 4% of total fiscal transfer, general transfers increase rapidly after 2001 as more tax revenues are centralized (Liu et al. 2009). As shown in Figure 8.13, this transfer increases from 874.6 billion yuan in 2008 to 3186.5 billion yuan in 2016, and the share in total fiscal transfers reaches 53.6%. General transfers include a variety of funds that serve multiple purposes, such as the equalization transfer, wage subsidies, the rural tax-to-fee reform fiscal transfer, funds transfer to resource-depleting cities, funds transfer for education, social security and health expenses. Though the names might imply special purposes, they share the same nature of formula-based calculation and redistribution and are thus classified as general transfers. Different from general transfers, the earmarked subsides are transferred based on negotiation and designed for specific purposes from infrastructure development and environmental protection, to disaster relief and operating funds for government administration. There is a downward trend in allocating the earmarked subsidies from the center to local governments. It accounts for 43% of total fiscal transfer in 2008 and drops to 34% in 2016. Different from the previous two transfer measures, tax refunds aim to compensate local governments instead of redistribution, which includes the value added tax and consumption tax rebate based on the growth of these two tax revenues and the fixed income tax base rebate. Over time, tax refunds as a share of total transfers declined from 18% to 11% during the period of 2008–2016.

However, these transfers mainly cover current spending and are more than enough to finance capital spending. The mismatch between large expenditure needs and small revenue sources coupled with tight restrictions on direct borrowing motivate local governments to create other channels to finance their operations, and this is widely known as the "land finance". Before the budget reform proposed in 2010, the local government extra-budgetary revenue reached 539.5 billion RMB and the share of local extra-budgetary expenditures is around 93% (Figure 8.14). The Budget Law of The People's Republic of China specifies that local governments are generally not allowed to issue local government bonds, unless the law or the State Council permits. However, the local government bond market is set up to finance infrastructure and support the ongoing rapid urbanization with recourse to bank loans, the Build-and-Transfer program and the issuance of local government bonds, mid-term bills and short-term financing securities. Notably, the local government bonds are issued mainly through government financing vehicles (LGFVs), urban development investment corporations or local government financing platforms. They are in some extent similar to public private partnerships (PPPs) in other countries. However, the funding of LGFVs is not only from the market but also from the fiscal system. Most LGFVs are transformed from or at least have state-owned enterprise backgrounds. They are endorsed by local governments to borrow from policy and commercial banks using land as collateral, and most LGFVs' profits from government subsidies, though they might be able to generate some revenues from infrastructure investment such as road tolls. The means of LGFV financing provides a partial solution to the issue of a lack of fiscal resources to finance infrastructure, but it also brings challenges and risks. Substantial fiscal risks are embedded because

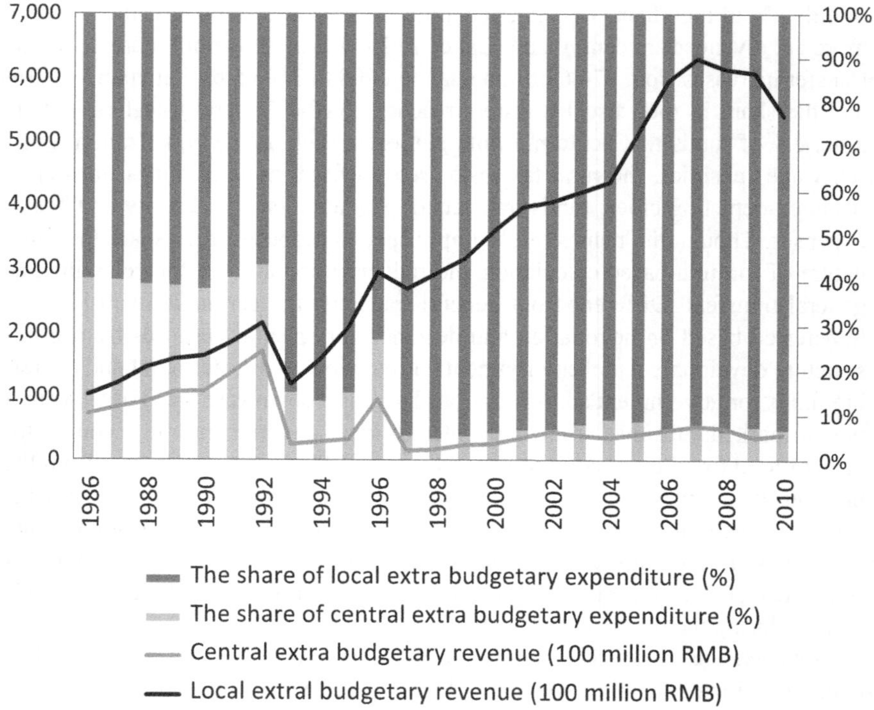

Figure 8.14 The central and local extra-budgetary revenue and expenditure

Source: The extra-budgetary expenditures and revenues are sourced from the Ministry of Finance in China. The shares are calculated by authors.

potential government liabilities are in many cases not transparently reported, closely monitored or systematically managed. As the most valuable asset for local governments, land is provided by local governments to LGFVs as collateral for borrowing. Land sales become a major source of extra-budgetary revenue before 2011, which also boost the on-budget fiscal revenue from direct taxes, such as urban land usage, deed and indirect taxes such as enterprise income taxes from construction and real estate companies. It plays an important role in relatively developed and fast emerging middle-income regions since land is attractive to real estate developers there. In this sense, the use of land as collateral to issue the urban investment bonds through LGFVS and direct land sales might contribute to the widening regional inequality and the local housing bubble, and this might bring about potential risks when the market starts to correct itself.

Although we have limited official data regarding local government debts, investment banks and research institutes have attempted to estimate the fiscal debt using the expanded definition of China's government and have constructed an augmented fiscal deficit series, incorporating the extra budgetary means of financing and local debt issuance through LGFVs.[4] The estimate from Zhang and Barnett's 2014 IMF Working Paper of central and local government debt over GDP is around 45% in 2012, which is considerably larger than the headline government deficit but broadly in line with other estimates because they use an expanded definition of government. Table 8.4 provides the debt statistics from the National Audit Office 2013 report. As of the end of 2012, the ratio of total government debts including direct and contingent liabilities to GDP (51894.2 billion RMB) is more than 50%. Table 8.5 reports the outstanding bonds in 31 Chinese provinces (Hongkong, Macau and Taiwan are excluded) as of 19 March 2018. We find that the most developed regions such as Beijing, Guangdong, Jiangsu and Shanghai have the largest stock of government debts compared to the underdeveloped regions such as Qinghai, Ningxia and Tibet. The rise of debts is indicative of potential fiscal risks, while the balance of debts is still within the sustainability threshold. The potential fiscal risks have already attracted the Chinese authority's attention, and a wide debate is ongoing to push forward a new round of fiscal reform.

The new round of fiscal reform has started, such as replacing the business tax with the value added tax, canceling the off- or extra-budgetary revenue and expenditure, incorporating land sales to the government-managed funding. All extra-budgetary categories have been canceled and clearly incorporated either into the general fiscal budget or the government-managed fund budget since 2011. Two more budget management systems have been established: one is the operating revenue and expenditure budget of state-owned capital, and the other is the social insurance fund budget. At the same time, the China Bank Regulatory Commission (CBRC) has worked together with fiscal departments at different levels of government to contain local government fiscal risks. Many LGFVs are reclassified based on their revenue-generating capacity, dependence on fiscal subsidy and restriction from entering the market for borrowing if their qualifications cannot meet the entry criteria. The next challenges to deepen the fiscal reform mainly stems from how to put in place a better institutional framework to better manage and monitor

Table 8.4 The center and local government liabilities

Year	*Administrative level*	*Direct liabilities (100 million Yuan)*	*Contingent liabilities (100 million Yuan)*	*Direct liabilities over GDP (%)*	*Contingent liabilities over GDP*
As of end of 2012	Center	94376.72	24456.87	18.2	4.7
	Local	96281.87	62576.45	18.6	12.1
	Total	190658.59	87033.32	36.8	16.8
As of June, 2013	Center	98129.48	25711.56	17.3	4.5
	Local	108859.17	70049.49	19.1	12.3
	Total	206988.65	95761.05	36.4	16.8

Note: This table is from the National Audit Office 2013 report, which is available from www.audit.gov.cn/n5/n25/c63642/part/27403.pdf.

Table 8.5 Outstanding bonds by region

Province (municipality)	*No. of bonds (number)*	*Proportion of bonds number (%)*	*Balance (CNY 100M)*	*Balance %*
Beijing	4275	11.50	234,262.15	30.95
Guangdong	2759	7.42	39,039.01	5.16
Jiangsu	3574	9.62	36,970.35	4.88
Shanghai	2046	5.51	33,186.29	4.38
Zhejiang	2655	7.14	26,296.07	3.47
Shandong	2295	6.18	23,790.05	3.14
Fujian	1514	4.07	19,491.05	2.57
Liaoning	1351	3.64	15,638.96	2.07
Sichuan	1371	3.69	15,258.01	2.02
Hunan	1007	2.71	14,472.30	1.91
Chongqing	1348	3.63	14,048.22	1.86
Tianjin	1154	3.11	13,169.15	1.74
Guizhou	830	2.23	12,240.67	1.62
Hubei	920	2.48	11,378.94	1.50
Henan	1099	2.96	11,313.53	1.49
Hebei	744	2.00	10,524.34	1.39
Anhui	819	2.20	10,476.06	1.38
Yunnan	714	1.92	9,350.82	1.24
Shannxi	576	1.55	9,177.14	1.21
Shanxi	952	2.56	8,207.55	1.08
Inner Mongolia	623	1.68	8,122.05	1.07
Guangxi	745	2.00	7,654.97	1.01
Jiangxi	621	1.67	7,368.89	0.97
Xinjiang	622	1.67	5,767.39	0.76
Heilongjiang	596	1.60	5,647.82	0.75
Jilin	596	1.60	5,383.77	0.71
Gansu	253	0.68	3,144.73	0.42
Hainan	190	0.51	2,319.74	0.31
Qinghai	187	0.50	1,985.37	0.26
Ningxia	204	0.55	1,663.34	0.22
Tibet	23	0.06	165.31	0.02

Note: The stock of local government bonds are collected from wind financial database as of 19 March 2018.

government borrowing and reduce the reliance of local government on land sales, and more importantly, from how to balance the fiscal relations among different layers of governments to match fiscal capacity with fiscal activity and how to use fiscal policies to achieve the goal of equalizing public good provision services across various regions.

8.4 Trade policy

8.4.1 Trade development in China

International trade has played an important role in facilitating China's economic development since the reform and opening up policy in 1979 was put in place.

Using data from the National Bureau Statistics of China during the period of 1979 to 2017, we show in Figure 8.15 the trend of trade development measured by the values of China's exports, imports and trade balance, respectively. Since the 1978 reform and opening up, the Chinese government has started to pursue an export-oriented economic development model. In 1992, China establishes the new foreign trade system, which greatly enlarges the scale of trade, with trading volume exceeding US$ 200 billion for the first time in 1994 and reaching US$ 509.65 billion in 2001 before entering the World Trade Organization (WTO), which marks a new stage of opening up. The trade volume has risen rapidly since then, until the occurrence of the global financial crisis. Due to the global economy downturn, China's trade surplus declined by 34%. However, with the resurgence of China and the world economy, China's foreign trade has been growing again, and it has made significant contributions in sustaining global economic growth. Although China's accession to WTO significantly boosts the aggregate volume of imports and exports, Figure 8.16 indicates that China's trade-dependent growth model has been gradually changing since 2006, with the trade dependence ratio declining from a peak level of 64% in 2006 to the current level of 34% in 2017.

In addition to the rising volume of exports and imports, there is an upward trend of foreign direct investment since 1978. We present in Figure 8.17 the distribution of China's outward and inward foreign direct investment (FDI) during 2003–2016. It shows that 68% of outward FDI flows out from China to her close neighbors in Asia, followed by the US (19%) and Europe (7%). Similarly, there are 70% inward FDI from Asia, 17% from the US and 6% from Europe. We also document the top 10 trading partners in Table 8.6 in 2017. Based on the total

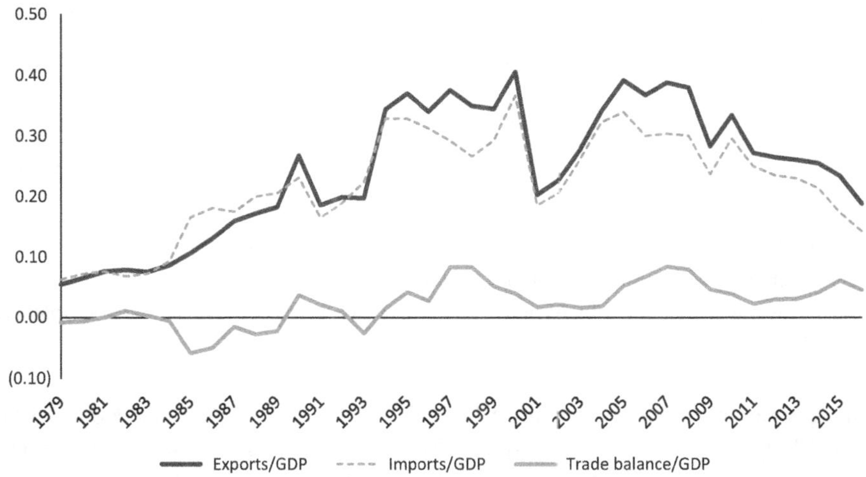

Figure 8.15 The development of trade in China (1979–2017)

Source: Values of exports and imports are sourced from General Administration of Customs, P.R. China; GDP is collected from the National Bureau of Statistics of China.

Figure 8.16 Trade dependence ratio in China (1979–2017) (%)

Source: Data is sourced from National Bureau of Statistics, China (1979–2017).

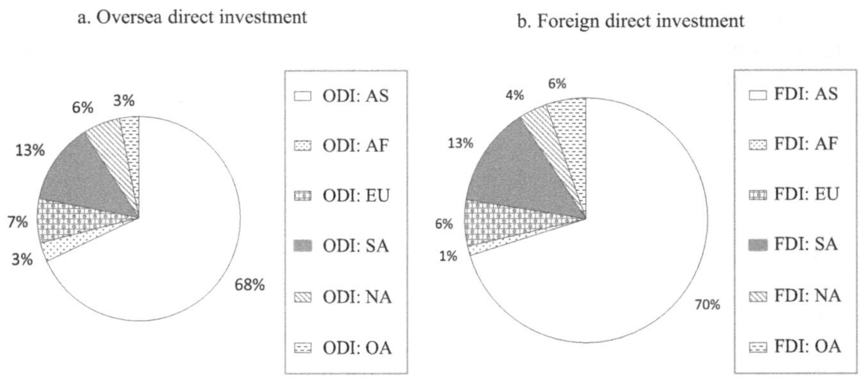

Figure 8.17 Distribution of China's outward and inward FDI (2003–2016)

Source: Data is sourced from National Bureau of Statistics of China (2003–2016).

Note: FDI indicates the inward foreign direct investment; ODI represents the outward foreign direct investment.

trade volume, it reports that the EU, the US., ASEAN, Japan and Hong Kong are China's top five trading partners. The top three export destinations are the US, EU and ASEAN, while most of China's imports are from the EU, ASEAN, Korea, Japan and Taiwan. This table partly reflects China's position as the world factory, where raw materials and intermediate goods are imported from neighboring nations and then exported to the US and the EU after having been turned into assembled products in China.

Table 8.6 China's major trading partners 2017 (in million USD)

Country/Region	*Export value*	*Import value*	*Trade surplus*	*Total trade volume*
EU	374441.93	245224.16	129217.77	619666.09
USA	433146.48	155177.27	277969.20	588323.75
ASEAN	282778.53	236159.56	46618.97	518938.09
Japan	137528.91	165782.66	–28253.75	303311.58
HK	282172.85	7576.79	274596.06	289749.64
Korea	103045.90	177572.71	–74526.81	280618.61
Taiwan	44029.41	155355.51	–111326.10	199384.92
Australia	41701.43	94581.23	–52879.81	136282.66
India	68143.36	16355.60	51787.76	84498.96
Singapore	46233.77	34225.90	12007.87	80459.66
Canada	31765.29	20348.05	11417.24	52113.34

Source: Data is sourced from General Administration of Customs (2017).

8.4.2 Evolution of trade policy

The Chinese government has come to realize that a country's trade policy is an essential part of economic policy and has implemented different trade facilitating strategies at difference phases of economic development. In general, China's international trade policy has experienced four phases of change, as shown in Figure 8.18, with the policy stance gradually shifting from trade protectionism to trade liberalization.

8.4.2.1 The first phase: 1979–1991

Since 1979, the Chinese government has abandoned the state monopoly system of foreign trade, and it has gradually established an export-oriented trade strategy with the trade policy shifting from "import substitution" to "export-oriented". Import restrictions have been implemented by means of tariff, import license, foreign exchange control, classification and management of import commodities. During this phase, China's mandatory plans and direct regulations on trade affairs stunted the working of the market mechanism. In 1988, China's "coastal area economic development" strategy, which strongly encourages coastal provinces to actively participate in the international division of labor, is put forward. Moreover, since 1991, the state has abolished financial subsidies for export, pushing foreign trade enterprises to embark on the development path of self-financing and self-management. To further promote export-oriented trading, the Chinese government also reduced the quotas and the license administration, lowered the general level of tariffs and deepened the reform of the internal operation of export-oriented enterprises.

8.4.2.2 The second phase: 1992–2000

China has initiated the market-oriented reform since 1992, and in the same time sped up the process of regional economic cooperation in the wave of economic globalization. At this stage, a series of trading strategies have been applied to

Figure 8.18 Evolution of trade policy (1979 up to now)

reduce trade barriers, create trade opportunities and promote the free mobility of goods, services, capital, technology and labor. At the same time, China took the initiative to reform the foreign exchange management system, establish the inter-bank foreign exchange market and improve the export tax rebate system in an attempt to create a favorable external environment to encourage foreign trade.

8.5.2.3 The third phase: 2001–2012

In December 2001, China became a full member of the World Trade Organization (WTO). Since then, China has further adjusted her foreign trade system, including lowering tariffs to meet WTO commitments. From 2001 to 2008, China's tariff level fell from 15.3% to 9.8%. Moreover, the Foreign Trade Law has been revised to establish the legal position for foreign trade. The reforms of RMB internationalization and interest rate liberalization have also been promoted. Since 2005, the central bank of China has implemented a manageable floating exchange rate system based on market supply and demand with reference to a basket of currencies. At the same time, foreign exchange management of overseas investment has been relaxed and the channels for domestic foreign exchange investment have been broadened. The outbreak of the global financial crisis in 2008 imposes serious challenges for trade development and leads to reduced global demand. The sharp decline in the trade volume after the global financial crisis reflects a series of problems in China's trading model, such as a heavy reliance on the traditional processing trade, with a large proportion of it in labor-intensive products. Besides, the value added for most export commodities is low. The traditional trading mode urgently requires industrial upgrading and transformation. In response, the Chinese government has revised multiple trade-related policies in an attempt to counterbalance the negative impacts of the crisis on economic growth. The details are summarized in Table 8.7.

8.5.2.4 The fourth phase: 2013-now

In 2013, President Xi Jinping initiates the national strategy of building the Silk Road Economic Belt and the 21st Century Maritime Silk Road (hereinafter referred to as the Belt and Road Initiative). This proposal has garnered widespread attention and support from the international community, since the Belt and Road (B&R) was proposed by 18th National Congress of the Communist Party of China in 2013 as the largest ever infrastructure and economic development

Table 8.7 Major trade policies (2008–2011)

Year	*Contents of major trade policies*
2005	The overall average applied MFN tariff was 9.7% and the average applied MFN tariff rates for agricultural and non-agricultural products were 15.3% and 8.8%; As of the end of 2005, the central government adopted, revised and abolished more than 2,000 pieces of laws, administrative regulations and department rules; China has, in accordance with the Information Technology Agreement (ITA), eliminated tariffs for all ITA products; The Chinese government attaches great importance to the protection of intellectual property rights (IPRs).
2006	The Regulations on Agricultural Tax that were enforced for 48 years were abolished; Tariff rate quota administration for vegetable oils was abolished; Export taxes applied to 51 textiles and clothing products and were levied at rates of RMB 0.2 to 4.0 per piece; all export taxes on textiles and clothing products were removed.
2007	China applied preferential tariffs unilaterally to 37 LDCs; the tariff averages ranged from 9.0% to 9.5%, depending on the origin of goods; The number of tariff lines subject to interim export duties almost doubled, VAT rebate rates on exports of some 2,800 lines (HS 8-digit) were eliminated or lowered in July, and the number of lines subject to export quotas and licensing requirements were increased.
2008	Elimination of export duties on 102 products including certain steel plates; Reduction of export duties on 23 products including, for example, yellow phosphorous; Export duties on five products (including apatite and silicon) were raised from 10% to 15%, or from 20% to 35%.
2009	Adjustment of the list of products subject to prohibition and restriction under processing trade; VAT rebate rates increased on exports of certain products including: iron and steel; non-ferrous metals; petrochemicals; electronic and information technology products; and some light industries; Cancelation of the policy of import duty reduction or exemption on imported products when these products were subject to trade remedy measures; Circular from the Ministry of Industry and Information Technology regulating its government procurement activities, under which it restates the practice of giving priority to domestic products, projects and services.
2010	Annual adjustment of the catalogue of items subject to automatic import licensing which included pork, chicken, vegetable oil, tobacco, paper, milk, minerals, chemicals, electrical products and certain steel products; Reduction of applied MFN import tariffs on six tariff lines; Elimination of export duties on 17 tariff lines.
2011	Tariff revenue accounted for 2.7% of total tax revenue, down from 2.8% in 2010; Bound rates ranged from zero to 65% for agricultural products and from zero to 50% for non-agricultural products; China's applied MFN tariff (including interim rates) consisted of 7,977 lines at the HS 2007 8-digit level.
2012	In July 2012, the Ministry of Commerce removed the automatic import licensing administration of 27 products and 130 products at HS 10-digit level. In May, 2012, the General Administration of Customs took the lead in implementing the pilot program of cross-border e-commerce business service in the cities of Shanghai, Chongqing, Hangzhou, Ningbo and Zhengzhou. In 2012, the Chinese Government released guiding documents concerning trade in services, such as The Outline for the Development and Planning of China's International Service Outsourcing Industry and The Opinions on Accelerating the Development of Foreign Culture Trade and has implemented relevant policies on the pilot program of levying Value Added Tax on certain service sectors in lieu of Business Tax.

Source: These contents are sourced from WTO document WT/TPR/OV/12 (2009)[1], WTO/OECD/UNCTAD (2010),[2] and Report on Trade Policy Review (2012)[3] and are summarized by authors.

program. In 2015, China issued The Vision and Actions[5] report on Jointly Building the Silk Road Economic Belt and the 21st Century Maritime Silk Road, which reveals the objectives of such an ambitious initiative. The Chinese government is working hard to promote policy coordination, connectivity of infrastructure and facilities, unimpeded trade, financial integration and interpersonal bonds with the participating countries while adhering to the principle of achieving shared growth through discussion and collaboration in pushing forward the Belt and Road construction. The proposal has attracted extensive participation from 71 countries as of 2017, and 56 economic and trade cooperation zones have been established by China and participating countries.[6] In 2015, China also initiated the construction of the Asian Infrastructure Investment Bank (AIIB). As of the end of 2017, 84 countries have become the members of AIIB. Figure 8.19 shows that the trade volume of countries along the Belt and Road accounts for 21.7% of the global trade in 2016. Figure 8.6 presents the top 10 trading partners along the Belt and Road in 2016, among which the top three are Singapore, India and Russia, respectively. The recent 19th congress report[7] further highlights that China will continue to focus on the B&R construction, carrying on the strategy of "going out" and "bringing in" to build an open pattern of two-way interaction between east and west and land and ocean. At present, China has signed 15 free trade agreements, covering 23 countries and regions and more than 8,000 commodities enjoy zero tariffs. Current evidence shows that the Belt and Road initiative has brought new opportunities in trade development not only for China but also for her trading partners.

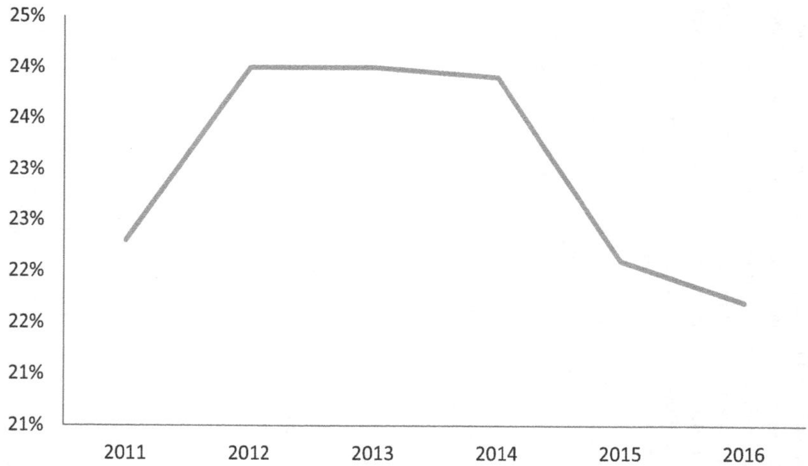

Figure 8.19 B&R countries' share in global trade

Source: Data is sourced from the 2017 Big Data Report of Trade Cooperation under the Belt and Road Initiative www.sic.gov.cn/archiver/SIC/UpFile/Files/Default/20170331094541370706.pdf (in Chinese).

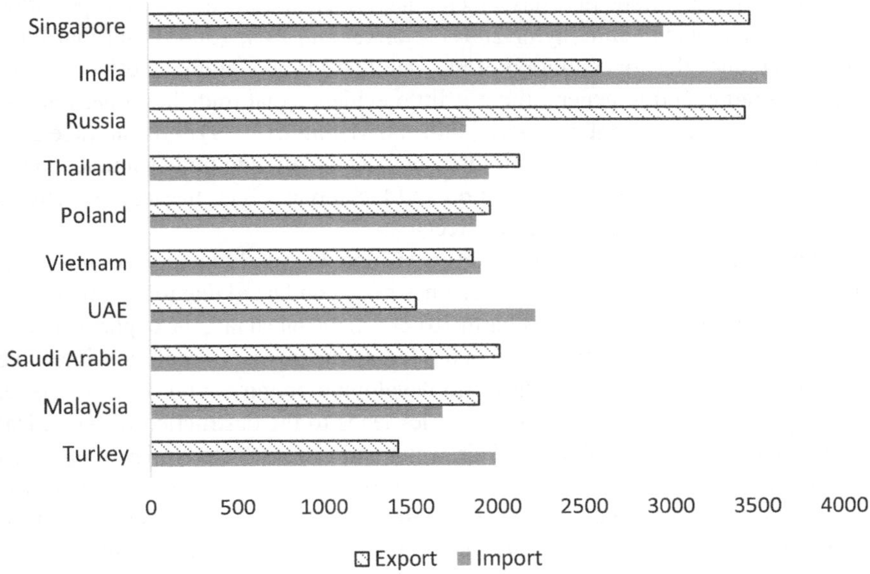

Figure 8.20 The rank of countries along belt and road in total trade volume in 2016 (US$ 100 million)

Source: Data is sourced from the 2017 Big Data Report of Trade Cooperation under the Belt and Road Initiative www.sic.gov.cn/archiver/SIC/UpFile/Files/Default/20170331094541370706.pdf (in Chinese).

8.4.3 Reflection on trade policy

The continuous development of global trade brings economic prosperity to the country but also brings about problems such as environmental degradation. The debate on the link between trade development and environment protection has become increasingly important in the policymaking process. Environmentalists argue that international trade might result in "leakage" as the efforts of reducing greenhouse gas emissions could be compromised because of the migration of carbon-intensive production to non-participating countries. Some studies such as Daly and Goodland (1994) explore the linkage between trade and environment, while focusing on the negative impact. They argue that out of cost considerations polluting industries have motives to move to the location with weak environmental policies, and the relocation exacerbates the local resource depletion and environmental pollution. Moreover, they are concerned that the trade policy promoting international trade and globalization might result in governments being less likely to enforce proper environmental standards that might weaken the competitive advantages of local firms. However, other researchers like Grossman and Krueger (1993) provide evidence that trade has a positive impact on the environment, as it increases real income and allows nations to afford better environmental policies. Additionally, trade also has a technique effect, which can result in pollution reduction (Copeland and Taylor 2004). Frankel and Rose (2005) find that trade tends to reduce the concentration of SO_2, but there is no significant effect on particulate matter, and in general there is little evidence that trade has a detrimental effect on the environment. Similarly, Jalil and Mahmud (2009) find that trade does not harm the environment. Essentially, when deconstructing trade's impact on the environment in the scale, composition and technique effect, the last two effects can compensate the negative scale effect.

The rapid growth of trade indeed brings China, the world factory, serious environmental problems, but little research has been conducted due to data unavailability (Li and Hewitt 2008; Eisenbarth 2017). On the one hand, the export-oriented industrial structure and labor division has led to the transfer of pollution-intensive industries from developed countries to developing countries; on the other hand, the expansion of export-oriented industries leads to the destruction of biological and mineral resources, pollution of air, water and increased stockpiles of unsorted solid waste. The resulting environmental problems are initially ignored in the pursuit of trade development and economic growth when China strives to promote growth of economy and is reluctant to enforce strict environmental regulation. Fortunately, in recent years the increasingly serious environmental issue has attracted public awareness and government attention. Eisenbarth (2017) finds that trade policies could indeed be used as a second-best environmental policy. For example, the export value added tax rebates encourage the conservation of natural resources such as minerals, metals, wood products and precious stones.

The Ministry of Environmental Protection, the Ministry of Commerce, the General Administration of Customs and the National Development and Reform Commission of China have jointly issued new regulations regarding the management of imported solid waste in 2011[8] and further strengthen the restriction and prohibition of importing solid waste from foreign countries and enlarge the scope of banned items in 2017. The series of reforming measures and actions demonstrate China's determination and dedication to improve environmental degradation using trade policies and provide future research directions in evaluating the effectiveness of trade policies on environmental protection.

8.5 Conclusions

We review three key aspects of economic policies in China, namely, the monetary policy, the fiscal policy and the trade policy and find out that the coherent themes underpinning these policies are growth and sustainability. As a country with a population of more than 1.3 billion, growth in terms of output has been the priority since the influential 1978 economic reform, which was highly successful in the aspect of alleviating the poverty ratio and improving economic welfare. Our analyses show that monetary, fiscal and trade policies have been counter-cyclical most of the time, driving economic growth during economic downturns and containing demand during economic booms. The three aspects of policies jointly shape the economic landscape of China with her growth model heavily relying on capital formation and exports. In addition, within a regionally decentralized authoritarian institutional framework, any form of policymaking and implementation has been the result of a play of politics and the rebalancing of interests between the central government and the subordinate lower-level governments. This institutional framework creates enough space for conducting bottom up economic experiments in the step-by-step economic reform process; nonetheless, it brings about distortion, inefficiency and disorder at the same time.

Economic prosperity comes not without a cost. It brings about many challenges such as high inequality across regions, groups of interests and individuals, environmental degradation and resources depletion. Looking forward, with economic growth gradually slowing down, we have the risk of falling into the middle-income trap. We also face demographic pressures related to an aging population with low fertility rate despite the relaxation of the one-child policy, and fast urbanization with insufficient and unequal public good provision in education and healthcare. Significant policy adjustments are imperative to make China's development more sustainable. In the 12th Five-Year Plan (2011–2015), the 13th Five-Year Plan (2016–2020) and the 19th Congress report, the annual growth rate target has been lowered to 7% and then to 6.5%, reflecting the refocus on the quality of growth and the rebalancing of the economy while still targeting to achieve a "moderately prosperous society" by 2020. These plans also highlight the Chinese government's dedication to develop measures to address environmental pollution, increase energy efficacy and improve education and healthcare accessibility. We do not intend to provide an exhaustive list of every aspect of economic policies, and the roles and effectiveness of other aspects of policies are not negligible, such as the industrial and innovation policy, which can help China narrow the income gap with Western countries through productivity growth and innovation that injects dynamism into the economy. Future research may focus on evaluating the effectiveness of these policies.

Notes

1 The People's Bank of China act was promulgated in 1995 at the third session of the 8th National Congress, which is available from www.pbc.gov.cn/rhwg/19981801.htm (in Chinese).

2 From 1988 to 1994, China adopted a dual-track system of exchange rate. From 1994 to July 2005, RMB was pegged to the US dollar. After the 2005 exchange rate reform, China adopted the manageable floating exchange rate regime. However, the Chinese currency was re-pegged to the dollar from July 2008 to May 2010 to boost export during the period of the Great Financial Crisis (Fan et al. 2011).

3 The 2016 Quarterly Monetary Policy Executive Reports are available from the People's Bank of China's official website www.pbc.gov.cn/english/130727/130879/3007494/3272842/index.html.

4 Some estimates of government liabilities are larger including IMF's because of their broad definition of general government which includes "augmented" fiscal activities. For example, all LGFVs' debts are incorporated into government debt while a large share of LGFVs' activities is commercial rather than fiscal. However, such detailed information is not accessible (Zhang and Barnett 2014).

5 The Vision and Actions report is available from www.yidaiyilu.gov.cn/wcm.files/upload/CMSydylgw/201706/201706200153032.pdf.
6 Data is available from www.yidaiyilu.gov.cn.
7 The 19th CCP report is available from http://ces.ustb.edu.cn/uploads/soft/171019/26_1651285121.pdf (in Chinese).
8 The 2011 regulation regarding the management of imported solid waste was based on the 2005 revised Law of Solid Waste Pollution Prevention in the People's Republic of China, and is available from www.customs.gov.cn/publish/portal0/tab515/info310245.htm. The 2017 prohibition mandate is available from www.waizi.org.cn/doc/22601.html.

References

Bahl, R. W. (1999), *Fiscal Policy in China: Taxation and Intergovernmental Fiscal Relations*, University of Michigan Press.

Bernanke, B. S., and A. S. Blinder (1992), "The Federal Funds Rate and the Channels of Monetary Transmission," *The American Economic Review*: 901–921.

Bernanke, B. S., and M. Gerler (1995), "Inside the Black Box: The Credit Channel of Monetary Policy Transmission," *Journal of Economic Perspectives* 9(4): 27–48.

Bernanke, B. S., and I. Mihov (1998), "Measuring Monetary Policy," *The Quarterly Journal of Economics* 113(3): 869–902.

Copeland, B. R., and M. S. Taylor (2004), "Trade, Growth, and the Environment," *Journal of Economic literature* 42(1): 7–71.

Daly, H., and R. Goodland (1994), "An Ecological-economic Assessment of Deregulation of International Commerce Under GATT Part I," *Population and Environment* 15(5): 395–427.

Dickinson, D., and J. Liu (2007), "The Real Effects of Monetary Policy in China: An Empirical Analysis," *China Economic Review* 18(1): 87–111.

Eisenbarth, S. (2017), "Is Chinese Trade Policy Motivated by Environmental Concerns?" *Journal of Environmental Economics and Management* 82: 74–103.

Fan, L., Y. Yu, and C. Zhang (2011), "An Empirical Evaluation of China's Monetary Policies," *Journal of Macroeconomics* 33(2): 358–371.

Frankel, J. A., and A. K. Rose (2005), "Is Trade Good or Bad for the Environment? Sorting Out the Causality," *Review of Economics and Statistics* 87(1): 85–91.

Groves, T., Y. Hong, J. McMillan, and B. Naughton (1994), "Autonomy and Incentives in Chinese State Enterprises," *The Quarterly Journal of Economics* 109(1): 183–209.

Grossman, G. M., and A. B. Krueger (1993), "Environmental Impacts of a North American Free Trade Agreement," in: P. Garber (ed.), *The US-Mexico Free Trade Agreement*, Cambridge: MIT Press, 1655177.

He, D., and L. L. Pauwel (2008), "What Prompts the People's Bank of China to Change Its Monetary Policy Stance? Evidence from a Discrete Choice Model," *China & World Economy* 16(6): 1–21.

Hsieh, C. T., and P. J. Klenow (2009), "Misallocation and Manufacturing TFP in China and India," *The Quarterly Journal of Economics* 124(4): 1403–1448.

Jalil, A., and S. F. Mahmud (2009), "Environment Kuznets Curve for CO2 Emissions: A Cointegration Analysis for China," *Energy Policy* 37(12): 5167–5172.

Jin, H., Y. Qian, and B. R. Weingast (2005), "Regional Decentralization and Fiscal Incentives: Federalism, Chinese Style," *Journal of Public Economics* 89(9–10): 1719–1742.

Li, Y., and C. N. Hewitt (2008), "The Effect of Trade between China and the UK on National and Global Carbon Dioxide Emissions," *Energy Policy* 36(6): 1907–1914.

Liu, M., J. Wang, R. Tao, and R. Murphy (2009), "The Political Economy of Earmarked Transfers in a State-designated Poor County in western China: Central Policies and Local Responses," *The China Quarterly* 200: 973–994.

Oi, J. C. (1992), "Fiscal Reform and the Economic Foundations of Local State Corporatism in China," *World Politics* 45(1): 99–126.

Romer, C. D., and D. H. Romer (2004), "A New Measure of Monetary Shocks: Derivation and Implications," *American Economic Review* 94(4): 1055–1084.

Sun, G., and W. Li (2017), "Monetary Policy, Exchange Rate and Capital Flow," The People's Bank of China Working Paper Series No. 2017/3, Beijing.

Sun, L., J. L. Ford, and D. G. Dickinson (2010), "Bank Loans and the Effects of Monetary Policy in China: VAR/VECM Approach," *China Economic Review* 21(1): 65–97.

Sun, R. (2013), "Does Monetary Policy Matter in China? A Narrative Approach," *China Economic Review* 26: 56–74.

Sun, R. (2015), "What Measures Chinese Monetary Policy?" *Journal of International Money and Finance* 59: 263–286.

Xiong, W. (2012), "Measuring the Monetary Policy Stance of the People's Bank of China: An Ordered Probit Analysis," *China Economic Review* 23(3): 512–533.

Xu, C. (2011), "The Fundamental Institutions of China's Reforms and Development," *Journal of Economic Literature* 49(4): 1076–1151.

Yao, Shujie (2000), "Economic Development and Poverty Reduction in China over 20 Years of Reforms," *Economic Development and Cultural Change* 48(3): 447–474. doi:10.1086/452606.

Zhang, Y. Y., and S. Barnett (2014), "Fiscal Vulnerabilities and Risks from Local Government Finance in China," IMF Working Papers, WP/14/4.

9 Chinese infrastructure

Ming He and Yang Chen[1]

9.1 Introduction

China has achieved extensive economic growth in the past 30 years, along with infrastructure development. From 1995 to 2016, China's total infrastructure investment grew at 18.7% annually, outpacing GDP growth by 6.1%.[2] During the same period, the ratio of infrastructure investment to GDP has climbed steadily from 6.7% to 20.4%. These numbers suggest the increasing importance of infrastructure in total government spending. In 2009, when the government launched the generous 4 trillion RMB stimulus package to counteract the economic slowing down, the growth rate of infrastructure investment reached a stunning 42.2%. In absolute terms, China is now world's biggest spender on fixed assets, accounting for 24.8% of total investment worldwide in 2014 (Ansar et al. 2016). With such vibrant growth, China's infrastructure has improved rapidly since the early 1980s, from highly underdeveloped to what is now better than that of medium-income countries (Table 9.1). A recent World Bank report clearly indicates that superior infrastructure is a key enhancement to China's overall business environment (World Bank 2012).

Economic theories emphasize the pivotal role of infrastructure in economic development and poverty alleviation. Transport and telecommunication infrastructure connects firms to markets and suppliers; it also facilitates the transmission of tacit knowledge through face-to-face or remote communications. Such infrastructure also grants access of labor to various opportunities and creates better matching with employers. Other physical infrastructure warrants the functioning of modern urban area, where agglomeration of firms and labor takes place. As such, infrastructure is an important driver of agglomeration and productivity growth, which creates long-term social benefits that is beyond the immediate effects of fiscal spending on building infrastructure. This neoclassic view was first formulated and confirmed by Aschauer (1989a) and Munnel (1992). The Chinese Ministry of Communications (MOC) shared the same view. In a massive propaganda launched in early 1980s, peasants all over the nation were told to "build roads if you want to get rich."

Given China's sheer size in area and population, her recent achievements in infrastructure are impressive, especially when one considers that the government

Table 9.1 Cross country comparisons in infrastructure

	Annual air flight per person		*Phone subscribers per 100 people*		*Rail line kilos per square kilo*		*WEF quality index of ports*	
	1980	*2015*	*1980*	*2015*	*1980*	*2015*	*1980*	*2015*
China	0.003	0.318	0.218	108.6	0.005	0.007	–	4.549
India	0.009	0.076	0.308	80.05	0.021	0.022	–	4.207
Medium-income	0.033	0.246	1.466	107.1	0.005	0.006	–	3.599
OECD	0.533	1.553	26.71	153.4	0.016	0.016	–	5.064

Source: The World Bank Data Bank.

at all levels was facing tight budget constraints (Chapter 8, this volume). It is then important to understand how these massive investments were financed, how fast different types of infrastructure were built and to what extent. Based on these understandings, the next question is how China's economic development is affected by the infrastructure built. Which sector or region benefits more from a certain type of infrastructure? Are the benefits felt evenly across the nation? Do government's pilot plans meet their initiatives? What are the looming problems created during the process? Finally, what are the imminent questions that researchers need to answer in the near future?

To answer these questions, the rest of this chapter is divided into three parts. Section 9.2 investigates China's infrastructure development by sector. We identify the main stakeholders and methods of financing. We also provide summary statistics of the investment size and capacity. Section 9.3 analyzes the economic consequence of infrastructure. We conduct an extensive review of the literature and perform cross-country comparisons. Finally, Section 9.4 identifies a few unanswered questions and invites future research in these fields.

9.2 The facts

To begin with, let us present our definition of infrastructure sectors and assess their relative importance in total infrastructure spending.

9.2.1 Definition and decomposition

The National Bureau of Statistics (NBS) categorize the national economy into 1094 sectors in 20 broad categories (GB/T 4754–2011). According to NBS definition, infrastructure refers to sectors in the following categories: (1) production and supply of electricity, heat, gas and water; (2) transport, storage and post; (3) management of water, conservancy, environment and public facilities. Other definitions usually include the telecommunication sector as well.[3] Therefore, we decided to add a fourth sub-category to the NBS definition, which is information transmission. Their recent shares in total infrastructure investment are shown in Figure 9.1.

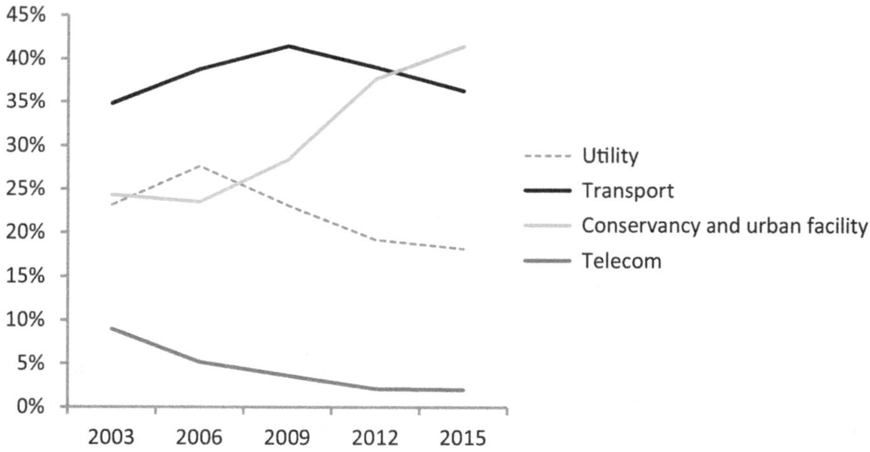

Figure 9.1 Infrastructure investment decomposition

Source: NBS; unit: percent.

It can be readily seen that categories 2 (transport related) and 3 (conservancy and urban facility) took the lion's share of all spending, and their weight is increasing steadily, from 65% in 2003 to 79% in 2015. Total infrastructure investment increased by 8.2 times (from 1,440 billion RMB to 13,198 billion RMB), which is similar to that of transport (7.9 times). The investment of conservancy and urban facility registered the highest growth (13.5 times). Further decomposition (Figure 9.2) of the investment spending in categories 2–4 reveals the dominant role of two sectors: highway transport and urban facility management; while in the telecom sector, the construction of mobile networks absorbs roughly 60% of all spending.

China's spending on highway infrastructure is generous, which reached 2,728.3 billion RMB in 2015, and it alone accounted for 18.0% of total infrastructure investment. This reflects a national strategic plan in developing a national highway network, which we shall discuss shortly. More impressive is China's spending on urban facility. It grew 15 times in 12 years and reached 4,618 billion RMB in 2015. It is the largest single sector in China's infrastructure investment. Obviously, this reflects China's rapid urbanization process during the same period of time (Chapter 5, this volume).

With these pictures in mind, the rest of this section will focus on highways and urban facilities. Given the competing role of railways in land transportation and their relative importance, we will also analyze China's railways in similar detail.

9.2.2 Highways

China had no expressway at all back in 1980, and the total length of her road network (excluding rural roads) was merely 0.89 million kilometers.[4] Compared to

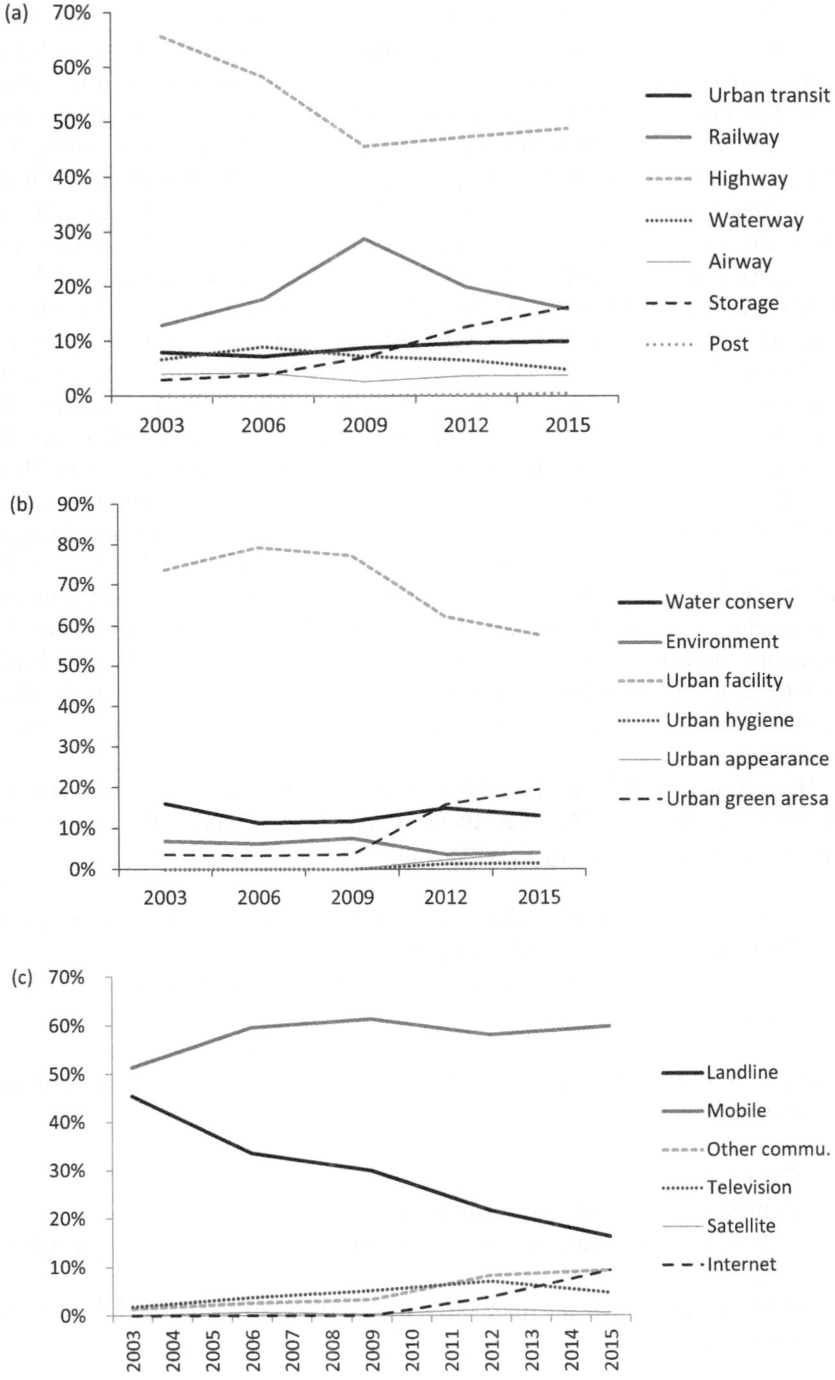

Figure 9.2 Further decomposition of infrastructure investment
Source: NBS. Unit: percent.

the 29,023 kilometers of highways and 8.6 million kilometers of non-rural roads in India at the same time, China's road network was severely underdeveloped. As the economic reform commenced in the early 1980s, the Chinese government started to upgrade her highway network, but it was not until 1988 that China had her first expressway built, which is 20.4 kilometers from Shanghai to Jiading. The sluggish progress in the 1980s might be explained by the limited amount of funding. Before 1980, all transport facility was planned and funded by the government. The central government was responsible for national or regional highways, and local government for local roads. Due to the limited fiscal resources at all levels (totally 122.9 billion RMB and 34.6 billion RMB allocated to infrastructure), it was virtually impossible for the government to carry out major highway projects.

Despite the far-reaching reform policies, there has been little change in the planning side of the nation's highway system. At the top of the hierarchy are the Ministry of Transport (MOT, formerly Ministry of Communication), the National Development and Reform Commission (NDRC, formerly State Planning Commission) and the State Council (SC). As the key player in the process, the Ministry of Transport drafts development plans for national and strategic regional highways. However, once a plan is approved by the NDRC and the SC, it is the Transport Department (TD) of each province that raises the money and conducts the actual construction; the provincial Transport Department also plans and builds the rest of the provincial highways. In contrast, the Transport Bureaus at lower levels take on far fewer responsibilities. It is no wonder that the majority of the highway projects are financed by the provincial governments.[5]

The reform period, however, did witness a drastic change in the highway financing policy. In 1984, the 54th executive meeting of the SC made three far-reaching decisions regarding highway development, which are:

- To levy vehicle purchase fee (tax) for use by the Ministry of Communication;
- To increase highway maintenance tax rate;
- To allow local governments and other entities to build highways using bank loans, and to repay with tolls.

As the reform deepened, the government gradually introduced additional financing channels, including:

- Gas tax (1999);
- Domestic and international capital (stock) market (1998);
- Aide or loans provided by foreign government or international organizations (1987);
- Other project financing method such as BOT, PFI, BT, and PPP (2014 onwards).

These decisions gave provincial TDs considerable latitude in funding highway projects.[6] User toll is a key feature of China's highways. As of 2015, almost all of China's expressways and a substantial fraction of grade one roads were tolled; many highways were tolled (owned) by non-government entitles (Table 9.2). Although toll rates in China must be approved by NDRC, they are comparable to those of developed countries (World Bank 2007). In 2016, toll revenue nationwide amounted to 454.9 billion RMB, of which 181.1 billion RMB was generated by highways operated by the government, and 273.8 billion RMB was taken by other investors. Tolls can be used to finance other highway projects directly, or they can be used to pay off current debts.[7] Tolls are also attractive to profit-seeking private investors and SOEs. Obviously, highway tolls give rise to a wide range of financing opportunities (Figure 9.3).

The National Trunk Highways System (NTHS) was the first ambitious strategic plan released by the MOT in 1992. It serves a few clear objectives:

- To connect all large cities (population $\geq$ 1 million) and most medium-sized cities (population $\geq$ 0.5 million) at the time;
- In coordination with other transport systems, to develop a fast, efficient and safe system of expressways, grade one and grade two roads that meets the needs of China's economic development.;

Table 9.2 Highway mileage by toll status and ownership (2015)

	Total mileage	*Tolled*	*Tolled by government*	*Tolled by non-government*
All roads	4,577.3	164.4	102.1	62.3
Expressway	123.5	117.0	65.8	51.2
Grade one	91.0	23.4	18.2	5.2
Grade two	360.4	22.9	17.8	5.0

Source: NBS and MOT; unit: 1,000 kilometers.

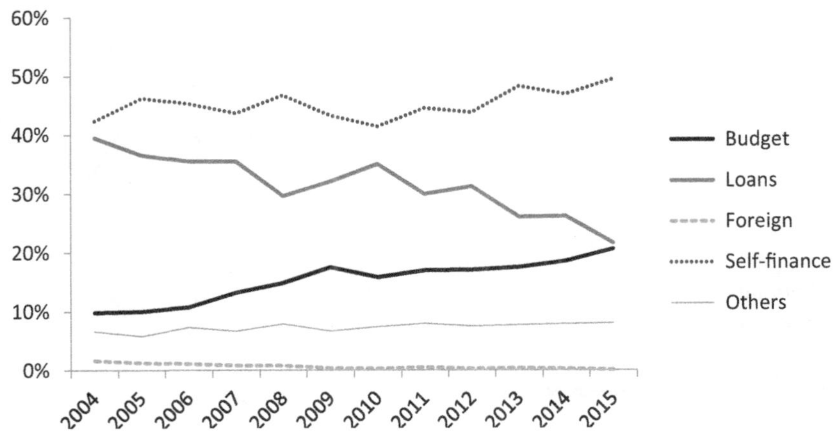

Figure 9.3 Source of highway investment funds

Source: NBS; Unit: percent.

Practically the project boils down to five north-south and seven east-west highways of a total length of 34,422 kilometers that spans the country's vast territory (Figure 9.4). It was planned that the majority (74.9%) of these highways would be built as expressways, 4.3% as grade one roads and 20.9% as grade two roads. The project was estimated to cost 900 billion RMB, taking 30 years (1991–2020) to complete.

The project was started in the late 1980s, when the MOT drafted the early versions of the blueprint. By the end of 1997, China had built 4,771 kilometers of expressways, 70% of which were NTHS highways. To counteract the 1998 financial crisis, the State Council decided to speed up infrastructure investment, highway construction included. In accordance with the decision made by the State Council, the MOT announced that it would "focus on two north-east roads and two east-west lines of NTHS, and prioritize the construction of high-traffic sections." With these decisions, the construction of NTHS highways accelerated, with at least 2,500 kilometers of new expressways built each year. In 2001, China's expressway network became one of the longest in the world, second only to the United States. By the end of 2007, the entire project was completed, 13 years ahead of the initial schedule.

The NTHS is just the beginning of MOT's ambition. Before it was finally built, the MOT released another plan exclusively for expressways, which was called the

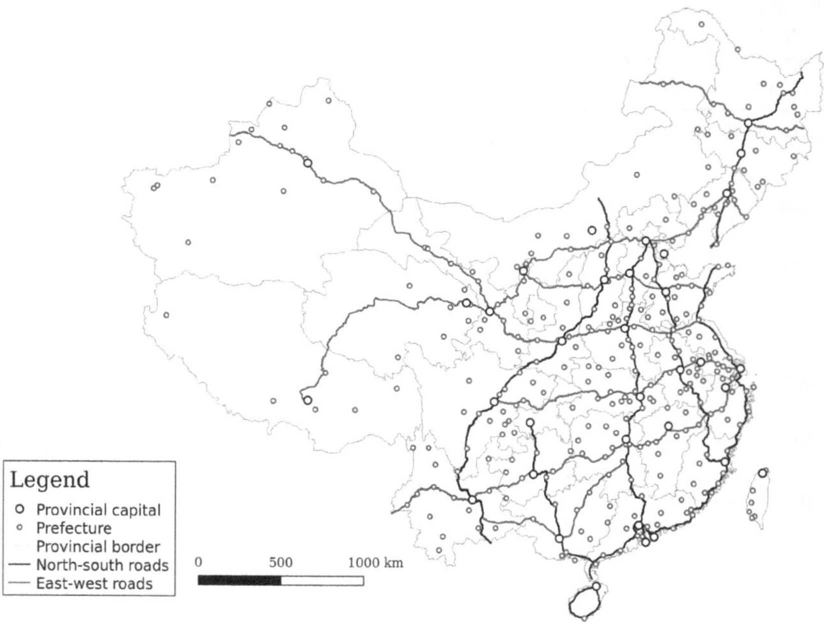

Figure 9.4 The national trunk highway system (1992)

Source: OpenStreetMap WikiProject China National Highway

National Expressway Network System (NENS). The pilot plan aims to achieve multiple economic and political objectives, which are:

- To connect all provincial capitals and to safeguard national security;
- To connect the major economic zones and to form an inter-province expressway network;
- To connect all large and medium-sized cities (population $\geq$ 200,000) and to form an inter-city expressway network;
- To connect neighboring countries and to form international transport corridors;
- To connect existing transport hubs (50 railway hubs, 67 major airports, 140 road transport hubs and 50 waterway hubs) and to form a highway based logistic network.

NENS comprise 34 artery expressways: seven radial lines from Beijing, nine north-south lines, and 18 east-west lines (Figure 9.5). The planned network had a total length of 85,000 kilometers, with 68,000 kilometers of artery lines and 17,000 kilometers of regional connection lines.[8] NENS is optimized for accessibility. One will be able to access NENS expressways in 30 minutes in the East, 60 minutes in Central China and two hours in the West. It is also designed to enhance efficiency and to reduce regional disparity. The most developed economic zones

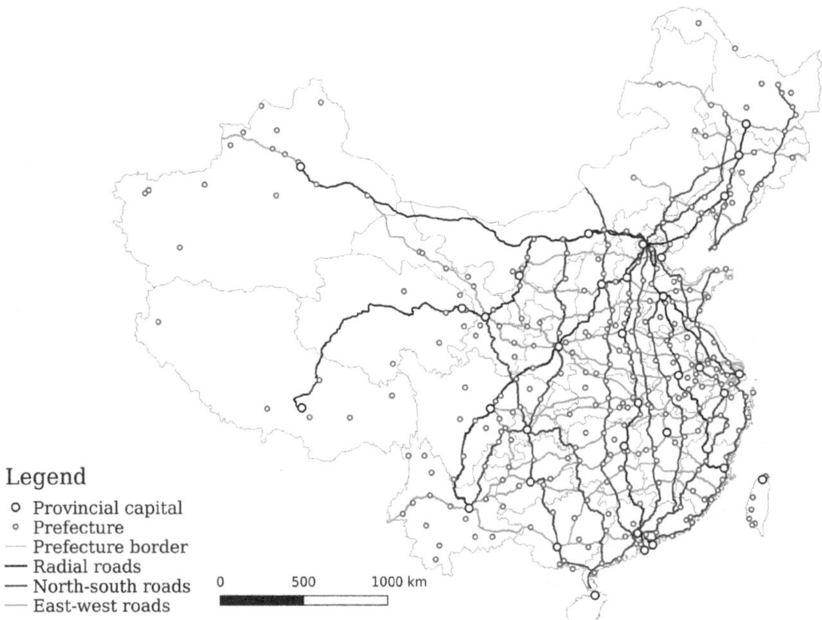

Figure 9.5 The national expressway network system (2013 plan)

Source: OpenStreetMap WikiProject Expressways of China

in the East will have at least three artery lines connecting each other; yet a substantial amount of lines are allocated to the Northeast and West, where connectivity was weak and the economic development was sluggish. By 2013, 71,000 kilometers of NENS expressways were built, 22,000 kilometers were under construction, and 25,000 kilometers were planned.[9] Without surprise, China will finish this grand project earlier than expected (2030).

As of 2015, China's highways reached 574,897 kilometers, of which 123,523 kilometers were expressways (Table 9.2). Figure 9.6 shows that the major boost of highway construction took place in the 2006–2010 period, during which the

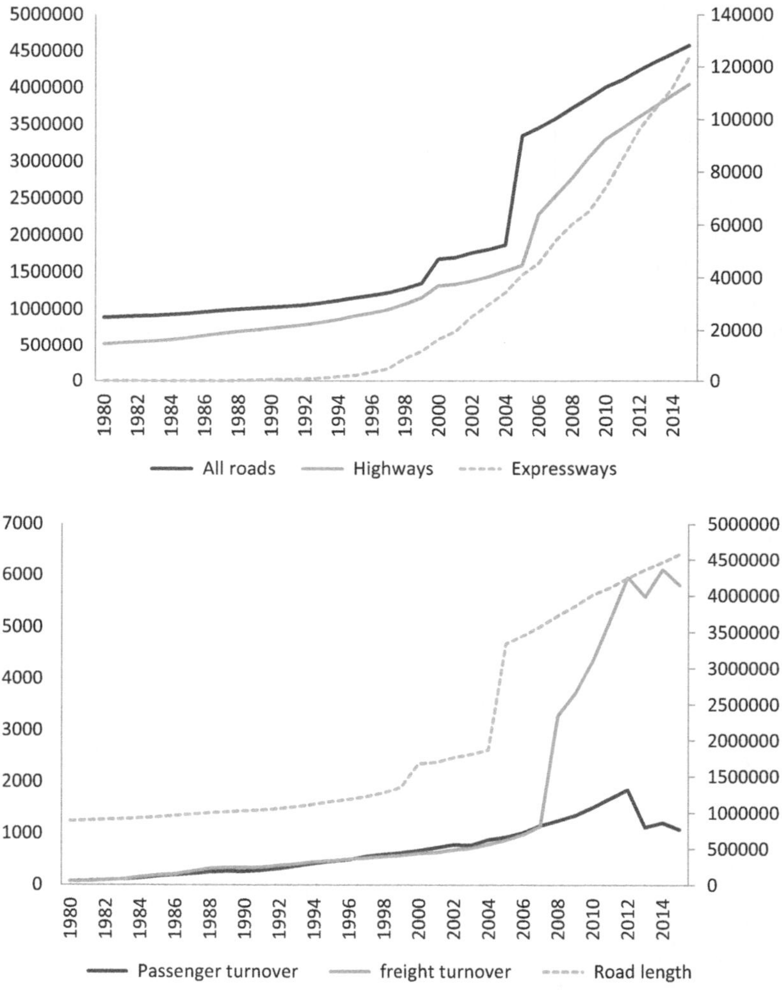

Figure 9.6 Growth in road length (top) and traffic turnover (bottom)

Source: NBS; Unit: kilometer (top), billion passenger-kilometer or billion ton-kilometer (bottom).

mileage was increasing at about 10% annually.[10] The mileage of expressways grew very fast before 2002 (48.4% annually) before it slowed down after 2007 (11.1% annually). On average, the length of highways and expressways grew at 6.0% and 30.2% annually over the 1980–2015 period. These numbers reflect Chinese government's dedication to expressway construction and the ample supply of various resources. Passenger and freight turnover were growing at higher rates than highway length (8.0% and 13.2% per annum), which suggests that the fast-growing road network is probably insufficient to meet the increasing needs of traffic.[11]

9.2.3 Railways

China was behind other major economies in railway development back in 1980. The total mileage of railways was 53,300 kilometers, which was shorter than that of India (61,200 kilometers) and the United States (265,800 kilometers). Nonetheless, China expanded her railway network considerably during the reform era. By the end of 2015, China had 121,000 kilometers of railways in operation, of which 74,700 kilometers were electrification lines and 19,800 kilometers were high-speed lines. They jointly delivered 1196.1 billion passenger-kilometers and 2375.4 billion ton-kilometers of (passenger and freight) turnover.

Until 2013, China's railway network was under the monolithic control of the Ministry of Railway (MOR), who is in charge of formulating regulations, planning routes, financing constructions, building new lines and manufacturing railway equipment. The actual daily operation of existing lines was conducted by 18 subordinate Regional Railway Administrations (RRA). The MOR underwent three waves of decentralization/marketization reforms. The 1991 Railway Law allows railways to be operated by local governments (local railways) or by joint ventures (joint railways); the law also encourages railway fares to be set on a commercial basis.[12] The 1991 law paved way for the Guangshen Railway Company and the Daqin Railway Company, which became listed companies either domestically or abroad. Starting from 1998, the MOR began to separate non-core activities and to transfer their control rights to other organizations; these activities include construction, manufacturing, design, telecommunication, education and social service. Correspondingly, the MOR was able to cut staff from 3.4 million to 2.1 million. The most recent reform took place in 2013, when the MOR was separated into the National Railway Administration (NRA) and the China Railway Corporation (CRC). The NRA inherits the administrative roles and it is now a branch of the MOT; the CRC takes over all remaining construction and management roles. The reform measures thus far were focused on structural change, but with very limited effects on ownership diversification.[13]

Because of the centralized management, railway investment was mainly conducted by the MOR, with limited involvement by local governments. This constitutes a sharp contrast against highways, on which we observe active local participation. We also observe that the MOR took the dominant role in managing existing lines. In 1980, there were 53,300 kilometers of railways, of which 93.6% (49,900 kilometers) were run by the MOR. It took 30 years for this percentage to reach 72.6%. Since the MOR was dismantled in 2013, the number dropped rapidly (59.9% in 2014). This observation suggests that many joint railways are in fact run by former MOR affiliates. Lack of participation by other entities may explain why total investment in railways has been considerably lower than that of highways (Figure 9.2, top).[14]

Prior to 2007, the major source of investment funds was self-raised funds (retained profits and surcharges) and the (central) government budget (Figure 9.7). However, bank loans increased sharply in 2008 and soon became the single largest source of funds. The timing matches the fiscal stimulus packages introduced in 2008. Because investment and management are highly centralized in the MOR, the soaring loans and likely increase in bond financing (in others) may put the MOR (and later CRC) under considerable financial pressure. Deleverage measures may explain the slowing down of railway investment activities in 2010 and 2015. In summary, the lack of diversified investors exposes the MOR to financial risk, and it may hinder major investment projects (World Bank 2007).

By 2008, China's national railway system was characterized by 16 artery lines, eight running north-south and another eight-running east-west (Figure 9.8). With 110,713 kilometers of railways, the system delivered 777.9 billion person-kilometers and 2,510.6 billion ton-kilometers of passenger and freight turnovers, respectively. The utilization rate is the highest in the world.[15]

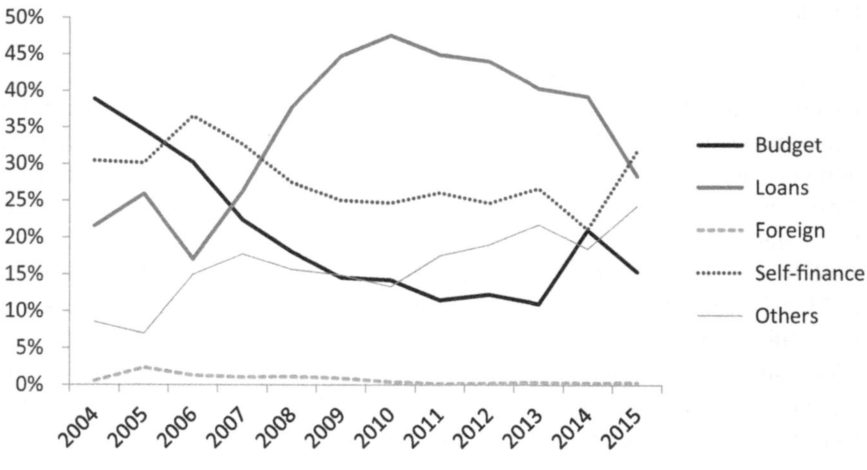

Figure 9.7 Source of railway investment funds

Source: the MOR railway statistical bulletin (2003–2016). Unit: percent.

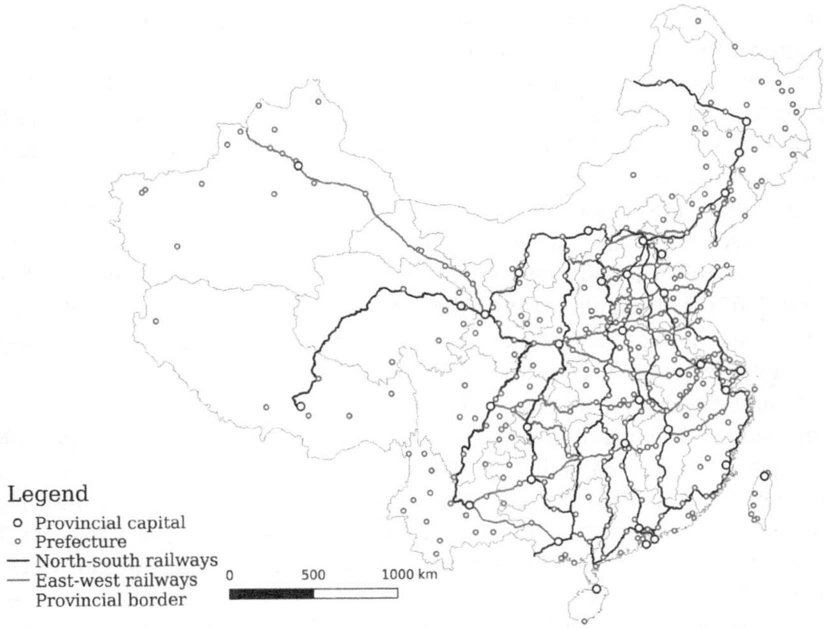

Figure 9.8 China's main railways (2008)

Source: OpenStreetMap WikiProject China Railways.

A recent major event in China's railway development is the Mid and Long-Term Railway Network Plan released in 2004 and revised in 2016. The plan features the following objectives:

- To build a railway network with wide coverage, which connects
    - all cities with 20 million or more population;
    - resource endowed regions;
    - logistic hubs;
    - main ports and boarder entries;
    - most county level jurisdictions;
- To build a modern high-speed railway network, which connects
    - major metropolitans;
    - most provincial capitals and cities with 50 million or more population;
- To build integrated transportation complex, which connects other means of transport.

According to this plan, China is to expand her railway network to 150,000 kilometers by 2020, and 200,000 kilometers by 2030. The project is expected to increase the turnover of the network to 1,600 billion person-kilometers and 3,100 billion ton-kilometers, a 100% increase in passenger turnover and a 23.4% increase in freight turnover over their 2008 values.

The plan is perhaps best known for its sub-plan on high-speed railways (HSR) dedicated to passenger traffic. The HSR network has 16 corridors, eight in the north-south direction and another eight-running east-west. As of 2016, China has built over 22,000 kilometers of HSR lines (Figure 9.9). When fully built, the total length of the HSR network is expected to reach 45,000 kilometers in 2030.

The size of the plan makes it the largest of its kind since the 19th century; the entire project is estimated to cost 100–150 billion RMB per annum (World Bank 2007). This combined with the 2008 stimulus package may explain why the amount of investment surged after 2008. As the plan itself pointed out, major reform measures are needed to explore new channels of project financing.

It can be seen from Figure 9.10 that the growth in the railway network was much slower than that of highways (2.3% vs. 6.0% per annum) during the 1980–2015 period. It was not until 2008 that it registered strong growth; yet almost all the growth was achieved by high speed railways. During the 1980–2015 period, total passenger turnover and freight turnover increased at 6.3% and 4.2% per year, respectively, which suggest that railway infrastructure investment was insufficient to meet the needs of the economy.

Inspections of the post-2011 data reveal a different story. It is interesting to observe that freight turnover started to decline in 2012, while the passenger

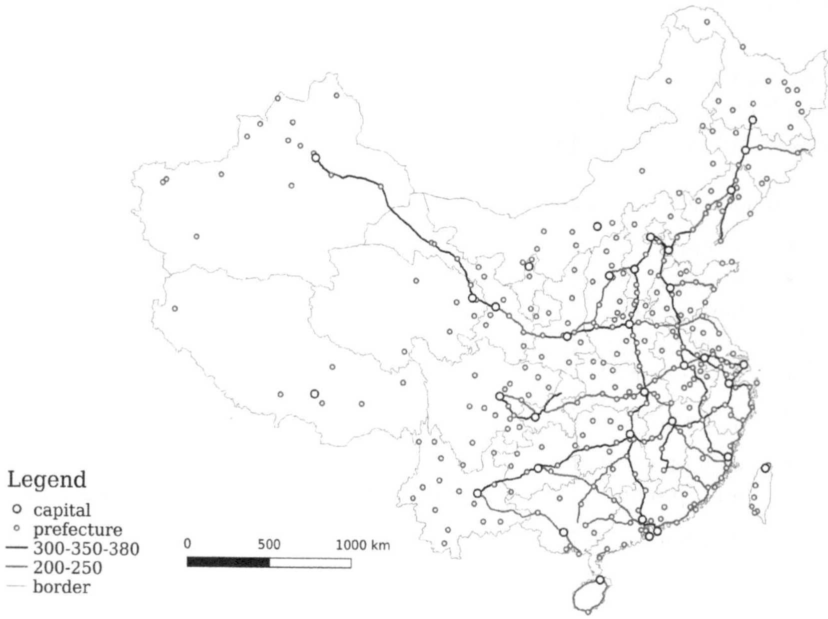

Figure 9.9 HSR lines in operation (2016)

Source: OpenStreetMap.

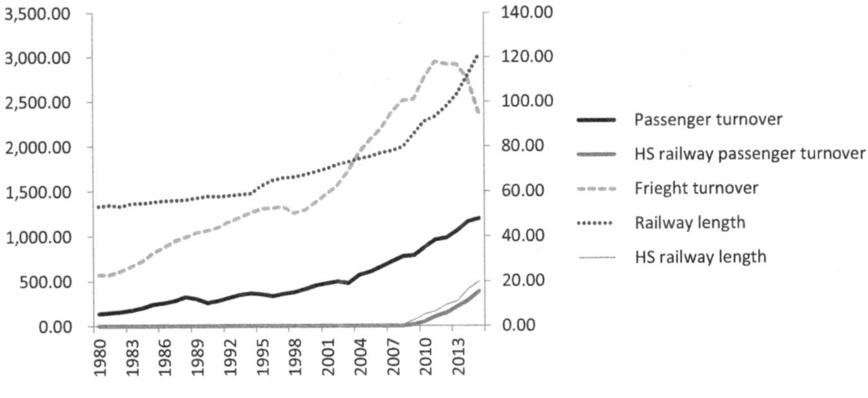

Figure 9.10 Growth of railway length and traffic

Source: NBS and MOT; Unit: billion passenger-kilometer or billion ton-kilometer (left axis), thousand kilometers (right axis).

turnover net of high speed railways also decreased slightly (from 855.4 billion passenger-kilometers in 2011 to 809.7 billion passenger-kilometers in 2015). These are likely the joint effects of the post-2011 economic slowdown and the general tendency that customers are gradually substituting highways for traditional railways in passenger and freight transportation because the former offers greater flexibility.[16] Although passenger and freight turnover by all modes of transportation continued to increase, the rate of highways far outpaced that of railways.[17] Consequently, railway turnover as a fraction of total passenger and freight turnover continued to decrease since 1980. In contrast, the gains by highways were substantial (Figure 9.11). Nevertheless, the passenger turnover was increasing for high speed railways, and it was increasing at the same speed as the length of the railway network (Figure 9.10).

To summarize, the gains of investment on the traditional railway network seemed to peak by 2011; afterwards the passenger and freight turnover started to decline despite the extension of the road network. Competition from other means of transport is strong and they became increasingly important relative to traditional railways. The high-speed railways, however, became the main driving force of passenger turnover growth in recent years.

9.2.4 Urban facilities

According to NBS definition, urban public infrastructure includes facilities in the following sectors: the supply of water, gas, and heat, public transit, urban roads and bridges, sewage, waste water disposal, flood prevention, green space and park maintenance, environmental hygiene and others. Their expenditure shares are illustrated by Figure 9.12 (top).

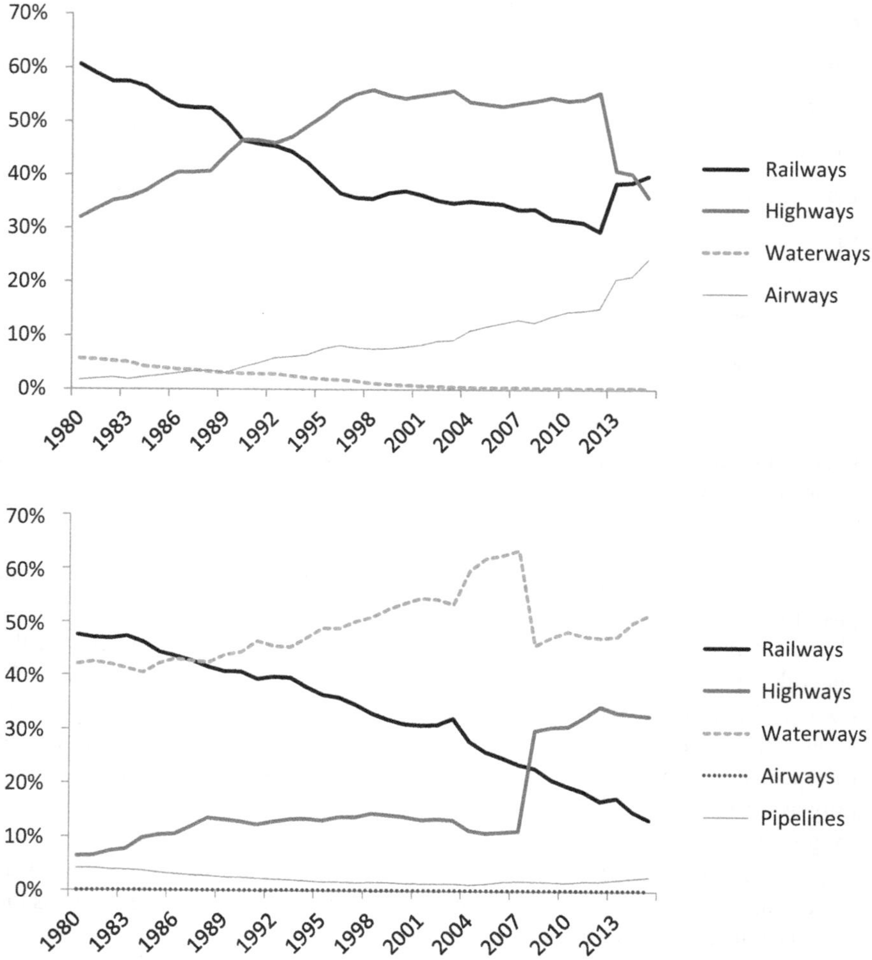

Figure 9.11 Turnover decomposition: passenger (top) and freight (bottom)

Source: MOT; Unit: percent.

The majority of the investment went to public transit and urban roads; data also show that the investment on urban roads and bridges increased particularly fast in the 2008–2010 period. This pattern resembles what we have seen in highways and railways, which suggests that on a regular basis as well as during fiscal expansions, the investment policy favors the broad transport sector, including urban transport. At the end of 2015, the total investment spending on urban infrastructure reached 1620.4 billion RMB, of which 370.7 billion RMB (22.9%) was spent on urban transit and 741.4 billion RMB (45.8%) was spent on urban roads and bridges.

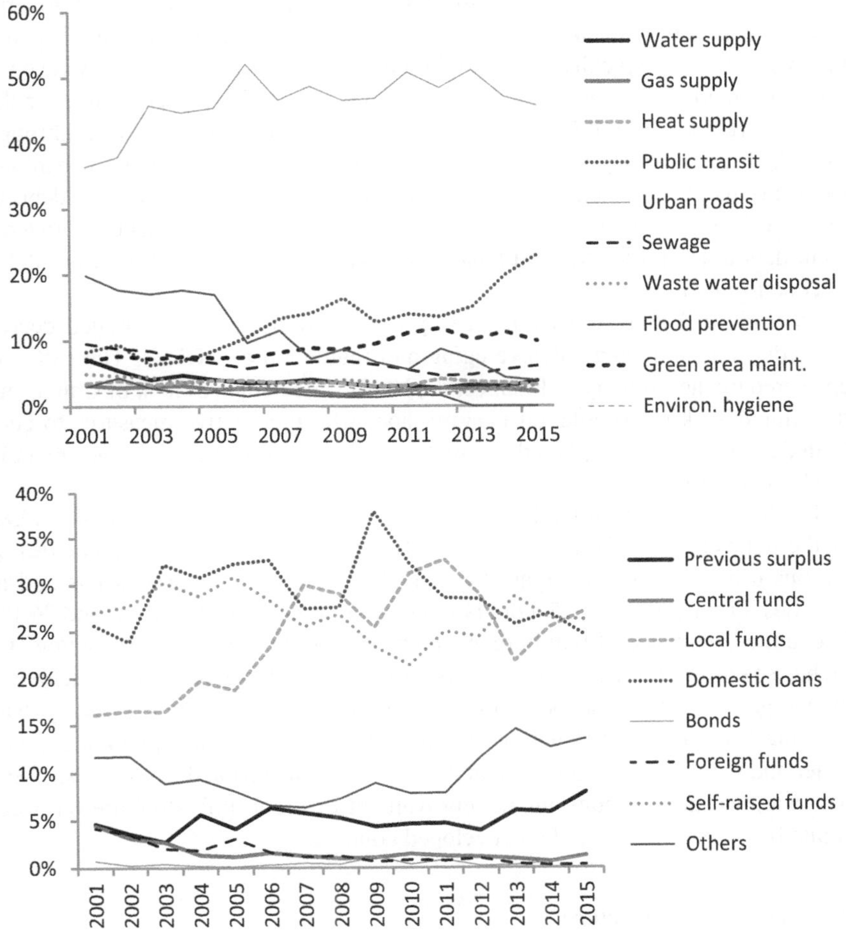

Figure 9.12 Decomposition of urban facility investment (top) and source of funds (bottom)

Source: The Ministry of Housing and Urban-Rural Development (MOHURD); Unit: percent.[19]

Unlike highways or railways, urban infrastructure is not managed by the provincial government. Instead, they are sole responsibilities of the city, county and township governments (hereafter local government). It is well known that the 1994 tax reform left a huge gap in provincial governments' budgets, and the situation is even severer among local governments (World Bank 2014).[18] Such imbalance has a far reaching consequence on the structure of urban infrastructure financing. In Figure 9.12 (bottom), we see that almost all (95.6%) budgetary funds came from local governments; yet there is a huge gap (1066.7 billion RMB or 64% of total investment spending in 2015) between budgetary funds and total expenditures that must be fulfilled otherwise. Bank loans (398.6 billion RMB in 2015) and self-financing (425.8 billion RMB in 2015) seem to be local governments' favorite instruments; they accounted for 24.6% and 26.3% of total spending, respectively. Typically, self-raised funds come from extra-budgetary revenue raised by land lease. Although direct borrowing from commercial banks or the bonds market was prohibited, local governments created huge borrowing through LGFVs. Besides, many local governments obtained credit from shadow banking (World Bank 2014). The 2008–2010 fiscal stimulus package created huge debts at the local level. By the end of 2011, it was estimated that the outstanding government debt at the provincial and local levels were 12,500 billion RMB, or 18.2% of concurrent GDP.

By mid-2010, the SC was alerted by the mounting debts and issued decree 19, requesting immediate deleveraging and regulation of LGFVs. The call was answered by the Ministry of Finance, the NDRC, the People's Bank of China, and the China Banking Regulation Commission, who took active measures to curb LGFV activity. These explain the slowdown of urban infrastructure investment in 2011 and afterwards.

The building of urban facilities does not seem to be affected by the fiscal gap or the deleveraging effort enforced in 2010. Figure 9.13 plots the capacities of various urban facilities compare to their 2002 values, in urban districts and in counties. From 2002 to 2015, population grew 32.8% in urban districts and 76.1% in counties, evidence of rapid urbanization. The built-up area was sprawling at a higher speed in both cases (100.6% vs 91.0%), and all urban facilities achieved higher growth rates than population. In particular, every single category was growing faster in counties than in urban districts, while sewage pipelines, waste water and solid-waste disposal capacity were more than tripled in counties. These observations indicate substantial improvement of urban infrastructure on a per capita basis, particularly in less developed counties.

9.2.5 Other infrastructure

China has achieved substantial improvement in other types of infrastructure. This section briefly discusses the development of airways, ports and telecom infrastructure.

9.2.5.1 Airways

In 1980, China had only 143 civilian airplanes; the total length of airways was 310,887 kilometers. The operation of airways and airports was conducted by the Civil Aviation Administration of China (CAAC), which was directly affiliated to the State Council. Like the MOR, the CAAC was not only a government administration, but also the only provider of flight service. The major marketization reform occurred in 1987, in which six airline companies were separated from the CAAC.[20] Since then, the provision of commercial flight service was handed over

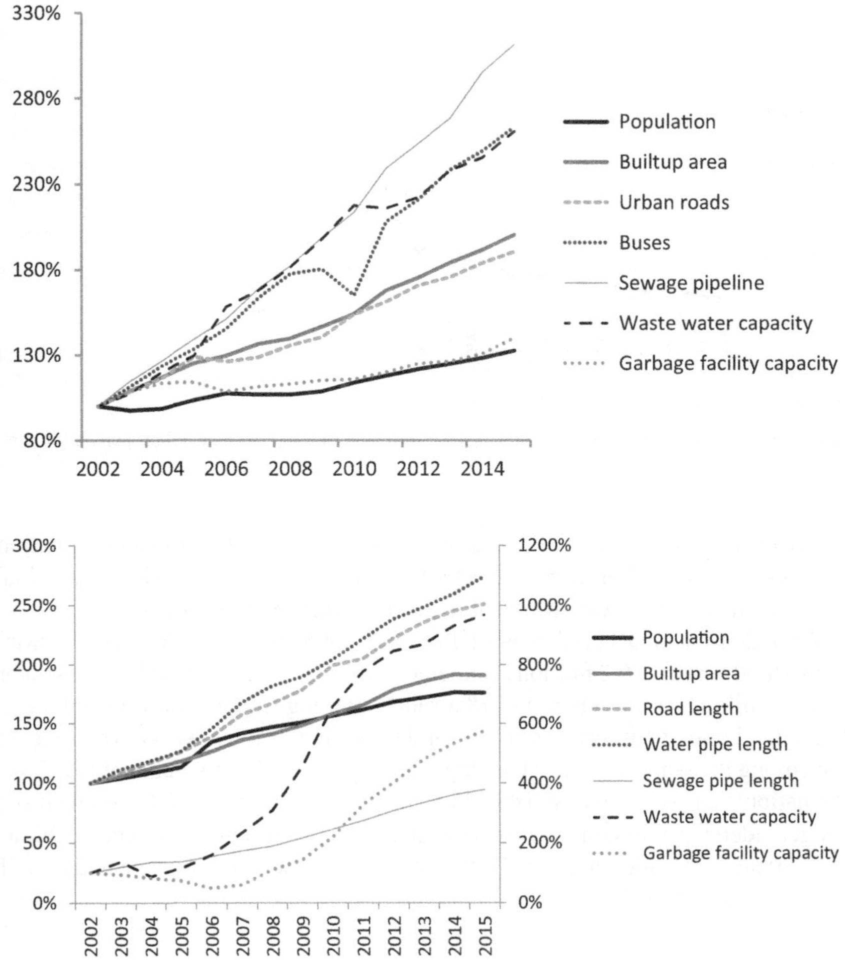

Figure 9.13 Growth of urban facilities in urban districts (top) and counties (bottom)

Source: NBS and MOHURD; the last three series of the bottom panel are shown on the right axis. Unit: percent.

to the six companies but CAAC was still in charge of airports. In 2002, the six companies were completely severed from the CAAC and the airports were also handed over to local governments. In 2008, the CAAC became a subsidiary of the MOT that oversees civil aviation.

China's air traffic grows hand-in-hand with her airline capacity (Figure 9.14). From 1980 to 2015, the total length of airways increased at an annual rate of 9.7%, from 0.3 million kilometers to 7.9 million kilometers. The growth rate of domestic airways was accelerated to 10.4% per annum after 2003, which is comparable to

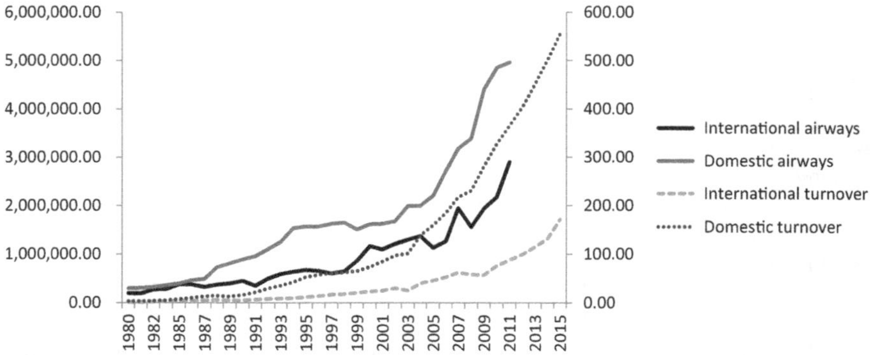

Figure 9.14 Length of airways and turnover

Source: China Transport Yearbook and CAAC. Units: kilometer (left) and billion person-kilometer (right).

the growth rate of air passenger turnover. Airways with international destinations were growing at a slightly higher rate than passenger turnover. These facts indicate that the capacity was sufficient to meet the market demand.

As of 2016, China's civil aviation fleet had 2,096 aircrafts flying 3,794 airways with a total length of 9.2 million kilometers. They delivered 0.49 billion passengers and 6.7 million tons of cargo in 218 airports. Beijing Capital Airport (ranking 2), Shanghai Pudong Airport (ranking 9) and Guanzhou Baiyun Airport (ranking 15) are among the world's busiest passenger airports. They jointly delivered 26.2% of the nation's air passengers and 49.6% of air cargo. It is predicted that total air passenger ridership will continue to grow at 10.4% per annum, reaching 1.5 billion in 2020 and 2.2 billion in 2025. Based on this forecast, China is expected to build another 136 airports by 2025.[21]

9.2.5.2 Ports

The development of port facility benefits from China's opening policy. In 1984, 14 coastal cities were designated by the SC as open cities.[22] In 1985, the SC released the Interim Provisions Concerning Preferential Treatment for Port and Terminal Development Projects Financed by Chinese and Foreign Joint Ventures, which allows foreign investors or joint ventures to lease, build, operate, or own berths and waterways. These measures sparked large-scale port construction, especially in the coastal open cities. Following China's WTO accession in 2001, port construction and freight turnover accelerated (Figure 9.15).

As of 2015, China had 5,899 sea berths, including 2,221 deep-water berths. They jointly delivered 8.1 billion tons of freight, including 189 million containers. Over 90% of imports and exports were shipped from ports. It is not a coincidence that China's export-oriented manufacturing centers such as the Pearl River Delta area and the Yangtze River Delta area all host major sea ports (Chapter 6, this volume).

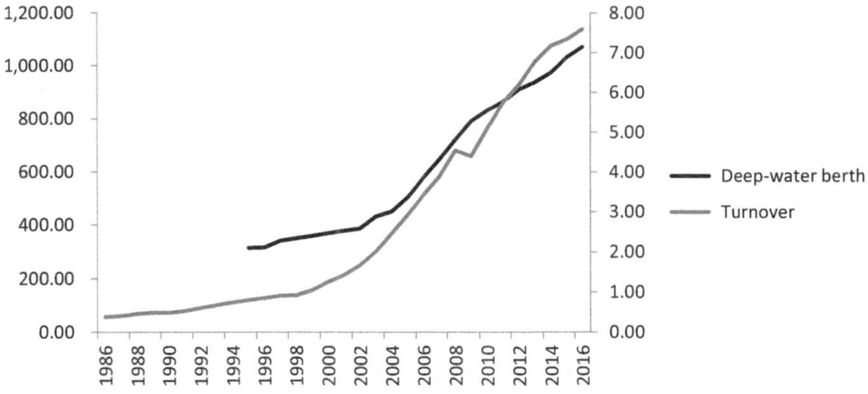

Figure 9.15 Deep-water berths and freight turnover of major sea ports

Source: NBS. Unit: billion tons (right)

Six Chinese ports are among the world's ten busiest container ports.[23] China currently has port facilities that are commensurate to her standing in international trade.

9.2.5.3 Telecom

Before 1994, China's telecom industry was under the monolithic control of the Ministry of Post and Telecommunications (MOPT), which was not only a government ministry, but also the nation's only telecom service provider (TSP). In 1994 an independent company, China Unicom, was established as a competitor of the MOPT. However, the MOPT still took the dominant market share. In a series of reforms during 1998–1999, the MOPT was divided into two parts. The administrative functions were taken over by the Ministry of Information Technology, while the corporative functions were assumed by three corporations: China Telecom, China Mobile and China Satcom. Later there were two more rounds of corporative restructuring. By 2008, only three TSPs were left, which were China Telecom, China Mobile and China Unicom. In 2015, *Forbes* magazine ranked China Mobile the world's top TSP and China Telecom the tenth.

Recent data demonstrate rapid development in China's telecom infrastructure. It can be seen from Figure 9.16 that total capacity of mobile switching centers more than doubled in ten years (from 1.14 billion in 2008 to 2.42 billion in 2017), which is commensurate to the growth of mobile phone users during the same period of time. As of 2017, the penetration rate of mobile phone as a percentage of population reached 102.5% in the nation, greater than that of the US (81.4%). On the contrary, the capacity of landline phone switching centers has decreased sharply since 2008, reflecting the decline in market demand. By 2017, the landline phone penetration rate dropped to 14%, half of its record high in 2006. The internet penetration rate reached 54.6% in 2017, which is slightly greater than the

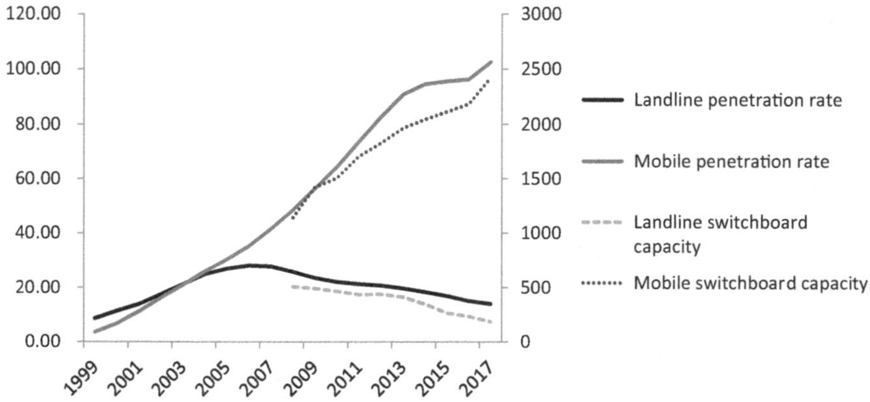

Figure 9.16 Telecom infrastructure capacity and penetration rate

Source: Ministry of Industry and Information Technology. Units: percent (left) and million (right).

world average (54.4%) but far lower than that of developed countries (80% or higher).

9.3 Economic impacts

Since the pioneer work of Aschauer (1989a), there has been an outpouring of literature that studies the economic impacts of infrastructure, including that of China. These studies explore a wide range of economic outcomes, from aggregate output and productivity, to trade volume, to wage and rental rates differential, and to sectoral development. However, these studies sometime generate conflicting conclusions, which cannot be easily reconciled unless we understand their theoretical background and empirical methodologies. Later on, we group the empirical findings according to the empirical model being used.

9.3.1 The aggregate production function approach

Macroeconomic theory view public infrastructure as a public good to the private sector that contributes to increasing returns to scale and higher aggregate productivity (Arrow and Kurz 1970; Barro 1990).[24] Public investment also has short-run effects because government uses fiscal policy to counteract business cycles (Arslanalp et al. 2010). The production function approach (Aschauer 1989a) views public infrastructure as an auxiliary input in the aggregate production function

$$y_t = \beta_0 + \beta_l l_t + \beta_k k_t + \beta_p p_t + u_t \qquad 9.1.$$

where y denotes aggregate output, k denotes private capital, l denotes labor input and p denotes infrastructure stock (all log-transformed). Empirically, this equation is often estimated in first difference (Shi and Huang 2014) or as a vector error correction model (Sahoo et al. 2010; Shi et al. 2017) to avoid spurious regression (Munnell 1992).

Using the aggregate production function approach, empirical studies of Chinese infrastructure corroborates the earlier findings that infrastructure are conducive to higher output. Sahoo et al. (2010) apply principle component analysis to six different type of infrastructure: railroads, paved roads, air freight, electricity use, fuel use and telephone lines. They build a national infrastructure index and supply it into a vector error correction model of Equation 9.1. Their estimated long-run output elasticity of infrastructure ranges from 0.27 to 0.41 over the period of 1975–2007. These values are similar to estimates using US national data (0.34–0.39, Munnell 1992). The same error correction model also reveals a two-way Granger causality between output and infrastructure. That is, the growth of the infrastructure index predicts the growth in output and *vice versa*. Shi et al. (2017) estimate another error correction model with several types of infrastructure at the same time. The estimated long-run output elasticity is 0.28–0.35 for electricity generating infrastructure, 0.22–0.31 for railways and 0.12–0.47 for telephone lines. Except for highways (insignificant), these estimates are again in line with the estimates using US data. However, these results must be interpreted with caution because the identified relationship does not represent causation.

Shi and Huang (2014) is a notable departure from the error correction model approach. They carefully address two issues: endogeneity and spatial spillover (Munnell 1992). Endogeneity arises because of two reasons. First, there are regional idiosyncrasies. Some areas, such as metropolitans receive more infrastructure than rural areas; output is higher in the former not only because of better infrastructure, but also other regional traits. Second, the government may build different amount of infrastructure based on local economic development. The relationship can be either positive or negative. On the one hand, economically developed or rapidly developing regions receive more infrastructure to support local economic activity; on the other hand, the government may build *more* infrastructure to counteract economic slowdown or to stimulate economic growth in less developed regions, which is especially true in China. Shi and Huang (2014) resolve the first endogeneity problem by estimating Equation 9.1 in first difference. Then they use a modified ACF estimator (Ackerberg et al. 2015) to tackle the second endogeneity problem. Using China's provincial data, their estimated output elasticity of infrastructure is 0.19 using OLS and 0.255 using ACF. The former value is remarkably similar to those estimated using US state data (0.15–0.20, Munnell 1992); it also suggests that previous studies are likely subject to the endogeneity bias. Shi and Huang (2014) model spatial spillover using a standard spatial Durbin error model. However, they fail to find any evidence of spillover effects for infrastructure.

The other contribution of Shi and Huang (2014) is their study of investment efficiency, i.e., the marginal product of infrastructure relative to private capital. If the ratio is greater than one, the economy benefits from more infrastructure investment; otherwise further infrastructure investment crowds out private investment and reduces aggregate output. They find that most Chinese provinces were underinvested in infrastructure in 1997. The large-scale infrastructure investment following the 1998 financial crisis improved China's investment efficiency and contributed to an additional 0.47% GDP growth rate by 2001. However, they also identify a persistent oversupply of infrastructure in western provinces since 2001, probably because of the "Western Development" plan. Meanwhile, the efficiency index remained above unity in some eastern and central provinces. Both observations indicate deteriorating investment efficiency after 2001.

An alternative approach to deal with the endogeneity problem is to model the levels of output and infrastructure in two or more simultaneous equations.[25] Fan et al. (2002) study the relationship between rural GDP and rural infrastructure using the simultaneous equation approach. In their model, output is assumed to depend on the level of infrastructure, whereas current infrastructure is assumed to be built on past infrastructure and current investment. The model also features a poverty equation which allows infrastructure to affect poverty through its effects on non-farm and agriculture incomes. Their estimates suggest that the output elasticity of road infrastructure is 0.079 for agriculture and 0.229 for the rural non-farming sector; rural telephone is 0.071 (agriculture) and 0.179 (non-farm), respectively. In the agriculture sector, the output elasticity of irrigation infrastructure is particularly large (0.412). Perhaps the most important finding is the prominent role played by rural R&D expenditure: on a dollar-to-dollar basis, R&D expenditure generates much higher returns than conventional infrastructure, such as irrigation, roads, and telephone. Besides, R&D and education expenditures are found to be more effective in poverty alleviation than spending on the conventional infrastructure.

A few articles study the growth effect of infrastructure. These studies are usually based on a growth model instead of an aggregate production function, while infrastructure is treated as an (exogenous) endowment that affects growth. The first of these studies is Demurger (2001), who uses a growth model augmented with infrastructure

$$g_t = \beta_0 + \beta_1 y_{t-1} + \beta_2 p_t, \qquad 9.2.$$

Where g_t is the growth rate of GDP per capita, y_{t-1} is the level of GDP per capita in the previous period. The model is regressed on provincial panel data during the period of 1985–1998. The estimates reveal a concave relationship between transport infrastructure and growth; the result also demonstrates a positive effect of telecommunication on growth. Hong et al. (2011) adopt the same growth model but improve Demurger's (2001) empirical strategy. They argue that infrastructure is likely endogenous because economic growth may have reverse causality on infrastructure. Their identification strategy is to instrument p_t with p_{t-1}, y_{t-2}, as well as other exogenous variables. The analysis confirms a downward bias in OLS estimates.[26] They find that land and water transport contribute to regional economic growth; the relationship is concave for land transport and convex for water transport, while the effect of air transport is insignificant throughout.

9.3.2 Transport infrastructure and monocentric cities

Another strand of the literature uses the monocentric city model to investigate the impact of transport infrastructure on the urban landscape. The model assumes that economic activities take place in the metropolitan area (CBD) because of access to long-range transportation facility or strong agglomerative economies at the center. Residents rent urban land from absentee land owners. Proximity to the CBD saves time and monetary commuting costs. Consequently, households have a higher willingness to pay for land close to the CBD, which results in a downward sloping bid-rent curve from the CBD. Each household must tradeoff lower commuting cost for higher land price for any parcel that is close to the CBD. The model also features an agriculture sector outside the city, which offers a constant rent to undeveloped land. The equilibrium is established when all residents achieve the same level of utility (from consumption and housing) and the land rent at the city boundary equals the agriculture rent. Following an increase in urban transport infrastructure (a reduction in commuting cost) or average income, the model predicts an increase in built-up area and a higher proportion of household choosing suburban residence.[27]

Deng et al. (2008) test the first hypothesis that better urban transport infrastructure causes urban sprawl. Using the closed-city version of the monocentric city model and Chinese city-level panel data in 1995–2000, they find that higher highway density causes the city to grow larger and terrain slope is negatively associated with city size. Ke et al. (2009) study the closed-city model and open-city model using city-level data in 2004. They find that four types of transport facility (urban road, highways, railroads, and airports) all contribute to urban sprawl. Specifically, a one percent increase in urban road per resident increases built-up area by 0.13–0.16%; one more highway that passes through the central city increases build-up area by 0.06–0.17%. Although these studies do not explicitly address the potential endogeneity problem, they do control for factors that may affect infrastructure supply, for instance built-up area in 1988 (Deng et al. 2008) and type of city (Ke et al. 2009).

Baum-Snow et al. (2017) test the second hypothesis that improved transport infrastructure causes suburbanization. Their study is based on the following empirical model:

$$y_t^C = \beta_0 + \beta_1 transport_t + \beta_2 y_t^P + u_t, \qquad 9.3.$$

where y_t^C denotes central city population; $transport_t$ is a measure of transport infrastructure; y_t^P is the population in the prefecture (the broad city). Given the population of the prefecture, the theory predicts that any additional road displaces central city population to the suburb ($\beta_1 < 0$). They study three types of transport infrastructure, namely radial highways, ring roads and radial railroads.

Their major contribution is their identification strategy. They argue that historically productive or attractive cities were allocated more transport infrastructure, so $\hat{\beta}_{1OLS}$ will be biased. Drawing on China's planning features, they instrument the highway network in 2010 by the 1962 road network. Even though the 1962 roads strongly predict the 2010 highways, they were not designed to serve the commuting pattern in 2010. Instead, they were built primary to connect cities to nearby farming regions. Thus, the 1962 roads satisfy the exclusion restriction. For a similar reason, the 1962 railroads were also built without regard to their impacts on post-reform cities, which justifies the practice of instrumenting the 2010 railroads with the 1962 railroads.

Baum-Snow et al. (2017) document strong population displacement by radial highways and ring roads. Each additional radial highway displaces 5.5–9.2% of central city population and each ring road displaces 20–30%. However, the effect of railroad on central city population is insignificant. Baum-Snow et al. (2017) extend the methodology to the suburbanization of industrial production. They find a similar displacement effect by ring roads and radial railroads. Each additional ring road displaces 51–65% of industrial GDP and each radial railroad displaces 26–33%. They further study employment decentralization by industrial sector. Industries with high weight-to-value ratios are found not to respond to transport infrastructure at all, while medium and low weight-to-value ratio industries generally exhibit decentralization, although they respond to different transport infrastructure. This result is consistent with Meyer et al.'s (1966) observation that heavy industries are difficult to relocate.

9.3.3 Transport infrastructure and new economic geography

Perhaps the single theory that receives most attention in the study of transport infrastructure is the new economic geography (NEG), which models regions separate in space as components of an integrated economic system that are interconnected by costly bilateral trade. At the heart of NEG models is the trade cost, which affects the demand and supply linkage between connected regions. Any change in transport infrastructure not only changes the trade cost between directly connected regions, but also changes the "demand capacity" and "supply capacity" of all inter-connected regions, generating system-wide perturbations. Therefore, any empirical study on transport infrastructure must be carefully based on a general equilibrium model.

There are two versions of the model, one assumes that labor is mobile across regions but immobile across sectors and another one assumes that labor is mobile across sectors but immobile across regions. When trade cost decreases, the first model predicts that the region with more manufacturing labor has higher demand capacity as well as higher supply capacity; thus, firms in this region are able to offer a higher nominal wage to labor, which results in higher real income. Manufacturing labor will reallocate to the manufacturing abundant region, forming a core-periphery configuration. With a similar mechanism, the second model predicts labor reallocating from the agricultural sector to the manufacturing sector in the manufacturing abundant region, forming another core-periphery configuration. Consequently, real income increases in the core and decreases in the periphery. In terms of welfare, the core and the periphery may gain or lose from further decrease in the trade cost, depending on parameter settings.[28]

Roberts et al. (2012) is one of the first to apply a general equilibrium NEG model to the study of China's highway network. Using detailed GIS data of the 2007 road network, they compute the shortest travel time between any pair of Chinese cities, based on which they define trade costs. Using these trade costs, they solve a general equilibrium model for regional wage rates, price indices, and income levels. The solution enables them to compute the real income and real wage rate in any city.

This procedure allows the comparison with a counterfactual outcome had the 2007 expressways not been built. For this purpose, they recompute trade costs using the road network without 2007 expressways. Then the general equilibrium model is solved again using the new trade costs, and the real incomes and real wage rates are recomputed.

The counterfactual analysis showed a strong effect of the 2007 expressways on regional income. Had the 2007 expressways not been built, China's nominal income would be 3.10% lower, and real income 5.98% lower. The benefit of the expressways, however, is not evenly felt across the nation. Following the building of the expressways, the percentage change in real income is larger in Eastern China where the "initial" real income level was high. Therefore, the expressway network may have aggravated the income disparity across the nation. They also find that the expressway network worsens the regional disparity in real urban wage rate but mitigates inequality in the real rural wage rate.

Faber (2014) studies the effect of NTHS highways on regional economic development. According to both versions of the NEG model, reduction in trade cost may form or strengthen the core-periphery configuration, resulting in lower level of economic activity in the periphery. To test this theory, Faber (2014) performs a difference-in-difference analysis on a sample of peripheral counties.[29] His estimation shows that connection to NTHS during 1992–2003 reduced local GDP growth by 20% over 1997–2006, growth of industrial value added reduced by 30%, and government revenue growth reduced by 26%. There was, however, no population relocation effect by NTHS connection. Faber (2014) conducts extensive investigation into a competing mechanism: industrial decentralization.[30] He includes a dummy variable for neighbors of NTHS connected counties and distance from NTHS highways into the difference-in-difference model. The estimates suggest no output or revenue effect in neighboring counties; the regressions also reveal the fact that the NTHS connection effect diminishes quickly as one moves away from NTHS highways. Thus, it must be the trade effect rather than the decentralization mechanism that governs the NTHS connection effect.[31]

One of Faber's (2014) major contributions is his innovative identification strategy. He argues that NTHS highway placement is not exogenous because the government favors politically important and economically developed regions in planning highways (Section 9.2.2). Instead of using historical transport routes, he constructs a least-building-cost highway network that spans the major nodes of NTHS. The counterfactual highway network assumes that minimizing building cost was the only motive when the government planned NTHS. The computation of least-building-cost routes utilizes rasterized surface data and Dijkstra's (1959) algorithm, while the construction of the least-cost spanning tree is based on Kruskal's (1956) algorithm. Similarly, he constructs an alternative least-cost spanning tree that is based on Euclidean distance. His instrument strategy has become a standard practice in related studies (Donaldson 2015; Yang 2016).

Yang (2016) studies the impact of NTHS on city productivity. His NEG model features immobile labor and potential entrant firms that are heterogeneous in productivity. Low productivity firms below a threshold value will be driven out of the market. The model predicts that cities with higher market access have higher threshold values, thus higher average productivity. The empirical study regresses firm TFP on Harris's (1954) market access. It is shown that a 1% increase in domestic market access increases firm TFP by 0.05%, while a 1% increase in foreign market access increases TFP by 0.09%. Yang (2016) decomposes the productivity gains and finds that entry of new firms explains 69–71% of the total gains from NTHS, while reallocation of resources among incumbent firms and exit of less productive firms are also important. Finally, he finds that industries with higher weight-to-value ratio and higher capital intensity are more affected by market access, which corroborates the findings of Duranton et al. (2014).

Yang (2016) extended Faber's (2014) identification strategy to allow a time-varying least-cost spanning tree. He first computes the actual length of NTHS constructed in each year, which is used as the exogenous constraint faced by the planner. He then uses Girvan and Newman's (2002) algorithm to decide the building time of each segment in the least-cost spanning tree, subject to the constraint. The time-varying instrumental variable thus reflects the planner's additional motive that more important highways should be built first.

Zheng and Kahn (2013a) study the effect of HSR on housing prices. They argue that the HSR network facilitates the decentralization of production with increased accessibility of peripheral cities. With HSR, firms can outsource nonessential activities to cheaper cities, resulting in growing housing price in the latter. Broadly speaking, their conceptual framework is similar to that of Donaldson and Hornbeck (2016) in the sense that both articles investigate the effect of transport infrastructure on the price of an immobile factor. They regress changes in housing price on changes in market access. Like many other researchers, they choose TSLS to resolve the endogeneity in HSR placement. Specifically, HSR lines are instrumented by historical railways and the locations of major military deployments. The latter instrumental variable is justified by the government's motive to transport troops by HSR. They demonstrate a strong price premium of HSR connection: a 1% increase in HSR market access increases housing price by 0.43%. On the contrary, no such effect is found for highway connection. The evidence thus supports the special role of HSR in facilitating firm fragmentation.

Lin (2017) studies the impact of China's HSR lines on urban specialization. His theoretical framework predicts that HSR connection creates market access for passengers, which benefits the growth of communication-intensive industries and industries that require non-routine cognitive skills. Empirically, he regresses regional employment on both HSR connection and HSR induced market access using a difference-in-difference model similar to that of Faber (2014). The result suggests that HSR connection increases local employment by 7%, while a 1% increase in HSR market access increases local employment by 2.2%. The employment effect of HSR market access is found to be most prominent on tourism (3.9%) and skilled employment (2.5%), but insignificant on other types of employment. On the contrary, highway access benefits manufacturing employment the most. These results support the prediction that HSR benefits industries intensive in non-routine cognitive skills, while highway network benefits industries intensive in routine skills. When market access is restricted to short distances (less than five-hour ride), the employment effects become much larger, indicating that the effect of HSR is more felt in short distances. Lin (2017) then performs the same analysis on 16 industries. He finds a clear positive relationship between the effect of HSR connectivity and the cognitive task content of the industry. These results further support the theoretical argument made earlier.

In Lin (2017), the endogeneity problem is addressed by a full set of controls. These include local government spending, public facilities, average GDP and population growth over the previous three years. The author performs event studies to demonstrate that the parallel trend assumption is satisfied.

9.3.4 Discussion

These studies, however, have their own limitations. Despite its large expenditure share (Figure 9.1), urban infrastructure is rarely studied. The only exceptions are Ke et al. (2009), who study urban roads and Zheng and Kahn (2013b), who study metro connection and urban green space. We hope more studies could reveal the economic impact of urban infrastructure, including urban roads, metro lines and other facilities.

Although the extant studies have demonstrated various economic impacts of infrastructure, the majority of them fail to answer the ultimate question whether these infrastructures should be built, i.e., whether the social benefit of infrastructures is large enough to offset the social cost of building them. Given the fact that infrastructure now accounts for 21.8% of China's total investment and this ratio keeps increasing, Shi and Huang's (2014) finding that the investment efficiency was already below unity in western provinces rings an alarm to China's future infrastructure plan. Ansar et al. (2016) provide micro evidence for the financial performance of Chinese infrastructure projects. Using data provided by the World Bank and Asian Development Bank, they study 95 road and rail projects carried out in China during the 1984–2008 period. Their criterion for economic efficiency is benefit-to-cost ratio (BCR). They find that 55% of the projects have BCR < 1;

the majority of which suffered from cost overruns and benefit shortfalls at the same time. Seven (nine) out of ten road (rail) projects experienced cost overrun, and the average cost overrun was 30.6%. On the other hand, 64.7% of the projects experienced lower than expected traffic after construction, the average traffic shortfall being 41.2%. Ansar et al. (2016) argue that optimism and strategic misrepresentation in public projects could severely undermine the economic return of infrastructure projects. In a separate study, Haughwout (2002) argues that infrastructure may generate producer benefits and consumer benefits at the same time; local prices (rent and wage rates) adjust so that firms and consumers become indifferent to regions with different endowments in infrastructure (Roback 1982). He points out that a positive output elasticity must not be treated as evidence that infrastructure is productive; rather, the conclusion must be based on a comparison between willingness to pay (WTP) and construction cost. Haughwout (2002) estimates the price differentials using a sample of large US cities and find large WTP for infrastructure. However, the WTP is not sufficient to offset the building cost. His study thus casts serious doubts on the popular view that infrastructure brings economic benefits. It would be interesting if further empirical evidence could be provided for China.

9.4 Concluding remarks

Since the early 1990s, China has become the world's largest investor in infrastructure, overtaking the US and the EU (Chen et al. 2013). China's massive infrastructure construction provides excellent opportunities for researchers to ascertain the economic impacts of infrastructure. In summary, infrastructure is found to contribute to output positively. The output elasticity of infrastructure is found to be 0.27–0.41 when using national data (Sahoo et al. 2010) and 0.19–0.26 when using provincial data (Shi and Huang 2014). At the macro level, studies also demonstrate the growth effect of infrastructure (Demurger 2001). Recent studies on economic geography focus on transport infrastructure and explore various types of economic impacts. It is found that highways and railways generate population and production decentralization in metropolitan areas (Baum-Snow 2017); while highways also generate backwash effects on peripheral counties (Faber 2014). Highway induced market access is also found to boost firm productivity, to increase aggregate income and to aggravate income inequality (Yang 2016; Roberts et al. 2012). HSR is found to increase housing price in connected cities and to stimulate specialization in communication-intensive industries (Zheng and Kahn 2013a; Lin 2017).

While most studies focus on the direct economic benefits or direct economic costs of infrastructure, few have considered its policy implications. First, infrastructure investment crowds out private investment. Given China's massive infrastructure investment (Section 9.1), the crowd-out effect could be considerable. While empirical evidence shows that infrastructure enhances the productivity of private capital (Section 9.3.1), it remains uncertain whether the productivity effects are enough to offset the private capital that has been crowded out. Thus, one is back to Aschauer's (1989b) old question "does public capital crowd out private capital?" Surprisingly, no empirical study has ever addressed this important question using Chinese data.

Second, China's infrastructure investment created huge public debt, especially among local governments (Chapter 8, this volume). As we presented in Section 9.2, China's infrastructure investment was largely financed by fiscal budget and internal sources, most of which ultimately became governmental debt (Ansar et al. 2016). According to an audit report issued by the National Auditing Office (NAO), outstanding government (central and local) debt was 20.7 trillion RMB in mid-2013, debt under governmental guarantee was 2.9 trillion RMB and explicit contingent liabilities were 6.7 trillion RMB.[32] These numbers together amounted to 50.9% of China's GDP in 2013. Local government debt is particularly worrisome. The 1994 tax reform left local governments with social responsibilities (including infrastructure building) that are far beyond their revenue capacity (Chang et al. 2013). Although local governments receive revenue transfers from the central government and collect off-budgetary revenues (e.g. land finance and fees collection), the fiscal gap becomes the ultimate source of local government debt. The situation is aggravated because local government officials, who face career incentives (Li and Zhou 2005), often promote major infrastructure projects.[33] Although it is difficult to ascertain the weight of infrastructure spending, local government debt increased rapidly in recent years. By the end of 2016, the total local government debt reached 15.3 trillion RMB, and the debt-to-revenue ratio reached 80.5%; a few local governments were already facing insolvency.[34]

The skyrocketing public debt raises an important question: What is the consequence of this debt risk? According to Ansar et al. (2016) and Chang et al. (2013), China is likely to face economic fragility. Thus, we have the follow-up question: how is the cost of future economic fragility compared to the short-run benefit of today's infrastructure? A targeted research is demanded to answer this question.

Notes

1 Xi'an Jiaotong Liverpool University, Suzhou, China. Email: ming.he@xjtlu.edu.cn. Yang Chen, Xi'an Jiaotong-Liverpool University, Suzhou, China. Email: yang.chen@xjtlu.edu.cn.

2 Total infrastructure investment is defined as gross capital formation in infrastructure (to be defined). We use nominal values for both infrastructure and GDP because the National Statistical Bureau (NBS) does not provide a deflator for infrastructure investment. 1995 is the first year that such data was available.

3 For instance, the National Research Council of United States defines physical infrastructure as "highways, streets, roads, and bridges; mass transit; airports and airways; water supply and water resources; wastewater management; solid-waste treatment and disposal; electric power generation and transmission; telecommunications; and hazardous waste management – and the combined system these modal elements comprise" (National Research Council 1987).

4 In China, roads are categorized into five classes according to their function, physical standard and designed capacity (JTG B01–2014). Expressways have fully controlled access and divided lanes, with a capacity over 25,000 vehicles per day (four lanes);

grade one roads have divided lanes but partially controlled access, with a capacity of 15,000–30,000 vehicles per day (four lanes); grade two roads have uncontrolled access and a capacity of 2,000–7,000 vehicles per day); grades three and four roads are country and township roads with significantly lower capacity. In this chapter, we use the word highway for designated national and regional trunk roads that are of strategic importance. They are called *Guo Dao* (national highway) and *Sheng Dao* (provincial highway), respectively. Physically they are all built as expressways, grade one or grade two roads.

5 In 2011, 96.5% of total road investment were made by local governments (World Bank 2014).

6 The vehicle purchasing tax became a central tax after 1994; the gas tax remained a central tax. The highway maintenance tax used to be collected by the local governments, but it was merged into the gas tax in 2009. Even though official statistics of individual taxes were seldom released, a report by Xinhua News Agency shows that China raised 180 billion RMB by vehicle tax alone in the first 15 years (Lin and Zhang 2000).

7 Prior to 2009, local governments are prohibited from making direct borrowings, either from bank or by issuing bonds. In response, they established thousands of Local Government Financial Vehicles (LGFV) to get credit from the market. These LGFVs usually take the form of Urban Investment and Construction Corporations, whose debts are endorsed by local governments. Starting from 2009, a selected group of provincial governments were allowed to issue bonds.

8 NENS was revised in 2013 and the total length was increased to 118,000 kilometers.

9 Many NENS expressways were simply NTHS expressways renamed or upgraded; some are upgraded from other existing roads.

10 The all roads data contains rural roads since 2004, which makes the pre-2004 data not comparable.

11 This is exactly the motive behind the 2013 revision of the NENS plan. It is nevertheless interesting to observe the sudden decline in passenger and freight turnover in 2013 and 2015, which may reflect the economic slowing down of the "new norm."

12 The prices still need approval by the State Council and NDRC. They were clearly kept low (Bai and Qian 2010).

13 Most joint railways are operated by SOEs separated from or affiliated to the MOR or RRAs. For instance, both the Guangshen Railway Company and the Daqin Railway Company remain subordinate of their RRAs.

14 In 2011, 85.3% of total railway investment was made by the central government (World Bank 2014). The total investment spending on highways was 2.51 trillion RMB in 2015, but that on railways was only 0.56 trillion RMB.

15 In 2014, the length of China's railway network (111,821 kilometers) was roughly half of that of the United States (228,218 kilometers), but the freight turnover was higher (2,753.0 vs 2,524.6 ton-kilometers).

16 Railways are advantageous in high-volume and long-distance transport; which is especially true for bulk goods. As of 2015, the average passenger traveling distance was 471.9 kilometers for railways, and only 66.4 kilometers for highways. Similarly, the average freight shipping distance was 707.4 kilometers by railway, while that of highways was 184.0 kilometers.

17 From 1980 to 1995, total railway passenger turnover increased from 0.14 billion passenger-kilometers to 1.20 billion passenger-kilometers, or 6% annually; that of freight turnover increased from 0.57 billion ton-kilometers to 2.38 billion ton-kilometers, or 4% annually. These numbers are 8% (passenger turnover) and 13% (freight turnover) for highways, respectively.

18 On the one hand, the tax revenue was centralized. The central government took most of the tax revenues, while the provincial and local governments had little discretion in setting their tax base or tax rates. On the other hand, the social responsibilities of the provincial and local governments have not been alleviated. The revenue-expenditure

imbalance is severer among local governments because provincial governments are inclined to keep most of the transfers from the central government.

19 The total investments reported by the MOHURD are roughly 83%-108% of those reported by NBS in 2006, 2009, and 2012 (Figure 9.2, center). However, the two sets of data differ substantially in 2003 and 2015 for unknown reasons. The exposition in section 9.2.4 is based on the MOHURD data.

20 They are Air China, China Eastern Airlines, China Southern Airlines, China Northwest Airlines, China Northern Airlines and China Southwest Airlines.

21 The National Civil Airport Plan (NDRC and CAAC 2015).

22 These cities are: Tianjin, Shanghai, Dalian, Qinghuangdao, Yantai, Qingdao, Lianyungang, Nantong, Ningbo, Wenzhou, Fuzhou, Guangzhou, Zhanjiang and Beihai.

23 They are Shanghai, Shenzhen, Ningbo-Zhoushan, Guangzhou, Qingdao and Tianjin.

24 Quoting Munnell (1992), "everyone agrees that public capital investment can expand the productive capacity of an area, both by increasing resources and by enhancing the productivity of existing resources."

25 This method was first implemented by Duffy-Deno et al. (1991) in their study of the infrastructure-output relationship.

26 That is, regions with high growth rates can build more infrastructure, and infrastructure is very responsive to economic growth.

27 Both the closed-city and open-city versions of the model make such predictions.

28 Please see Fujita et al. (1999) for details.

29 Specifically, his regression model is $y_{i2006} - y_{i1997} = \beta_0 + \beta_1 connect_i + u_i$, where y_i is the outcome variable under study, and $connect_i$ indicates whether county i was connected to NTHS highways between 1992 and 2003.

30 If NTHS connected peripheral counties decentralize their industrial production into their unconnected neighbors, then one should make the same observation on the connected counties.

31 Faber (2014) provides further evidence. The NEG theory predicts that peripheral counties with larger pre-existing market sizes or higher pre-existing trade costs will be less affected by the reduction in trade cost. Both predictions are supported by empirical evidence.

32 Source: the Audit Report on National Governmental Debt. Beijing: The National Audit Office.

33 For instance, World Bank (2010) points out that Chinese metro projects appear to be promoted as means to increase city GDP rather than the result of assessing problems. Chinese metro projects are often much larger than those elsewhere.

34 Source: Caixin Net (http://economy.caixin.com/2017-06-23/101105065.html).

References

Ackerberg, Daniel A., Kevin Caves, and Garth Frazer (2015), "Identification Properties of Recent Production Function Estimators," *Econometrica* 83(6): 2411–2451.

Ansar, Atif, Bent Flyvbjerg, Alexander Budzier, and Daniel Lunn (2016), "Does Infrastructure Investment Lead to Economic Growth or Economic Fragility? Evidence from China," *Oxford Review of Economic Policy* 32(3): 360–390.

Arrow, Kenneth J., and Mordecai Kruz (1970), *Public Investment, The Rate of Return, and Optimal Fiscal Policy*, Baltimore: Johns Hopkins University Press.

Arslanalp, Serkan, Fabian Bornhorst, Sanjeev Gupta, and Elsa Sze (2010), "Public Capital and Growth," IMF Working paper series No. 10/175, International Monetary Fund, Washington, DC.

Aschauer, David Alan (1989a), "Is Public Expenditure Productive?" *Journal of Monetary Econmics* 23(2): 177–200.

Aschauer, David Alan (1989b), "Does Public Capital Crowd Out Private Capital?" *Journal of Monetary Economics* 24(2): 171–188.

Bai, Chong-En, and Yingyi Qian (2010), "Infrastructure Development in China: The Cases of Electricity, Highways, and Railways," *Journal of Comparative Economics* 38(1): 34–51.

Barro, Robert J. (1990), "Government Spending in a Simple Model of Endogeneous Growth," *Journal of Political Economy* 98(5): S103–S125.

Baum-Snow, Nathaniel, Loren Brandt, J. Vernon Henderson, Matthew A. Turner, and Qinghua Zhang (2017), "Roads, Railroads and Decentralization of Chinese Cities," *Review of Economics and Statistics* 99(3): 435–448.

Chang, Jian, Lingxiu Yang, and Yiping Huang (2013), "How Big is the Chinese Government Debt?" *China Economic Journal* 6(2–3): 152–171.

Chen, Youguang, Stefan Matzinger, and Jonathan Woetzel (2013), *Chinese Infrastructure: The Big Picture*." Hong Kong: McKinsey & Company.

Démurger, S. (2001), "Infrastructure Development and Economic Growth: An Explanation for Regional Disparities in China?" *Journal of Comparative Economics* 29(1): 95–117.

Deng, Xiangzheng, Jikun Huang, Scott Rozelle, and Emi Uchida (2008), "Growth, Population and Industrialization, and Urban Land Expansion of China," *Journal of Urban Economics* 63(1): 96–115.

Dijkstra, Edsger W. (1959), "A Note on Two Problems in Connexion with Graphs," *Numerische Mathematic* 1(1): 269–271.

Donaldson, Dave (2015), "Railroads of the Raj: Estimating the Impact of Transportation Infrastructure," *American Economic Review*, forthcoming.

Donaldson, Dave, and Richard Hornbeck (2016), "Railroads and American Economic Growth: A Market Access Approach," *The Quarterly Journal of Economics* 131(2): 799–858.

Duffy-Deno, Kevin T., and Randall W. Eberts (1991), "Public Infrastructure and Regional Economic Development: A Simultaneous Equations Approach," *Journal of Urban Economics* 30(3): 329–343.

Duranton, Gilles, Peter M. Morrow, and Matthew A. Turner (2014), "Roads and Trade: Evidence from the US," *Review of Economic Studies* 81(2): 681–724.

Faber, Benjamin (2014), "Trade Integration, Market Size, and Industrialization: Evidence from China's National Trunk Highway System," *Review of Economic Studies* 81(3): 1046–1070.

Fan, Shenggen, Linxiu Zhang, and Xiaobo Zhang (2002), "Growth, Inequality, and Poverty in Rural China: The Role of Public Investments," IFPRI research report No. 125. Washington, DC: International Food Policy Research Institute.

Fujita, Masahisa, Paul R. Krugman, and Anthony J. Venables (1999), *The Spatial Economy: Cities, Regions and International Trade*, Cambridge: MIT Press.

Girvan, Michelle, and Mark E. J. Newman (2002), "Community Structure in Social and Biological Networks," *Proceedings of the National Academy of Sciences* 99(12): 7821–7826.

Harris, Chauncy D. (1954), "The Market as a Factor in the Localization of Industry in the United States," *Annals of the Association of American Geographers* 44(4): 315–348.

Haughwout, Andrew F. (2002), "Public Infrastructure Investments, Productivity and Welfare in Fixed Geographic Areas," *Journal of Public Economics* 83(3): 405–428.

Hong, Junjie, Zhaofang Chu, and Qiang Wang (2011), "Transport Infrastructure and Regional Economic Growth: Evidence from China," *Transportation* 38(5): 737–752.

Ke, Shanzi, Yan Song, and Ming He (2009), "Determinants of Urban Spatial Scale: Chinese Cities in Transition," *Urban Studies* 46(13): 2795–2813.

Kruskal, Joseph B. (1956), "On the Shortest Spanning Subtree of a Graph and the Traveling Salesman Problem," *Proceedings of the American Mathematical Society* 7(1): 48–50.

Li, Hongbin, and Li-An Zhou (2005), "Political Turnover and Economic Performance: The Incentive Role of Personnel Control in China," *Journal of Public Economics* 89(9–10): 1743–1762.

Lin, Hongmei, and Xiaosong Zhang (2000), "Where Comes the Highway Construction Fund?" The Xinhua Net, Available at: www.people.com.cn/GB/channel1/10/20001221/358112.html.

Lin, Yatang (2017), "Travel Costs and Urban Specialization Patterns: Evidence from China's High Speed Railway System," *Journal of Urban Economics* 98: 98–123.

Meyer, John Robert, John F. Kain, and Martin Wohl (1966), *The Urban Transportation Problem*, Cambridge: Harvard University Press.

Munnell, Alicia H. (1992), "Policy Watch: Infrastructure Investment and Economic Growth," *Journal of Economic Perspectives* 6(4): 189–198.

National Development and Reform Commission and, The National Civil Airport Plan. (2015), http://www.ndrc.gov.cn/zcfb/zcfbghwb/201703/W020170315444446628935.pdf.

National Research Council (1987), *Infrastructure for the 21st Century: Framework for a Research Agenda*, Washington, DC: The National Academies Press.

Roback, Jennifer (1982), "Wages, Rents, and the Quality of Life," *Journal of Political Economy* 90(6): 1257–1278.

Roberts, Mark, Uwe Deichmann, Bernard Fingleton, and Tuo Shi (2012), "Evaluating China's Road to Prosperity: A New Economic Geography Approach," *Regional Science and Urban Economics* 42(4): 580–594.

Sahoo, Pravakar, Ranjan Kumar Dash, and Geethanjali Nataraj (2010), *Infrastructure Development and Economic Growth in China*, IDE Discussion Paper No. 261, Institute of Developing Economics, Chiba.

Shi, Hao, and Shaoqing Huang (2014), "How Much Infrastructure is Too Much? A New Approach and Evidence from China," *World Development* 56: 272–286.

Shi, Yingying, Shen Guo, and Puyang Sun (2017), "The Role of Infrastructure in China's Regional Economic Growth," *Journal of Asian Economics* 49: 26–41.

World Bank (2007), *An Overview of China's Transport Sector – 2007*, Washington, DC: The World Bank.

World Bank (2010), *Urban Rail Development in China: Issues and Options*, Washington, DC: The World Bank.

World Bank (2012), *Enterprise Surveys: China Country Profile 2012*, Washington, DC: The World Bank.

World Bank (2014), *Urban China: Toward Efficient, Inclusive, and Sustainable Urbanization*, Washington, DC: The World Bank.

Yang, Yang (2016), "Transport Infrastructure, City Productivity Growth and Sectoral Reallocation: Evidence from China," Working paper, University of California at Los Angeles.

Zheng, Siqi, and Matthew E. Kahn (2013a), "China's Bullet Trains Facilitate Market Integration and Mitigate the Cost of Megacity Growth," *Proceedings of the National Academy of Sciences* 110(14): E1248–E1253.

Zheng, Siqi, and Matthew E. Kahn (2013b), "Does Government Investment in Local Public Goods Spur Gentrification? Evidence from Beijing," *Real Estate Economics* 41(1): 1–28.

Part IV

Future connections and sustainability

10 Demography and inequality in China

Charles van Marrewijk[1]

10.1 Introduction

After analysing historical, geographical, and policy connections in the previous nine chapters, this chapter in combination with the next two chapters look at the sustainability of China's future.[2] Inspired by the previous (policy) analysis, this chapter will briefly analyze two stories of China's successful economic development. One story is based on economic policy and openness, the other story is based on the demographic transition. Associated with these two stories we analyze two main problems, namely Chinese inequality and China's ageing population. The chapter structure is briefly outlined in Figure 10.1.

We start in Sections 10.2 and 10.3 by providing some background information for our two stories, namely a general overview of issues relevant for global competitiveness and an overview of the development of world population in general and for some main countries and regions in particular. These sections can be brief in light of the analysis already available in Chapters 1–9. We then continue with story one (economic policy and openness) and problem one (inequality) in Sections 10.4 and 10.5. To illustrate this story and problem, we use data from the World Bank (2017) and the UNU-WIDER (2017a) World Income Inequality Database 3.4 (WIID 3.4). Next, Section 10.6 provides an intermezzo on demographic transition, which allows us to continue with story two (demographic dividend) and problem two (population ageing) in Sections 10.7 and 10.8. To illustrate this story and problem, we combine data from the World Bank (2017) with data from the United Nations Population Division (2015). Our discussion on China's population ageing problem in Section 10.8 immediately provides a proper international perspective. We do the same regarding China's inequality problems in Section 10.9. Finally, Section 10.10 concludes with a brief evaluation of the merits of the two stories and the relevance of the two problems for China's future successful economic development.

10.2 Background one: global competitiveness

Many aspects are important for economic growth and development. We can emphasize the role of capital accumulation in the growth process, the need to educate workers and raise human capital levels, and the need to innovate and benefit

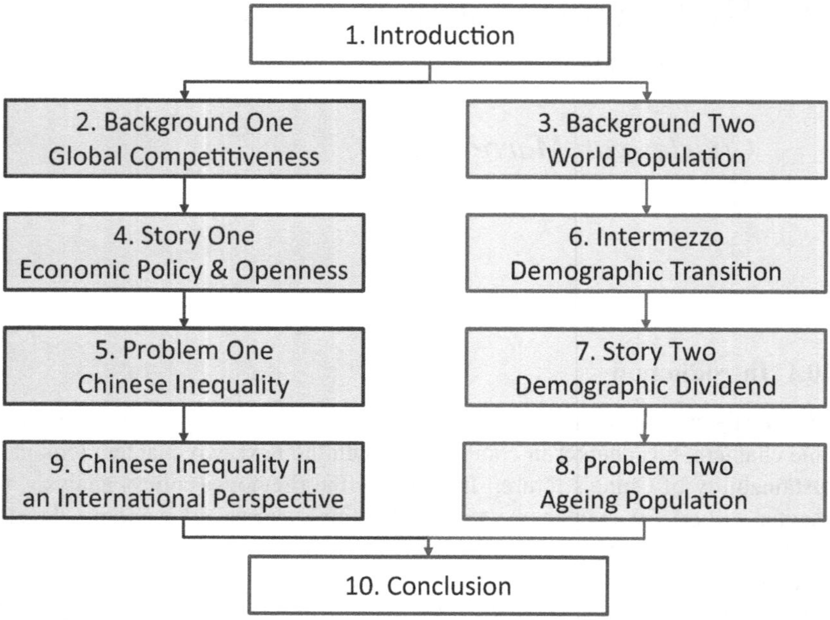

Figure 10.1 Chapter structure

from international knowledge spill overs. In addition, we should mention the role of institutions to lay a solid foundation for the economic growth process and the role of finance for development. Moreover, workers need to be healthy, well-trained, and educated in order to function properly in our increasingly complex society, and so on. This section provides an overview of the main issues that are at stake in order for an economy to be globally competitive, also at different stages of development, based on the Global Competitiveness Report (World Economic Forum 2015), which uses a specific methodology discussed later.

The 2015 Global Competitiveness Index (GCI) framework distinguishes between 12 different so-called pillars of competitiveness for three main types of economies, at different stages of economic development: factor-driven economies, efficiency-driven economies, and innovation-driven economies. Associated with each type of economy is a sub-index contributing to overall competitiveness, namely a basic requirements sub-index (consisting of four pillars), an efficiency enhancer sub-index (consisting of six pillars), and an innovation and sophistication sub-index (consisting of two pillars), as follows:

A *Factor-driven* economies; *basic requirements* sub-index

1 Institutions
2 Infrastructure

3 Macroeconomic environment
4 Health and primary education

B *Efficiency-driven* economies; *efficiency enhancers* sub-index

5 Higher education and training
6 Goods market efficiency
7 Labour market efficiency
8 Financial market development
9 Technological readiness
10 Market size

C *Innovation-driven* economies; *innovation and sophistication* sub-index

11 Business sophistication
12 Innovation

This approach thus acknowledges that many different aspects are important for determining a country's competitiveness and economic growth. The relative importance of individual components for total competitiveness is, of course, up for discussion. The GCI, however, uses detailed information to estimate how well a country is scoring on each of the individual components. The institutions pillar, for example, is estimated using 21 different indicators, including property rights, diversion of public funds, judicial independence, organized crime, ethical behaviour of firms, and so on. As another example, the business sophistication pillar is estimated using 11 different indicators, including local supplier quantity, local supplier quality, value chain breadth, extent of marketing, and so on. It is similar for the other 10 pillars.

The GCI also takes into consideration the relative importance of different pillars for countries in different stages of economic development, as measured by income per capita (see Figure 10.2). For factor-driven economies (income per capita up to 2,000), the weight for the basic requirements index is 60%, for the efficiency enhancers is 35%, and for innovation and sophistication is 5%. There is then a transition (income per capita in between 2,000 and 3,000) to the next stage for efficiency-driven economies (income per capita between 3,000 and 9,000), where the weight for the basic requirements index is 40%, for the efficiency enhancers is 50%, and for innovation and sophistication is 10%. Finally, there is a transition (income per capita in between 9,000 and 17,000) to the next stage for innovation-driven economies (income per capita above 17,000), where the weight for the basic requirements index is 20%, for the efficiency enhancers is 50%, and for innovation and sophistication is 30%.

Figure 10.3 provides an indication for the score on each of the 12 pillars for four sample countries in four panels using a radar diagram. For each pillar the score ranges from 0 to 7, where a higher score indicates better performance. A low score for a particular pillar is reflected in an observation close to the radar centre for that particular pillar, and a good score far away from that centre. Each panel in

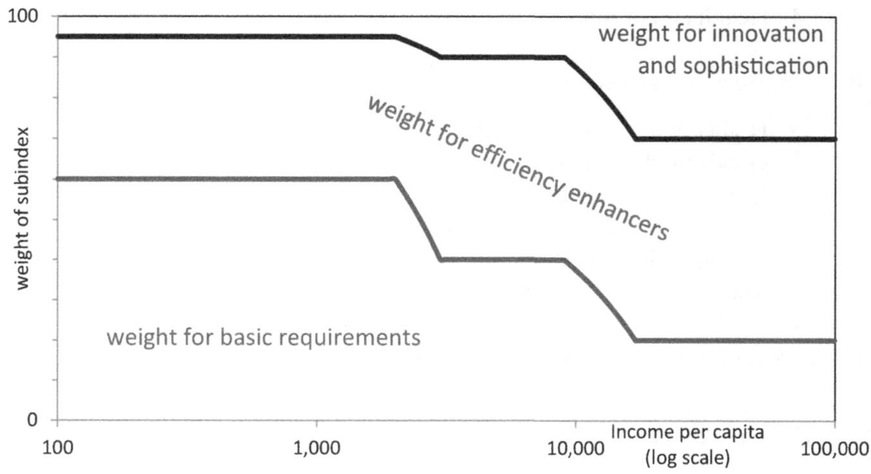

Figure 10.2 Stages of development and sub-index weights in global competitiveness

Source: Based on data from World Economic Forum (2015).

Figure 10.3 also shows the average score for all countries (in grey) for all pillars for ease of reference.

Panel *a* depicts the score for Switzerland, the country with the highest GCI. Switzerland scores above the world average for all pillars, and thus essentially has no weak spots. Switzerland's weakest point in relative terms (that is compared to the world average score for that pillar) is for health, followed by market size. Switzerland's relatively strong points are innovation, followed by infrastructure. Panel *b* depicts the score for the US, number 3 in the ranking. With the exception of the macroeconomic environment (which is therefore its relatively weakest point) the US scores above the world average for all pillars. The US's relatively strongest point is market size, followed by innovation. Panel *c* depicts the score for China, number 28 in the ranking. With the exception of technological readiness (which is therefore its relatively weakest point) China also scores above the world average for all pillars, although only marginally so in six cases. China's relatively strongest point is market size, followed by the macroeconomic environment. Panel *d*, finally, depicts the score for Nigeria, number 124 in the ranking. With the exception of market size and labour efficiency (which are therefore its relatively strongest points) Nigeria scores below the world average for all pillars. Nigeria's lowest scores in relative terms are for health and infrastructure. As this discussion shows, one of the advantages of the GCI approach is that it helps countries to identify which pillars of economic growth and competitiveness need improvement, particularly in their specific stage of development.

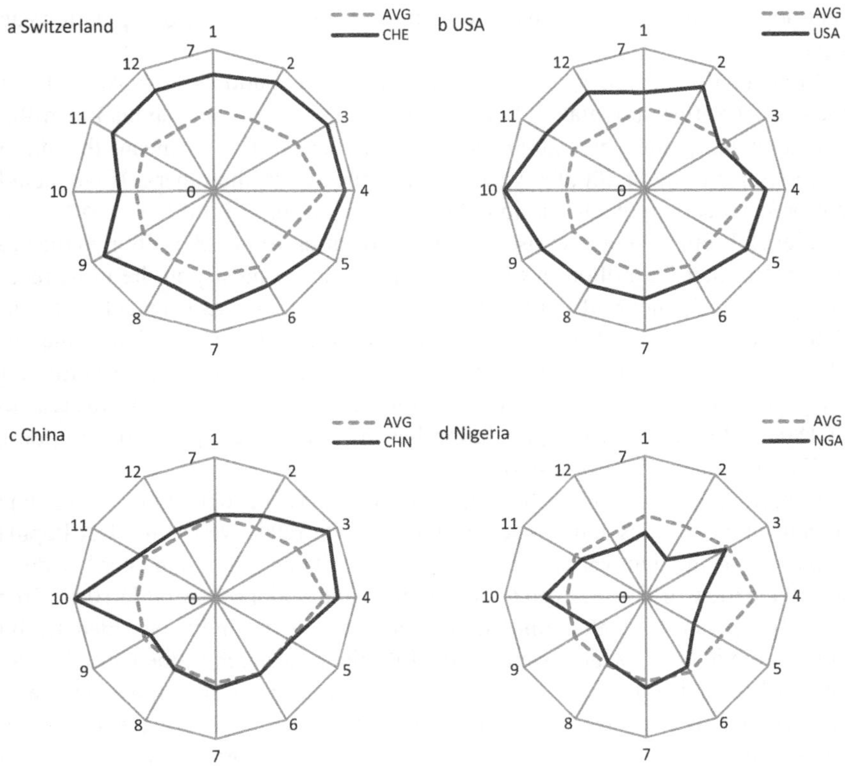

Figure 10.3 Global competitiveness in 12 pillars for four countries, 2015

Source: Based on data from World Economic Forum (2015)

Notes: The pillars 1–12 are listed in the main text; the score for each pillar ranges from 0 (lowest) to 7 (highest); AVG = world average score, for reference.

The broad message of the approach is clear. Global competitiveness depends on an appropriate mix of many different economic policies at appropriate different stages in the development process. The success of an economy thus largely depends on the viability of its policy mix.

10.3 Background two: world population

According to the United Nations Population Division (2015), the total world population will reach 7.5 billion in 2017; the midpoint estimate on 1 July 2017 is 7,515 million people. This is a substantial increase of about 1.11% over the estimate one year earlier on 1 July 2016. It means that more than 226,000 people are added to the world population *each day*, leading to a total increase of about

82.6 million people *per year*. This, in turn, means that more than the entire current population of a country like Germany is added to the world population each year.

From an historical perspective, this increase in population is high. According to the United Nations Population Division (1999), there were only about 300 million people on our planet some 2000 years ago (in the year 0). This means that it took Homo Sapiens about 200,000 years to reach the 300 million mark. If we include our predecessors in the discussion, it took mankind some 7 million years to reach that level. From then on, the rise in world population from 300 million in the year 0 to more than 7.5 billion in the year 2017 occurred mostly in the most recent 200 years, see panel *a* of Figure 10.4. World population was stagnant in the first thousand years, rising from 300 million in the year 0 to 310 million in the year 1000. It began to increase slowly in the next 500 years (rising from 310 million in the year 1000 to 500 million in the year 1500). The one billion mark was reached in 1804, after which world population began to increase rapidly to 2 billion in 1927, 3 billion in 1960, and so on.

Regarding information on the distribution of the world population among major regions and countries and projected future growth rates, we use the UN Population Division medium variant up to the year 2050 in the discussion later.[3] To do so, we divide the world into seven main countries and regions (see Table 10.1). From a country perspective, the population of both China and India exceeded 1.3 billion people in 2015, which is more than four times as much as the United States, the third-ranked country. So, for the sheer size of their population we include the countries China and India separately. The other entities are mostly the main continents (Africa, Europe, and Latin America), with the exception of what is labelled *Offshoots* in Table 10.1, which groups together four countries (United States, Canada, Australia, and New Zealand) with a similar demographic and historical experience. In this perspective we follow Angus Maddison (2001), who refers to

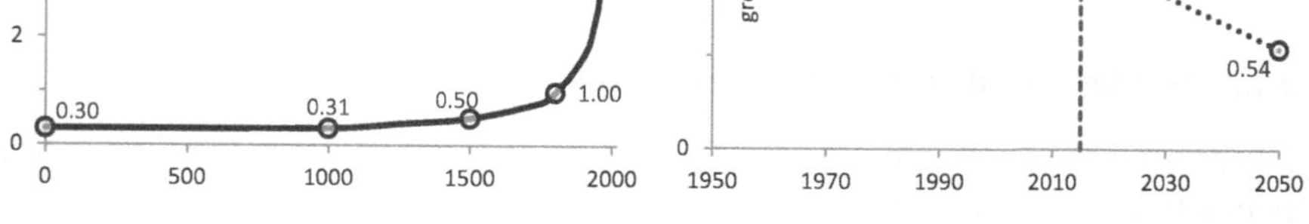

Figure 10.4 World population (0–2017) and world population growth rate (1950–2050)

Source: Based on data from UN Population Division (1999), The World at Six Billion, and (2015) World Population Prospects: The 2015 Revision; projections are for the medium variant.

Table 10.1 Population in main countries and regions: 1950, 2015 and 2050 projection

Region	*Total population (million)*			*Percent of world total*		
	1950	*2015*	*2050*	*1950*	*2015*	*2050*
China	544	1,376	1,348	21.5	18.7	13.9
India	376	1,311	1,705	14.9	17.8	17.5
Africa	229	1,186	2,478	9.1	16.1	25.5
Latin America	169	634	784	6.7	8.6	8.1
Offshoots	182	386	472	7.2	5.3	4.9
Europe	549	738	707	21.7	10.0	7.3
Other Asia	476	1,717	2,231	18.9	23.4	22.9
World	2,525	7,349	9,725	100.0	100.0	100.0

Source: Based on data from UN Population Division World Population Prospects: The 2015 Revision; projection for 2015 based on medium variant; Offshoots are: US, Canada, Australia, and New Zealand; Latin America includes Caribbean (LAC); Other Asia includes small populations from Oceania (less than 1% of the total)

these four countries as the *Western Offshoots*. The remaining (rest of the world) region is called *Other Asia*, as it consists mainly of Asian countries (excluding China and India), combined with small populations from Oceania (less than 1% of its total population).

Figure 10.5 illustrates the population developments in the seven main regions from 1950 to 2050, both in an absolute sense (millions, see panel *a*) and a relative sense (percent of world total, panel *b*). Similarly, Table 10.1 provides the absolute and relative numbers for three time periods: 1950, 2015, and 2050. We summarize our findings of a closer look at the figures and percentages from the figure and table for two main periods, namely actual developments and projected developments.

Actual developments for the period 1950–2015:

- The population level was growing in all main countries and regions.
- The growth rate was much lower in Europe than in the world as a whole, namely about 0.5% per year compared to 1.6% per year, leading to a substantial reduction of Europe's share in world population (from almost 22% to 10%).
- The growth rate was somewhat lower than the world average in the Offshoots and China (namely about 1.2% and 1.4% per year, respectively), leading to a decline in the share of world population of about 2% for the Offshoots and 3% for China.
- The growth rate was higher than the world average for Africa, Latin America, Other Asia, and India, which therefore have a rising population share. This holds for Africa, which had the highest growth rate (2.5% per year) and increased its share of the world population by 7 percentage points (from 9.1% to 16.1%).

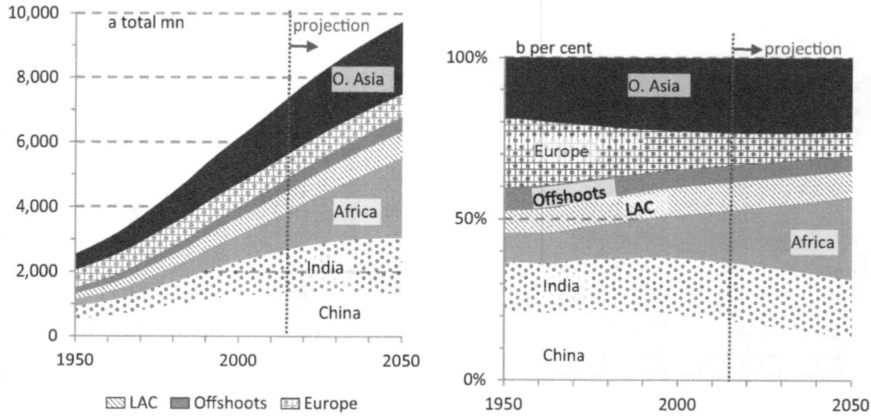

Figure 10.5 Population projections of main countries and regions, 1950–2050

Source: Based on data from UN Population Division, World Population Prospects: The 2015 Revision; projections from 2015 onwards based on medium variant; Offshoots are: US, Canada, Australia, and New Zealand; Latin America includes Caribbean (LAC); Other Asia includes small populations from Oceania.

Projected developments for the period 2015–2050:

- The population level is expected to decline in China (by 2%) and in Europe (by 4%), while a rise is expected in all other main countries and regions.
- The growth rate is expected to be *below* the world average (of 0.8% per year) for *all* countries and regions, except for *Africa* (with a growth rate of 2.5% per year). Therefore, Africa's share of the world population is expected to rise substantially from 16.1% in 2015 to 25.5% in 2050.

Combining the previous observations, we note that the developments in Europe and China contrast strongly with the developments in Africa. We analyse the dynamics of these developments (in terms of birth rate and death rate) in more detail in Section 10.6, but first we discuss the first story of economic development.

10.4 Story one: economic policy and openness

Our first story on Chinese economic development focuses on the importance of (economic) policies. We have analysed the impact of various policies throughout this book, particularly in Chapters 7–9. In this section we will focus on the importance of economic policies in general and international contacts and interactions in particular, see also Chapter 3 and Chapter 6. China is a large country with an impressive cultural, economic, and military history, dating back thousands of years, see also Chapter 1. Since we want to get a feel for the importance of international contacts through trade and capital flows, and openness to the outside world, even for such a large country as China, we will measure economic development in China relative to the outside world. To this end, Figure 10.6 depicts China's income per capita as a percentage of world average income per capita in any given year (in constant 2010 USD),[4] as well as China's export of goods and services as a percentage of GDP,[5] both on a log scale.

In 1949, Mao Zedong proclaimed the founding of the People's Republic of China and installed a new political and economic order modelled on the Soviet model. In 1958, Mao broke with the Soviet model and started a new economic programme called the *Great Leap Forward.* Its aim was to raise industrial and agricultural production by forming large cooperatives and building 'backyard factories'. The results of the market disruption and poor planning, leading to the production of unsaleable goods, were disastrous. Within a year, starvation appeared even in fertile agricultural areas, resulting in famine from 1960 to 1961. The relationship with the Soviet Union deteriorated sharply, leading to the restriction of the flow of scientific and technological information to China, and the withdrawal of all Soviet personnel in 1960. When compared to the world average, the impact of the Great Leap Forward shows up in Figure 10.6 as a deterioration of China's living standards from an already low 5.20%in 1960 to an even lower 3.35%in 1962 (a relative decline of 36%!).

In the early 1960s Liu Shaoqi and his protégé Deng Xiaoping took over direction of the party and adopted pragmatic economic policies at odds with Mao's revolutionary vision. In 1966, when the Chinese economy had almost recuperated from the consequences of the Great Leap Forward and Chinese per capita income had bounced back to 4.43% of the world average, Mao started the *Cultural*

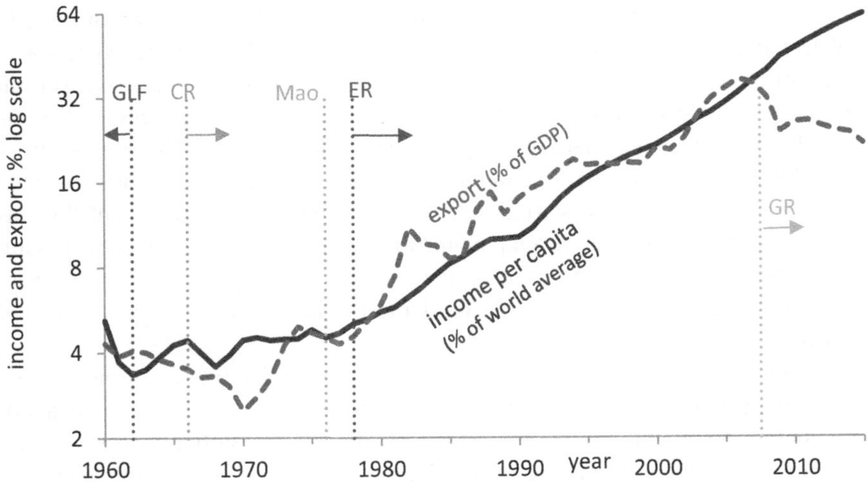

Figure 10.6 Economic development in China, 1960–2015

Source: World Development Indicators online; income per capita is GDP in constant 2010 USD (relative to world average of that year in percent); exports of goods and services as percent of GDP; GLF = end Great Leap Forward; CR = start Cultural Revolution; Mao = Mao's death; ER = start Economic Reform; GR = start Great Recession.

Revolution, a political attack on the pragmatists who were dragging China back towards capitalism. The Red Guards, radical youth organizations, attacked party and state organizations at all levels. Again, Mao's insightful ideas were disastrous to the Chinese standard of living, which dropped to 3.57% of the world average in 1968 (this time a relative decline of 'only' 19%). The Chinese political situation stabilized after some years along complex factional lines, resulting in living standards of around 4.5% of the world average. Deng Xiaoping was reinstated in 1975 but then stripped of all official positions one year later by the Gang of Four (Mao's wife and three associates).

Mao's death in September 1976 set off a scramble for succession, leading to the arrest of the Gang of Four and the reinstatement of Deng Xiaoping in August of 1977. In a pivotal meeting in December 1978, the new leadership adopted *Economic Reform* policies to expand rural incentives, encourage enterprise autonomy, reduce central planning, open up to international trade flows with the outside world, establish foreign direct investment in China, and pass new legal codes in June 1979. The positive consequences of the economic reforms, which were continued with some interruptions by successive governments, for the Chinese standard of living were enormous, dramatically illustrating the dynamic costs of trade restrictions. In relative terms, income per capita in China increased more than 12-fold in 37 years, from 5.06% of the world average in 1978 to 63.44% in 2015. A monumental achievement indeed, with enormous consequences for more than one billion people.

The policy of openness, or lack thereof, is illustrated in Figure 10.6 by exports of goods and services relative to income. During the inward-looking policies of the Great Leap Forward and the Cultural Revolution, the share of exports declined from 4.31% of income in 1960 to its minimum of 2.49% of income in 1970 (a relative decline of 42%). After a recovery to about 4.5% in 1978, exports as a share of income started to rise rapidly as a consequence of the Economic Reform process, reaching a peak of more than 37% of income in 2006. Remember that this is a sharply increasing share of a rapidly rising income level. These trade flows have been vital for Chinese economic development. Relative exports declined once the *Great Recession* started in 2007 (to about 22% in 2015), but this has not slowed down Chinese development. Apparently, China was rather successful in its transition process to the next stages of economic development (see Section 10.2), such that it can also rely on domestic factors for continued economic growth (see also Section 10.7).

Another indicator of the policy of openness is provided by the Foreign Direct Investment (FDI) flows relative to income in Figure 10.7. There are no data available before 1982, but we can be sure that FDI flows were virtually absent before that time. After the economic reforms, FDI into China rose rapidly from a meagre 0.21% of income in 1982 to an average level almost 4% from 1992 to 2015, with a declining time trend to reflect the rising importance of domestic factors for Chinese economic development. Associated with these investments is an enormous transfer of knowledge by multinational firms. After a brief initial peak in FDI

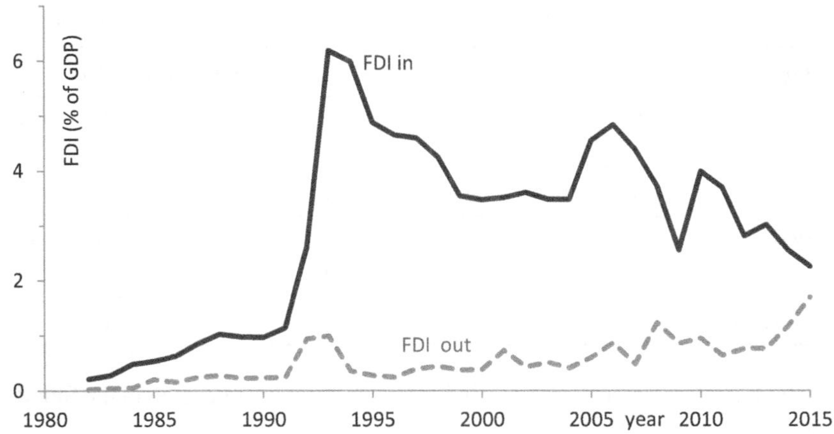

Figure 10.7 China; FDI inflows and outflows (% of GDP), 1982–2015

Source: World Development Indicators online; FDI = Foreign Direct Investment.

outflows in the early 1990s (associated with the peak in inflows), China is also increasingly active as an investor in the rest of the world since 1996, particularly after 2013. FDI outflows increased from about 0.24% of income in 1996 to 1.7% in 2015. The more decentralized and outward-oriented economic policies that started around 1980 have been enormously important for China's economic development.

Box 10.1 Development, inequality, and conflict

Our indicator of success in Sections 10.4 and 10.7 is China's income level per capita in a year relative to the world average income level per capita in that year. This indicator provides no information regarding the distribution of the gains within society. We discuss this (as summarized in Table 10.2) for *Marconia*, a hypothetical country with two groups of identical people: the Small group (consisting of 25 million people) and the Big group (consisting of 75 million people). In the base year, the income level for everyone in the Small group is 12% of the world average, while the income level for everyone in the Big group is 8% of the world average. As a consequence, the average income level in Marconia is 9% of the world average in the base year ($0.25 \times 12\ 12 + 0.75 \times 8 = 9$). There are, of course, several indicators of inequality possible in this setting, but we focus on the ratio of income of a person in the Small group relative to income of a person in the Big group,

Table 10.2 Marconia example of economic development and distribution of gains

Population	*Small group*		*Big group*		*Relative income (%)*	
	25 million		*75 million*		*Country vs world*	*Small vs big*
	Income	*(gain %)*	*Income*	*(gain %)*		
Base year	12		8		9	150
Situation 1	24	(100)	16	(100)	18	150
Situation 2	36	(200)	12	(50)	18	300
Situation 3	48	(300)	8	(0)	18	600

which is 150% in the base year, indicating that the income level in the Small group is 50% higher than in the Big group.

In situation 1, the income level for everyone in Marconia rises by 100%, for the Small group from 12 to 24 and for the Big group from 8 to 16. As a consequence, the ratio of small vs big income per capita within the country remains 150%. Since everyone gains and the distribution of income remains the same, the drastic change in economic policy is likely to receive wide support from everyone.

In situation 2, the income level of the Small group rises by 200% (from 12 to 36) while the income level of the Big group rises by only 50% (from eight to 12). Consequently, the ratio of small vs big income per capita rises drastically from 150% to 300%. The people in the Small group are strong supporters of the drastic economic policy change, but the people of the Big group have mixed feelings. On the one hand their income level rises substantially (which they like), but on the other hand the income level of other people rises much more and creates rising inequality (which they resent). This is likely to create envy and conflict within society.

In situation 3, all gains from the drastic economic policy change accrue to the Small group, where income rises by 300% (from 12 to 48), while the income level for the Big group does not rise at all. As a consequence, the ratio of small vs big income per capita rises enormously from 150% to 600%. This clearly undermines public support for the drastic economic policy change in view of the unequal distribution of gains.

10.5 Problem one: Chinese inequality

An important potential problem threatening China's impressive economic development is rising income inequality. Remember that our indicator of success is China's income level per capita relative to the world average. This indicator provides no information regarding the distribution of the gains within society, which might create conflicts (see Box 10.1).

Our analysis is based on the UNU-WIDER World Income Inequality Database (WIID), which collects information on inequality estimates for almost all countries in the world from 1867 onwards. The latest version (January 2017, WIID 3.4) has 8817 estimates for 182 countries, of which 175 estimates are for China, starting in 1953. Of these observations 42% are classified as low quality, 41% as average quality, 18% as high quality, and 12% as unknown quality. As expected, the quality of the observations tends to increase over time (see panel *a* of Figure 10.8) even though the first unknown classification occurs in 2006. Our discussion is based on all different types of quality available, but we clearly identify the level of quality in the graphs to follow.

Several issues need to be taken into consideration when compiling inequality measures, see UNU-WIDER (2017b). First, we need to know if the inequality measure is on an income or consumption/expenditure basis. There are advantages of and advocates for either approach; Deaton and Zaidi (2002) favour the consumption approach, while Atkinson and Bourguignon (2000) do not. Second, we must be clear on what to include in the definition of income and consumption. Regarding income-based inequality measures, it is preferred if these are based on disposable income rather than total income, if available. Third, there are some conceptual issues. The household should be the basis for the analysis, while the household size should be taken into consideration, since we are interested in the economic well-being of individuals, not of households.[6] Finally, we should choose an appropriate income inequality measure. Although various options satisfying certain restrictions (anonymity, scale independence, population independence, and satisfying the transfer principle) are available (such as the mean log deviation, the Theil index, and the generalized entropy measures), we focus on the Gini index since it is widely used, satisfies the restrictions, and is a distribution-free inequality index that represents the views on inequality of a society with very general distributional preferences (Sen 1974).

The early inequality measures available tend to be based on gross income as a welfare definition (12% of the observations), while later measures are based on disposable income (67% of the observations). Consumption-based estimates (15% of the observations) are more recent; see panel *b* of Figure 10.8. The remaining 10% of the observations are based on other welfare definitions. Regarding the equivalence scale used, household per capita estimates are by far the most common (87% of the observations), while 5% are without adjustment and 9% are in another category. The data also indicate if there are age restrictions for the included people in the study (for China there never is, so all studies are based on 'all' population) and the type of area covered, classified as 'all' for the country as a whole (27% of the observations), 'urban' (37% of the observations), and 'rural' (35% of the observations).

On the basis of the previous information and in view of our interest in the change of income inequality over time, we will focus on inequality measures

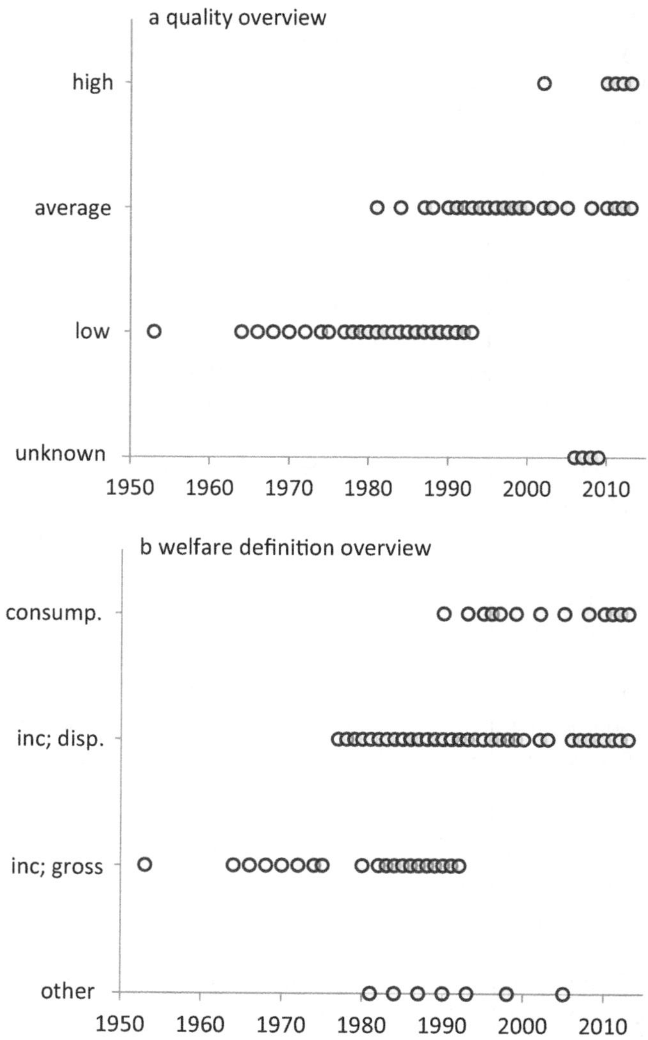

Figure 10.8 China inequality information; quality and welfare, 1953–2015

Source: Based on data from UNU-WIDER (2017a); inc. = income; disp. = disposable; consump. = consumption.

based on disposable income using household per capita as equivalence scale. This implies we use the preferred income measure (disposable income), which is most widely available, and the preferred equivalence scale (household per capita), which is also most widely available, but cannot include the earliest income inequality measures in the period 1953–1975 (since these are based on gross income instead of disposable income). We must, of course, distinguish the different types of studies regarding area covered. In total, there are 114 studies with a Gini index available meeting our criteria, namely 21 studies for the country as a whole, 46 rural studies, and 47 urban studies. These are illustrated in panels *a*, *b*, and *c*, respectively, in Figure 10.9 and discussed later.

We start with an analysis of the Gini index (on a scale from 0 to 100) for the country as a whole (see panel *a* of Figure 10.9). The first observation is in 1978 on the start of the Economic Reform process and the last observation is in 2012. The early observations are of low quality, most of the middle observations are of average quality, and a large share of the recent observations are of high quality, combined with several observations of unknown quality. Although there are, of course, variations between the studies, there is a consistent trend visible over time, supported by studies of different quality classifications. The Gini index of income inequality in China rises substantially over time. The regression line provided in panel *a* explains 74% of the variation in the Gini coefficient and has a slope of 0.7122 (see Table 10.3). Based on the regression line, which combines information from all available studies, the Gini index for China as a whole rose from 26.5 percentage points in 1978 at the start of the Economic Reform process to 52.9 percentage points in 2015.

Panel *b* of Figure 10.9 shows the Gini index for studies on rural income inequality in China. The first observation is again in 1978 and the last observation in 2012. As for the country as a whole, the quality of the studies tends to improve over time and the Gini index tends to rise over time. The regression line provided in panel *b* explains 78% of the variation in the Gini coefficient and has a slope of 0.5070 (see Table 10.3). Based on this regression line, the Gini index for rural China rose from 24.3 percentage points in 1978 to 43.1 percentage points in 2015. The increase is thus less sharp for rural China than for the country as a whole.

Panel *c* of Figure 10.9 shows the Gini index for studies on urban income inequality in China. The first observation is in 1977 and the last observation in 2012. As for the country as a whole and for rural China, the quality of the studies tends to improve over time and the Gini index tends to rise over time. The regression line provided in panel *c* explains 82% of the variation in the Gini coefficient and has a slope of 0.8114 (see Table 10.3). On the basis of this regression line, the Gini index for urban China rose from 12.2 percentage points in 1978 to 42.3 percentage points in 2015. The increase for urban China is thus sharper than for the country as a whole and much sharper than for rural China.

We briefly summarize our findings for disposable income inequality based on the Gini index as follows:

- China's overall income inequality has risen substantially since 1978.
- China's rural income inequality has also risen substantially since 1978, but slower than for China as a whole.

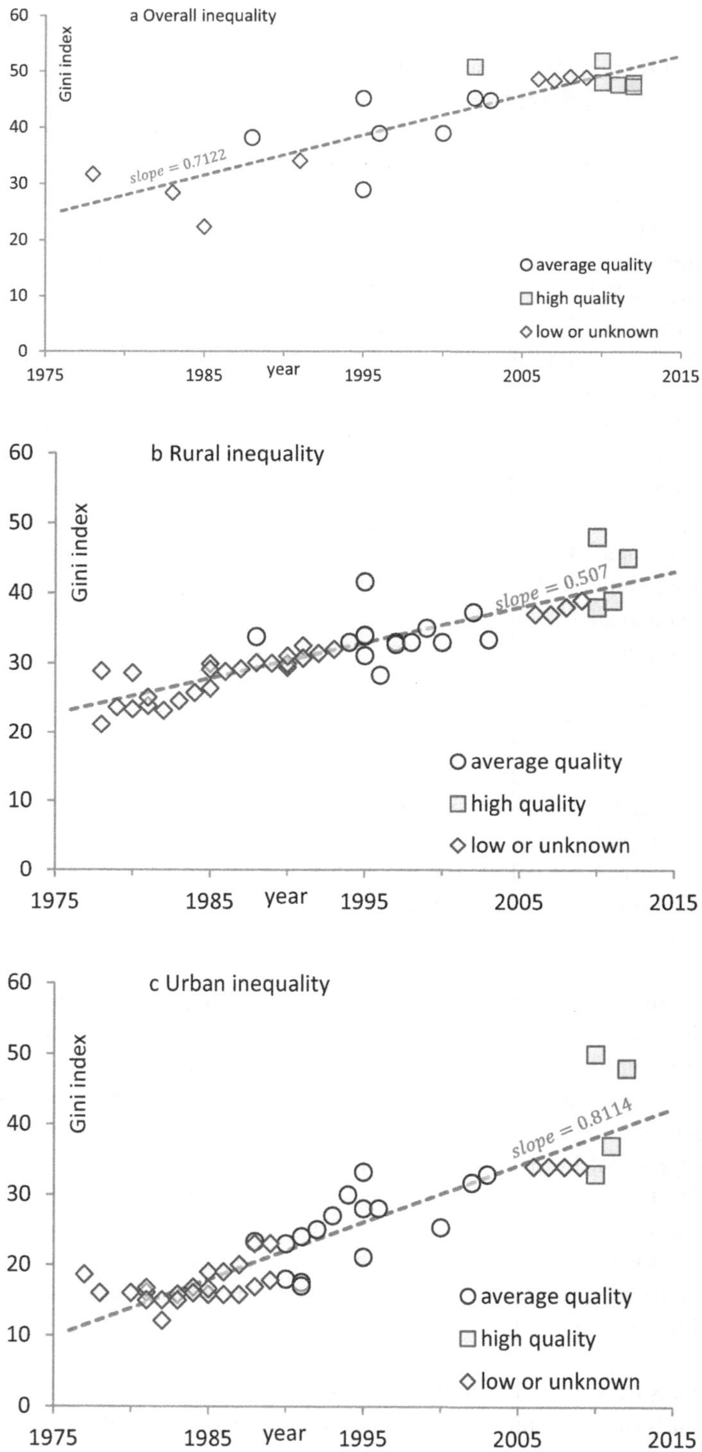

Figure 10.9 Chinese inequality; Gini coefficient, 1975–2015

Source: Based on data from UNU-WIDER (2017a); regression explains 74.1%, 78.0%, and 82.2% of variance for panels *a-c*, respectively; number of observations is 21, 46, and 47 for panels *a-c*, respectively; dashed lines are regression lines.

Table 10.3 China Gini index regressions, 1977–2015

	Country	*Rural*	*Urban*
Intercept	–1382	–979	–1593
(t value)	(–7.16)	(–12.10)	(–14.19)
Slope	0.7122	0.5070	0.8114
(t value)	(7.38)	(12.49)	(14.40)
R^2	0.741	0.780	0.822
# observations	21	46	47

Source: Time regressions based on UNU-WIDER (2017a) data; disposable income studies only; dependent variable is Gini index (scale from 0 to 100).

- China's urban income inequality was low in 1978 but has been rising faster since then relative to China as a whole and much faster relative to rural China.
- At the moment (2017), China's urban disposable income inequality is about equal to China's rural disposable income inequality.[7]

The remark that China's urban inequality was low in 1978 is clear when we compare panels *b* and *c* of Figure 10.9, and further discussed in Section 10.9. Note that China's overall income inequality is higher than either the rural or the urban inequality because of the differences in income levels in these areas.[8] China's rapid economic development has thus been accompanied by rising disposable income inequality. This is not a new phenomenon, see Box 10.2.

Box 10.2 Development and income inequality

The World Bank's 2009 World Development Report was entitled *Reshaping Economic Geography* and focused on the links between economic development on the one hand and the advantages of physical geography (resources, waterways, climate; first-nature geography) and man-made geography (clustering, agglomeration, and spill-overs; second-nature geography) on the other hand. The role of concentration of economic activities in specific locations for development plays an important role in this study.

Countries embarking on a successful development path generally concentrate economic activity more and more in cities and specific clusters of activity, which attract migration flows from the country side, usually create slums, and may grow into large agglomerations. During this initial stage of development income inequality measures within the country and between regions in the country generally increase. At later stages of development, the migration flows slow down or stop, the worst slum problems are addressed, and measures of income inequality decline again. This is illustrated in Figure 10.10 for the US in 1840–1960 (the arrows for the US

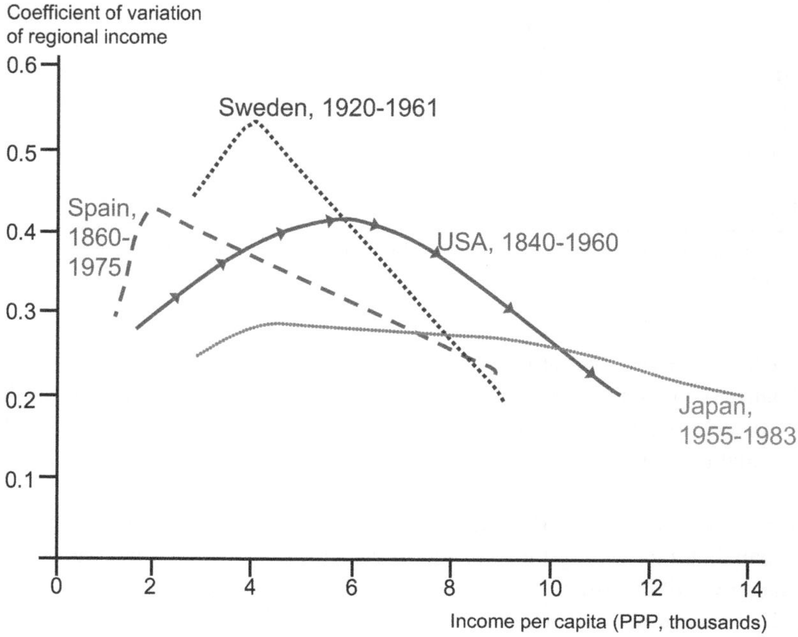

Figure 10.10 Development and income inequality, some historical examples

Source: Based on World Bank (2009).

indicate a time-direction: per capita income rises over time; similarly for the other countries), for Spain in 1860–1975, for Sweden in 1920–1961, and for Japan in 1955–1983. In all cases, but to varying degrees and at varying speeds, regional income inequality first rises and then reaches a peak before declining again. This parallels the current developments in China, where income inequality has been rising since 1978 along with the concentration of economic activity in rapidly growing, large cities.

10.6 Intermezzo: demographic transition

Before we continue with our next story on Chinese economic development and its associated next problem, we briefly provide some information on the demographic transition model in this section. Demographers use a variety of precisely defined terms in their models to adequately express and predict expected changes in population developments. We will focus on the size of the population as determined by the population growth rate. This, in turn, depends on three main variables: the crude birth rate, the crude death rate, and the net migration rate (equal to immigration minus emigration). All these variables are expressed as a number per 1000 population. As Equation 10.1 indicates, the population growth rate (per 1000) is the difference between the crude birth rate and the crude death rate (also known as the rate of natural increase) plus the net migration rate. We focus on (crude) birth and death rates, which are empirically more important for determining population growth rates than net migration rates for most countries in the world (van Marrewijk et al. forthcoming, Chapter 12).

$$\text{population growth rate} = \text{crude birth rate} - \text{crude death rate} + \text{net migration rate} \qquad 10.1.$$

From Section 10.3, we know that the world population at first grew slowly for many years, after which the growth *rate* increased rapidly around 1800, reached a peak around 1968 and then started to decline again. Moreover, we know that expected population trends up to 2050 differ widely for the main countries and regions. The *demographic transition* model connects population developments with economic developments. It is based on empirical observations of birth and death rates made at the beginning of the 20th century by the American Warren Thompson (1887–1973) and Adolphe Landry (1874–1956) of France. The model is illustrated in Figure 10.11 using four stages.[9]

- Stage one. Birth and death rates are high and volatile, such that population growth is low and fluctuating. It is a stage of low economic development (before the industrial revolution), with mostly agricultural workers.
- Stage two. The death rate starts to fall, especially among children, as a result of improvements in health care and sanitation. It is a stage of starting economic development in which birth rates remain high. Consequently, the difference between birth and death rates starts to rise and the population starts to grow more quickly.
- Stage three. Birth rates start to fall as well, not only because of the availability of contraceptives and an increase of women's status, but also because fewer children are needed on the farm to work as a result of mechanization. It is a more advanced stage of economic development in which the population still rises rapidly, but the speed of population growth starts to decline towards the end of this stage as the gap between birth rate and death rate narrows.
- Stage four. Birth rates and death rates are both low, stabilizing the population at a higher level than before the demographic transition began. It is a stage of higher economic development with, on average, an older population.

During the demographic transition the structure of the population changes, with a rising share of young people and a falling share of older people in stage two,

Figure 10.11 Demographic transition

followed by a declining share of young people and a rising share of older people in stages three and four. To illustrate the (projected) relevance of demographic transition, we use information on birth rate and death rate for the world as a whole and for China and Africa for the period 1950–2050, as shown in panels *a-c* of Figure 10.12. We briefly discuss each panel in turn and remind the reader that birth rates and death rates are per 1000 population and that all panels have the same scale.[10]

Panel *a* shows the developments for the *world* as a whole. In 1950 the world birth rate was about 37 and the death rate about 19, leading to a rate of natural increase of around 18. The world birth rate declines for the whole period; rapidly in the period 1950–2015 (from 37 to 20) and more slowly since then (to 15 in 2050). Note that there are some fluctuations in the decline of the birth rate in the first half of the 1960s and second half of the 1980s. These are largely related to developments in China, see panel *c*. The world death rate declines from 1950 to 2015 (from 19 to eight) and is expected to rise (because of an ageing world population) to about nine in 2050. As a result, the rate of natural increase peaked at 21 in 1968 and declines to six in 2050. The rate of natural increase is indicated clearly in the figure by the shaded area. For ease of reference, the world birth and world death lines are included in light grey in panels *b* and *c* of Figure 10.12.

Panel *b* shows the demographic developments in *Africa*. The birth rate is much higher than the world average throughout the whole period. Although the African birth rate is declining steadily, starting at 48 in 1950 and declining to 36 in 2015 and 24 in 2050, the gap with the world average birth line is steadily rising until the early 2000s and only starts to decline from there on. Africa's death rate is also

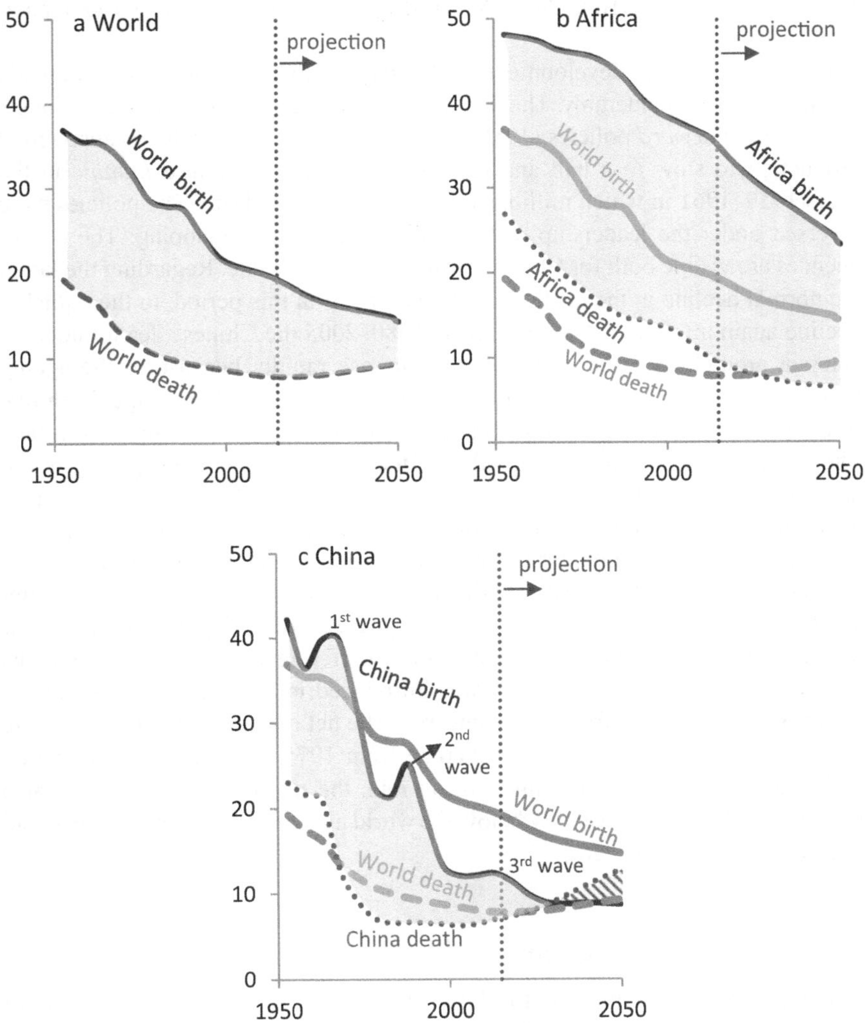

Figure 10.12 Crude birth and death rates; selected countries and regions, 1950–2050

Source: Based on data from UN Population Division, World Population Prospects: The 2015 Revision; projections from 2015 onwards based on medium variant; five-year averages projected in centre year; shaded area is rate of natural increase, striped if it is a decline.

higher than the world average in 1950 (27 compared to 19) due to poor health care and sanitation. Improvements in these conditions combined with a young population implies that death rates in Africa decline for the whole period (to 10 in 2015 and six in 2050) and are expected to drop below the world average in the second half of the 2020s. As a consequence of these developments, the rate of natural increase is much higher than the world average for the whole period, namely 21 in 1950, 26 in 2015, and 18 in 2050. As a result, Africa's share of the world population is rising rapidly.

Panel *c* shows the developments in *China*, which are clearly more dramatic and fluctuating considerably. The fluctuations are mostly related to Mao Zedong's *Great Leap Forward* policies (1958–1962, see Section 10.4), which caused food production to slow to a halt and resulted in the *Great Chinese Famine* in the years 1959–1961 in which millions of people starved to death. The policies were reversed under the leadership of Liu Shiaoqu and Deng Xiaoping. The consequences are visible both for China's birth rate and death rate. Regarding the latter, the normal decline in the death rate came to a halt in this period, to then quickly decline again afterwards.[11] In the period 1980–2005 the Chinese death rate stagnates at around six, after which it starts to rise rapidly because of the ageing population to 13 in 2050; it is expected to be above the world average death rate from 2020 onwards. The fluctuations are even more visible in China's birth rate. There is a strong decline in births during the Great Famine as people try not to have children when the circumstances are bleak, followed by a peak to (partially) make up for lost children in the period immediately afterwards (second part of the 1960s). This large number of births then leads to a new peak some 25 years later (second part of the 1980s), which in turn leads to a more modest peak after another 25 years (around 2015). A new, even more modest, ripple effect will occur in the second half of the 2030s, and so on. Interfering with these developments is China's one-child policy, which was introduced in 1979 and is beginning to be formally phased out from 2015 onwards. The net result is a wildly fluctuating birth rate that is below the world average from 1975 onwards. In combination with the developments for China's death rate, the rate of natural increase also fluctuates wildly, is consistently below the world average from 1990 onwards, and negative from 2030 onwards.

10.7 Story two: demographic dividend

A popular and instructive way to illustrate the changing population structure of a country or region during the demographic transition is to construct a so-called population pyramid. An example of three such pyramids for the world as a whole in 1990, 2015, and 2050 is given in Figure 10.13. The size of the population (in millions) is measured on the horizontal axis; for males to the right of the origin and for females to the left of the origin. The population of both sexes is divided into five-year age groups, namely 0–4 years old, 5–9 years old, and so on. All people above 100 years old are grouped together.[12] The age groups are depicted on the vertical axis, from zero to 100. The figure also indicates three broader age groups, labelled *young* (0–14 years old), *working age* (15–64 years old), and *old* (65 years and older). This distinction is analyzed in more detail later on.

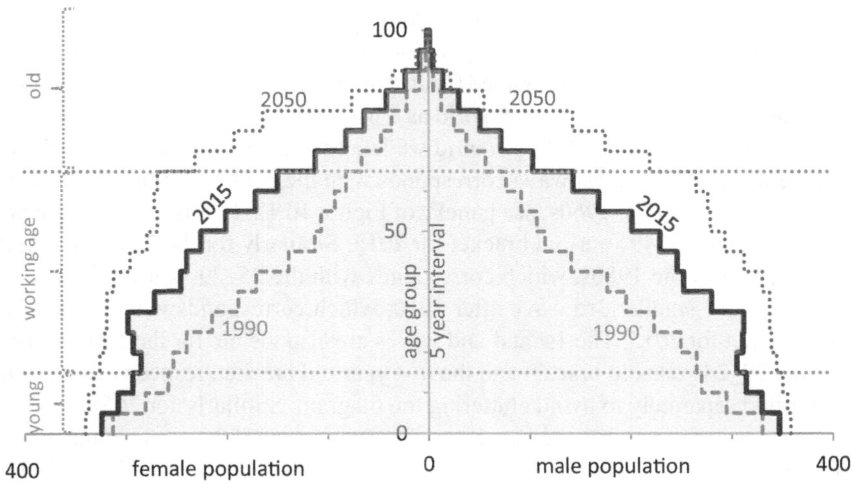

Figure 10.13 World population pyramids; 1990, 2015, and 2050

Source: Based on data from UN Population Division, World Population Prospects: The 2015 Revision; projections for 2050 based on medium variant; million population per five-year age group.

The sharpest (most 'pointy') population pyramid in Figure 10.13 is the 1990 pyramid, in which each older age cohort is clearly smaller than the previous one. There were, for example, 313 million females in the 0–4 year age group in 1990, followed by 281 million females in the 5–9 year age group, 258 million in the 10–14 year age group, and so on. The respective numbers for males in 1990 are: 330, 294, and 270 million. Such a sharp pyramid is indicative of a rapidly rising population, with a large fraction of young people and a small fraction of older people. More specifically, about 33% of the population in 1990 was in the young category (0–14 years old) and only 6% in the old category (65+), leaving about 61% in the working age category (15–64 years old).

The 2015 population pyramid is shaded for clarity. It is bigger and less sharp than the 1990 pyramid. The fact that it is bigger indicates that the world population is increasing, because the sum of all areas represents the entire world population. The fact that it is less sharp indicates that the population growth rate is declining, resulting in a smaller share of young people (26% compared to 33% in 1990) and the share of older people is rising (more than 8% compared to 6% in 1990). The net result is a rise in the working age population (close to 66%, rather than 61% in 1990).

The 2050 population pyramid is again bigger than the 2015 pyramid (so the population level is still rising) and even less sharp (so the population growth rate is still declining). By 2050 the share of young people will have declined below

22% and the share of older people will have risen above 14%. The net result is a decline in the working age population from 66% to 64%.

Figure 10.14 provides similar population pyramids for China in 1990, 2015, and 2050.[13] We first focus on the shaded China 'pyramid' of 2015, which does not look like the regular pyramids for the world as a whole discussed earlier because of the peaks and gaps. For the 2015 pyramid we label the peaks 1st, 2nd, and 3rd wave on the male side. The 1st wave corresponds with the peak in China's birth rate in the second half of the 1960s; see panel *c* of Figure 10.12. It thus relates to the population in the 45–49 year-old bracket for 2015. Similarly for the 2nd[d] wave in the second half of the 1980s, which corresponds with the 25–29 year old bracket for 2015 and the smaller 3rd wave after 2010, which corresponds with the 0–4 year old bracket for 2015. The 1st and 2nd waves are also visible for the 1990 pyramid (in the 20–24 year-old bracket and the 0–4 year old bracket, respectively), but not identified separately to avoid cluttering the diagram. Similarly for 2050.

The corresponding broader age categories (in percent of the total population) for young–working age–old are 29–66–5 in 1990, 17–73–10 in 2015, and 14–62–24 in 2050. This indicates a rapidly declining young population and a rapidly rising older population, with initially a rising share of the working age population and then a declining share of working age population (see the following and next section).

$$income\ per\ capita = \frac{income}{population} = \underbrace{\left(\frac{working\ age\ population}{population}\right)}_{A} \underbrace{\left(\frac{workers}{working\ age}\right)}_{B} \underbrace{\left(\frac{income}{workers}\right)}_{C} \quad 10.2.$$

Figure 10.15 shows the share of the working age population for the world, Africa, and China for the period 1950–2015.[14] For the world as a whole, the share of the working age population reached a minimum of 57% around 1965 and has been rising since then to a peak of almost 66% around 2010. Since income per capita is by definition the product of three ratios, see Equation 10.2, this means that for a given income per worker (*C*) and share of workers in the working age population (*B*), a rise in the share of the working age population (*A*) directly translates into rising income per capita levels. In a dynamic perspective (for a given growth rate of income per worker and a given share of workers in the working age population), a rise in the share of the working age population translates into a rise in the growth rate of income per capita (Rougoor and van Marrewijk 2015). As such, a rise in the share of the working age population during the demographic transition implies a boost in income per capita levels and growth rates, which is referred to as the *demographic dividend*; see Bloom et al. (2003) for an overview. There does not seem to be a generally accepted term for the opposite of a demographic dividend when the share of the working age population is low.[15] For clarity of exposition, we take the world's share of the working age population as a benchmark and use the term *dividend* if a country's share is higher than the world average and the

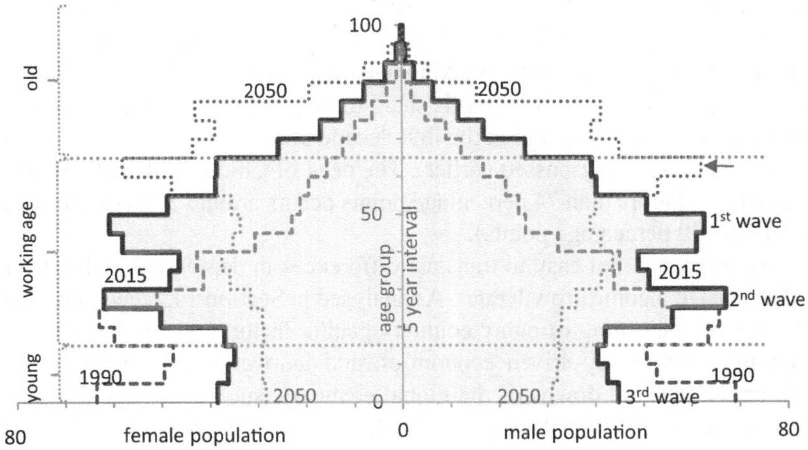

Figure 10.14 China population pyramids; 1990, 2015, and 2050

Source: Based on data from UN Population Division, World Population Prospects: The 2015 Revision; projections for 2050 based on medium variant; million population per five-year age group.

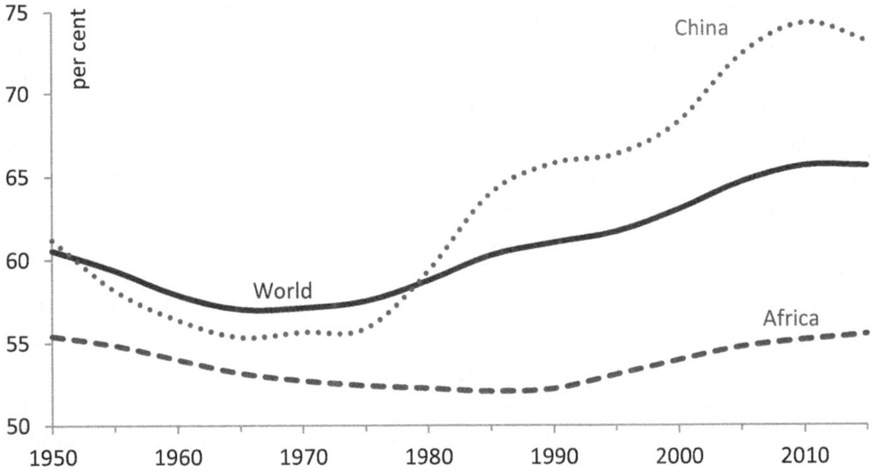

Figure 10.15 Working age (15–65) population; percent of total, 1950–2015

Source: Based on data from UN Population Division, World Population Prospects: The 2015 Revision.

Note: Vertical scale does not start at zero.

term *reverse dividend* if it is lower. We measure the dividend and reverse dividend in percentage point deviations from the world average.

Africa deviates substantially from the world average in Figure 10.15 and has a large reverse dividend for the whole period 1950–2015. In fact, Africa's share of the working age population reached a minimum of 52% in 1985 (at which stage the reverse dividend was more than 8 percentage points) and has been rising steadily since then to about 56% in 2015. Africa's reverse dividend is more than 10 percentage points for the period 2005–2015. Chinese developments are quite different. China's share of the working age population is fairly close to the world average up to 1980, after which this share rapidly rises above the world average, particularly in the 1980s and in the first decade of the new millennium (related to the two birth waves discussed earlier). The peak of China's share of working age population of more than 74 percentage points occurs around 2010 (a demographic dividend of 9 percentage points).

It is, of course, not easy to translate differences in demographic dividend into differences in income growth rates. As analysed in Section 10.2, economic growth depends on the timing of many country-specific factors, related to factor-driven economies, efficiency-driven economies, and innovation-driven economies, as well as the ups and downs of the global economy, such as the rapid restoration after the destructions of World War II, the global oil price shocks, or the trade decline after the Great Recession of 2008. One way to illustrate the demographic dividend, while controlling for global effects, is to analyse income developments relative to the world as a whole. To do so, we define relative income as a country's income per capita (GDP in constant 2010 USD) divided by the world average income per capita in that year, using percentage points and a log scale, as we did in Section 10.4.

Figure 10.16 illustrates the connection between the demographic dividend and relative income for China (panel *a*) and Sub-Sahara Africa (panel *b*). We use Sub-Sahara Africa, rather than Africa, for our illustration as the income per capita information provided by the World Bank focuses on the Sub-Sahara part of Africa, which excludes countries in North Africa (where demographics and economic developments tend to be different from the rest of Africa). Data are available from 1960 onwards. We combine this, obviously, with Sub-Sahara Africa's demographic dividend, which differs slightly from that of Africa as a whole as given in Figure 10.15.

In China there is a mild reverse dividend in the 1960s and first part of the 1970s. As panel *a* of Figure 10.16 shows, relative income in China slightly declines (with considerable variations related to the *Great Leap Forward* and *Cultural Revolution* policies) from 5.2% of the world average in 1960 to 4.5% in 1976 (the year Mao Zedong dies). From then on, China develops an enormous demographic dividend relative to the world as a whole, with an associated sharp rise in relative income levels, from 4.5% of the world average in 1976 to 63.4% in 2015. Panel *b* of Figure 10.16 shows that Sub-Sahara Africa has a large and growing reverse demographic dividend relative to the world as a whole for the entire period, which leads to a decline of relative income from 29.1% of the world average in 1960 to 16.2% in 2015. The implication of this story is thus that the demographic dividend contributed considerably to the rapid Chinese economic development in the period 1978–2015, like Africa's reverse dividend can explain part of its relative decline.

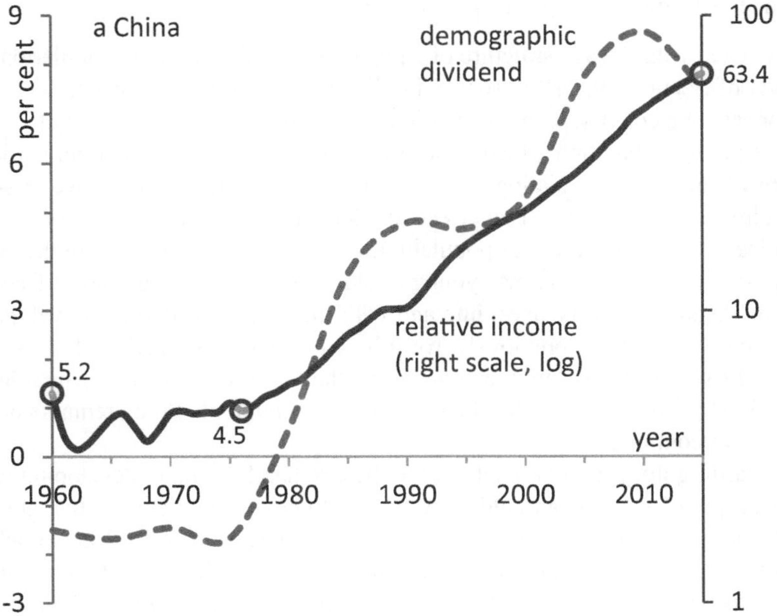

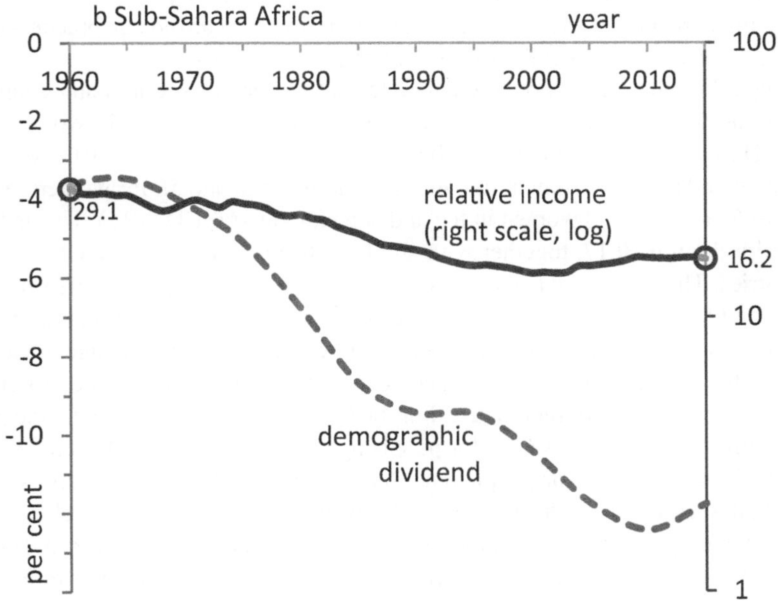

Figure 10.16 Demographic dividend for China and Sub-Sahara Africa, 1960–2015

Source: Based on data from UN Population Division, World Population Prospects: The 2015 Revision and World Development Indicators online; demographic dividend is a country's share of 15–64 year old population in percent minus the world's share of 15–64 year old population, five-year observations; relative income is income per capita (GDP in constant 2010 USD) relative to the world average income per capita in percentage points.

10.8 Problem two: ageing population

Associated with the age structure of a population as shown in the population pyramids of Section 10.7 is a broader implication regarding the economic growth prospects of a country. If the population of a country is rapidly growing the share of the young population which is not yet economically active is large, while the share of the older population which is no longer economically active is small. We already saw that these two effects do not cancel out for the share of the economically active working age population, which actually varies during the demographic transition. The terms 'young', 'old', and 'working age' are, of course, debatable and may vary over time and with the level of economic development of a country. As noted previously, we follow the standard practice of classifying the 0–14 year-old population as young and the 65+ bracket as old, which leaves the 15–64 year-old bracket for the working age population. Some remarks on this before we continue.

Regarding the young population. On the one hand, in many developing countries people of 15 years and older are (forced to be) economically active at work, at the farm, or otherwise because they no longer (can afford to) go to school. Likewise, in many (economically) advanced countries the mandatory minimum schooling age is up to 18 years old, while most people continue their studies into their 20s. On the other hand, many people in the 15–19 year-old age bracket continue to go to school, also (and increasingly so) in developing countries. Similarly, many people in advanced countries in the 15–24 year-old age brackets go to school *and* are economically active through part-time jobs.

Regarding the older population. The formal retirement age in many countries is around 65 years old for men and (on average) a few years less for women. The OECD average retirement age for basic or minimum pensions in 2014 was 64.7 for men and 63.5 for women, ranging from 60 for men and 58 for women in Turkey to 67 for men and women in Iceland and Norway (OECD 2015). This is illustrated in Figure 10.17, together with similar information for selected developing countries. The retirement age is the same for men and women in China (60), India (58), and Indonesia (55). It is higher for men than for women in Brazil (65 vs 60) and Russia (60 vs 55). Many countries are increasing the retirement age in view of longer life expectancies. Whether people actually stop working at the retirement age is, of course, a different matter. For the OECD countries as a whole, the average employment rate was 67% for people aged 55–59, falling to 44% for people aged 60–64, and 20% for people aged 65–69, see OECD (2015). There is again substantial variation, with employment levels in these three categories close to the OECD averages for Canada, much higher in Japan, and much lower in Turkey. Many poor developing countries have no effective pension scheme or retirement age, so people stop formal employment if they are no longer physically able to do so or no longer in demand by employers. They may then still be economically active in the informal sector, growing food close to home, taking care of grandchildren, and so on.

The previous discussion shows that the age borderlines of 15 and 65 to determine dependency ratios of young vs working age population or old vs working

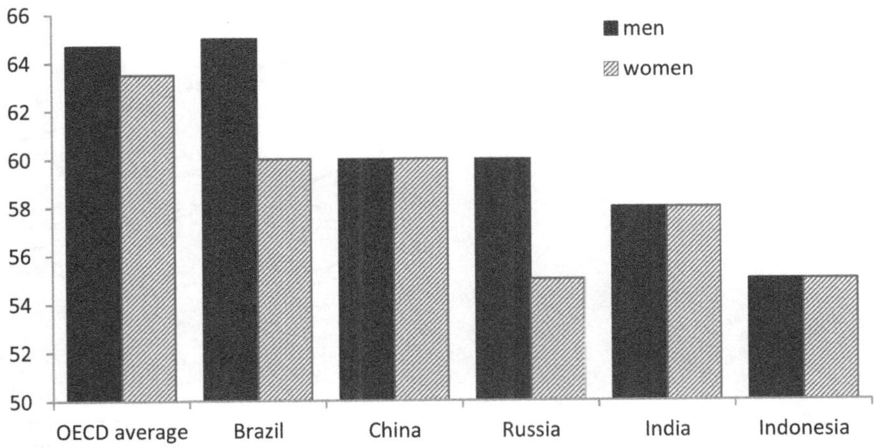

Figure 10.17 Retirement ages for basic and minimum pensions, 2014

Source: Based on data from OECD (2015).

Note: Vertical scale does not start at zero.

age population or total dependents (young + old) vs working age population are vague and to some extent arbitrary. It is clear, however, that in general younger people are not yet economically active and are dependent on others for food, clothing, care, and shelter. Similarly, older people tend to become no longer economically active and become more dependent on others (although not necessarily financially) for food, clothing, care, and shelter. We can, of course, alter the borderline ages of 15 and 65, but this does not change the main message analysed later.

Figure 10.18 illustrates the evolution of the share of the young population (panel *a*) and the old population (panel *b*) from 1950 to 2050 for the world as a whole and a selection of regions and countries. To avoid cluttering the diagram, we grouped together Europe and the Offshoots (with a rather similar age structure from 1975 onwards), as well as Latin America and Other Asia (with a rather similar age structure from 1985 onwards).[16] For the world as a whole, the share of the young population peaked at 38% in 1965, declined to 26% in 2015, and will continue to decline below 22% by 2050. The opposite holds for the share of the old population, which reached a minimum of 5% in 1960, increased to 8% in 2015, and will continue to rise above 14% by 2050.

For the main regions and countries, the developments are (on average) rather similar to the world trends in Latin America, India, and Other Asia. The share of the *young* population is *lower* than the world average and the share of the *old* population is *higher* than the world average throughout the entire period for Europe and the Offshoots. These countries thus have a relatively old population. The reverse holds for Africa, which has a higher young population and a smaller old population. The developments are most dramatic in China, where the share

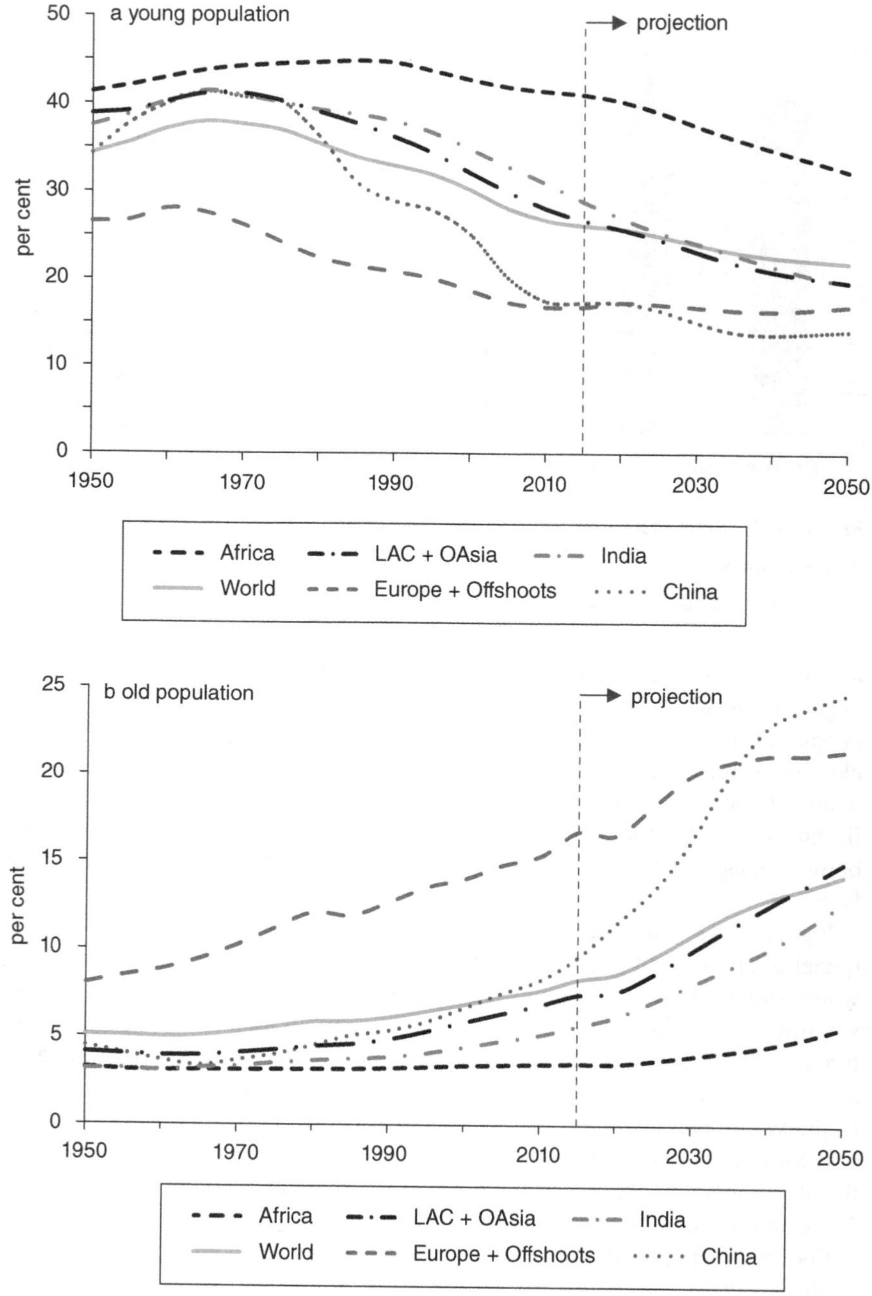

Figure 10.18 Young (0–14) and old (65+) population; percent of total, 1950–2050

Source: Based on data from UN Population Division, World Population Prospects: The 2015 Revision; projections from 2015 onwards based on medium variant; Offshoots are: US, Canada, Australia, and New Zealand; LAC+OAsia = Latin America and Caribbean plus Other Asia.

of the young population is initially higher than the world average, reaches a peak above 41% in 1965, declines below the world average in the 1980s, reaches 17% in 2015, reaches a minimum below 14% around 2040, and then slowly starts to rise again. Almost the opposite holds for the share of the old population in China, which is initially below the world average, reaches a minimum close to 3% around 1965, rises above the world average in the early 2000s, is almost 10% in 2015, and approaches 25% by 2050. The share of the young population in China even declines below that of Europe and the Offshoots in the 2020s, while the share of the old population in China even rises above that of Europe and the Offshoots at the end of the 2030s. In the years ahead (2015–2050), China thus has by far the most rapidly ageing population.

Figure 10.19 shows the consequences for the share of working age population and is an extended version of Figure 10.15, as it includes more regions/countries and predictions for the period 2015–2050. We see that there is a small reverse dividend for Latin America, India, and Other Asia for the period 1950–2015, while there will be a small dividend for the period 2015–2050, particularly for India. The opposite holds for Europe and the Offshoots, where there was a demographic dividend up to 2015 and there will be a reverse dividend from then on. We already discussed Africa in Section 10.7. Note that Africa is expected to continue to have a reverse dividend throughout the period 2015–2050.

We also analysed China already in Section 10.7 for the period 1950–2015. Note that China's recent enormous demographic dividend is predicted to disappear rapidly and will become a reverse dividend at the end of the 2030s. A particularly

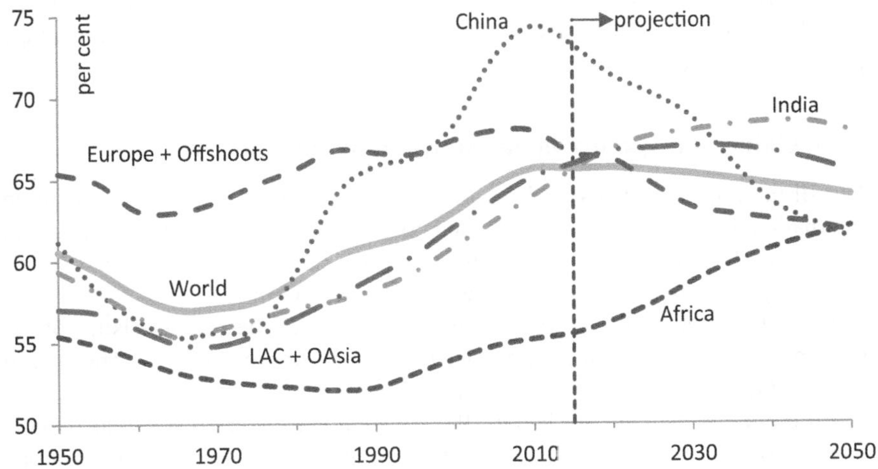

Figure 10.19 Working age (15–65) population; percent of total, 1950–2050

Source: Based on data from UN Population Division, World Population Prospects: The 2015 Revision; projections from 2015 onwards based on medium variant; Offshoots are: US, Canada, Australia, and New Zealand; LAC+OAsia = Latin America and Caribbean plus Other Asia.

Note: Vertical scale does not start at zero.

large ageing problem faces China around 2050, as identified by the arrow pointing to the 60–64 year old male population for the 2050 pyramid in Figure 10.14. This age bracket is clearly large in 2050 as it relates to the 2nd wave; in fact, by this time the male and female population in the 60–64 year old bracket is 9.4% of the total Chinese population. In the next five years (from 2050 to 2055) it will be replaced in the working-age share of the population by the much smaller 10–14 year old age bracket of 2050, which implies an enormous decline in the share of the working age population by almost three percentage points in a period of just five years. A similar drastic reduction in the share of the working age population is related to the 1st wave and will occur at the end of the 2030s (causing the switch from dividend to reverse dividend).

The implications of this analysis regarding the demographic dividend of the main regions and countries for the period 2015–2050 are as follows. First, in view of a switch from dividend to reverse dividend around 2015, it will become increasingly difficult for Europe and the Offshoots to keep up with income per capita developments in the world as a whole. Second, in view of a sharp decline in demographic dividend and return to a reverse dividend at the end of the 2030s, China's high income per capita growth rates can be expected to decline sharply in the 2020s and 2030s, while remaining above the world average. From around 2040 onwards a relative decline of China's income is likely. Third, in view of its continued reverse dividend, it will be hard for Africa to keep up with income per capita growth rates in the rest of the world. In fact, Africa's switch to a demographic dividend region is only expected around 2060. Fourth, in view of its rising demographic dividend, income per capita growth rates in India are likely to be above the world average in the decades to come; India's peak of demographic dividend is around 4 percentage points in the 2040s.

10.9 Chinese inequality in an international perspective

Our discussion of China's ageing problem in Section 10.8 already put it in an international perspective by comparing to developments in other regions and countries. Despite Box 10.2, we did not yet do something similar for China's inequality problem. This section remedies that shortcoming.

We start in Table 10.4 by providing an overview of the characteristics of the Gini index for all 8782 available studies for all countries in WIID 3.4. The overall average Gini is 39.30, varying from a minimum of 12.1 to a maximum of 78.6. The minimum is actually reached in 1982 for an urban China study included in the analysis of Section 10.5.[17] This supports the suggestion that inequality in urban China in the 1970s and early 1980s was very low at the start of the Economic Reform process.

Table 10.4 also provides information regarding the welfare definition, quality level, and equivalence scale for four main categories each in panels *a-c*, respectively. In addition, it provides information in panel *d* on the type of studies we use

Table 10.4 Overview of WIID 3.4 Gini index

	Gini av	*Deviation*	*Share*	*Gini min*	*Gini max*
All (8782 observations)	*39.30*	*0*	*100*	*12.1*	*78.6*
a. Welfare definition					
Consumption	36.91	–6.1	15.1	16.2	74.3
Disposable income	38.74	–1.4	46.3	12.1	69.4
Gross income	39.89	+1.5	21.9	15.5	78.6
Other	42.25	+7.5	16.7	14.6	70.0
b. Quality					
Low	41.32	+5.1	21.6	12.1	78.6
Average	37.23	–5.3	30.8	15.5	65.8
High	39.56	+0.7	45.2	18.5	77.1
Unknown	43.35	+10.3	2.3	19.3	63.7
c. Equivalence scale					
Household adult equivalent	35.66	–9.3	21.8	16.6	72.0
Household per capita	41.96	+6.8	44.2	12.1	78.6
Without adjustment	38.24	–2.7	24.7	15.5	70.0
All other	38.02	–3.3	9.3	14.6	69.0
d. Disposable income and household per capita					
All studies	45.29	+15.2	19.5	12.1	69.4
Area all (country)	45.28	+15.2	11.5	18.0	69.4
Rural	46.32	+17.8	3.0	21.2	67.8
Urban	46.17	+17.5	4.6	12.1	62.8
Area other*	28.08	–28.6	0.4	21.3	32.6

Source: Calculations based on UNU-WIDER (2017a) data; av = average; min = minimum; max = maximum; deviation = percentage deviation from overall average; share = percent of all observations; area other refers to 36 German studies.

in Section 10.5, based on disposable income and household per capita. We will focus attention on the *deviation* column in the table, which provides the percentage deviation of the average Gini score in a particular category from the overall average of 39.30 for all studies combined.

Regarding the welfare definition, we see that studies based on disposable income result in somewhat lower inequality estimates (–1.4%) and studies based on gross income result in somewhat higher inequality estimates (+1.5%). The deviations are more substantial for consumption-based inequality measures (–6.1%) and other welfare definitions (+7.5%).

Regarding the quality level of the studies, we see that high-quality studies tend to have somewhat higher inequality estimates (+0.7%) and low-quality studies substantially higher inequality estimates (+5.1%). Consequently, the average quality studies have substantially lower inequality estimates (–5.3%). Note that the unknown quality studies are a small fraction of the total only (2.3% of all studies), such that its substantial deviation (+10.3%) does not yet lead to clear conclusions. We already noted that there is a clear time dimension for the quality of the studies.

Regarding equivalence scale used, we see that household per capita studies lead to substantially higher inequality estimates (+6.8%) relative to all other types of equivalence scales, particularly relative to household adult equivalent scales which lead to substantially lower inequality estimates (–9.3%).

On the basis of the information provided in panels *a-c* alone, one would expect the average Gini index for the type of studies we analyse for China, which are based on disposable income (–1.4%) and household per capita (+6.8%) to be, on average, about 5% above the overall average. This is not true, as indicated in panel *d* of Table 10.4, and thus a reminder that one has to be careful not to jump to conclusions when different types of characteristics are combined. As indicated in panel *d*, the overall average Gini coefficient for all studies based on disposable income and household per capita is 15.2% higher than the overall average (substantially more, therefore, than the earlier guess of 5%). This is the same at the country level and a bit higher at the rural and urban level (+17.8 and +17.5%, respectively).

What does this mean for our analysis in Section 10.5? The actual overall Gini average for all studies included in the analysis for China in Section 10.5 is equal to 29.23, which is substantially below the average of 45.29 listed in panel *d* of Table 10.4 for similar studies for all countries in the database (deviation is −35%). Similar remarks hold for the *area all* studies, the *rural* studies, and the *urban* studies in panel *d*, with deviations for China relative to those benchmarks of −7, −31, and −49%. This simply indicates that for the period as a whole, Chinese inequality is lower than it is in most other parts of the world.

Our analysis for China in Section 10.5 focuses on the development over time of Chinese inequality in the period 1978–2015. To provide a proper international perspective of these developments, we therefore have to compare Chinese developments over time with appropriate indicators for other countries. We do this in two steps, as illustrated in Figure 10.20.

In step 1 (panel *a* of the figure) we calculate a five-year moving average Gini index for each year for all observations available in the WIID 3.4 database. The left-hand-side of the graph depicts the Gini level in year x based on the average for year $x - 4$ up to year x (the last observation in year 2015 is thus based on observations for the period 2011–2015), while the right-hand-scale of the graph indicates the number of observations on which a particular average Gini value is based. As panel *a* illustrates, the number of available observations is low initially and rises rapidly in the second half of the 1980s, while the average Gini coefficient fluctuates around 39.3; more specifically, the average Gini is below 38.99 in the period 1975–1994, as indicated by the arrows in panel *a*, and above this value for all earlier and later periods.[18] Since most *average* quality studies are in the period 1975–1994 (as illustrated various times earlier), this explains the negative deviation for studies of average quality and the positive deviations for studies of low and high quality in panel *b* of Table 10.4. Our discussion previously, however, indicates that we have to be careful not to jump to conclusions when we are

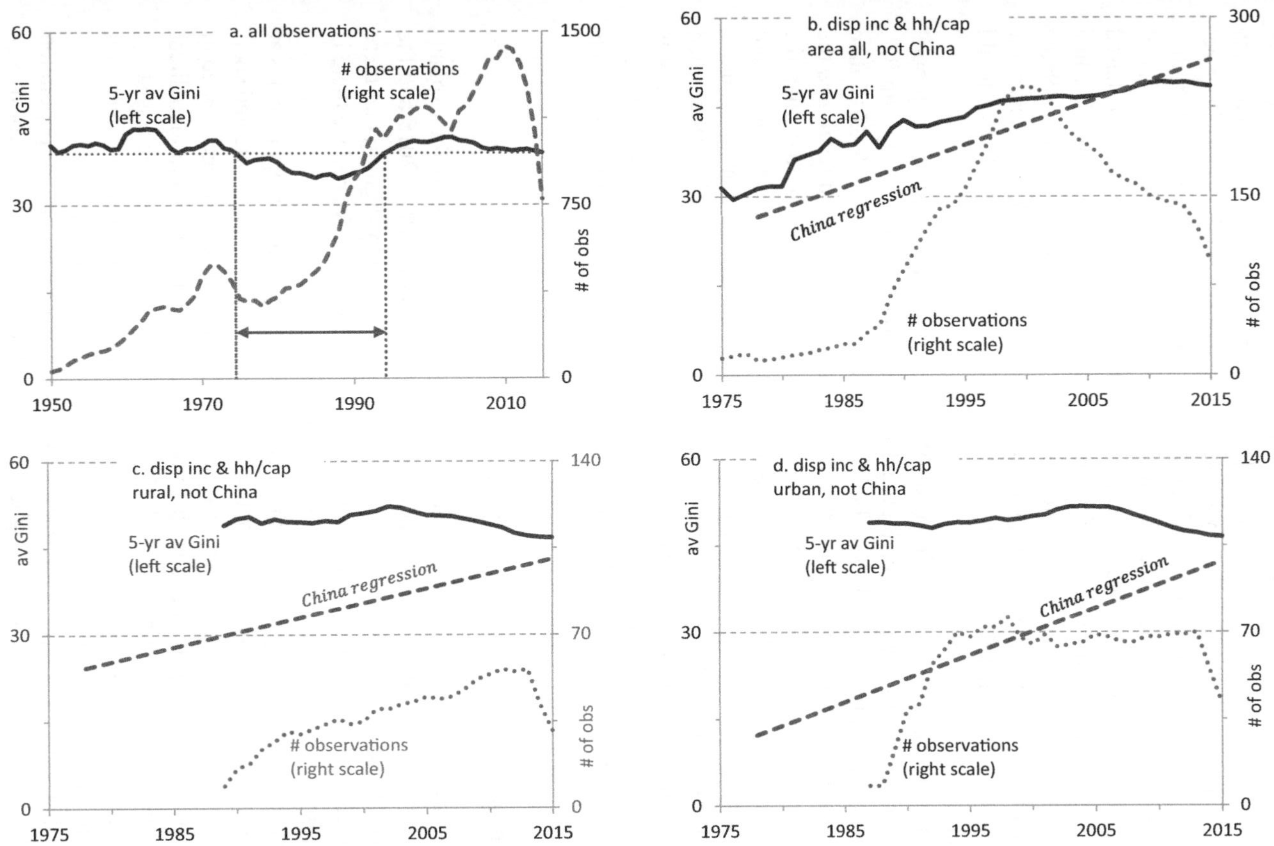

Figure 10.20 The Gini index over time in the WIID 3.4 database, 1950–2015

Source: Based on UNU-WIDER (2017a) data; yr = year; av = average; disp = disposable; hh/cap = household per capita; obs = observations; 5-yr av for year x refers to the period from $x - 4$ to x; see main text for details.

combining different types of studies. As such, the average Gini illustrated in panel *a* of Figure 10.20 cannot be used as a basis for an international comparison for our study for China.

In step 2 (panels *b-d* of the figure), we provide an international benchmark for Chinese inequality by calculating the five-year moving average Gini index (similar as for panel *a*) for all disposable income studies based on household per capita for all countries in the world, excluding China; namely for all area studies in panel *b*, for rural studies in panel *c*, and for urban studies in panel *d*. Each panel also shows the number of observations on which an average Gini value is based (right-hand-scale) and, for ease of reference, the relevant China regression line from our analysis in Section 10.5. Note that the number of observations available to calculate an average benchmark Gini index is low before 1990, particularly for rural studies.[19] Conclusions relative to the early period, say, 1975–1985, should be made with some caution.

When we compare the development of Chinese inequality with the appropriate benchmark in panels *b-d* of Figure 10.20, the conclusion is always similar: Chinese inequality is initially low but rises faster in the period 1978–2015 than the relevant international benchmark at the country level, the rural level, *and* the urban level. At the country level, Chinese inequality is higher in 2015 than the international benchmark. This is not yet the case at the rural and urban level, but this switch is imminent if current trends continue. Also note that at the country level the benchmark Gini index is rising over time (particularly before 1990 when only a limited number of observations are available), but Chinese inequality is rising *faster* over time in this period. This is not the case for the rural and urban benchmark Gini indices, which both are not rising over time, in contrast to their relevant Chinese equivalents.

10.10 Evaluation and conclusions

What have we learned in the previous analysis on the two stories for explaining China's successful economic development in the period 1978–2015 and the related two main problems? We could vary on an old quote by arguing that there are three sides to this story: story one, story two, and the truth. We believe there is value in both stories and that they mutually reinforce each other.

The formidable change in economic policy initiated by Deng Xiaoping that is at the heart of story one, and the move towards a more open, outward-oriented society that benefits from the interactions and connections with knowledge created in other parts of the world, embedded in traded goods and services and foreign direct investments into the country, is undoubtedly a big part of China's success story. In fact, it is hard to imagine China could have been even remotely as successful without such a policy change of economic liberalization and openness.

Similarly, the dramatic demographic events that created a unique population profile for China and by far the highest demographic dividend in the world, particularly in the period 1990–2025, must have contributed to an important extent to China's economic success story. In 2010, at the peak of the demographic dividend,

China's share of the working age population is more than 74% of the total population, which is about 9 percentage points above the world average and more than 19 percentage points above Africa's share of working age population. Again, it is hard to imagine that China could have been even remotely as successful without this enormous demographic dividend.

When evaluating the merits of the two stories, it seems clear that they partially caused each other and mutually reinforced each other. An important cause of China's unique population profile are the dramatic consequences of Mao's Great Leap Forward policies (1958–1962), which were instrumental in creating China's large demographic dividend some 30 years later and beyond (in the period 1990–2025). The rapid rise in China's share of working age population starts around 1975, but a demographic dividend relative to the rest of the world is only created around 1980 and initially still small; it only reaches a more substantial level of around 5 percentage points around 1990.

In this perspective, it is hard to contribute most of China's successful development in the period 1978–1990, when China's income per capita level doubles from 5.06% of the world average to 10.21%, to demographic forces. Instead, we think credit in this period should be duly given to Deng Xiaping's Economic Reform process and the opening up of the economy to trade and investment flows. Fortunately for China, just when Deng Xiaoping's 1978 kickstart for Chinese economic development might have started to slow down, around 1990, the demographic dividend (story two) kicks in and takes over in two waves. The first wave is around 5 percentage points in the period 1990–2000, while the second wave is more than 7 percentage points in the period 2000–2015. As noted, the peak of 9 percentage points is around 2010, perfectly timed to mitigate the adverse consequences of the Great Recession. Note that the continuation of China's successful economic development of course also requires continued adjustment of its economic policies, in line with our arguments in Sections 10.2 and 10.4. These adjustments become easier as a result of the demographic dividend. In this sense, the two stories reinforce each other.

We also think that, associated with the two stories, there is value in the two main problems we analyse. At the start of the Economic Reform process (1978), Chinese disposable income inequality (household per capita) is low in an international perspective; this holds for the country as a whole, for rural inequality, and (in particular) for urban inequality. Since then, Chinese income inequality has been rising rapidly at the rural level, very rapidly at the country level, and extremely rapidly at the urban level. Consequently, urban inequality is now about the same as rural inequality, while China's overall inequality is now higher than the average for all other countries in the world. Although we argue that rising inequality is quite common during a period of rapid economic development, inequality has now been rising for almost four decades, which creates envy and conflict within society and undermines support for continued, much needed new economic policy adjustments.

There is, essentially, no escape from China's ageing population problem, but there is, fortunately, some time left before it really kicks in. The demographic dividend, to which China has become accustomed and which has eased the adjustment of economic policies, will decline in the years to come and eventually switch to a reverse dividend at the end of the 2030s. The fact that the demographic dividend remains high up to 2025 and remains positive until the end of the 2030s means that China's economy can continue to grow more rapidly than the rest of the world for another two decades or so, although the opportunities are smaller in the 2030s when the demographic dividend starts to decline rapidly as the first population wave caused by the Great Leap Forward policies start to retire. From 2040 onwards, China is faced with a reverse dividend, which will make it harder to keep up with economic developments in the rest of the world. This will be particularly challenging after 2050 when the reverse dividend exacerbates rapidly as the second population wave of the Great Leap Forward policies also start to retire.

We argued earlier that the two stories of China's successful economic development process interact and mutually reinforce each other. In a similar vein, we would like to point out that the two main problems identified and analysed previously might exacerbate each other in their impact on the Chinese economy in a negative spiral. Since 1990 China's powerful demographic dividend has made it easier to continue the economic reform process that is required to keep China globally competitive as the character of its economy changes over time, as outlined in Section 10.2. China continues to benefit strongly from this demographic dividend up to around 2025 and weakly thereafter in the 2030s. This means China should grab the opportunity for the next 10–15 years to address the inequality problem and the ageing population problem, as it will become much harder to do so from 2030 onwards. The Chinese government is aware of both problems and argues that it is trying to reverse the process of rising inequality. According

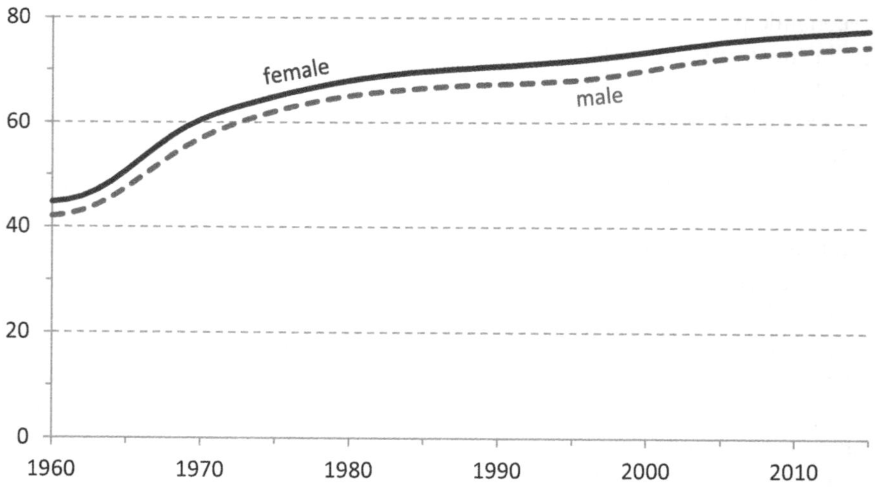

Figure 10.21 Life expectancy at birth; China (years)

Source: Based on World Bank (2017) data.

to some studies they are succeeding, see Cai and Du (2011), but our analysis in Section 10.5 shows that it is too early to reach that conclusion.

There is no effective way for the Chinese government to address the ageing population problem itself. The government can, however, alleviate the economic consequences of this problem, particularly if we take the continued rise in life expectancy at birth into consideration. In 2015 average life expectancy at birth for Chinese men was 74.5 years and for women 77.5 years. This is a substantial increase from the respective numbers in 1960, namely 42.0 years for men and 44.8 years for women. The average increase in life expectancy at birth in the period 1960–2015 was therefore an astounding 0.6 years per year. As Figure 10.21 shows, however, that number is deceptive as most of the increase was in the period 1962–1977 when the country was recovering from the consequences of the Great Leap Forward. The average rise in life expectancy at birth in the most recent three decades is about 0.26 years per year (still an addition of more than three months per year). In any case, as life expectancy has been rising for decades and is likely to continue to do so, an important way for the Chinese government to alleviate the population ageing problem is to start to increase the pension age in steps to keep up with rising life expectancy,[20] as well as stimulating older people to continue to work until they reach retirement.

Notes

1 Utrecht University School of Economics, Adam Smith Hall 2.10, Kriekenpitplein 21–22, 3584 EC, Utrecht, The Netherlands. Telephone: *31 30 253 7109. Email: j.g.m.vanmarrewijk@uu.nl.
2 This chapter is partially based on van Marrewijk (2017, Ch. 17), Rougoor and van Marrewijk (2015), and van Marrewijk et al. (forthcoming, Chapters 10 and 12).
3 The UN Population Division analyses eight main variants which differ in assumed fertility, death, and migration. The medium variant represents its best guesstimate of what is going to happen. Uncertainty is high after 2050.
4 It is, unfortunately, not possible to use the superior PPP income data as it is not available in 1960–1990.
5 We could have chosen the share of imports (as a percent of GDP) or the share of total trade (based on imports and exports as a percent of GDP) as alternative measures of openness. The graph looks very similar to Figure 10-6.
6 Since various and changing ‘equivalence scales’ are used, UNU-WIDER prefers to focus on income per capita estimates, also because they are the most widely available.
7 If you take the regression results (too) seriously, then urban inequality surpasses rural inequality in July 2017.
8 In the new millennium, using NBS data, urban average income is about three times higher than rural average income. The UNU-WIDER data provide no solid basis for analyzing the change in urban vs rural average (or median) income over time, since only few studies provide data (the earliest is 1995) and different sources provide quite different results for the same year.
9 Sometimes five stages are identified, but the fifth stage is then uncertain, so it is excluded here.
10 Dividing the numbers by 10 therefore gives percentage growth rates.
11 Note that the graphs are based on five-year averages, which mitigates the enormous peak in the death rate of 1960.

12 The UN Population Division does not provide a detailed breakdown for the 80+ population before 1990, which is the reason to choose 1990 as the first year.
13 Detailed examples of population pyramids for all countries in the world for all years from 1950 up to 2100 are available at www.populationpyramid.net.
14 Some demographic literature prefers to discuss dependency ratios, a monotone transformation defined as the share of (young, old, or total) dependents divided by the share of working age population. We prefer to focus on the more direct measure of the share of the working age population, see also Rougoor and van Marrewijk (2015).
15 The term demographic deficit cannot be used as it seems to have different meanings for different researchers.
16 Similarity in age structure in this context refers to the share of working age population.
17 The maximum is reached for Mali as a whole in 1994 in a study based on gross income.
18 The value 38.99 is chosen, rather than 39.00, because the average Gini for 2015 is 38.997.
19 An average Gini based on a very low number of observations is not reliable, so we imposed a minimum of eight observations in order to be included in the average Gini calculation; this is relevant for panels *c* and *d* only.
20 We think the retirement age should keep up with life expectancy in a relative sense and not (as in the Netherlands) in an absolute sense. If, for example, the current retirement age is 65 and current life expectancy is 80, then if life expectancy rises to 85 the retirement age should rise to $65 \times (85/80) = 69$, and not to 70.

References

Atkinson, A. B., and F. Bourguignon (2000), "Introduction: Income Distribution and Economics," in: A. B. Atkinson and F. Bourguignon (eds.), *Handbook of Income Distribution*, Vol. 1, Amsterdam: Elsevier.

Bloom, D. E., D. Canning, and J. Sevilla (2003), *The Demographic Dividend: A New Perspective on the Economic Consequences of Population Change*, Santa Monica: Rand.

Cai, F., and Y. Du (2011), "Wage Increases, Wage Convergence, and the Lewis Turning Point in China," *China Economic Review* 22: 601–610.

C. van Marrewijk (2017), *International Trade*, Oxford: Oxford University Press.

C. van Marrewijk (2018), *International Money: Interest, Exchange Rates, and Policy*, mimeo: Utrecht University.

C. van Marrewijk, S. Brakman, and J. Swart (forthcoming), *The Economics of Developing and Emerging Markets* (working title), Cambridge: Cambridge University Press.

Deaton, A., and S. Zaidi (2002), "Guidelines for Constructing Consumption Aggregates for Welfare Analysis," LSMS Working Paper No.135. Washington, DC: World Bank.

Maddison, A. (2001), *The World Economy: A Millenial Perspective*, Paris: OECD Publishing.

OECD (2015), *Pensions at a Glance 2015: OECD and G20 Indicators*, Paris: OECD Publishing.

Rougoor, W., and C. van Marrewijk (2015), "Demography, Growth, and Global Income Inequality," *World Development* 74: 220–232.

Sen, A. (1974), "International Bases of Alternative Welfare Approaches: Aggregation and Income Distribution," *Journal of Public Economics* 3: 387–403.

United Nations Population Division (1999), *The World at Six Billion*, New York: United Nations, Available at: see www.un.org/esa/population/publications/sixbillion/sixbillion.htm.

United Nations Population Division (2015), *World Population Prospects: The 2015 Revision*, New York: United Nations, Available at; see https://esa.un.org/unpd/wpp/.

UNU-WIDER (2017a), *World Income Inequality Database* (WIID 3.4), January 2017, Helsinki, Finland: UNU-WIDER.

UNU-WIDER (2017b), *World Income Inequality Database (WIID) Version 3.4 User Guide and Data Sources*, January 2017, Helsinki, Finland: UNU-WIDER.

World Bank (2009), *World Development Report 2009: Reshaping Economic Geography*, Washington, DC: World Bank.

World Economic Forum (2015), *The Global Competitiveness Report 2015–2016*, Geneva: World Economic Forum.

World Bank (2017), *World Development Indicators online*, selected variables downloaded in the period April-July 2017 from www.worldbank.org.

11 Sustainability in China

Julia Swart[1]

11.1 Introduction

The previous chapter analyzed sustainability of China's future by looking at economic policy, openness, and the demographic transition. In this chapter we focus on China's dependence on natural resources and on environmental pollution to better understand the implications of economic growth in a long-term perspective. Pollution has a negative impact on human health and the environment. Water pollution, for example, is associated with stomach illness, liver illness, and neurological problems. Land contamination has been linked to cancer and birth defects. Air pollution (e.g. ambient particulate matter) is the fifth risk factor for total deaths from all causes for all ages and sexes worldwide (Health Effects Institute 2017a).

Figure 11.1 shows that death rates attributable to ambient particulate matter is significantly higher in China than in Europe and the Americas, although declining at a faster rate. In absolute terms, more than one million people in China died in 2015 because of exposure to ambient particulate matter. In this chapter we will focus on the effects of pollution on the quality of life in China through its direct impact on human health. Overall, however, the total effect of pollution is much larger once we take into account all indirect effects through climate change (such as more frequent episodes of flooding and drought).

This chapter also exploits China's current dependence on natural resources. Chapters 2 and 3 showed the dramatic changes in the Chinese economy since the Economic Reform processes started in 1978. In this chapter we will see that while the beginning of these changes was not accompanied by a significant increase in the use of natural resources, this picture altered drastically in the new millennium. For many natural resources the increase in use occurred at an increasing rate. This is the case for the main energy sources (coal and oil), which together with the other energy sources translates in an approximately 150% increase in energy use per capita from the year 2000 to 2014. Figure 11.2 shows a sharp correlation between China's income per capita and energy use in the period 1970–2014.

We will link the sustainability challenges to economic growth in China and the high growth rates at the country level but must realize that China is an exceptional country from a size perspective. China is the home of over 1.4 billion people, whose income (on average) is rapidly increasing. The number of poor people, for example, decreased from 755.8 million in 1990 to 25.1 million in 2013 (World

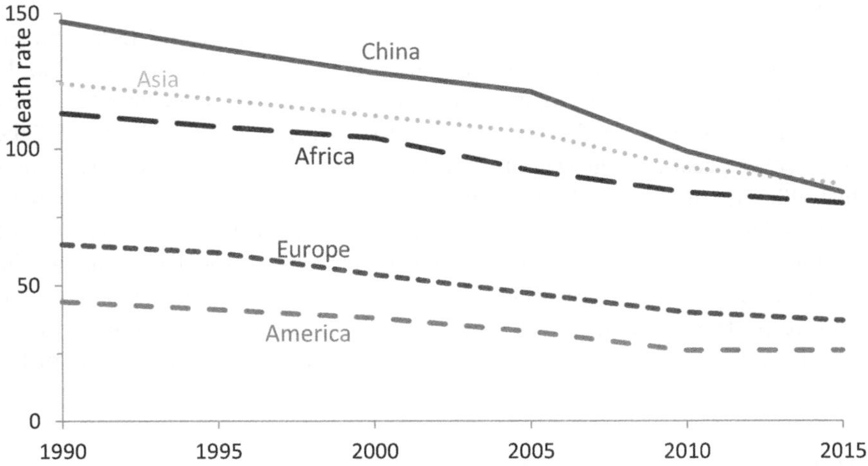

Figure 11.1 Death rate attributable to fine ambient particulate matter pollution

Source: Created using data from the Health Effects Institute (2017b); death rate per 100,000 people; fine ambient particulate matter. $PM_{2.5}$

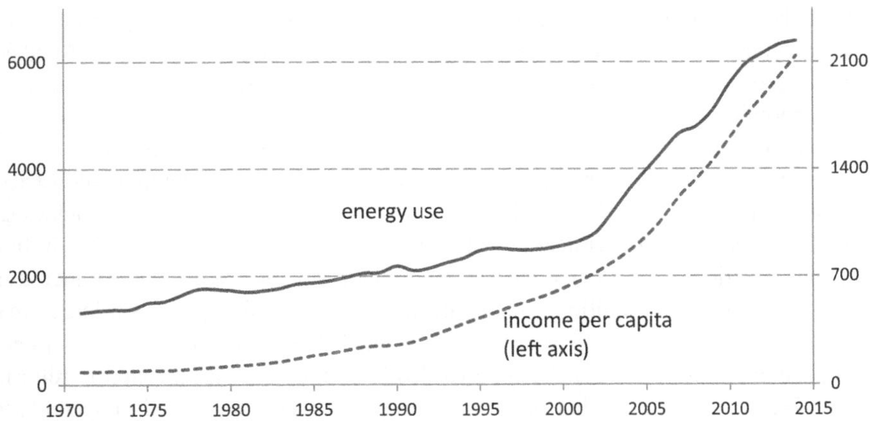

Figure 11.2 China; income per capita and energy use, 1971–2014

Source: Created using data from the World Development Indicators online; income in GDP per capita in constant 2010 USD; energy use in kg of oil equivalent per capita.

Bank 2017). More affluence and improvements in the standard of living have as a side-effect more pressure on the environment, unless, enough instruments are created to circumvent this down side of wealth. Up until today, the Chinese story is one in which population size and higher income levels have transformed the economy in terms of consumption of natural resources and energy. Besides the peculiarity of a big population and rising income, China is also an increasingly main player in the international economy. Therefore, pollution generated, and natural resources used, in China are part of a complex international chain of trade and investment relations.

This chapter makes extensive use of World Bank data (World Development Indicators 2017) and United Nations (2017) data. We focus on recent (mainly since 1990) historical development of main environmental indicators for China as a whole. We start in Section 11.2 by providing an overall indication of the link between economic growth in China and the environment. Section 11.3 shows that although in absolute terms China is wealthy in terms of natural resources, its population size and industrialization process implied increasing dependence on foreign supply of main natural resources. Sections 11.4 and 11.5 analyse the recent developments and issues in terms of water availability and forest conservation, respectively. The next two sections focus on two types of pollution: waste and air pollution. Finally, Section 11.8 concludes with a brief evaluation of the sustainability challenges and opportunities for a greener future for China.

11.2 Economic growth and the environment

Since the economic reform process started in 1978, China has experienced sustained economic growth which has largely come hand-in-hand with social development. As a reflection of this progress, China is experiencing an increase in the middle-class population. Simultaneously, as analysed in the previous chapter, the social transformations in China have also been linked to high inequality as the urban working force increased their standards of living faster than the rural work force. Another side of economic prosperity has been a deepening of the environmental challenges.

Economic growth is associated with an endless list of environmental problems in China. The industrialization process in China is not a contemporary phenomenon. It can be traced back to the beginning of the 20th century. One of the main industries behind Chinese economic growth in the 1940s was the heavy industry (including steel, machinery, and chemical industries), which are highly polluting. This initial industrialization process in China was thus undoubtedly associated with an increase in (air) pollution. In addition, to support the industrialization process a large area of forests was devastated during the 1950s and 1960s. Nonetheless, environmental problems only started to become evidently serious after the economic reform of 1978, even though at that time, these problems were considered of secondary importance. We analyse the relationship between economic development and environmental degradation in China, focusing on the period from 1978 until today.

The aforementioned link between economic development and environmental degradation is in line with the Environmental Kuznets Hypothesis, which states that at low levels of economic development environmental degradation is low because production activities are limited. However, as economic development rises, environmental problems worsen. This positive relationship between economic development and environmental degradation eventually reaches a maximum, such that at a high enough income level, environmental problems start to receive more priority and become less severe. Thus, according to the Environmental Kuznets Hypothesis, wealthier countries will dedicate more resources to alleviate environmental problems.

Table 11.1 Income per capita, population, and environmental indicators, 2014–2016

Country	*Income per capita*		*Population size*		*Income per unit of energy*		*Alternative & nuclear energy*		CO_2 *emission per capita*		$PM_{2.5}$ *air pollution*	
	value	*rank*	*value*	*rank*	*value*	*rank*	*value*	*rank*	*value*	*rank*	*value*	*rank*
Norway	89,818	1	5.2	116	9.79	45	41.3	6	9.27	13	9.1	113
Switzerland	75,726	2	8.4	98	17.03	6	43.6	5	4.31	46	12.9	105
Denmark	60,268	3	5.7	111	14.26	9	7.5	38	5.94	31	11.0	110
Sweden	56,319	4	9.9	88	8.45	53	48.5	4	4.48	44	6.2	117
Australia	55,671	5	24.1	53	7.85	61	2.6	63	15.40	4	5.9	118
Singapore	52,601	6	5.6	113	16.09	7	0.0	94	10.31	10	18.7	88
USA	52,195	7	323.1	3	7.39	69	12.1	27	16.49	3	8.4	114
Japan	47,608	11	127.0	11	10.41	38	2.8	59	9.54	12	13.3	104
Germany	45,552	12	82.7	16	10.89	32	11.7	29	8.89	17	14.0	100
Korea	25,459	22	51.2	27	6.22	76	15.5	22	11.57	9	28.7	51
Turkey	14,071	31	79.5	18	14.03	10	7.1	40	4.49	43	36.4	36
Russia	11,099	33	144.3	9	4.95	85	8.8	33	11.86	8	16.6	93
Malaysia	11,028	34	31.2	45	7.86	60	1.3	72	8.03	21	15.6	96
Brazil	10,826	32	207.7	5	10.63	35	12.5	26	2.59	57	11.4	109
Mexico	9,707	37	127.5	10	10.41	39	5.2	47	3.87	50	20.2	79
Colombia	7,526	42	48.7	28	17.30	4	12.6	25	1.76	65	18.0	89
S. Africa	7,504	41	55.9	24	4.75	88	2.7	61	9.05	16	29.6	49
China	*6,894*	*47*	*1,378.7*	*1*	*5.40*	*83*	*5.4*	*45*	*7.54*	*23*	*58.4*	*12*
Thailand	5,901	53	68.9	20	7.42	68	0.5	83	4.62	41	26.4	59
Indonesia	3,974	60	261.1	4	11.17	29	8.2	34	1.82	64	15.4	97
Philippines	2,753	72	103.3	12	13.87	11	20.3	15	1.06	74	23.5	65
Egypt	2,724	71	95.7	14	11.75	23	1.8	69	2.20	59	104.7	2
Nigeria	2,458	73	186.0	7	7.03	71	0.3	84	0.55	87	38.0	32
India	1,861	80	1,324.2	2	8.36	55	3.0	56	1.73	67	74.3	6
Vietnam	1,770	82	92.7	15	7.67	66	7.5	37	1.84	63	28.3	52
Pakistan	1,182	89	193.2	6	9.14	50	4.5	52	0.90	76	65.0	8
Bangladesh	1,030	94	163.0	8	13.17	14	0.2	87	0.46	90	89.4	3
Tanzania	867	98	55.6	25	4.74	89	0.9	77	0.22	102	23.3	66
Ethiopia	511	111	102.4	13	2.68	97	1.7	70	0.12	109	35.7	38
D.R.Congo	387	116	78.7	19	1.78	100	2.6	62	0.06	114	46.3	21
# countries		118		124		100		99		117		118

Notes: Income per capita: GDP, constant 2010 USD in 2016; population in millions in 2016; income per unit of energy (GDP in constant 2011 PPP USD per kg of oil equivalent) in 2013; alternative & nuclear energy (% of total energy use) in 2014; $\boldsymbol{CO_2}$ emissions (metric tons per capita) in 2014; $\boldsymbol{PM_{2.5}}$ air pollution, mean annual exposure (micrograms per cubic meter) in 2015; data included for countries with more than 5 million inhabitants in 2016; World Development Indicators (2017), The World Bank.

Table 11.1 compares China with a selection of other countries with respect to income per capita, population, and four environmental indicators. Despite the impressive economic growth process of the last 40 years, the standard of living in China (as measured by income per capita) is still far below those of advanced countries (such as Norway, the US, and Japan) and some emerging countries (such as Russia, Brazil, and South Africa). Based on the Environmental Kuznets Curve, China should thus be a relatively high polluting country. In line with that, Table 11.1 shows that China has a relatively low energy efficiency, despite the sharp decrease of 66% of energy consumption per unit of GDP in the period from 1980 to 2008 (Wei and Liao 2016). Similarly, the last three columns of Table 11.1 show that emissions are high in China, while the country relies modestly on alternative and nuclear energy, which could alleviate these high levels of emissions. The combination of high emissions and low reliance on renewable energy sources is largely a result of the extensive consumption of coal, which raised at an astonishing rate from 2002 onwards. In 2002 consumption of total primary coal was equivalent to approximately 1693 million short ton, whereas in 2015 this figure had raised to 4376 million short tons, a 158% increase.[2] The share of coal in total energy sources in China represented approximately 67% in the year 2009.

Despite the increase in energy use in China (particularly oil and coal) and the associated CO_2 emissions (the *scale effect*), recent studies focusing on China and air pollution have found evidence for an Environmental Kuznets Curve (Auffhammer and Carson 2008; Jalil and Mahmud 2009; Jalil and Feridun 2011; Jayanthakumaran et al. 2012). These results are, however, not unanimous. Other literature (Yue et al. 2007, or Hu and Huang 2008) do not find evidence for an inverted-U-relationship for China. There are many reasons for this difference (including methodology and time-frame), but a main issue when analysing the Environmental Kuznets curve is to consider the different channels through which economic development affects the environment. The Environmental Kuznets Curve hypothesis bases its prediction on two different stages of development (low development with increasing pollution; high development with decreasing pollution), where the possible decreasing environmental degradation can be a result of different aspects, such as improvements in abatement technologies, technological progress, structural changes, education, and whether a pollutant has local or regional impact. Underlying these factors, political decisions, rules, and regulations (when well enforced), can facilitate structural changes and technological improvements which are more conducive to a greener economy. Finally, as discussed in Chapter 8, openness to trade also has an impact on the environment, which can be either positive or negative. To fully access this impact, one needs to decompose the impact of trade on three components: the scale effect; the composition effect; and the technique effect. Whereas clearly, the scale effect impacts the environment negatively, this can be outweighed by the composition effect (specialization in cleaner goods) and the technique effect (adoption of cleaner technologies). The empirical results are mixed, and further research needs to be carried out to evaluate the overall impact that trade has on the environment in China (see Chapter 8).

Chapter 7 analysed the development of the Chinese institutions in a long-term perspective. Many institutional changes have taken place in China in the last 35 years, which have facilitated a sustained period of high growth rates. Nonetheless, as economic development took place environmental degradation became more prominent, raising the urgency of political measures to protect the environment. We argue in Section 11.8 that environmental concern is a recent issue in the Chinese political agenda. Therefore, decoupling of environmental degradation (and natural resource use) and economic growth will take time before it is convincingly observed in the data. The next sections will use recent data to analyse the trends in environmental indicators. Overall, we find that the period of rapid economic growth in China has been at the cost of the environment, leading to a political challenge to revert this trend.

Section 11.3 analyses the impact of Chinese economic growth on the demand for natural resources. We will see that China is becoming increasingly dependent on foreign supply to meet its demand of natural resources. Despite a clear improving trend on China's materials intensity (ratio of domestic materials consumption relative to production) in the period 1970 to 2000, from 2000 onwards materials intensity stabilized at around approximately 10 kg per USD, which is more than twice the global average. These figures suggest no decoupling of natural resource use with economic development, providing evidence against an Environmental Kuznets Curve in China (West et al. 2013). This has the dual negative impact on natural resource depletion and environmental degradation.

11.3 Natural resources: metals, minerals, and energy sources

In absolute terms China is a wealthy country with respect to many natural resources (such as iron, lead, and coal), being an important supplier for domestic use. With the intensification of the industrialization process, China's demand for natural resources significantly increased. At the same time, the composition of demand for these resources also changed. Whereas in the 1970s biomass encompassed about 63% of the domestic material consumption, and construction minerals encompassed about 8%, these figures switched around in the 1980s: only 15% of all domestic material consumption related to biomass and 63% to construction minerals (West et al. 2013). The high domestic consumption of construction minerals reflects the vast investments in infrastructure in China. Overall, the demand for natural resources in China is unprecedented in history.

In per capita terms, China is a relatively resource-poor country with respect to many important natural resources, such as renewable water, oil, minerals, and metals. Figure 11.3 shows the Chinese dependence on natural resources imports from 1992 until 2016. Throughout this period, on average, about 40% of all Chinese imports consisted of commodities which are either natural resources or resource-intensive commodities (such as articles based on stone and minerals). The high import share of natural resources is a reflection of China's resource-intensive growth and the relatively low domestic supply of these resources. This growth model has intensified in particular from 2000 onwards when China joined the World Trade Organization. As a result of this affiliation, China's exports grew significantly, favouring high investment in manufacturing plants and equipment (Dollar 2016). After the 2008 crises, with the decrease in exports, the Chinese government invested heavily in infrastructure, continuing on the heavy-investment growth strategy. Consequently, the demand for natural resources continued at high levels.

Figure 11.3 also illustrates the recent decline in imports as a result of China's slower economic growth rate since 2014. At the same time China started to shift the composition of income towards consumption and away from investment, which will likely have an effect on China's import share of natural resources. The expectation is that China's demand for natural resources will stabilize in the short run at the level observed in the 2000s (Dollar 2016). While from the industrial

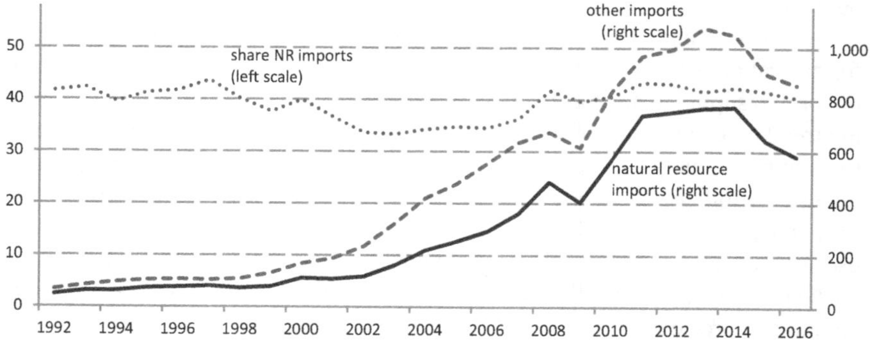

Figure 11.3 China imports of natural resources and other commodities

Source: Created using United Nations, Commodity Trade Statistics Database; imports of natural resources include: vegetables, foodstuff, wood, textile inputs, stone, glass, minerals, oil, and metals; value in constant 2010 USD billion (right-axis); left axis indicates the percent (in value) of China's import consisting of natural resources.

production side we can expect lower demand for natural resources, the rising affluence of the Chinese population is nowadays placing the highest demand for natural resources.

Figure 11.4 disaggregates the data of Natural Resources, by focusing on four groups: *i.* metals, *ii.* minerals, *iii.* stone and glass, and *iv.* vegetables, foodstuff, and wood. The figure illustrates the impressive increase in China's imports of natural resources, in particular of minerals, where fuels and oil represent on average more than 90% of the commodities in this group. Striking in this figure as well is the significant drop of imports of minerals since 2014. The decrease in income growth is a factor, as well as the sharp drop in oil prices.

From an international perspective, China is one of the biggest importers of natural resources. Taking the European Union as one entity, China ranked as the fourth biggest importer of natural resources in 2008, which represented about 10% of the world's imports (Ruta and Venables 2012). Within the different groups of natural resources, China is a bigger player in terms of trade of metals than energy trade (Dollar 2016). China is an important importer of iron, copper, and zinc, among others. About half of the global demand for major base metals is from China (IMF 2015). Accordingly, Figure 11.4 illustrates the sharp rise in Chinese imports of metals from 2000 onwards. At the same time, domestic extraction still fulfils most of China's demand for metals. China is simultaneously a major consumer and producer of metals worldwide. In the case of iron-ore (the most important base metal from an economic perspective), for example, China is the leading producer country while consuming more than half of the world's production (IMF 2015). Out of the four most important metals (iron-ore, copper, primary aluminium, and nickel), China is the major producer of iron-ore and primary aluminium. China is, moreover, the main consumer of all these metals, accounting approximately

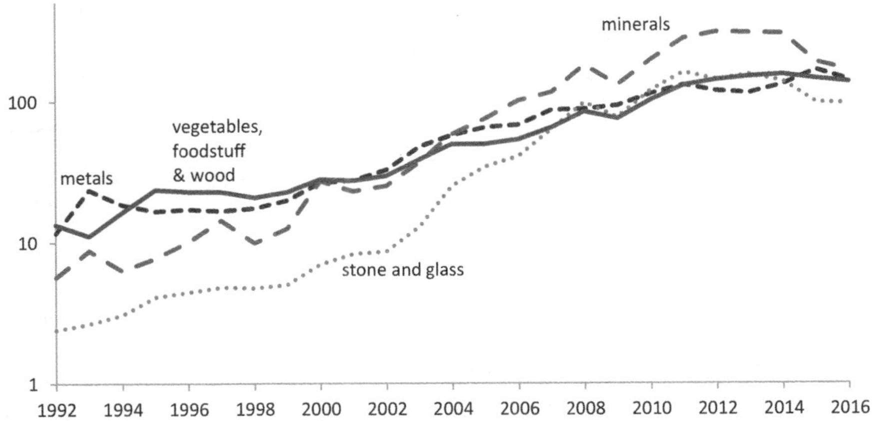

Figure 11.4 China; import of natural resources, by natural resource type (log scale)

Source: Created using United Nations, Commodity Trade Statistics Database; classification based on the Atlas of Economic Complexity (Centre for International Development at Harvard University); minerals include commodities like petroleum and derivatives, coal, copper ore, and so on; values in constant 2010 USD billion, log scale.

for half of the world's consumption. This high demand for metals is a relatively new phenomenon in China. China's metal consumption share increased rapidly from 2000 onwards. From a supply side, concomitant with this resource-intensive growth model of China, the domestic supply of energy and minerals were declining after 2000 (Dollar 2016), which spurred China's investment in mines abroad as well as in trade agreements with relatively resource abundant countries.

Associated with a larger external presence in the natural resources market, the large dependence on natural resources and the challenges related to the extraction and use of natural resources, stimulated China to become more resource efficient. From 1970 onwards, China increased resource efficiency significantly, in particular energy efficiency, which improved at an annual compound growth rate of close to 4% from 1970 to 2009 (significantly higher than the global gain of 0.7%). Nonetheless, relative to the world, China's energy efficiency is still low, requiring close to 2.5 times more energy per unit of economic output than the world average (West et al. 2013).

The rise in resource efficiency in China has been the result of the adoption of modern technologies and institutional changes. Most of the energy efficiency improvement occurred from 1975 onwards and was led by the industrial sector. Industries have invested in new, more efficient plants which reduced the energy requirements. This consolidated investment suggests that less sharp improvements will occur in the near future. Indeed, from 2000 onwards the improvement in energy efficiency has stabilized. Without significant structural changes in the Chinese economy, the demand for energy will not decrease.

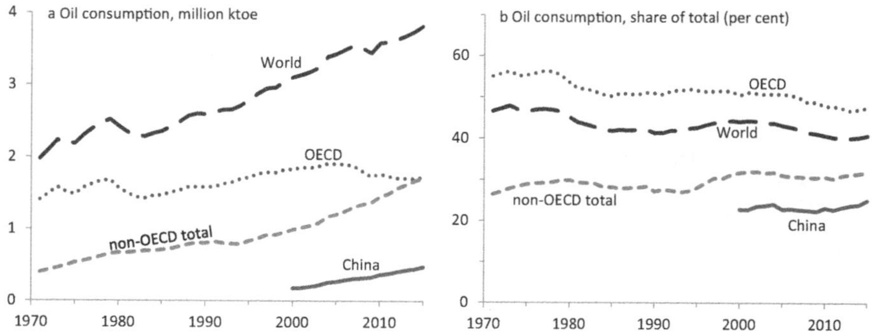

Figure 11.5 Oil consumption; China and selected regions, 1971–2015

Source: Created using International Energy Agency data (2017; www.iea.org/statistics); panel a: total oil consumption in million ktoe; panel b: oil consumption as share of total energy consumption (percent).

We can expect a continuous increase in the demand for oil in China, as well an increase in the demand for oil relative to metals, which are largely used for industrial production and construction, whereas oil demand comes predominantly from the transportation sector. The recent switch in Chinese growth to domestic consumption, combined with the rise in income per capita, explains this expected rising trend for oil. Car ownership in China, for example, grew at over 18% per year compounding from 2003 to 2008 (West et al. 2013). Figure 11.5 illustrates the increase in consumption of oil products in China, from 1971 until 2015. Whereas in 2000 China's consumption of oil products represented around 5.7% of world consumption, in 2015 this figure had increased to 12.5%.

Overall, this section shows that China's consumption of natural resources increased at much faster rates than the global average. Despite being a resource-rich country in absolute terms, China has increasingly depended on imports of natural resources from abroad. Institutional changes towards a more efficient economy are starting to emerge and significant modernization of the Chinese economy has translated to an increase in resource efficiency. Nonetheless, China still has much to catch up in terms of greening its economy by making more efficient use of its natural resources, and by doing so, also limiting the environmental impact from resource extraction and use. In the next section, we analyse water, another crucial natural resource, which is already a scarce resource in many parts in China.

11.4 Water

Water is a vital natural resource. Humans depend directly on freshwater for survival, but also indirectly in many ways, such as agriculture, sanitation, and hygiene. Water scarcity affects approximately 40 percent of the world population and because of non-sustainable use of it, this percentage is expected to rise. In China water shortage is a critical challenge. In 2014 China had 2,062 cubic meters of renewable internal freshwater resources per capita, which is about 35% of the world average, less than half of the amount in East Asia and Pacific (4,525 cubic meters per capita), and far below the amount of its neighbouring country Russia (29,982 cubic meters per capita). In 2014 China had approximately 6.6% of the world's renewable freshwater resources, compared to 19% of the world population. The problem is getting worse because of limited supply and rising demand. The World Resources Institute estimates that around 678 million people in China were living in areas considered highly water-stressed in 2010 (Wang et al. 2017). The two biggest drivers of this are industrialization and urbanization.

Figure 11.6 shows that the agricultural sector withdrew most of the water from 1982 onwards. However, in the last 10 years, industry and domestic withdrawals increased their relative importance. While in 1982 the agricultural sector accounted for 88% of total freshwater withdrawals, in 2014 this had dropped to approximately 65%. Figure 11.7 completes this picture by showing the absolute levels of withdrawals (in billion cubic meters). Overall, China experienced a 37% increase in the annual freshwater withdrawals from 1982 to 2014. Across the three sectors, the most impressive increase in this same period was from the domestic sector (approximately 11 times higher in 2014 than 1982), followed by the industrial sector (approximately three times higher in 2014 than 1982), whereas no significant change was observed in the agricultural sector. An important driver of the water withdrawal increase by the domestic sector is income growth. However, the improvement in water source (such as piped water on premises and public taps), in particular in the rural areas has also played an important role in this increase. In 1990, only 56% of the Chinese rural population had access to improved water

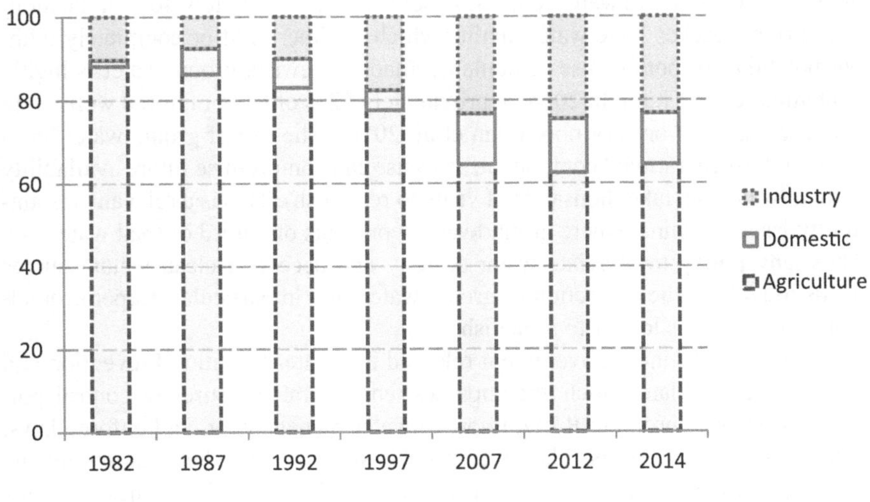

Figure 11.6 China; distribution of freshwater withdrawals (percent of total)

Source: Created using World Development Indicators online; withdrawals in billion cubic meters.

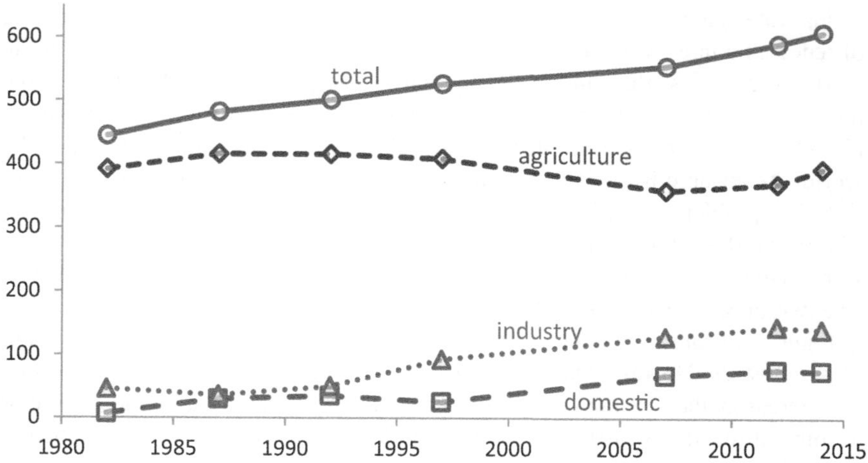

Figure 11.7 China; annual freshwater withdrawals, 1982–2014

Source: Created using World Development Indicators online; withdrawals in billion cubic meters.

sources, compared to 93% in 2015. This improvement in the rural area has significantly decreased the gap with the urban counterpart, where approximately 97% of the population had access to improved water sources throughout the 1990–2015 period.

Apart from being a relatively scarce country in terms of water, China also faces the problem of rising water pollution, which is one of the most severe in the world. According to recent statistics, around 200 million people in the country do not have access to safe water sources. In addition, approximately 46% of the monitored river reaches have water quality which is either unfit or completely without potential for potable use or human contact. Likewise, groundwater is highly contaminated in China. In 2014, approximately 62% of the monitored wells were classified as poor or very poor (Han et al. 2016). The use of groundwater has a strong inter-generational component, as its use can compromise future availability (groundwater can take thousands of years to replenish). This is a relevant sustainability issue in China, where groundwater represents one-third of total water use. Thus, any policy to alleviate water scarcity and access to clean water sources needs to address the protection of groundwater, and in particular deeper groundwater, which takes longer to replenish.

In 2015, the Chinese government released the Water Pollution Prevention and Control Action Plan, which encompasses ten general measures to control pollution discharge, promote R&D, improve water management, and enforce laws, among others. The Action Plan is comprehensive and sets sharp targets for the coming years. By focusing on both prevention and control, the Chinese authorities indicate their commitment to a more sustainable use of water. There are ample opportunities to make better use of the current water supply, such as policies to improve water-use efficiency and to stimulate cultivation of crops which are less water-intensive. Some progress can already be seen, for instance, the decrease in the total irrigation water withdrawal as a result of adoption of more water-efficient equipment. However, given the rising demand for water, the effort to increase water efficiency and decrease water pollution in China has to be massive if the country is to give more water access to the 678 million people in China living in areas considered highly water-stressed.

11.5 Forests

Forests provide diverse social benefits, which are spread throughout the vicinities of the forest, but also transcends to whole countries, continents or the world. Forests provide a diversity of environmental services, which affect the climate, the amount of rain, and the quality of the soil. Forests are the home of different species of plants, trees, and animals. Biodiversity, in turn, is fundamental to increase the productivity of our ecosystem because it safeguards the sustainability for all life forms and facilitates the recovery from natural disasters. Finally, forests provide a range of biological products such as food, wood, and medicinal resources. The acknowledgement that biodiversity preservation is fundamental for sustainability, led to the adoption of the Convention of Biological Diversity in 1992 by 193 countries, including China. During the Convention, the large dependency of the world economy, and in particular of poor households, on biological resources was emphasized.

China is one of the top 12 countries in the world relative to biodiversity, which is guaranteed by the large forest area. In 2015 forest area in China accounted for approximately 22% of the total land area in the country, which is 33% higher than in 1990 (16.7%). Such an impressive increase in a relatively short period of time, makes China the top country in the world regarding the net gain in forest area. From 1990 to 2015 China added 512 thousand km^2 of forest area, which is far beyond the second top country in this respect (the United States with 76 thousand km^2). Plantation projects are ongoing in China since 1980. These projects are based on plantation-style forests, which means that a large part of the "new forest" does not constitute of natural regeneration of forests. Natural forests have, in fact, declined from 1950 to 1995. Zhang et al. (2000) report that natural forests constituted only 30% of the total forest area in 1995.

Deforestation has, therefore, prevailed over a longer time frame. Until the 1950s agricultural production was associated with intensive conversion of forest area to crop land. The Chinese government forest policy implemented in the 1970s focused on economic development rather than environmental sustainability, in particular the maximization of timber production (Zhang et al. 2000). As a result, China's forest area represents a small fraction of the world's forest area, which is in contrast to China's territory size (China is the second largest country in the world in terms of land area). Figure 11.8 shows that across the 1990–2015 period, China had approximately 4 to 5% of the world's forest area. In comparison, the United States (third largest country), had approximately 7 to 8% of the world's forest area.

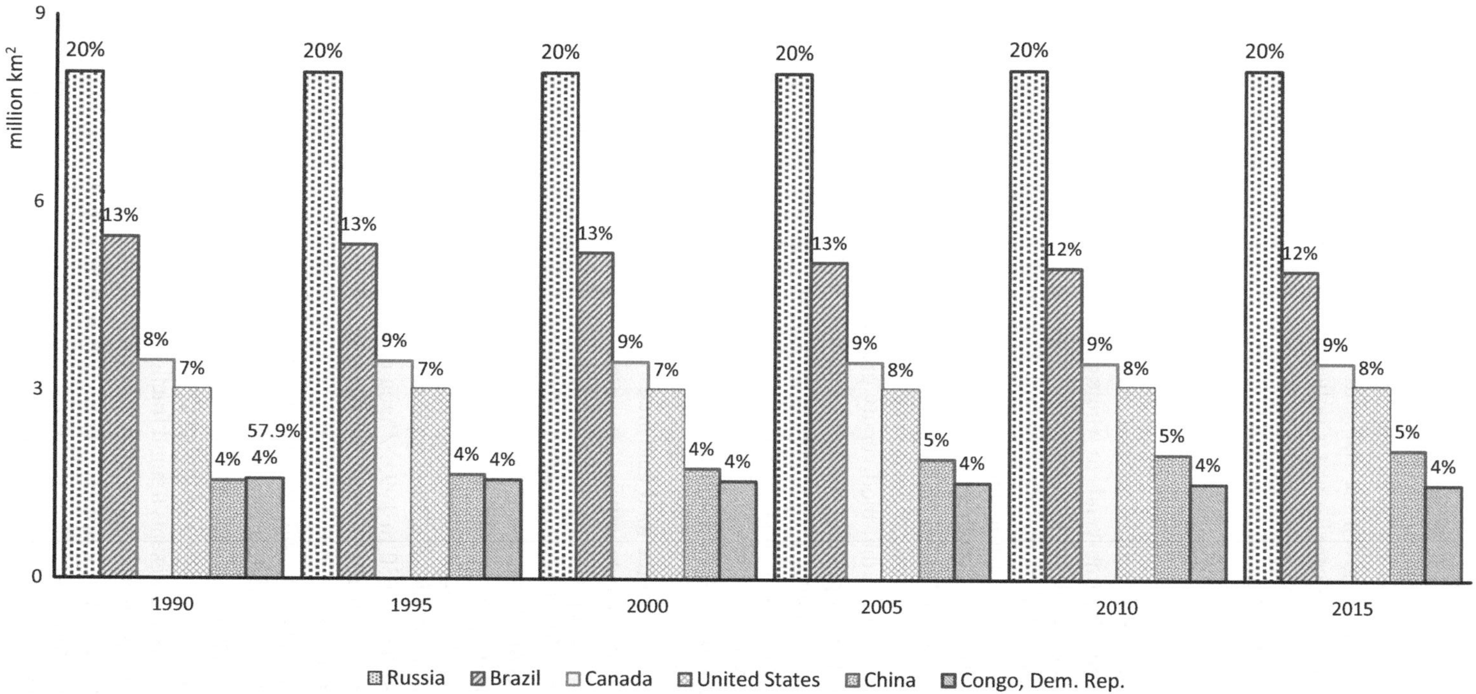

Figure 11.8 Forest area in six leading countries, 1990–2015

Source: Created using World Development Indicators online data; forest area in million km^2; labels indicate forest area relative to the global forest area in that year (percent).

The deforestation practice which held largely until the 1990s had a big burden on the Chinese environment, affecting the sustainability practices of forestry management. Problems of loss of biodiversity, soil erosion and flooding were directly linked to the loss of natural forests. These acknowledgements led to the replacement of the forest policy in 1998. Since then, forestry development in China has received a high priority in the policy sphere. The new forest policy encompassed both further protection and restoration of natural forest as well as the amplification of forest plantation. The policy is however, less effective in preventing deforestation in other countries, which is problematic when taking into account the increasing demand for wood products (in particular timber).

The Chinese imports of "Wood and articles of word; wood charcoal" increased yearly on average by 13% from 1992 to 2016 (Data from the United Nations, Comtrade). In 2016, China matched the United States in terms of the value of imports of wood products (see Figure 11.9). Together, these two countries accounted for almost 40% of world's imports of wood products. The main exporters of wood and wood products to China are Russia and the United States. Table 11.2 shows that China represents the main market for the exports of wood products in Russia, New Zealand, Thailand, and Australia. In all these four countries exports to China account for over 50% of each country's exports of wood products. Three major wood products exporters to China (Russia, Thailand, and Indonesia) still face many challenges with respect to sustainable forest management, which implies that the Chinese demand for wood has a negative impact on the world's forest sustainability.

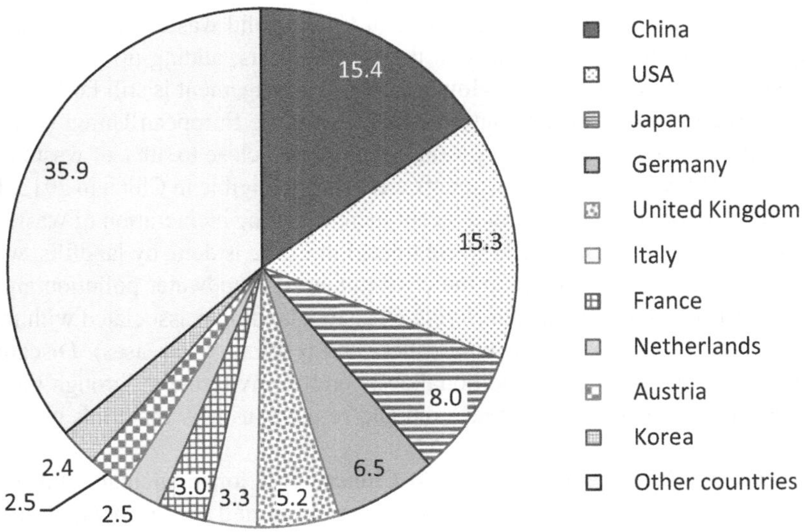

Figure 11.9 Share of world import of wood and articles of wood; wood charcoal, 2016 (percent)

Source: Created using United Nations, Comtrade (2017) data; top ten countries, percent of total imports.

Table 11.2 China imports of wood, articles of wood, and wood charcoal, 2016

Exporter	*Trade value (billion USD)*	*Percent of China imports*	*Income per capita*	*Percent of partner exports*
Russia	3.68	18.8	11,099	56.4
USA	2.52	12.8	52,195	27.9
New Zealand	1.55	7.9	36,842	53.7
Thailand	1.54	7.8	5,901	63.0
Canada	1.34	6.8	50,232	10.2
Australia	1.13	5.8	55,671	80.9
Indonesia	9.53	4.9	3,974	24.6

Source: Created using data from World Bank, WDI (2017) for income (GDP per capita, constant 2010 USD) and United Nations, Comtrade (2017) for trade variables.

11.6 Waste

Waste is inevitably generated as a side product of economic activity. Figure 11.10 shows the relation between waste collected and income (both in logs) for a sample of 112 advanced and developing countries. The associated regression line explains 83% in the variance of waste collected and has a slope of 0.78, which implies that if income rises by 10% than collected waste rises on average by 7.8%. The figure identifies some countries, such as Niger, Cameroon, Moldova, and China, which are clearly above the regression line and thus collect more waste than expected on the basis of their income level.

Besides affluence, waste generation is also highly correlated with urbanization and population growth. Urban areas generate significantly more waste than rural areas. Given the rapid urbanization rate in China, solid waste generation is also expected to increase significantly in the coming years, adding up to the current rising trend (see Figure 11.11). However, waste management is still far below the practices adopted in most advanced countries. In the European Union (EU-28), for example, recycling and composting[3] represented close to 40% of waste treatment in 2014, whereas such treatments were still negligible in China in 2012. Figure 11.12 shows that apart from a recent increase in the incineration of waste, the majority of the municipal solid waste treated in China is done by landfills, which imposes a significant burden on the environment (groundwater pollution and air pollution) and on human health (living close to a landfill is associated with many health problems, in particular lung cancer and respiratory diseases). Discarding waste in this way also puts additional costs on the environment through the loss of resources which could be recovered and re-used (as new materials or energy sources).

Figure 11.10 to Figure 11.12 report Chinese data for municipal solid waste. Overall, the conclusion is that economic growth and the associated social-economic effects are resulting in increasing waste generation, which are not being properly treated. Both increase of waste and waste management are problematic from an environmental and public health perspective. Furthermore, the type of waste plays an important role in defining the level of concern arising from waste

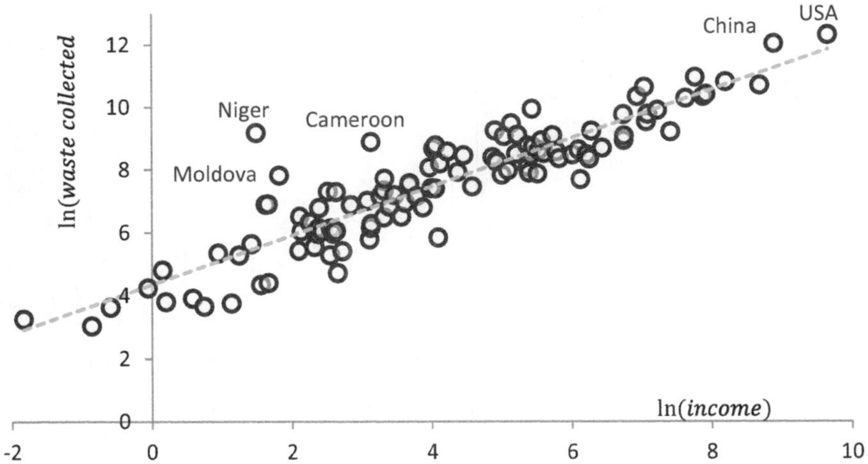

Figure 11.10 Municipal waste collection and economic development, around 2012

Source: Created using World Bank Development Indicators online (for income) and United Nations Statistics Division (2017; https://unstats.un.org/unsd/environment/time%20series.htm); collected waste in million tons, most recent year available; income is GDP in constant 2010 USD billion, matching year; median observations in the year 2012, most recent in 2014, latest in 2000; dashed line is a regression line with slope (elasticity) equal to 0.7792; this explains 83.1% of the variance in ln*(waste collected)*.

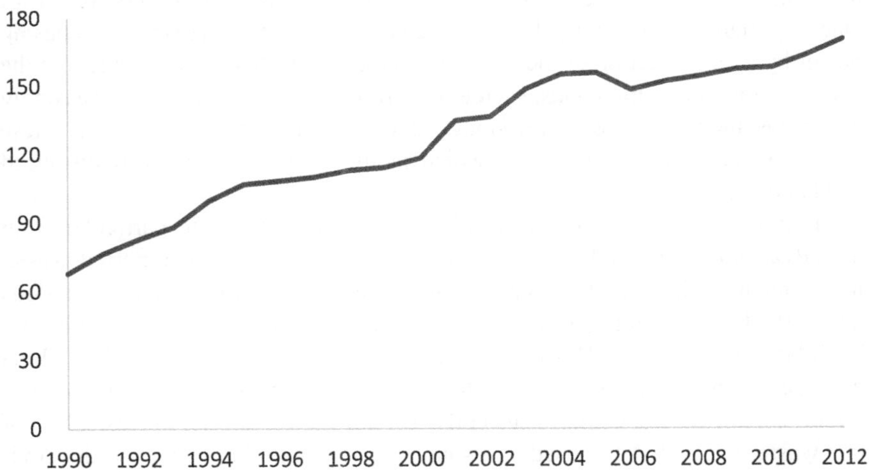

Figure 11.11 Municipal waste generated in China; million tons, 1990–2012

Source: Created using OECD Statistics (2017, https://stats.oecd.org/Index.aspx?DataSetCode=MUNW#).

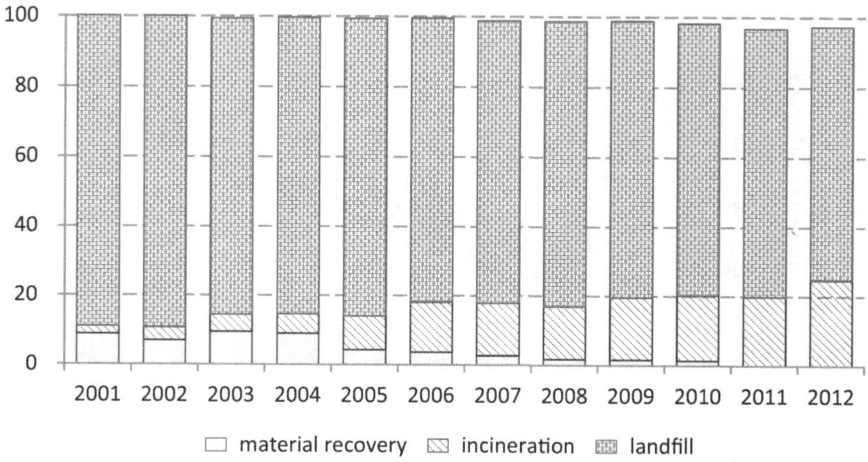

Figure 11.12 Municipal solid waste treated in China; by treatment (percent), 2001–2012

Source: Created using OECD Statistics (2017, https://stats.oecd.org/Index.aspx?DataSetCode=MUNW#); *material recovery is recycling and composting.*

generation. Municipal solid waste can be classified in two main groups: hazardous waste and non-hazardous waste. Hazardous waste has properties related to toxicity and flammability which pose a potential or actual danger to the environment and to the health of human beings and/or other living organisms. Figure 11.13 shows the sharp increase in hazardous waste generation in China from 2006 onwards. One important factor driving this increase is e-waste. The increase of purchasing power by a large fraction of the Chinese population, is driving a sharp rise in the consumption of durable goods, such as electronics. Chinese are now increasingly discarding mobile phones, televisions, computers, and other electronics. These goods contain hazardous materials which should therefore be properly displaced and handled.

China has imported waste from abroad for a long time, in particular from the advanced world (pollution transfer). In the 1980s China imported waste, including household garbage and medical waste, containing many hazardous materials. In 1991 China ratified the Basel Convention on the Control of Transboundary Movements of Hazardous Wastes and their Disposal. Since then China has become more active in controlling the types of waste which the country imports. Nonetheless, China is currently still the major importer of waste. Part of this waste is recycled and used as a source of new material. However, the environmental impact from the import of waste is massive. Unlike many advanced countries which adopt modern technologies to dispose and recycle waste, in China hazardous residues from waste materials are usually displaced directly onto the land.

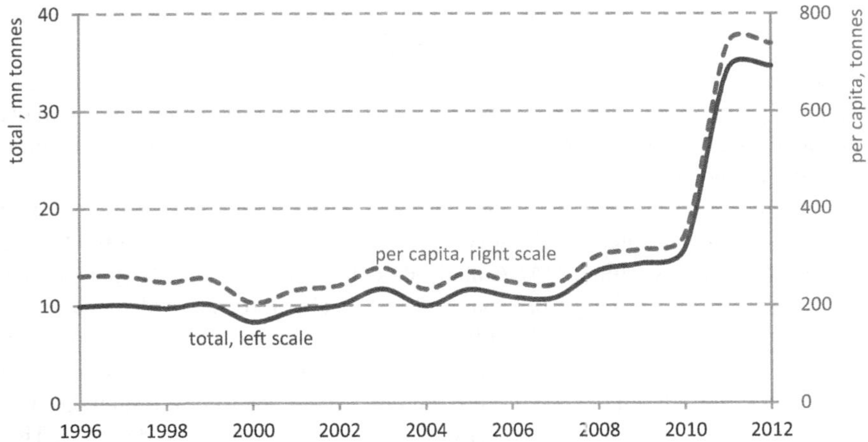

Figure 11.13 China; hazardous waste generated, 1996–2012

Source: Created using data from United Nations Statistics Division (2017); total in million tons; per capita in tons per person; https://unstats.un.org/unsd/environment/time%20series.htm

On December 2017 China announced to the World Trade Organization (WTO) that it will ban 24 types of solid waste imports (such as plastics waste and textile materials) as of January 1, 2018. China recognizes that mixed with this type of non-hazardous waste, it is common to find hazardous materials which are highly polluting. The objective of this ban is therefore environmental protection and improvement of human health and safety in China. As a consequence, advanced countries will have to find another way to cope with the million tons of waste they used to ship to China. This ban comes as a response to the poorly enforced *Law of the People's Republic of China on Prevention and Control of Environmental Pollution by Solid Wastes* from 2005, which forbids dumping of solid wastes into China, unless this waste can be used as raw material. Gradually, China is sending out the message to the world that it does not want to take all the environmental burden associated to the living standards of other parts of the world.

11.7 Air pollution

The two most important components of local air pollution are particulate matter and nitrogen dioxide. Within particulate matter, two are widely measured in main cities throughout the world: PM_{10} (particles with diameters of 10 micrometres and smaller) and $PM_{2.5}$ (also called fine particles, with diameters of 2.5 micrometres and smaller). Particulate matter originates from diverse sources (such as construction, agriculture, and industrial processes) and are made of a variety of chemicals.

Transportation (in particular road traffic), power plants and industrial facilities are the main sources of nitrogen dioxide (NO_2) in the atmosphere. Besides contributing to air pollution, when nitrogen dioxide interacts with oxygen and water it results in acid rain, which negatively affects the environment. Together nitrogen dioxide, particulate matter and other local air pollutants have a direct effect on the quality of life of those exposed to it (in particular, because they can lead to respiratory and cardiovascular diseases).

In the period from 1995 until 2015 nitrogen oxides were the air pollutant with the highest growth rates in China (Cui et al. 2016). However, this growth was not uniform across China. NASA analyses density change of nitrogen dioxide around the world. Looking from space, NASA is able to observe changes in key pollutants, including nitrogen dioxide, on a regional and local scale. By looking at changes from the period 2005–2014 in China, NASA found that whereas cities in the North Central Plain observed sharp increases in the levels of nitrogen dioxide, main cities such as Shanghai and Beijing experienced a significant decrease. This finding indicates that environmental regulation in China is beginning to have an impact on the quality of the environment.[4] World Bank data on $\boldsymbol{PM_{2.5}}$ air pollution (mean annual exposure) shows that after a period of rapid growth from 1990 to 2005 levels of this pollutant have stabilized, although at a high level (close to 60 μg/m^3 in 2015).[5]

The World Health Organization (WHO) advices on a maximum of 10 μg/m^3 annual mean for $\boldsymbol{PM_{2.5}}$ and of 20 μg/m^3 annual mean for $\boldsymbol{PM_{10}}$.[6] Based on this guideline and data from the same organization,[7] none of the 210 cities in China with measured data on particulate matter, were considered as healthy cities in terms of $\boldsymbol{PM_{2.5}}$. Only two of the 210 cities in China had less than 20 μg/m^3 annual mean for $\boldsymbol{PM_{10}}$. Figure 11.14 shows that in China many cities face a high level of concentration of particulate matter.

Zhang and Cao (2015) report similar findings for $\boldsymbol{PM_{2.5}}$ in 190 cities in China. The authors report a population-weighted mean of 61 μg/m^3 in Chinese cities, which is approximately three times higher than the global population-weighted mean. Moreover, the authors state that less than one percent of the 500 largest cities of China have met the health guidelines relative to air quality proposed by the WHO.

Overall, concentration of particulate matter varies with season, temperatures and time of the day, but among the main drivers are burning coal, cement production and steel production. China still relies heavily on coal for the provision of energy and for industrial production, which has a strong negative impact on the local environment and health, besides contributing to climate change. Additionally, cement and steel production have increased rapidly from 1990 onwards. From 2011 to 2013, for example, China used more cement than the United States did in the entire 20th century.[8] This is a result of the rapid urbanization process which China is going through. Eventually, this process will smooth out and cement production will decrease. Environmental regulation will serve as an incentive for further improvements in air quality. Given the current high level of emissions, in particular in the main cities, air pollution will likely remain a troublesome reality of main Chinese cities for many years to come.

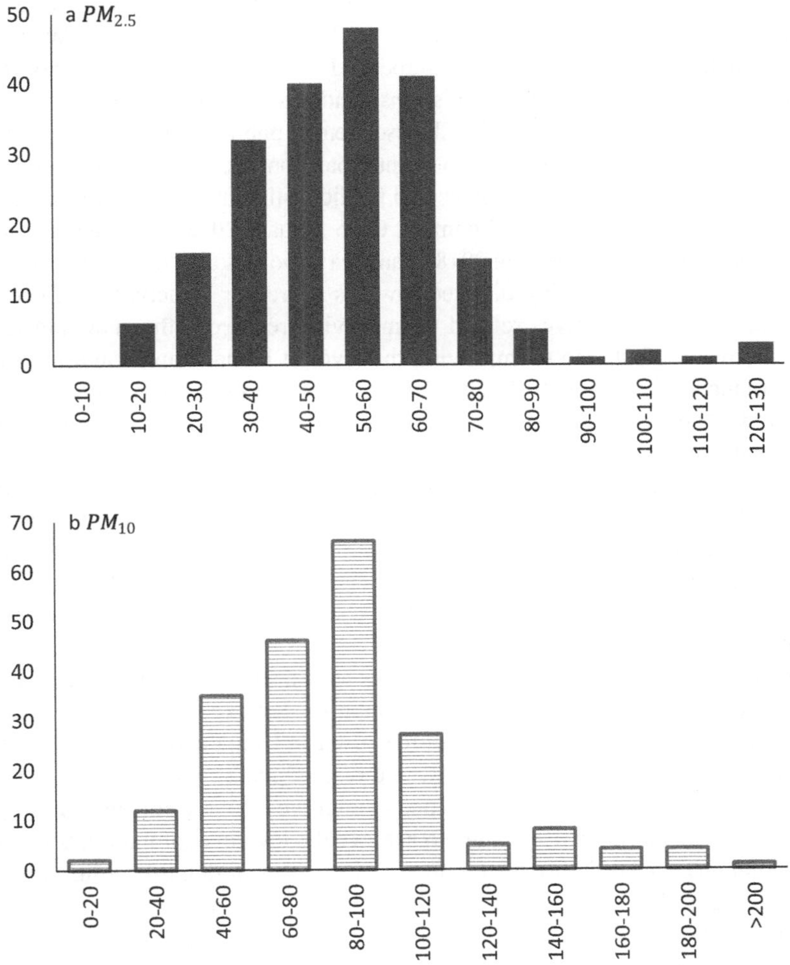

Figure 11.14 Chinese cities and particulate matter; $PM_{2.5}$ and PM_{10}, histogram 2013–2014

Source: Created using WHO ambient (outdoor) air pollution database; 210 Chinese cities included; data refer to either 2013 or 2014; annual mean micrograms per cubic meter for $PM_{2.5}$ and PM_{10}.

11.8 Evaluation and conclusions

China's economic growth process in the last 30 years has been unmatched in history. The lives of millions of Chinese people have been directly or indirectly affected by the economic transformation which the country has passed throughout this period. However, while people have been walking up the ladder to higher standards of living, the environment has taken the opposite route. Environmental degradation and resource depletion are now compromising a sustainable development process in China's future. China is now a middle-income country (income per capita in 2016 was about 13% of that of the US). If China is to raise the standards of living of its population to the levels of high income countries, the consequences for the environment would be dramatic, unless the right policies are in place.

Environmental regulations in China are advancing on a fast pace. West et al. (2013) point out that China recently introduced policies in a variety of sectors (such as renewable energy and vehicle emissions standards) to improve resource efficiency and decrease pollution. In 2014 the Chinese Premier publicly declared "war on pollution" (Branigan 2014). A new Environment Protection Tax became effective on January 1, 2018, which taxes companies and public institutions for discharging certain pollutants directly into the environment. On 5 January 2018 China announced the intention to plant new forests in 2018 in an area of no less than 6.6 million hectares.

Concomitant to a policy directed towards a greener society, China needs to translate this to objectives related to improving resource efficiency and fostering innovation, but also to improving the level of human capital and increasing governance capacity. On 9 October 2017 China's president stated that China has entered a "new era", during which China would "take centre stage in the world". The question which now remains is whether this will also hold in the environmental sphere. The recently announced environmental targets and plans suggest that it will. All in all, this chapter shows that the first steps have been taken to increase the greenness of the Chinese economy, but there are still many challenges to be addressed and opportunities to be seized. Timing of the policies also needs to be considered. We should not expect a radical change in environmental indicators, as effects take time to be observed.

Finally, China's sustainability challenges have a strong global perspective. The rapid economic growth since 1978 has mainly been export oriented. Therefore, a significant part of the natural resources used in China end up in consumption goods for other parts of the world. Even though China should continue its recent effort to decrease materials intensity and to improve resource efficiency more generally, we should not expect China to achieve the low level of materials intensity from countries who do not have intensive industries in domestic soil. Similarly, part of the pollution generated in China is realized in order to satisfy the global demand for goods. Thus, part of the solution to the sustainability issues in China need to be acted upon on a global scale, through, for example, fostering the consumption of greener products. This requires a global shift in behaviour towards consuming less and accepting to pay a higher price for more-polluting goods. In combination with that, one of the crucial sustainability issues of the present days is climate change. The high levels of greenhouse gases emissions in China have an effect in the global climate, which again, requires a combined action that goes beyond the Chinese policy sphere alone.

Notes

1 Utrecht University School of Economics, Adam Smith Hall 2.07a, Kriekenpitplein 21–22, 3584 EC, Utrecht, The Netherlands. Telephone: *31 30 253 9413. Email: j.swart@uu.nl. I would like to thank Charles van Marrewijk for useful comments and suggestions and for assistance with the graphs of this chapter.

2 Source: based on data from the International Energy Agency.

3 Source: Eurostat, http://ec.europa.eu/eurostat/data/database. Data for non-hazardous waste under treatment type: recovery other than energy recovery- except backfilling.
4 https://earthobservatory.nasa.gov/IOTD/view.php?id=87392
5 For comparison, in Europe and Central Asia, the level for the same year was approximately 19 μg/m^3)
6 www.who.int/mediacentre/factsheets/fs313/en/
7 Source: based on WHO urban air quality database, ambient (outdoor) air pollution database 2016.
8 Source: www.washingtonpost.com/news/wonk/wp/2015/03/24/how-china-used-more-cement-in-3-years-than-the-u-s-did-in-the-entire-20th-century/?utm_term=.55431702f833

References

Auffhammer, M. and Carson, R.T. (2008), "Forecasting the path of China's CO2 emissions using province-level information," *Journal of Environmental Economics and Management* 55(3): 229–247.

Branigan, T. (2014), "Chinese premier declares war on pollution in economic overhaul." *The Guardian*. Available at: https://www.theguardian.com/world/2014/mar/05/china-pollution-economic-reform-growth-target (Accessed 20 December 2017).

Cui, Y., J. Lin, C. Song, M. Liu, Y. Yan, Y. Xu, and B. Huang (2016), "Rapid Growth in Nitrogen Dioxide Pollution over Western China, 2005–2013," *Atmospheric Chemistry and Physics* 16: 6207–6221.

Dollar (2016), *China's Engagement with Africa: From Natural Resources to Human Resources*, Washington, DC: Brookings Report.

Han, D., M. J. Currell, and G. Cao (2016), "Deep Challenges for China's War on Water Pollution," *Environmental Pollution* 218: 1222–1233.

Health Effects Institute (2017a), *State of Global Air 2017*. Special Report. Boston, MA: Health Effects Institute.

Health Effects Institute (2017b), *Global Burden of Disease Study 2015*. IHME, 2016. Available at: www.stateofglobalair.org (Accessed 16 October 2017).

Hu, C., and X. J. Huang (2008), "Characteristics of Carbon Emission in China and Analysis on Its Cause," *China, Population, Resources and Environment* 18(3): 38–42.

IMF (2015), "Adjusting to Lower Commodity Prices." *World Economic Outlook*, Commodity special feature, October 2015.

Jalil, A., and M. Feridun (2011), "The Impact of Growth, Energy and Financial Development on the Environment in China: A Cointegration Analysis," *Energy Economics* 33(2): 284–291.

Jalil, A., and S. F. Mahmud (2009), "Environmental Kuznets Curve for CO2 Emissions: A Cointegration Analysis for China," *Energy Policy* 37(12): 5167–5172.

Jayanthakumaran, K., R. Verna, and Y. Liu (2012), "CO_2 Emissions, Energy Consumption, Trade and Income: A Comparative Analysis of China and India," *Energy Policy* 42: 450–460.

Ruta, M., and A. J. Venables (2012), "International Trade in Natural Resources: Practice and Policy," *Annual Review of Resource Economics* 4: 331–352.

United Nations (2017), *United Nations Statistics Divisio, UN Comtrade*, selected variables downloaded in the period April-December 2017 from https://comtrade.un.org/data/.

Wang, J., L. Zhong, and C. Iceland (2017), *China's Water Stress is on the Rise*, World Resources Institute www.wri.org/blog/2017/01/chinas-water-stress-rise (Accessed 16 November 2017).

Wei, Y. M., and H. Liao (2016), *Energy Economics: Energy Efficiency in China*, Switzerland: Springer International Publishing AG.

West, J., H. Schandl, S. Heyenga, and S. Chen (2013), "Resource Efficiency: Economics and Outlook for China," UNEP, Bangkok, Thailand.

World Bank (2017), *World Development Indicators online*, selected variables downloaded in the period April-July 2017 from www.worldbank.org.

Yue, Y., T. Sonobe, and K. Otsuka (2007), "Beyond the Environmental Kuznets Curve: A Comparative Study of SO2 and CO2 Emissions between Japan and China," *Environmental and Development Economics* 12(3): 445–470.

Zhang, P., G. Shao, G. Zhao, D. C. Le Master, G. R. Parker, J. B. Dunning, and O. Li (2000), "China's Forest Policy for the 21st Century," *Science* 288.

Zhang, Y. L., and F. Cao (2015), "Fine Particulate Matter ($PM_{2.5}$) in China at a City Level," *Scientific Reports* 5.

12 China's emerging global role

Peter J. Morgan[1]

12.1 Introduction

China's re-integration with the global economy has served it well over the past three decades. By steadily intensifying its trade, investment, and financial links with the global economy over the next two decades, China will be able to benefit from further specialization, increased investment opportunities and higher returns to capital, and a mutually beneficial flow of ideas and knowledge. As a key stakeholder in the global economy, China should actively promote further liberalization of trade and support a multilateral agreement on investment flows. Integrating the Chinese financial sector with the global financial system requires further opening of the capital account. This needs to be undertaken steadily and cautiously, but this liberalization will be a key step toward internationalizing the renminbi as a global reserve currency. Finally, China should play a central role in engaging with its partners in multilateral settings to shape the global governance agenda and address pressing global economic issues such as climate change, global financial stability, and a more effective international aid architecture.

As a result of its outstanding growth performance, China is entering a more confident and engaged stage of its involvement with the global economy and financial system. Section 12.2 describes China's re-entry into the global economy, including foreign direct investment (FDI) and trade. Section 12.3 covers China's re-entry into the global financial system, including capital market opening and economic reforms. Section 12.4 describes China's participation in the international financial architecture, including the Group of Twenty (G20) and international financial institutions. Section 12.5 covers China's role in the provision of global goods, including control of climate change. Section 12.6 concludes.

12.2 China's re-entry to the global economy

China began to open up to FDI and trade as part of the reform process that began in 1978, in sharp contrast to autarkic policies pursued during the Mao Zedong period. With the establishment of special economic zones, Deng Xiaoping's remarks during his famous South China tour, and accession to the World Trade Organization (WTO) as milestones, China expanded and deepened its economic integration with the global economy. This policy paid off handsomely for China, bringing investments, advanced technologies, and managerial expertise; opening the international market for China's goods and services; and giving a boost to China's internal economic reforms. The proximity of Hong Kong and Taiwan, helped, as did a large Chinese diaspora dispersed across the globe (World Bank 2013).

12.2.1 Foreign direct investment policies

China adopted FDI-friendly policies since 1980, beginning with permitting FDI in Special Economic Zones but steadily broadening it to the rest of the nation. As a result, China is now host to over 700,000 partly foreign-owned companies with accumulated foreign direct investment of US$ 1.354 trillion as of 2016 (UNCTAD 2017). These companies account for 22% of tax revenue, 28% of industrial value added, 55% of exports, 69% of the trade surplus and 50% of technology imports. Foreign direct investment has enabled China to integrate into global manufacturing networks (global value chains), as well as contributing substantially to exports, employment, technology imports and institutional reform (World Bank 2013).[2]

FDI outflows have risen rapidly since inauguration of the "Going Global" policies in the late 1990s, from US$ 1 billion in 2000 to US$ 128 billion in 2016 (UNCTAD 2017). China's total FDI outflows over the period were greater than for any other emerging markets except Russia and Hungary. Since 2003, almost 55% of China's greenfield FDI and 27% of M&A transactions have been in the mining sector, compared with 10% in M&A transactions from advanced countries (World Bank 2013).

China's FDI outflows have increased at about the same annual rate of growth as outflows from Japan and Korea, to take regional examples that have achieved rapid growth (beginning from the year that these countries' outflows exceeded US$ 1 billion), but less than outflows from Malaysia. Given China's huge size, FDI outflows could quickly rise to high levels. For example, by 2030, China's per capita GDP is expected to exceed US$ 10,000. If China's FDI outflows relative to GDP equaled the level of Japan's at a similar level of income (about 0.5%), then China's outflows would almost double to US$ 75 billion (World Bank 2013).

China's investment outflows have raised concerns among some commentators in host countries, and efforts by Chinese firms to purchase foreign companies and to operate in foreign countries have in some cases met political opposition. For example, the state-owned China National Offshore Oil Corporation withdrew its bid for Union Oil Company of California (Unocal) in the face of political opposition in the United States. A 2008 deal to double Aluminum Corporation of China's (Chinalco) stake in Rio Tinto, an Anglo-Australian iron ore producer, was scrapped due to opposition from Australian lawmakers (Xu 2009). However, despite its rapid growth, China's outward FDI remains a small share of total FDI flows and a minuscule amount compared with total investment in most host countries (World Bank 2013).

Other issues may be more important. Chinese firms' lack of experience means that they may lack the political networks and knowledge of host-country cultures necessary to avoid mistakes in public relations, branding, and management. Sometimes Chinese companies have made mistakes that led to opposition. For example, some observers have expressed concerns about the environmental impact of investments by Chinese firms. Governments or political interests who view China as a long-term threat to other countries' security interests may not welcome investment by Chinese firms. The government's support for outward investment, including subsidies for investments in natural resources, tax breaks, and low-interest financing from state-owned banks (Luo et al. 2010), has raised perceptions that these practices are unfair, although some of them are hardly unique to China (World Bank 2013).

Moreover, the prominent role played by State-Owned Enterprises (SOEs) rather than private firms sometimes creates suspicion in host countries about potential strategic behavior by Chinese investors. More than two-thirds of FDI outflows were from centrally controlled SOEs in 2009, and a portion of the remainder came from firms partially owned or controlled by the state or by provincial or municipal governments (Salidjanova 2011). The important role played by SOEs in China's foreign investment is not surprising – most of the large Chinese companies that have the resources and expertise to invest abroad are owned by the state. Relatively few of the 115 Chinese companies in the Fortune 500 list of the largest global firms in 2017 are privately owned (China Daily 2017). The government needs to ensure that private firms are given the same opportunity to invest abroad by avoiding burdensome approval processes that might inhibit such investment.

Chinese FDI policy has focused on international treaties to protect foreign investors. Since the early 1980s, China has signed 127 bilateral investment treaties (BITs) (through May 2010) and 112 double taxation treaties (through May 2009) (Davies 2010). Since 2000, China's bilateral investment treaties, mostly concluded with developing countries that are the main destinations for Chinese FDI, have expanded protections for investors. These include commitments by host countries to treat foreign investors, once established in the country, equally with domestic investors, and to provide investors with nearly unrestricted access to international tribunals (such as the World Bank's International Centre for the Settlement of Investment Disputes) when disputes develop (Berger 2008). The latest Chinese BITs do allow for the continuation of existing provisions that discriminate against existing foreign investors, subject to a "best effort" commitment to roll back such measures over time (World Bank 2013).

The rise of China and other emerging-market and developing economies has also challenged the global systems for investment and trade in some cases by contributing to stalled multilateralism, global and regional fragmentation and changing the nature of global trade through the formation of global production networks – something to which the World Trade Organization (WTO) and other global and regional bodies are struggling to adapt. To be sure, the United States also began to pursue more protectionist policy following President Trump's election in 2016.

The rise of these economies has meant a greater focus on the issues that are important to them. Negotiations around agriculture and non-agricultural market access have seen talks stall in the WTO. Work on a multilateral investment framework has not made any progress, instead being advanced through a network of bilateral agreements, regional initiatives like the ASEAN Investment Area and specific multilateral agreements such as trade-related investment measures (TRIMs) and the negotiation of bilateral investment treaties. Some recent analysis suggests the north-south divide is likely a key factor in this slow progress as developing nations become increasingly wary of the risks associated with investment frameworks, particularly because of investor protection clauses (Drysdale et al. 2017).

12.2.2 Trade

The development of China's trade is described in detail in Chapter 8. The beginning of export-oriented policies in 1978 clearly had a huge impact on China's growth acceleration since then. Moreover, China's accession to the World Trade Organization in 2001 triggered economy-wide improvements in efficiency and spurred technology acquisition and adaptation. More recently, the phasing out of incentives that had favored foreign investors stimulated competition by leveling the playing field with domestically owned firms (World Bank 2013). China's entry into the WTO in 2001 also led to the adoption of many new economic laws and the amendment of others. The adoption of laws such as the Administrative Litigation Law (1989), the State Compensation Law (1994) and the Administrative Licensing Law (2003) were important landmarks (OECD 2005).

12.2.3 Impacts of China's role in world trade

China now plays such a large role in world trade that many nations are vulnerable to the negative impact of a significant slowdown in Chinese growth, either through direct trade impacts or indirect impacts via declines in commodity prices. For example, Zhai and Morgan (2018) used a multi-sectoral global computable general equilibrium model, to quantitatively investigate the impacts of a growth slowdown in the PRC for emerging Asian economies through trade linkages. The results suggested that a GDP growth slowdown of 1.6 percentage points in the PRC would bring about a growth deceleration of 0.26 percentage points in developing Asia as a whole. However, the impacts vary dramatically by economy within developing Asia and elsewhere, reflecting their differences in economic and trade structure. Within Asia, Taiwan and Hong Kong are most vulnerable to the PRC's economic downturn, while South Asia is the most isolated from changes in the PRC. Latin America is also expected to see a relatively large impact (Table 12.1).

Given the enormous importance of the PRC in global commodity markets, the effects of the PRC's slowdown on commodity demand and prices are likely to be significant as well. For example, Zhai and Morgan (2018) estimated that the PRC's growth slowdown would lower the PRC's demand for coal and oil and gas

Table 12.1 Effects of the PRC's slowdown on GDP and trade, 2016–2020

	GDP	*Exports*	*Imports*	*Trade balance as % of GDP*
Australia and New Zealand	– 0.37	– 0.80	– 0.31	– 0.35
Japan	– 0.24	– 0.61	– 0.30	– 0.18
PRC	– 1.59	0.05	– 2.01	1.45
Developing Asia (excl. the PRC)	**– 0.26**	**– 0.50**	**– 0.35**	**– 0.25**
Hong Kong	– 0.51	– 0.66	– 0.49	– 0.38
Republic of Korea	– 0.26	– 0.51	– 0.42	– 0.28
Taiwan	– 0.54	– 0.72	– 0.64	– 0.37
Indonesia	– 0.29	– 0.58	– 0.20	– 0.29
Malaysia	– 0.42	– 0.53	– 0.41	– 0.34
Philippines	– 0.47	– 0.75	– 0.45	– 0.29
Singapore	– 0.34	– 0.40	– 0.37	– 0.32
Thailand	– 0.27	– 0.39	– 0.33	– 0.24
Viet Nam	– 0.35	– 0.40	– 0.30	– 0.30
Other Southeast Asia	– 0.31	– 0.58	– 0.29	– 0.24
India	– 0.14	– 0.35	– 0.19	– 0.13
Other South Asia	– 0.22	– 0.34	– 0.17	– 0.12
Canada	– 0.19	– 0.32	– 0.18	– 0.16
United States	– 0.17	– 0.40	– 0.16	– 0.10
European Union	– 0.19	– 0.31	– 0.23	– 0.14
Latin America	– 0.29	– 0.51	– 0.24	– 0.19
Rest of the world	– 0.36	– 0.46	– 0.27	– 0.29
The World	**– 0.42**	**– 0.35**	**– 0.42**	**0.00**

GDP = gross domestic product; PRC = People's Republic of China.

Source: Zhai and Morgan (2018).

Note: Percentage point changes in annual growth rates relative to the baseline except for trade balance.

by 6.9% and 5.8% in 2020, respectively. As a result of spillover effects to other economies, global demand for these two energy goods would fall by 3.8% and 2.0%, respectively. They would experience price drops of 1.6% and 0.9%, respectively, reflecting a more elastic coal supply in the world. Global grain demand is estimated to fall by 1.6% in 2020 relative to the baseline. The PRC's grain consumption would contract by 4.4%, contributing to around 60% of the global demand reduction. The world real price of grain, deflated by the numéraire of the model, would fall by 0.6% in 2020 relative to the baseline.

Using a GVAR modeling approach, Inoue et al. (2018) find that, in response to a 1% slowdown in the PRC's GDP, every country in Asia except the Philippines experiences a negative shock either in the short term or in the long term; however, the level and extent of the shocks differ greatly. Indonesia is by far the most negatively impacted country both in the short term as well as the long term, with a long-term decline of −0.12%. It is followed by Thailand (–0.095% in the long term), the Republic of Korea (–0.07%), Singapore (–0.05%), Malaysia (–0.05%), and Australia (–0.05%). The impact of a negative PRC real GDP shock is less marked for India (–0.018%).

12.3 Deeper integration into the global financial system

China has proceeded much more cautiously in liberalizing its capital markets than its foreign trade regime. A tightly managed exchange rate and extensive capital controls have been linchpins of China's economic policies. These policies have helped support spectacular export-led growth and supported financial stability. This policy mix has also played an important role in insulating the economy from the global financial crisis of 2008–2009, although the impacts on exports were still large. However, Chinese authorities see the need to gradually liberalize both their financial system and their capital markets, and to move toward a more flexible and market-determined exchange rate to promote efficient allocation of resources.

China's official exchange rate depreciated sharply in 1994 with the unification of the previous dual-exchange-rate system (see Figure 12.1). Thereafter, the government basically fixed the renminbi/dollar rate until July 2005 when a managed floating exchange rate regime was adopted, and the renminbi gradually appreciated. By October 2011, the real effective exchange rate had appreciated 66% compared with that of January 1994, and 31% compared with that of January 2005. The managed exchange-rate policy required maintaining a relatively closed capital account, so that the domestic monetary policies could be more independent and effective. (World Bank 2013).

In recent years, the Chinese government has pursued a policy of increasing the acceptance of the renminbi as a global currency. This requires development along several dimensions. For a currency to be accepted in international transactions by other countries and held as assets by foreigners, the country's shares in international trade and financial transactions have to be significant. Inflation and inflation expectations need to be low in order to maintain confidence that the currency is

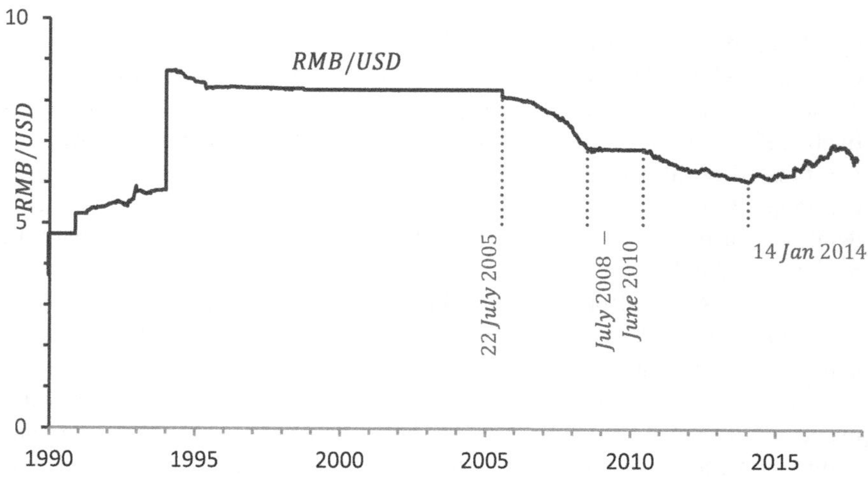

Figure 12.1 Movements of renminbi/US dollar rate

Source: Van Marrewijk (2018) based on data from https://fred.stlouisfed.org.

a reliable store of value. Nonresidents should have confidence in the independence and competence of monetary authorities. Domestic capital markets need to be deep and liquid so that investors can buy and sell large volumes of securities without greatly affecting the market price. Markets need to include a broad range of financial instruments with different risk-return characteristics.

China currently meets only some of these necessary conditions. The country is now the largest trading economy in the world. Officially recorded consumer-price inflation was only 1.6% in 2017, actually below the government's target. However, in most respects the renminbi is not yet a suitable international reserve currency. While the Chinese authorities' management of inflation has contributed to the credibility of stabilization policies, the monetary policy decision-making regime still lacks transparency, which makes it difficult for market participants to anticipate changes. The transparency of China's monetary policy has improved substantially in the early part of the last decade but is not high by international comparison. Further moves to improve the independence of the central bank and to increase the transparency of monetary policy decision making are needed to support greater international acceptance of the renminbi (World Bank 2013).

To be sure, the International Monetary Fund (IMF) decided to include the renminbi as a reserve currency in its special drawing rights (SDR) basket starting in October 2016 (IMF 2016). One of the key criteria for inclusion in the SDR basket is that the currency must be regarded as "freely usable." This clearly holds for trade-related transactions but is still very much a work in progress regarding financial transactions. Therefore, the IMF seems to have stretched the criterion somewhat on the basis of recent improvements in "reforms to China's monetary, foreign exchange, and financial systems and . . . advances made in liberalizing, integrating, and improving the infrastructure of its financial markets" (IMF 2016, 1). However, China still has a long way to go before it can claim to have an open capital account.

Government policies have encouraged the use of renminbi in trade and financial transactions. On the trade side, settlement in renminbi grew rapidly, accounting for nearly 30% of total trade in 2015, up from only 2.5% in 2010 (see Figure 12.2). However, the share then fell sharply to only 16% in 2017, reflecting diminished expectations of renminbi appreciation. This suggests that the demand for renminbi settlement had a strong speculative element, rather than being based just on convenience or cost. Moreover, the pattern of settlement in renminbi is very unbalanced, with almost 90% of the settlements on the import side. The share of the renminbi in total foreign exchange transactions, including capital account transactions, is increasing rapidly but from a very low base, and still was only 2% in 2016 (ranked 8th), according to BIS data (BIS 2016).[3]

The government is also undertaking cautious steps toward allowing foreigners to participate in capital account transactions denominated in renminbi. Some qualified investors, including international development institutions in China, have been allowed to issue bonds in China's domestic market (Makin 2011), and some foreign participation in the domestic banking system has been allowed, although foreign banks' share of financial assets remains below 2%, and their

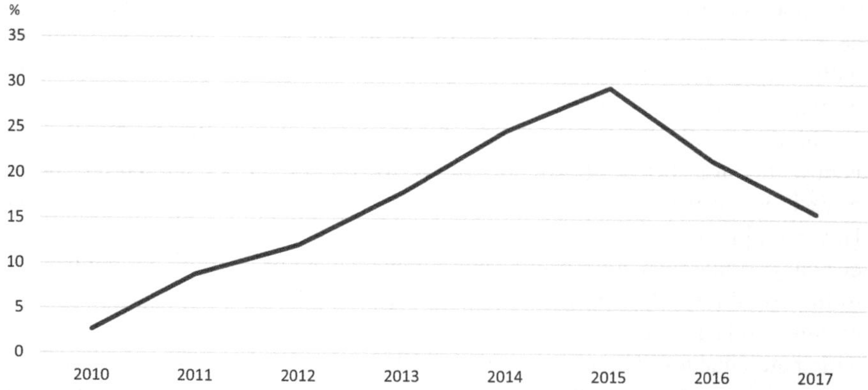

Figure 12.2 Share of total Chinese trade settled in renminbi (%)

Source: People's Bank of China, PRC General Administration of Customs, author's estimates.

activities are restricted. The government has developed offshore markets in renminbi in Hong Kong and elsewhere, including provision for renminbi balances to be held by foreigners, the development of instruments for hedging currency risk, and the issuance of renminbi-denominated government bonds (Huang 2010). The goal has been to develop an offshore market while maintaining capital account restrictions (He and McCauley 2010). Some Chinese companies have issued renminbi-denominated bonds in Hong Kong, but the size of the available renminbi-denominated assets is still small, resulting in the bulk of the trade settlements held in deposits in the Hong Kong clearing bank. Since October 2010, China has allowed three types of foreign institutions, including foreign central banks or monetary authorities – renminbi clearing banks in Hong Kong and Macao, and foreign banks participating in cross-border renminbi trade settlements – to invest in domestic Chinese interbank bond markets using renminbi (World Bank 2013). Since 2002, foreign investors have been allowed to buy and sell RMB denominated shares in China's mainland stock exchanges through the qualified foreign institutional investor (QFII) scheme, while Chinese institutions can invest abroad under the qualified domestic institutional investor (QDII) scheme. Commercial credit inflow and outflow restrictions were lifted in 2013. However, cross-border investment by individuals remain tightly controlled.

Nonetheless, China's capital account is still assessed to remain relatively closed. According to data from the Chinn-Ito index of capital account liberalization (Chinn and Ito 2006), a *de jure* measure based on information from the IMF on exchange rate regimes, China's score as of 2015 was −1.195, unchanged since 1993, indicating a relatively closed account.[4] This puts it on a par with countries such as India, Pakistan and Thailand.

Also, liberalization of capital flows has not always proceeded smoothly. Chinese authorities tightened exchange controls in 2016 when they were concerned about capital outflows. As a result, the share of the renminbi in total international payments fell to 1.7% in December 2016 (ranking 6th) compared with 2.3% in December 2015 (ranking 5th) (Swift 2018).

12.3.1 Dual-track systems and financial repression

Perhaps the greatest challenge that China faces in expanding the cross-border use of the renminbi is its underdeveloped financial system. China lacks the diversified financial instruments and secondary markets that would enable investors to quickly and cheaply convert their renminbi assets into cash, even if capital controls were removed. Low efficiency, high transaction costs, and weak supervision and regulation are major limitations on financial sector development (Wu et al. 2010). Financial market infrastructure is improving but remains challenged: bankruptcy procedures are not widely understood, modern accounting standards are not applied uniformly, and issues often lack transparency. Restrictions on the kinds of foreign institutions allowed to buy domestic securities, on the size of investments, and on the pace of repatriation still limit foreigners' access to China's financial markets (World Bank 2013).

Huang and Wang (2017) argue that China's financial sector has been characterized by three dual-track systems during the reform period in China. The first dual-track reform strategy was between the state and non-state sectors, reflecting the need to protect SOEs because of their weaker financial condition and political importance in key economic sectors. This led to the second dual track liberalization approach between product and factor markets, as the government needs to intervene in factor markets in order to support the less efficient SOEs. Financial repression, including privileged access to finance by SOEs, is an important form of factor market distortion. This led to a third dual-track system, namely that between the formal and informal financial sectors. The core of this approach is to continue to protect the SOEs while facilitating non-SOEs to grow rapidly.

The third dual track is particularly relevant for the financial sector. Financial policies aimed at protecting SOEs had the effect of discriminating against privately owned firms. Therefore, even though China already has very large financial markets, small and medium-sized enterprises (SMEs) and low-income households still have inadequate access to formal finance from the state-owned banks (SOBs), primarily bank loans. In response, the informal financial sector emerged, mainly in the forms of curb markets and shadow banking. The recent development of digital finance such as peer-to-peer (P2P) lending may also be regarded as part of the informal market. The two sectors co-exist, with the formal sector mainly serving large companies and wealthy households but with pricing and allocation of financial resources heavily distorted, and the informal sector mainly serving SMEs and low-income households with pricing and allocation of financial resources mainly market-driven. While the informal sector makes an important contribution to financial intermediation, it has often been unregulated, unstable and relatively small, although this situation is gradually changing. In particular, SMEs face high costs of funds that inhibit their potential to invest, raise productivity and innovate, although this has eased somewhat as a result of the emergence of P2P lending platforms.

12.3.2 Need for further reforms

China needs to further push ahead with financial reform. In November 2013, the Chinese leaders unveiled a program of comprehensive financial reform in 11 specific areas. They fell into three broad categories: creating a level-playing field (such as allowing private banks and developing inclusive finance), freeing up the market mechanism (such as reforming the interest rate and exchange rate regimes and achieving capital account convertibility) and improving regulation. The most important objectives of these three policy steps are to make the market work and to enforce market discipline, which, if carried out, could end the three-dual-track system.

A level-playing field is necessary for market economies. This principle should apply to enterprises and households as well as financial institutions. While it was justifiable for political and economic reasons that the government chose to protect the SOEs at the initial stage of reform, this policy is no longer an optimal choice, as government guarantees for SOEs generated much distorted behavior in financial markets. These distortions discourage new private sector entrants and reduce competition and innovation (World Bank 2013, 398).

China has benefited from adopting international regulatory norms for banks. China accelerated its program to implement Basel standards in the late 1990s, as a guide for the recapitalization of state-owned banks in response to the large amount of nonperforming loans (NPLs). Adopting international norms provided a useful benchmark and a means of enhancing the credibility of the government's program. Authorities combined elements of the implementation of Basel I (such as capital requirements) with elements from Basel II (supervisory review and disclosure procedures), in what officials of the China Bank Regulatory Commission (CBRC) sometimes called "Basel 1.5." As a result of this process and strong economic growth, the banks' estimated NPLs dropped from a staggering 23% of GDP in 2000 (Allen and others 2009) to below 2% in January 2010 (World Bank 2013, 405–406).

In a free-market system, financial institutions can compete equally, and pricing and allocation of financial resources are determined by the market. In late 2015, the People's Bank of China (PBoC) removed the last restriction, the ceiling on deposit rates. However, the central bank noted that it would have to take at least two more steps to complete interest rate liberalization – strengthening risk pricing capability of financial institutions and improving the transmission mechanism of monetary policy (Tan et al. 2016). In other words, a new monetary policy framework and a functioning financial market are necessary for the market-determined interest rate regime.

Prudent regulation is also an important condition because financial liberalization could at times cause market volatility and instability. The government is revamping the regulatory model in order to improve coordination of regulatory policies. The general expectation is that PBoC will likely take on more responsibilities in macro-prudential regulation and that the three specialized regulators, China Banking Regulatory Commission (CBRC), China Securities Regulatory Commission (CSRC) and China Insurance Regulatory Commission (CIRC), will likely be merged to some extent. However, China's regulatory system is still not independent. Moreover, regulators are responsible for both financial sector development and financial stability, goals which may sometime contradict each other. To improve the quality of regulation, regulators should be made independent, professional and authoritative. The regulations should focus on functions not institutions. And the policy objectives should be limited to maintaining financial stability (Huang and Wang 2017).

Although this reform program is both comprehensive and ambitious, it is still too early to conclude that it will succeed. First, when the authorities released the comprehensive reform program at the end of 2013, they indicated that it should make critical progress before 2020. However, there was no timeline for implementation of different reform steps. The pace of financial reform, in particular, depends on progress in many other areas, such as SOE reform.

Also, financial reform needs to be coordinated with liberalization of the capital account of the balance of payments. In recent past years, the authorities made serious efforts trying to internationalize the renminbi and liberalize the capital account. However, the exchange rate regime is not yet sufficiently flexible, interest rates are not market-determined, and governance of the state-owned commercial banks is still not in line with the market environment. When domestic and international economic and financial market conditions become volatile, the government often has to backpedal on liberalization by intervening in markets more aggressively.

Finally, successful SOE reform is the key to significant reform of the financial sector. SOEs are still an important source of financial inefficiency and risks. The government has continued to support SOEs because they provide millions of jobs and occupy strategic points of the socialist market economy. The employment argument has weakened significantly over time, but the political argument is still important for policymakers. It is critical to wean SOEs off of their preferred financial treatment, but any such move will likely face strong resistance from vested interests.

12.4 Participation in international financial institutions

In line with its rapid growth and status as the world's second largest economy, China has taken an increasing role in international governance. Traditionally this has been exercised through its participation in multilateral institutions such as the Group of Twenty (G20), the International Monetary Fund, the World Bank, the World Trade Organization and the Asian Development Bank. The middle three constitute the main Bretton Woods institutions established after World War II. China was a founding member of these institutions in 1945, but the People's

Republic of China did not take over the memberships of the IMF and the World Bank until April 1980. Accession to the WTO did not take place until 2001.

12.4.1 Re-entry to international financial institutions

Since 1980, China has developed deep links with these "traditional" global governance institutions, varying in nature between the respective institutions. The World Bank's development-financing role has generated less tension in China than the IMF's exchange rate surveillance of the renminbi, for example. Yet China has remained engaged in active dialogue with both processes, disagreements notwithstanding. (Jorgensen and Strube 2014)

China graduated from the World Bank's financing program for the world's poorest countries, the International Development Association (IDA), in 1999. Having achieved middle-income status, China was the third-largest recipient of new commitments made by the International Bank for Reconstruction and Development (IBRD), the World Bank's main lending arm for such countries, and the fourth-largest beneficiary of commitments from the World Bank's International Finance Corporation (IFC) in 2013. China has also received significant technical assistance from the World Bank since its admission as a member (Jorgensen and Strube 2014). The PRC joined the Asian Development Bank in 1986 and became one of the largest recipients of ADB lending programs.

12.4.2 Reform of international financial institutions

The reform agenda for the international financial architecture includes several major elements, most of which relate to the IMF and the G20. As one of the three important Bretton Woods international organizations responsible for an international economic order that has changed so rapidly, the IMF is in need of urgent reform, especially in the areas of representation of the emerging powers, the effectiveness of its policy recommendations to developing countries and the dominant position of the United States within the Fund (Drysdale et al. 2017).

China's role in these institutions (aside from the G20), as expressed by voting share, has not increased commensurately with its economic importance, chiefly due to resistance to change from other members who stand to lose voting share as a result of such an adjustment of shares. The 2008 global financial crisis provided modest momentum for accelerating Bretton Woods institutions governance reform. Specifically, it produced a modest improvement in the representation of emerging market and developing countries in the World Bank and the IMF. In line with commitments made at the Pittsburgh G20 Summit in 2009, both organizations agreed to an increase of about 3% to the voting power for developing and transition countries. The reforms would elevate China to the status of third-largest member by voting share in both the IMF (6.07% of voting shares) and the IBRD (5.55% of voting power), still relatively modest relative to China's economic size. However, the US Congress failed to pass the

IMF reform legislation in mid-2014, which brought the reform process to a halt (Drysdale et al. 2017).

12.4.3 Participation in the G20

The G20 provides China with opportunities to shape global economic governance that are not provided by legacy processes. First, China is an original member of the G20, with an involvement stretching back to the forum's establishment as a finance ministers and central bank governors' process in 1999. China's equal "historical ownership" over the process is politically and symbolically important for Chinese participants. Second, as opposed to the "G8+5" or a "G7+China" model, the G20 is, by and large, composed of economies selected mainly on the criterion of size. Because the other emerging economies within the G20 are also foundational members, engaging with the G20 process does not weaken China's claim to be a "developing economy." Third, the G20 affords China a pre-eminent yet informal space where it can regularly engage with other G20 members as it grows into a more significant leadership role in the global economy (Jorgensen and Strube 2014). Fourth, the G20 provides an important venue for negotiations on global economic governance matters between China and the United States, i.e., the "G2." The agenda-setting ability of the G2 was recently highlighted at the conclusion of the APEC 2014 meeting, where a China-US agreement on carbon emissions gave a significant boost to global climate change negotiations. (Jorgensen and Strube 2014)

12.4.4 China-sponsored international financial institutions

The lack of progress of reform of governance of the existing Bretton Woods international institutions naturally has caused frustration for China and has led it to seek other outlets for international governance which give it a more prominent and self-determined role. This has manifested itself most obviously in the establishment of two new multilateral development banks, the Asia Infrastructure Investment Bank (AIIB) and the New Development Bank (NDB, formerly known as the BRICS Development Bank). The key issue about these new development banks is the extent to they will function as multilateral banks, or they will basically follow the dictates of Chinese policy. A second question is the extent to which the new institutions will review prospective projects with sufficient concerns about environmental and social impacts. Concerns about these two issues have been raised in the case of the AIIB, for example, since China holds the largest voting share by far, and there is no executive board. In contrast, voting shares in the NDB are equal for the five members.

The primary task of the AIIB, according to Chinese President Xi Jinping, is to provide capital for the Belt and Road Initiative (BRI; Xinhua 2015; see Section 12.5 for a discussion of the BRI). While the governance structure of the AIIB and the diverse objectives of the BRI qualify the direct correspondence between these initiatives, there is clearly some intended connection between them.

With a subscribed capital base of $93 billion and 84 members as of 2018, the AIIB will enhance China's ability to work with fellow AIIB participants in financing Asian infrastructure projects. According to the articles of agreement (AOA) of the bank, China will hold a total voting share of over 26.9% due to its contribution of US$ 29.78 billion. China is the largest investor in the AIIB and its largest shareholder (the next largest shareholder is India at 7.74%). As written in the AOA, at least 75% of total votes are required in order to amend the AOA, adjust the capital shares of regional members, increase the capital base of the bank and make other major changes. Thus, China has the de facto veto power in the bank (Yu 2017).

The major multilateral development institutions have all started to work with the AIIB in providing loans and sharing their professional expertise in order to construct much needed infrastructure in the region. Although the AIIB will find it hard to avoid competition with the existing international organizations in financing infrastructure projects, the infrastructure construction market should be large enough for the AIIB, World Bank and the ADB to compete amicably (Yu 2017).

China has also actively pursued the establishment of the $100 billion NDB under the BRICS' authority, as well as a new contingent reserve arrangement (similar to the Chiang Mai initiative). The NDB announcement shows China is prepared to push for the BRICS' evolution as a practically focused process. The equal division between BRICS members in terms of their equity stakes in the NDB contrasts with the proportional World Bank and IMF governance structures outlined earlier. How sustainable the NDB's "equitable" financing arrangements will be in the long term remains to be seen; South Africa evidently will struggle to provide the same kind of long-term financial backing as China (Jorgensen and Strube 2014).

12.4.5 China's participation in regional financial architecture

China also maintains an important role in regional multilateral institutions such as the Asia-Pacific Economic Cooperation (APEC), the Association of Southeast Nations plus Six (ASEAN+6) and the East Asian Summit and, earlier, the Chiang Mai Initiative Multilateralization (CMIM), a regional financial safety net. The share of China (including Hong Kong) in the CMIM equals 32%, the same as that of Japan.

12.5 Global public goods

China's future prosperity depends to a large extent on the preservation of global public goods – issues that are important for many countries where market forces cannot be relied upon to achieve efficient outcomes. Such cases require coordinated government policies to ensure the efficient provision of global public goods. For example, the market cannot be relied upon to limit environmental damage, either domestically or cross-border, so issues such as climate change and threats to the ozone layer can be resolved only through international coordination and mechanisms to internalize externalities. Similarly, preservation of global resources such as ocean fisheries, seabed minerals, and the Antarctic requires coordinated interventions by governments. The benefits of communications networks increase with the number of users, so international agreements and domestic regulations that promote efficient Internet use, for example, are in everyone's interest. International trade and financial transactions require a framework of rules to promote cooperation; reductions in import barriers and steps to ensure global financial stability often require international discussion. Efforts to reduce global poverty, thereby enhancing global stability, will be more effective if all countries with sufficient resources are encouraged to participate. The term "global public goods" is somewhat misleading: much of the work involves establishing effective institutions that consider the global impact of the provision of goods and services. While all of these issues touch on domestic policies, they all also involve international coordination (World Bank 2013).

12.5.1 Climate change

The global economy faces an enormous challenge in reducing carbon emissions to avoid the worst effects of climate change. Absent changes in policies to reduce emission intensity, the increase in average global temperatures over the next several decades could be calamitous, with a rise in the sea level that would inundate vast regions where millions of people live as well as the degradation of agricultural land that millions of poor people depend on for their livelihood. China will be severely affected, both directly in some regions and indirectly as the global economy deteriorates (World Bank 2013).

China is the largest source of carbon emissions, accounting for 23% of global carbon dioxide (CO2) emissions (although note that China's large export sector means that a significant portion of the goods produced in generating these emissions are actually consumed abroad). Moreover, during the next 20 years, China is expected to be responsible for one-quarter of the increase in emissions, even in a baseline scenario that assumes a significant shift toward the service sectors in China. Effective global policies are not feasible without China's participation, both because limiting China's emissions is critical and because other countries are unlikely to participate in the absence of the largest source of carbon emissions.

It is in China's interest to reduce carbon emissions significantly; otherwise, China would create an artificial comparative advantage in energy-intensive production and be stuck with the current emission structure, making the country even more dependent on future energy supply. Over the long term, the supply of energy is one of the most binding constraints on growth potential, so having a comparative advantage in energy-intensive production is not desirable. In addition, greater reliance on energy-intensive production would worsen China's already considerable environmental challenges (World Bank 2013).

12.5.2 Belt and Road Initiative (BRI)

The concepts of the Silk Road Economic Belt and the Maritime Silk Road were first introduced by Chinese President Xi Jinping during his visits to Kazakhstan and Indonesia in 2013. The Central Government has since then further elaborated on the idea of building the Silk Road Economic Belt and the 21st Century Maritime Silk Road. The concept is now most often abbreviated as the "Belt and Road" Initiative or BRI.

On 28 March 2015, China's National Development and Reform Commission, in conjunction with China's Foreign Ministry and Commerce Ministry, issued an action plan for the Belt and Road, bringing the concept one important step closer to realization. Titled the "Vision and Actions on Jointly Building Silk Road Economic Belt and 21st Century Maritime Silk Road," the official document lays out the basic goals of the "One Belt One Road" Initiative: "It is aimed at promoting orderly and free flow of economic factors, highly efficient allocation of resources and deep integration of markets; encouraging the countries along the Belt and Road to achieve economic policy coordination and carry out broader and more in-depth regional cooperation of higher standards; and jointly creating an open, inclusive and balanced regional economic cooperation architecture that benefits all" (NDRC 2015). The BRI's priority is infrastructure connectivity. Towards that end, the Chinese government has facilitated the establishment of the AIIB (as described earlier) and set up a US$ 40 billion Silk Road Fund. The Fund is expected to be similar to the World Bank's investment arm the International Finance Corp and the African Development Bank's mutual development fund. Financed by a small group of investors, the Fund targets infrastructure construction, exploration of natural resources, and industrial and financial cooperation.

On land, the BRI will focus on jointly building a new Eurasian Land Bridge and developing the China-Mongolia-Russia, China-Central Asia-West Asia and China-Indochina Peninsula economic corridors by taking advantage of international transport routes, relying on core cities along the Belt and Road and using key economic industrial parks as cooperation platforms (see Figure 12.3). This should have a substantial impact in boosting trade among Central Asian countries located between China and Europe. At sea, the BRI will focus on jointly building smooth, secure and efficient transport routes connecting major sea ports along the Belt and Road. The China-Pakistan Economic Corridor and the Bangladesh-China-India-Myanmar Economic Corridor are closely related to the BRI (NDRC 2015).

The BRI encompasses both hard infrastructure investment and soft connectivity, including trade facilitation, trade and investment agreements, maintenance of closer economic ties, deepening of political trust and enhancement of cultural exchanges. In addition to roads, railways and ports, hard infrastructure also includes pipelines and telecommunications networks (NDRC 2015).

Chinese companies, most of which are state-owned, have been active in implementing the BRI initiatives, and have made huge investments in transportation and other infrastructure projects located in the Silk Road countries. Investment in ports is one example. Chinese firms have constructed many container ports and been granted exclusive management rights. These ports are located in strategic positions along China's Silk Road, which enables China to control transportation of goods and people. (Yu 2017).

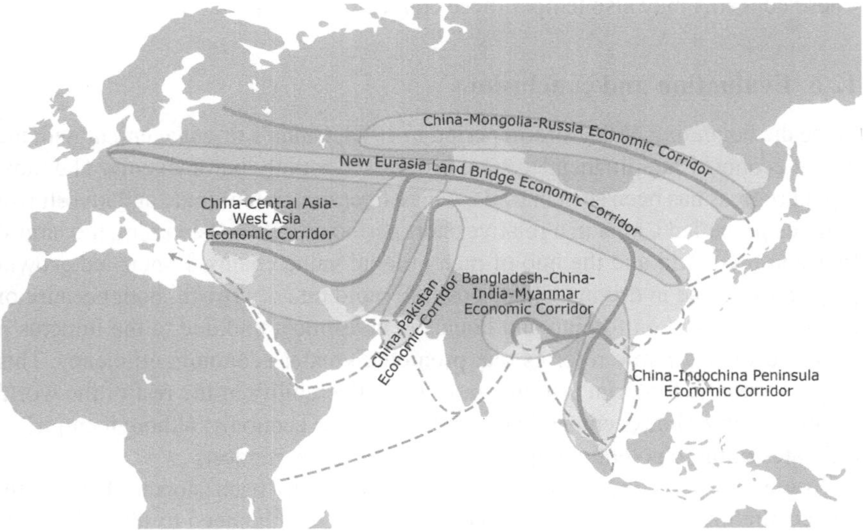

Figure 12.3 Map of belt and road routes

Source: www.silkroutes.net/OBOR/9MapWallStreetJounal.jpg

Nonetheless, China faces both internal and external challenges to implementation of its BRI initiatives. From the internal perspective, China has yet to establish an effective central leadership structure to coordinate Silk Road-related activities and the various government departments have failed to come up with unified strategy for implementing the BRI proposals abroad. For example, the Ministry of Commerce is primarily interested in bilateral trade and investment, while the NDRC is primarily concerned with inter-regional infrastructure construction projects with the region. Intensifying local competition represents an additional concern for China, as two southwestern Chinese provinces, Yunnan and Guangxi, both claim to be China's gateway towards Southeast Asia and are engaged in intense competition over preferential policies from the Chinese central government (Yu 2017). Externally, although China's bilateral trade and economic ties with the ASEAN countries are increasing, relations between China and many member countries have been damaged by ongoing maritime disputes in the South China Sea.

The BRI could be seen as a reflection of China's growing maritime power and its aim to project its sea power and naval capabilities globally. India for one is concerned about China's emerging power and has not joined the BRI. Other countries are engaged in territorial disputes with China, centered mainly on competing claims for sovereignty over areas of the South China Sea such as the Spratly Islands and the Paracel Islands, including Brunei, Malaysia, the Philippines, Taiwan and Viet Nam. China's claims in that region are summarized in the "nine-dash line" map that covers almost all of the South China Sea (BBC 2016). These concerns may also temper those countries' participation in the BRI.

12.6 Evaluation and conclusions

Since the beginning of the reform period in 1978, China's re-engagement with the global economy and financial system progressed rapidly but unevenly. The most rapid progress has been seen in trade, where liberalization of trade and investment regimes propelled China in a relative short period of time to becoming the largest trader in the world and the hub of many global value chains. Export-led growth played a key role in driving China's overall rapid rate of growth, both because of the direct impacts on foreign and domestic investment and due to the impetus it provided for economic reforms that promoted greater economic efficiency. This larger economic footprint also increases the vulnerability of the rest of the world to any possible shocks emanating from the Chinese economy, although empirical estimates of these potential impacts are still relatively modest.

Progress in terms of liberalizing capital flows has been slower. This partly reflects the link between capital account opening and the need to liberalize China's domestic financial sector, and partly shows caution about the impacts of full capital-account opening on the independence of monetary policy and possible capital volatility resulting either from domestic or external shocks. Progress of liberalization of the financial system has proceeded relatively slowly partly because of reluctance of the government to completely dismantle the current apparatus where state-owned financial institutions give favorable treatment to SOEs in order to carry out state policy. The timetable for creating a truly level-playing field between SOEs and privately-owned enterprises is still unclear.

Since China's capital account remains relatively closed, this puts a damper on the use of the renminbi as an international currency. Even though the IMF has anointed the renminbi as a "freely usable" currency by virtue of including it in the SDR basket, this is clearly not the case for capital-account transactions, and such free use still looks rather far off.

China's economic success and emergence as the world's second largest economy, and the prospect of becoming the world's largest economy in the near future,[5] have given the government greater confidence in taking a more assertive role in global governance. This tendency was reinforced by the perceived weakening influence of the advanced economies following the debacle of the global financial crisis of 2008–2009. The Chinese government is happy to provide economic development lessons for the rest of the world which may differ significantly from those of the "Washington consensus."

As part of this thrust, China has sought to increase the voting shares of it and other emerging economies in the main international financial institutions, including the IMF and the World Bank. However, progress on this front has not been commensurate with China's rising economic power, due largely to resistance from current advanced-country members. As a result, China has developed an independent approach, including establishing new international financial institutions such as the AIIB and NDB and promoting the Belt and Road Initiative as a way to improve trade and other linkages between China and its trading partners on the Eurasian continent and in Africa. The BRI is very ambitious, but the overall plan is still somewhat vague and subject to change. The extent to which China can derive "soft power" from this investment program also remains unclear.

The one thing that remains clear is that China's influence on the world stage will continue to increase in line with its economic and financial power. This will partly depend on how successfully it deals with domestic issues such as resource constraints, pollution and financial reform, but the basic trend is unlikely to alter for the foreseeable future. The key point is that such influence and power be wielded in ways that benefit other countries as well as China. The two most obvious ways of doing so are in the areas of international trade and climate change control. Following the abdication of the US from its leading role in trade liberalization under the Trump administration, China has a great opportunity to play the role of a champion of free or freer trade. China must also make a key contribution to limiting the emission of greenhouse gases if targets for limiting global warming are to be achieved. If it can contribute meaningfully to international cooperation in this area, this would be a major achievement.

To be sure, economic issues are very important, but geopolitical issues will also claim attention. How China deals with issues such as territorial claims in the South China Sea, denuclearization of the Korean peninsula and, most importantly, its developing rivalry with the US, will critically shape its global role in the coming decade.

Notes

1 Asian Development Bank Institute, Tokyo, Japan. Email: pmorgan@adbi.org. I thank Charles van Marrewijk for permission to use Figure 12.1.
2 See Chapter 8 for a more detailed description of the trends of China's inward and outward FDI.
3 The reported share was 4% out of a total of 200%, since two currencies are involved in every transaction.
4 The index ranges from -1.90 (most closed) to 2.37 (completely open).
5 The World Bank estimates that China's GDP is already the world's largest in purchasing-power parity terms. Estimates of when it will become the largest in US dollar terms range from 2025 to 2030.

References

Allen, F., J. Qian, M. Qian, and M. Zhao (2009), "A Review of China's Financial System and Initiatives for the Future," in: J. Barth, J. Tatom and G. Yago (eds.), *China's Emerging Financial Markets, The Milken Institute Series on Financial Innovation and Economic Growth*, New York: Springer.

Bank for International Settlements (BIS) (2016), *Triennial Central Bank Survey of Foreign Exchange and OTC Derivatives Markets in 2016*. Basel: Bank for International Settlements. Available at: www.bis.org/statistics/d11_3.pdf

Berger, A. (2008), "China and the Global Governance of Foreign Direct Investment: The Emerging Liberal Bilateral Investment Treaty Approach." Discussion Paper 10/2008, German Development Institute, Bonn.

British Broadcasting Company (BBC) (2016), *Why is the South China Sea Contentious?* London: British Broadcasting Company. 12 July. Available at: www.bbc.com/news/world-asia-pacific-13748349

China Daily (2017), *China Brightens Fortune 500 List*. Beijing: China Daily. July 22. Available at: www.chinadaily.com.cn/business/2017-07/22/content_30209599.htm

Chinn, M., and H. Ito (2006), "What Matters for Financial Development? Capital Controls, Institutions, and Interactions," *Journal of Development Economics* 81(1): 163–192.

Davies, K (2010), "Outward FDI from China and Its Policy Context," Columbia FDI Profiles, Vale Columbia Center on Sustainable International Investment, New York.

Drysdale, P., A. Triggs, and J. Wang (2017), "China's New Role in the International Financial Architecture," *Asian Economic Policy Review* 12(2): 258–281

He, D., and R. McCauley (2010), "Offshore Markets for the Domestic Currency: Monetary and Financial Stability Issues," Working Paper 02/2010, Hong Kong Monetary Authority, Hong Kong (March).

Huang, Y. (2010), "RMB Policy and the Global Currency System." Working Paper 2010–03, Peking University, China Center for Economic Research, Beijing.

Huang, Y., and X. Wang (2017), "Building an Efficient Financial System in China: A Need for Stronger Market Discipline," *Asian Economic Policy Review* 12(2): 188–209.

Inoue, T., D. Kaya, and H. Ohshige (2018), "Estimating the Impact of Slower PRC Growth on the Asia Pacific Region: GVAR Model Approach," in: J. Lin, G. Wan, and P. Morgan (eds.), *Slowdown in the People's Republic of China: Structural Factors and the Implications for Asia*, Tokyo: ADBI Press.

International Monetary Fund (IMF) (2016), *IMF Adds Chinese Renminbi to Special Drawing Rights Basket*, Washington, DC: International Monetary Fund. Available at: www.imf.org/en/News/Articles/2016/09/29/AM16-NA093016IMF-Adds-Chinese-Renminbi-to-Special-Drawing-Rights-Basket

Jorgensen, H., and D. Strube (2014), *China, the G20 and Global Economic Governance*, Sydney, Australia: The Lowy Institute, November.

Luo, Y., Q. Xue, and B. Han. (2010), "How Emerging Market Governments Promote Outward FDI: Experience from China," *Journal of World Business* 45: 68–79.

Makin, J. H. (2011), "Can China's Currency Go Global?" *Economic Outlook, American Enterprise Institute for Public Policy Research*, Washington, DC (January).

National Development Reform Commission (NDRC), Ministry of Finance and Ministry of Commerce (2015), *Vision and Actions on Jointly Building Silk Road Economic Belt and 21st-Century Maritime Silk Road*. Beijing: National Development Reform Commission. March 28. Available at: http://en.ndrc.gov.cn/newsrelease/201503/t20150330_669367.html

Organization for Cooperation and Development (OECD) (2005), *Governance in China*, Paris: OECD.

Salidjanova, N. (2011), "Going Out: An Overview of China's Outward Foreign Direct Investment," *US-China Economic and Security Review Commission Staff Research Report*, Washington, DC (March 30).

Swift (2018), *Follow the Internationalisation of China's Currency*. New York: Swift. Available at: www.swift.com/our-solutions/compliance-and-shared-services/business-intelligence/renminbi/rmb-tracker

Tan, Y., Y. Ji, and Y. Huang (2016), "Completing China's Interest Rate Liberalization," *China & World Economy* 24(2): 1–22.

United Nations Conference on Trade and Development (UNCTAD) (2017), *World Investment Report 2017: Annex Tables*. New York: United Nations. Available at: http://unctad.org/en/Pages/DIAE/World%20Investment%20Report/Annex-Tables.aspx

World Bank (2013), *China 2030: Building a Modern, Harmonious and Creative Society*, Washington, DC: World Bank.

Wu, F., R. Pan, and D. Wang (2010), "Renminbi's Potential to Become a Global Currency," *China and World Economy* 18 (1): 63–81.

Xinhua News Agency (2015), "China Focus: Xi Stresses Implementing Central Economic Policies," 9 July.

Xu, J. (2009), "Rio Tinto-Chinalco: China Is Not Amused," *Wall Street Journal Blogs*, 4 June.

Yu, Ho. (2017), "Motivation behind China's 'One Belt, One Road' Initiatives and Establishment of the Asian Infrastructure Investment Bank," *Journal of Contemporary China* 26(105): 353–368.

Zhai, F., and P. Morgan (2018), "Impact of the People's Republic of China's Growth Slowdown on Emerging Asia: A General Equilibrium Analysis," in: J. Lin, G. Wan, and P. Morgan (eds.), *Slowdown in the People's Republic of China: Structural Factors and the Implications for Asia*. Tokyo: ADBI Press.

Index

Note: Page numbers in *italics* indicate figures; those in **bold** indicate tables.